THE LAST
MAGNIFICENT WAR

THE LAST MAGNIFICENT WAR

Rare Journalistic and Eyewitness Accounts of World War I

EDITED BY

Harold Elk Straubing

PARAGON HOUSE
New York

First edition, 1989

Published in the United States by

Paragon House Publishers
90 Fifth Avenue
New York, NY 10011

Manufactured in the United States of America

Library of Congress Cataloging-in-Publication Data

The Last magnificent war: rare journalistic and eyewitness accounts
of World War I/compiled and edited by Harold Elk Straubing.—
1st ed.
p. cm
Includes index.
ISBN 1-55778-030-7
1. World War, 1914–1918—Sources. 2. World War, 1914–1918—
Personal narratives. I. Straubing, Harold Elk, 1918–
D505.L37 1989   11-11457
940.3—dc19   CIP

*Lovingly dedicated
to the two women in my life,
Helen and Michelle,
for their inspiration,
encouragement and patience.*

Contents

PART III. PROPAGANDA

PART IV. RECRUITMENT AND CAMP LIFE

PART V. NAVIES AT WAR

PART VI. WAR BY THE PARTICIPANTS

CONCLUSION. THE ARMISTICE

Introduction

In the beginning of the twentieth century, what started out as an attempt at a limited military action erupted into the largest war the world had known to that time. In 1914 weaponry had outdistanced military tactics and caused a slaughter of men and animals on the grandest scale. Conservative estimates of the casualties at the end of the war were ten million dead and twenty million wounded.

The unprecedented savage butchery had its seeds in the imperialistic and economic rivalries set in motion in the nineteenth century by the territorial and economic expansion of the British, German and Russian empires. The growth of nationalism and the Industrial Revolution were the most powerful factors in promoting these rivalries. The Franco-Prussian war of 1870–71 deprived France of the provinces of Alsace and Lorraine and left it dreaming of revenge. Germany was unified, and after dismissing Bismarck (1890), the new Emperor, William II, pursued a course of colonial and naval policies that clashed with British interests. The decay of the Ottoman Empire brought the opposition between German and Anglo-French interests into focus and led to nationalistic rivalries in the Balkans where Pan Slavism, encouraged by Russia, menaced the existence of the multinational Austro-Hungarian Monarchy.

Religious conditions in the Balkans were as complicated as racial relations. In Bulgaria, a branch of the Bulgarian citizenry was Islamic, as were half a million Turks and colonists of the Eastern lowlands. And while the Albanians were largely Islamic, the bulk of the population of the Balkans professed the Greek Orthodox faith. Greek Catholics prayed for the day when Constantinople would be rescued from the infidel and the cross once again would be raised over the mosque of St. Sophia as the followers of Mohammed labored for the spread of Islam. And along the Western coast of the Balkan Peninsula, Roman Catholics were numerous.

The international crises over Morocco and Bosnia and Hercegovina (the Balkan Wars 1912–1913) and many lesser incidents were fateful symptoms of the explosive state of Europe. They were accompanied by a mad-paced armaments race.

Two opposing coalitions emerged in the diplomatic shifts that began in 1879—The Triple Alliance (formed in 1882 by Germany, Austria and Italy), and the Triple Entente, formed in 1907 when Britain joined in alliance with France and Russia—but they seemed evenly balanced. Moreover, the dynastic and personal ties of the rulers of Europe cut across the alliances and favored the peaceful settlements of disputes at the highest level. It could be said that in 1914 not a statesman or ruler wanted a general conflict; yet many toyed with the idea of a limited war. The spark that set off the powder keg was the assassination on June 28, 1914 of Archduke Francis Ferdinand (heir to the throne of Austria-Hungary), and his morganatic wife, the Duchess of Hohenberg.

The war that followed exceeded the wildest expectations of politicians, soldiers, and civilians. To some it brought paralyzing fear; to others, intoxication with excitement, exhilaration; but to all, an eventual devastation that could never be repaired, forgiven or forgotten. Everyone witnessed a change in the family, friends became estranged, there were heart-wrenching uprootings, and to so many, it was the end of life's road.

War tends to bring out man's basest emotions; violence digs deep into the character of an individual so that under the cover of combat conditions, people act in a brutally aggressive manner and commit atrocities they would never dream of acting out in a peacetime society. National pride, racial and religious intolerance stir cruel actions. Armed with rifle and bayonet, and wearing a uniform that spells some measure of authority by force, it is suddenly blameless to attack churches and congregations who pray to a different god. People of another skin color are also fair game for wrongs real or imagined.

The war that erupted in 1914, originally concerned with commerce, colonies and boundary lines, in a short time spilled over to cater to every hate group, and the slaughter of innocents was appalling.

And yet this period preceding the war years was one of elegance and grace, of art and music. The leaders of the countries that were soon to be locked in the deadly struggle were from elite European society, schooled in all the graces. The politicians and the military were well educated, sophisticated and religious. Even the United States was being led by a university professor. There were no barroom brawlers, street fighters, or disgruntled wild-eyed godless anarchists in this group.

At the turn of the century the world was heading into an era of magnificent culture. World War I reversed the direction. Well bred leaders turned their back on art and music. They gave way to poison gas and the bayoneting of children. These magnificent people of a magnificent generation had their last magnificent war, a depraved carnage of bloodletting on a scale that still staggers the imagination.

Generally a book of the era deals with material digested by an author then spit up neatly and spread before the reader like plates before diners, each in its perfect place. What is lacking is the immediacy of the exciting material. What did the people know? When did they know it? How was it presented? What words inflamed national pride and hatred for fellow men to the point of committing murder?

The stories that follow are some of the reading material that was exposed to the citizens of the world preceding and during the war. These words were the inspiration that would keep men fighting, others working in factories and fields, would "make the world safe for democracy," and help win "the war that would end all wars."

The material reproduced here is as it appeared and was offered before the public. Some of it is reported fact, some of it was fictionalized to rally support, and some of it outrageous propaganda. In the light of the intervening years, we can now make our own judgements as to the type of information, misinformation and disinformation fed to the people of the world during those very terrible and frightful years.

PART I
WAR'S CRYSTAL BALL

At the turn of the century the stench of war permeated throughout Europe. There was a general feeling that war was imminent, and it was a guessing game among politicians and military leaders as to when and how it would start. A senior German general's book on Germany's military future frightened and angered people all over the world, and once the war came, politicians used the book to predict tragedies on a grand scale in order to rally public support.

Germany and the Next War

General Friedrich von Bernhardi
Translated by Allen H. Powles

"THE RIGHT TO MAKE WAR"
LONGMANS, GREEN & CO., 1912

Europe boiled with unrest for almost one hundred years before erupting into the setting of a giant battlefield for World War I. After four years of intense fighting, the world powers retreated to lick their wounds—and in the process planted the seeds for World War II. There was an intermission—a hiatus of eighteen years between the two wars, enough time for a new generation of man-children to bear arms, and then the death and destruction continued. Weapons were refined; made more deadly. The brutality practiced on civilians was sharpened. People had learned to inflict suffering on humankind to a degree never before seen or endured in the civilized world.

But in the century before World War I the imperial powers felt a growing need for colonization so that they could expand their markets, harvest new crops and promote commerce in distant lands.

As far back as 1823, John Quincy Adams, then Secretary of State under James Monroe, wrote the President that it should be clearly understood that the American continents were not to be considered as subjects for future colonization by any European powers. These were the exact words that President Monroe repeated in his doctrine that grew out of two diplomatic problems: A minor clash with Russia concerning the northeast coast of North America, and a fear that the reactionary European governments, commonly called the Holy Alliance, might seek to conquer Latin American countries that had recently revolted from Spain.

There was more trouble for Spain in Cuba where revolution broke out, and with the sinking of the Maine, the United States declared war. Hostilities ended in 1898, Spain was out, and Cuba was established as an independent republic under U. S. protection.

Inspired by the Cuban revolt, the Filipinos rebelled in 1896 which led to a shaky peace with Spain. This did not last long for the insurgents accepted American aid when the Spanish-American War broke out. The victory of Admiral Dewey in Manila Bay in 1898 led the Filipinos to believe that they would be set up as a republic, but instead the treaty that closed the war simply transferred the Philippines to the United States. The revolution turned its anger upon the United States, but fizzled in two years when the rebel leader, Aquinaldo, was captured.

The United States had caught the colonization fever, and held on to the Philippines, using it for commerce, trade, and producing material that would be of value to itself.

Europe, cut off from colonizing in the Americas, turned its full attention to Africa where it had a free hand. It was in this continent that the seeds of war were sown. In particular, the incidents in Morocco peaked the competition and fanned the flames of hatred.

Morocco was an ideal country for colonizing: Its population was concentrated in the coastal regions where rainfall was plentiful. Wheat and other cereals could be raised without irrigation, and on the Atlantic side they grew olives, citrus fruits and grapes. Fish was plentiful and part of the population fished for a livelihood. In the northern foothills there were phosphates, zinc, copper, lead, cobalt and coal.

And the government was corrupt, the inhabitants restless.

In 1904 France concluded a secret treaty with Spain to partition Morocco and agreed with Great Britain not to oppose British aims in Egypt in exchange for a free hand in Morocco.

In 1905 France asked the Sultan of Morocco for a protectorate, but Germany moved dramatically by having its Emperor land at Tangier from his yacht and declare the independence of Morocco.

On German insistence the Algeciras Conference (January–March 1906) was called to consider the Moroccan question. German investments were assured protection, but French and Spanish interests were given high recognition by the decision to allow France and Spain to police Morocco. Under the claim of effecting pacification, the French steadily annexed territory.

In 1908, the friction emitted sparks in Casablanca under French occupation when the German consul gave refuge to deserters from the French Foreign Legion. The dispute was eventually settled by the Hague Tribunal.

Abdu-L-Hafid tossed his brother off the throne in a coup d'etat and then had trouble maintaining order. He sought and obtained help from France and Spain that became especially necessary when the revolt broke out in 1911.

In the middle of this situation the German warship, Panther, made its appearance at Agadir on 1 July 1911. Its arrival was interpreted as a threat of war and speeded a final adjustment of imperial rivalries. On 4 November 1911 Germany agreed to a French protectorate in Morocco in exchange for the cession of French territory in equatorial Africa.

But not all Germans were satisfied with this settlement. They felt that their honor had been impugned and they were being tossed a bone while Spain, France, and Britain carved up the continent.

One of the most vocal critics was General Friedrich von Bernhardi. He felt that all patriotic sections of the German people were greatly excited by *the Moroccan dispute. This was not a simple commercial or colonial question; the honor and the future of the German nation was at stake.*

A deep rift opened between the feeling of the nation and the diplomatic action of the government. The public wanted Germany to assert itself but there didn't appear any understanding of the dangers of such a political position and the sacrifices which a boldly outlined policy would have demanded.

The General wasn't sure if the majority of people would answer a call to arms—would they be ready to bear permanent and heavy burdens of taxation? He felt that Germany had reached a crisis in national and political development. Because of the country's science, literature, and warlike achievements of the past, the General claimed he was proudly conscious of belonging to a great civilized nation which, in spite of all the weakness and mistakes of bygone days, would assuredly win a glorious future. Out of the conviction of his "German heart" he wrote a book, Germany and the Next War, *which was widely circulated in 1912, and incensed the citizens, diplomats, and politicians of many countries.*

The General decried the political and moral development of humankind because the value of war was unappreciated. If the ideas about perpetual peace kept on being disseminated in Germany, the nation could lose its enthusiasm for war which constituted its greatness in history. He sneered at those citizens who had increased their wealth and lived for the moment, incapable of sacrificing enjoyment to the service of great conceptions.

The Germans, he claimed, were formerly the best fighting men in the most warlike nation in Europe. For a long time they proved themselves to be the ruling people of the continent by the power of their arms and the loftiness of their ideas. Germans had bled and conquered on countless battlefields in every part of the world, he said, and in late years had shown that the heroism of their ancestors still lived in the descendents.

In striking contrast to this military aptitude the German people displayed in the past, they had become peace-loving—an almost too peace-loving nation. A rude shock, he suggested, was needed to awaken their warlike instincts, and compel them to show their military strength.

Undoubtedly Adolf Hitler read and studied the book, Germany and the Next War, *for much of* Mein Kampf, *his own treatise on Germany's destiny, rings with the same strong nationalist feelings, the superiority of German people and culture, and its glorious future in world conquest.*

Since 1795, when Immanuel Kant published in his old age his treatise on "Perpetual Peace," many have considered it an established fact that war is the destruction of all good and the origin of all evil. In spite of all that history teaches, no conviction is felt that the struggle between nations is inevitable, and the growth of civilization is credited with a power to which war must yield. But, undisturbed by such human theories and the change of times war has again and again marched from country to country with the clash of arms, and has proved its destructive as well as creative and purifying power. It has not succeeded in teaching mankind what its real nature is. Long periods of war, far from convincing men of the necessity of war, have, on the contrary, always revived the wish to exclude war, where possible, from the political intercourse of nations.

This wish and this hope are widely disseminated even today. The maintenance of peace is lauded as the only goal at which statesmanship should aim. This unqualified desire for peace has obtained in our days a quite peculiar power over men's spirits. This aspiration finds its public expression in peace leagues and peace congresses; the Press of every country and of every party opens its columns to it. The current in this direction is, indeed, so strong that the majority of Governments profess—outwardly, at any rate—that the necessity for maintaining peace is the real aim of their policy; while when a war breaks out the aggressor is universally stigmatized, and all Governments exert themselves, partly in reality, partly in pretence, to extinguish the conflagration.

Pacific ideals, to be sure, are seldom the real motive of their action. They usually employ the need of peace as a cloak under which to promote their own political aims. This was the real position of affairs at the Hague Congresses, and this is also the meaning of the action of the United States of America, who in recent times have earnestly tried to conclude treaties for the establishment of Arbitration Courts, first and foremost with England, but also with Japan, France, and Germany. No practical results, it must be said, have so far been achieved.

We can hardly assume that a real love of peace prompts these efforts. This is shown by the fact that precisely those Powers which, as the weaker, are exposed to aggression, and therefore were in the greatest need of international protection, have been completely passed over in the American proposals for Arbitration Courts. It must consequently be assumed that very matter-of-fact political motives led the Americans, with their commercial instincts, to take such steps, and induced "perfidious Albion" to accede to the proposals. We may suppose that England intended to protect her rear in event of war with Germany, but that America wished to have a free hand in order to follow her policy of sovereignty in Central America without hindrance, and to carry out her plans regarding the Panama Canal in the exclusive interests of America. Both countries certainly entertained the hope of gaining advantage over the other signatory of the treaty, and of winning the lion's share for themselves. Theorists and fanatics imagine that they see in the efforts of President Taft a great step forward on the path to perpetual peace, and enthusiastically agree with him. Even the Minister for Foreign Affairs in England, with well-affected idealism, termed the procedure of the United States an era in the history of mankind.

This desire for peace has rendered most civilized nations anaemic, and marks a decay of spirit and political courage such as has often been shown by a race of Epigoni. "It has always been," H. von Treitschke tells us, "the weary, spiritless, and exhausted ages which have played with the dream of perpetual peace."

Everyone will, within certain limits, admit that the endeavours to diminish the dangers of war and to mitigate the sufferings which war entails are justifiable. It is an incontestable fact that war temporarily disturbs industrial life, interrupts quiet economic development, brings widespread misery with it, and emphasizes the primitive brutality of man. It is therefore a most desirable consummation if wars for trivial reasons should be rendered impossible, and if efforts are made to restrict the evils which follow necessarily in the train of war, so far as is compatible with the essential nature of war. All that the Hague Peace Congress has accomplished in this limited sphere deserves, like every permissable humanization of war, universal acknowledgment. But it is quite another matter if the object is to abolish war entirely, and to deny its necessary place in historical development.

This aspiration is directly antagonistic to the great universal laws which rule all life. War is a biological necessity of the first importance, a regulative element in the life of mankind which cannot be dispensed with, since without it an unhealthy development will follow, which excludes every advancement of the race, and therefore all real civilization. War is the father of all things. The sages of antiquity long before Darwin recognized this.

The struggle for existence is, in the life of Nature, the basis of all healthy development. All existing things show themselves to be the result of contesting forces. So in the life of man the struggle is not merely the destructive, but the life-giving principle. "To supplant or to be supplanted is the essence of life," says Goethe, and the strong life gains the upper hand. The law of the stronger holds good everywhere. Those forms survive which are able to procure themselves the most favourable conditions of life, and to assert themselves in the universal economy of Nature. The weaker succumb. This struggle is regulated and restrained by the unconscious sway of biological laws and by the interplay of opposite forces. In the plant world and the animal world this process is worked out in unconscious tragedy. In the human race it is consciously carried out, and regulated by social ordinances. The man of strong will and strong intellect tries by every means to assert himself, the ambitious strive to rise and in this effort the individual is far from being guided merely by the consciousness of right. The life-work and the life-struggle of many men are determined, doubtless, by unselfish and ideal motives, but to a far greater extent the less noble passions—craving for possessions, enjoyment and honour, envy and the thirst for revenge—determine men's actions. Still more often, perhaps, is the need to live which brings down even natures of a higher mould into the universal struggle for existence and enjoyment.

Struggle is, therefore, a universal law of Nature, and the instinct of self-preservation which leads to struggle is acknowledged to be a natural condition of existence. "Man is a fighter." Self-sacrifice is a renunciation of life, whether in the existence of the individual or in the life of States, which are agglomerations of individuals. The first and paramount law is the assertion of one's own independent existence. By self-assertion alone can the State maintain the conditions of life for its citizens, and ensure them the legal protection which each man is entitled to claim from it. This duty of self-assertion is by no means satisfied by the mere repulse of hostile attacks; it includes the obligation to assure the possibility of life and development to the whole body of the nation embraced by the State.

Strong, healthy, and flourishing nations increase in numbers. From a given moment they require a continual expansion of their frontiers, they require new territory for the accommodation of their surplus population. Since almost every part of the globe is inhabited, new territory must, as a rule, be obtained at the cost of its possessors—that is to say, by conquest, which thus becomes a law of necessity.

The right of conquest is universally acknowledged. At first the procedure is pacific. Over-populated countries pour a stream of emigrants into other States and territories. These submit to the legislature of the new country, but try to obtain favourable conditions of existence for themselves at the cost of the original inhabitants, with whom they compete. This amounts to conquest.

The right of colonization is also recognized. Vast territories inhabited by uncivilized masses are occupied by more highly civilized States, and made subject to their rule. Higher civilizations and the correspondingly greater power are the foundations of the right to annexation. This right is, it is true, a very indefinite one, and it is impossible to determine what degree of civilization justifies annexation and subjugation. The impossibility of finding a legitimate limit to these international relations has been the cause of many wars. The subjugated nation does not recognize this right of subjugation, and the more powerful civilized nation refuses to admit the claim of the subjected to independence. This situation becomes peculiarly critical when the conditions of civilization have changed in the course of time. The subject nation has, perhaps, adopted higher methods and conceptions of life, and the difference in civilization has consequently lessened. Such a state of things is growing ripe in British India.

Lastly, in all times the right of conquest by war has been admitted. It may be that a growing people cannot win colonies from uncivilized races, and yet the State wishes to retain the surplus population which the mother-country can no longer feed. Then the only course left is to acquire the necessary territory by war. Thus the instinct of self-preservation leads inevitably to war, and the conquest of foreign soil. It is not the possessor, but the victor, who then has the right. The threatened people will see the point of Goethe's lines:

> That which thou didst inherit from thy sires,
> In order to possess it, must be won.

The procedure of Italy in Tripoli furnishes an example of such conditions, while Germany in the Morocco question could not rouse herself to a similar resolution.*

In such cases might gives the right to occupy or to conquer. Might is at once the supreme right, and the dispute as to what is right is decided by the arbitrament of war. War gives a biologically just decision, since its decisions rest on the very nature of things. . . . We cannot reject the possibility that a State, under the necessity of providing remunerative work for its population, may be driven into war. If more valuable advantages than even now is the case had been at stake in Morocco, and had our export trade been seriously menaced, Germany would hardly have conceded to France the most favourable position in the Morocco market without a struggle. England, doubtless, would not shrink from a war to the knife, just as she fought for the ownership of the South African goldfields and diamond mines, if any attack threatened her Indian market, the control of which is the foundation of her world sovereignty. The knowledge, therefore, that war depends on biological laws leads to the conclusion that every attempt to exclude it from international relations must be demonstrably untenable. But it is not only a biological law, but a moral obligation, and, as such, an indispensable factor in civilization.

The attitude which is adopted towards this idea is closely connected with the view of life generally.

If we regard the life of the individual or of the nation as something purely material, as an incident which terminates in death and outward decay, we must logically consider that the highest goal which man can attain is the enjoyment of the most happy life and the greatest possible diminution of all bodily suffering. The State will be regarded as a sort of assurance office, which guarantees a life of undisturbed possession and enjoyment in the widest meaning of the word. We must endorse the view which Wilhelm von Humboldt professed in his treatise on the limits of the activity of the State. The compulsory functions of the State must be limited to the assurance of property and life. The State will be considered as a law-court, and the individual will be inclined to shun war as the greatest conceivable evil.

If, on the contrary, we consider the life of men and of States as merely

---

* This does not imply that Germany could and ought to have occupied part of Morocco. On more than one ground I think that it was imperative to maintain the actual sovereignty of this State on the basis of the Algeciras Convention. Among other advantages which need not be discussed here, Germany would have had the country secured to her as a possible sphere of colonization. That would have set up justifiable claims for the future.

a fraction of a collective existence, whose final purpose does not rest on enjoyment, but on the development of intellectual and moral powers, and if we look upon all enjoyment merely as an accessory of the chequered conditions of life, the task of the State will appear in a very different light. The State will not be to us merely a legal and social insurance office, political union will not seem to us to have the one object of bringing the advantages of civilization within the reach of the individual; we shall assign to it the nobler task of raising the intellectual and moral powers of a nation to the highest expansion, and of securing for them that influence on the world which tends to the combined progress of humanity. We shall see in the State, as Fichte taught, an exponent of liberty to the human race, whose task it is to put into practice the moral duty on earth. "The State," says Treitschke (in "Deutsche Geschichte"), "is a moral community. It is called upon to educate the human race by positive achievement, and its ultimate object is that a nation should develop in it and through it into a real character; that is, alike for nation and individuals, the highest moral task."

This highest expansion can never be realized in pure individualism. Man can only develop his highest capacities when he takes his part in a community, in a social organism, for which he lives and works. He must be in a family, in a society, in the State, which draws the individual out of the narrow circles in which he otherwise would pass his life, and makes him a worker in the great common interests of humanity. The State alone, so Schleiermacher once taught, gives the individual the highest degree of life.*

War from this standpoint will be regarded as a moral necessity, if it is waged to protect the highest and most valuable interests of a nation. As human life is not constituted, it is political idealism which calls for war, while materialism—in theory, at least—repudiates it.

If we grasp the conception of the State from this higher aspect, we shall soon see that it cannot attain its great moral ends unless its political power increases. The higher object at which it aims is closely correlated to the advancement of its material interests. It is only the State which strives after an enlarged sphere of influence that creates the conditions under which mankind develops into the most splendid perfection. The development of all the best human capabilities and qualities can only find scope on the great stage of action which power creates. But when the State renounces all extension of power, and recoils from every war which is necessary for its expansion; when it is content to exist, and no longer wishes to grow; when "at peace on sluggard's couch it lies," then its citizens become

---

* Since expanding the idea of the State into that of humanity, and thus entrusting apparently higher duties to the individual, leads to error the human race should be conceived as a whole struggle and, by implication, the most essential vital principle should be ruled out. Any action in favor of collective humanity outside the limits of the State and nationality is impossible. Such conceptions belong to the wide domain of Utopias.

stunted. The efforts of each individual are cramped, and the broad aspect of things is lost. This is sufficiently exemplified by the pitiable existence of all small States, and every great power that mistrusts itself falls victim to the same curse.

All petty and personal interests force their way to the front during a long period of peace. Selfishness and intrigue run riot, and luxury obliterates idealism. Money acquires an excessive and unjustifiable power, and character does not obtain due respect.

"Wars are terrible, but necessary, for they save the State from social petrifaction and stagnation. It is well that the transitoriness of the goods of this world is not only preached, but is learnt by experience. War alone teaches this lesson."*

War, in opposition to peace, does more to arouse national life and to expand national power than any other means known to history. It certainly brings much material and mental distress in its train, but at the same time it evokes the noblest activities of the human nature. This is especially so under present-day conditions, when it can be regarded not merely as the affair of Sovereigns and Governments, but as the expression of the united will of a whole nation.

All petty private interests shrink into insignificance before the grave decision which a war involves. The common danger unites all in a common effort, and the man who shirks this duty to the community is deservedly spurned. This union contains a liberating power which produces happy and permanent results in the national life. We need only recall the uniting power of the War of Liberation or the Franco-German War and their historical consequences. The brutal incidents inseparable from every war vanish completely before the idealism of the main result. All the sham reputations which a long spell of peace undoubtedly fosters are unmasked. Great personalities take their proper place; strength, truth, and honour come to the front and are put into play. "A thousand touching traits testify to the sacred power of the love which a righteous war awakes in noble nations."†

The individual can perform no nobler action than to pledge his life on his convictions, and to devote his own existence to the cause which he serves, or even to the conception of the value of ideals to personal morality. Similarly, nations and States can achieve no loftier consummation than to stake their whole power on upholding their independence, their honour and their reputation.

Such sentiments, however, can only be put into practice in war. The possibility of war is required to give the national character that stimulus from which these sentiments spring, and thus only are nations enabled to

---

* Kuno Fischer, "Hegel," i., p. 737
† Treitschke, "Deutsche Geschichte," i., p. 482

do justice to the highest duties of civilization by the fullest development of their moral forces. An intellectual and vigorous nation can experience no worse destiny than to be lulled into a Phaeacian existence by the undisputed enjoyment of peace.

From this point of view, efforts to secure peace are extraordinarily detrimental to the national health so soon as they influence politics. The States which from various considerations are always active in this direction are sapping the roots of their own strength. The United States of America, *e.g.*, in June 1911, championed the ideas of universal peace in order to be able to devote their undisturbed attention to money-making and the enjoyment of wealth, and to save the three hundred million dollars which they spend on their army and navy; they thus incur a great danger, not so much from the possibility of a war with England or Japan, but precisely because they try to exclude all chance of contest with opponents of their own strength, and thus avoid the stress of great political emotions, without which the moral development of the national character is impossible. If they advance farther on this road, they will one day pay dearly for such a policy.

Again, from the Christian standpoint we arrive at the same conclusion. Christian morality is based, indeed, on the law of love. "Love God above all things and thy neighbour as thyself." This law can claim no significance for the relations of one country to another, since its application to politics would lead to a conflict of duties. The love which a man showed to another country as such would imply a want of love for his own countrymen. Such a system of politics must inevitably lead men astray. Christian morality is personal and social, and in its nature cannot be political. Its object is to promote morality of the individual, in order to strengthen him to work unselfishly in the interests of the community. It tells us to love our individual enemies, but does not remove the conception of enmity. Christ Himself said: "I am not come to send peace on earth, but a sword." His teaching can never be adduced as an argument against the universal law of struggle. There never was a religion which was more combative than Christianity. Combat, moral combat, is its very essence. If we transfer the ideas of Christianity to the sphere of politics, we can claim to raise the power of the State—power in the widest sense, not merely from the material aspect—to the highest degree, with the object of the moral advancement of humanity, and under certain conditions the sacrifice may be made which a war demands. Thus, according to Christianity, we cannot disapprove of war in itself, but must admit that it is justified morally and historically.

Reflection thus shows not only that war is an unqualified necessity, but that it is justifiable from every point of view. The practical methods which the adherents of the peace idea have proposed for the prevention of war are shown to be absolutely ineffective.

The Character of Our Next War

If we look at our general political position, we cannot expect support from any one in carrying out our positive political plans. England, France, and Russia have a common interest in breaking down our power. This interest will sooner or later be asserted by arms. It is not therefore the interest of any nation to increase Germany's power. If we wish to attain an extension of our power, as is natural in our position, we must win it by the sword against vastly superior foes. Our alliances are defensive, not merely in form, but essentially so. I have already shown that this is a cause of their weakness. Neither Austria nor Italy are in any way bound to support by armed force a German policy directed towards an increase of power. We are not even sure of their diplomatic help, as the conduct of Italy at the conference of Algeciras sufficiently demonstrated. It even seems questionable at the present moment whether we can always reckon on the support of the members of the Triple Alliance in a defensive war. The recent *rapprochement* of Italy with France and England goes far beyond the idea of an "extra turn." If we consider how difficult Italy would find it to make her forces fit to cope with France, and to protect her coasts against hostile attacks, and if we think how the annexation of Tripoli has created a new possession, which is not easily defended against France and England, we may fairly doubt whether Italy would take part in a war in which England and France were allied against us. Austria is undoubtedly a loyal ally. Her interests are closely connected with our own, and her policy is dominated by the same spirit of loyalty and integrity as ours towards Austria. Nevertheless there is cause for anxiety, because in a conglomerate State like Austria, which contains numerous Slavonic elements, patriotism may not be strong enough to allow the Government to fight to the death with Russia, were the latter to defeat us. The occurrence of such an event is not improbable. When enumerating the possibilities that might affect our policy, we cannot leave this one out of consideration.

We shall therefore some day, perhaps, be faced with the necessity of standing isolated in a great war of the nations, as once Frederick the Great stood, when he was basely deserted by England in the middle of the struggle, and shall have to trust to our own strength and our own resolution for victory.

Such a war—for us more than for any other nation—must be a war for our political and national existence. This must be so, for our opponents can only attain their political aims by almost annihilating us by land and by sea. If the victory is only half won, they would have to expect continuous renewals of the contest, which would be contrary to their interests. They know that well enough, and therefore avoid the contest, since we shall certainly defend ourselves with the utmost bitterness and obstinacy. If, notwithstanding, circumstances make the war inevitable, then the intention of our enemies to crush us to the ground, and our own resolve to maintain our position victoriously, will make it a war of desperation. A war fought and lost under such circumstances would destroy our laboriously gained political importance, would jeopardize the whole future of our nation, would throw us back for centuries, would shake the influence of German thought in the civilized world, and thus check the general progress of mankind in its healthy development, for which a flourishing Germany is the essential condition. Our next war will be fought for the highest interests of our country and of mankind. This will invest it with importance in the world's history. "World power or downfall!" will be our rallying cry.

Keeping this idea before us, we must prepare for war with the confident intention of conquering, and with the iron resolve to persevere to the end, come what may.

We must therefore prepare not only for a short war, but for a protracted campaign. We must be armed in order to complete the overthrow of our enemies, should the victory be ours; and, if worsted, to continue to defend ourselves in the very heart of our country until success at last is won.

It is therefore by no means enough to maintain a certain numerical equality with our opponents. On the contrary, we must strive to call up the entire forces of the nation, and prepare and arm for the great decision which impends. We must try also to gain a certain superiority over our opponents in the crucial points, so that we may hold some winning trumps in our hand in a contest unequal from the very first. We must bear these two points in mind when preparing for war. Only by continually realizing the duties thus laid on us can we carry out our preparedness to the fullest, and satisfy the demands which the future makes on us. A nation of 65,000,000 which stakes *all* her forces on winning herself a position, and on keeping that position, cannot be conquered. But it is an evil day for her if she relies on the semblance of power, or, miscalculating her enemies' strength, is content with half-measures, and looks to luck or chance for that which can only be attained by the exertion and development of all her powers.

Financial and Political Preparation

We must consider England, as well as France and Russia. We must expect not only an attack by sea on our North Sea coasts, but a landing of English forces on the continent of Europe and a violation of Belgo-Dutch neutrality by our enemies. It is also not inconceivable that England may land troops in Schleswig or Jutland, and try to force Denmark into war with us. It seems further questionable whether Austria will be in a position to support us with all her forces, whether she will not rather be compelled to safeguard her own particular interests on her south and south-east frontiers. An attack by France through Switzerland is also increasingly probable, if a complete reorganization of the grouping of the European States is effected. Finally, we should be seriously menaced in the Baltic if Russia gains time to reconstruct her fleet.

All these unfavourable conditions will certainly not occur simultaneously, but under certain not impossible political combinations they are more or less probable, and must be taken into account from the military aspect. The military situation thus created is very unfavourable.

If under such uncertain conditions it should be necessary to place the army on a war footing, only one course is left: we must meet the situation by calling out strategic reserves, which must be all the stronger since the political conditions are so complicated and obscure, and those opponents so strong on whose possible share in the war we must count. The strategic reserve will be to some extent a political one also. A series of protective measures, necessary in any case, would have to be at once set on foot, but the mass of the army would not be directed to any definite point until the entire situation was clear and all necessary steps could be considered. Until that moment the troops of the strategic reserve would be left in their garrisons or collected along the railway lines and at railway centres in such a way that, when occasion arose, they could be despatched in any direction. On the same principle the rolling-stock on the lines would have to be kept in readiness, the necessary time-tables for the different transport arrangements drawn up, and stores secured in safe depots on as many different lines of march as possible. Previous arrangments for unloading at the railway stations must be made in accordance with the most various political prospects. We should in any case be forced to adopt a waiting policy, a strategic defensive, which under present conditions is extremely unfavourable; we should not be able to prevent an invasion by one or other of our enemies.

No proof is necessary to show that a war thus begun cannot hold out good prospects of success. The very bravest army must succumb if led against a crushingly superior force under most unfavourable conditions. A military investigation of the situation shows that a plan of campaign, such as would be required here on the inner line, presents, under the modern system of "mass" armies, tremendous difficulties, and has to cope with strategic conditions of the most unfavourable kind.

The disadvantages of such a situation can only be avoided by a policy which makes it feasible to act on the offensive, and, if possible, to overthrow the one antagonist before the other can actively interfere. On this initiative our safety now depends, just as it did in the days of Frederick the Great. We must look this truth boldly in the face. Of course, it can be urged that an attack is just what would produce an unfavourable position for us, since it creates the conditions on which the Franco-Russian alliance would be brought into activity. If we attacked France or Russia, the ally would be compelled to bring help, and we should be in a far worse position than if we had only one enemy to fight. Let it then be the task of our diplomacy so to shuffle the cards that we may be attacked by France, for then there would be reasonable prospect that Russia for a time would remain neutral.

This view undoubtedly deserves attention, but we must not hope to bring about this attack by waiting passively. Neither France nor Russia nor England need to attack in order to further their interest. So long as we shrink from attack, they can force us to submit to their will by diplomacy, as the upshot of the Morocco negotiation shows.

If we wish to bring about an attack by our opponents, we must initiate an active policy which, without attacking France, will so prejudice her interest or those of England, that both these States would feel themselves compelled to attack us. Opportunities for such procedure are offered both in Africa and Europe, and anyone who has attentively studied prominent political utterances can easily satisfy himself on this point.

In opposition to these ideas the view is frequently put forward that we should wait quietly and let time fight for us, since from the force of circumstances many prizes will fall into our laps which we have now to struggle hard for. Unfortunately such politicians always forget to state clearly and definitely what facts are really working in their own interests and what advantages will accrue to us therefrom. Such political wisdom is not to be taken seriously, for it has no solid foundation. We must reckon with the definitely given conditions, and realize that timidity and *laissez-aller* have never led to great results.

It is impossible for anyone not close at hand to decide what steps and measures are imposed upon our foreign policy, in order to secure a favourable political situation should the pending questions so momentous to Germany's existence come to be settled by an appeal to arms. This requires a full and accurate knowledge of the political and diplomatic position which I do not possess. One thing only can be justly said: Beyond the confusion and contradictions of the present situation we must keep before us the great issues which will not lose their importance as time goes on.

Italy, which has used a favourable moment in order to acquire settlements for her very rapidly increasing population (487,000 persons emigrated from Italy in 1908), can never combine with France and England to fulfill her political ambition of winning the supremacy in the Mediterranean, since both these States themselves claim the place. The effort to break up the Triple Alliance has momentarily favoured the Italian policy of expansion. But this incident does not alter in the least the fact that the true interest of Italy demands adherence to the Triple Alliance, which alone can procure her Tunis and Biserta. The importance of these considerations will continue to be felt.

Turkey also cannot permanently go hand-in-hand with England, France, and Russia, whose policy must always aim directly at the annihilation of present-day Turkey. Islam has now as ever her most powerful enemies in England and Russia, and will, sooner or later, be forced to join the Central European Alliance, although we committed the undoubted blunder of abandoning her in Morocco.

There is no true community of interests between Russia and England; in Central Asia, in Persia, as in the Mediterranean, their ambitions clash in spite of all conventions, and the state of affairs in Japan and China is forcing on a crisis which is vital to Russian interests and to some degree ties her hands.

All these matters open out a wide vista to German statesmanship, if it is equal to its task, and make the general outlook less gloomy than recent political events seemed to indicate. And, then, our policy can count on a factor of strength such as no other State possesses—on an army whose military efficiency, I am convinced, cannot be sufficiently valued. Not that it is perfect in all its arrangements and details. We have amply shown the contrary. But the spirit which animates the troops, the ardour of attack, the heroism, the loyalty which prevail amongst them, justify the highest expectations. I am certain that if they are soon to be summoned to arms, their exploits will astonish the world, provided only that they are led with skill and determination. The German nation, too—of this I am equally convinced—will rise to the height of its great duty. A mighty force which only awaits the summons sleeps in its soul. Whoever to-day can awaken the slumbering idealism of this people, and rouse the national enthusiasm by placing before its eyes a worthy and comprehensible ambition, will be able to sweep this people on in united strength to the highest efforts and sacrifices, and will achieve a truly magnificent result.

In the consciousness of being able at any time to call up these forces, and in the sure trust that they will not fail in the hour of danger, our Government can firmly tread the path which leads to a splendid future; but it will not be able to liberate all the forces of Germany unless it wins her confidence by successful action and takes for its motto the brave words of Goethe:

> Bid defiance to every power!
> Ever valiant, never cower!
> To the brave soldier open flies
> The golden gate of Paradise.

Europe—After the War

Dr. Ivan Yovitchévitch
Secretary General of the Council
of State of Montenegro

THE AMERICAN REVIEW OF REVIEWS, March 1915

A prognostication about Europe after the war came as early as 1915 from a Balkan statesman who attempted to predict the war's duration and the adjustments that would follow. His analysis of the situation was mailed from Detinje which is about twenty miles from Podgorica—now called Titograd, Montenegro's capital. His letter went through the Italian postal service in Albania to Review of Reviews *Magazine in New York City. Basically it was an appeal for United States relief for the food shortage and poverty in Montenegro due to the war conditions.*

Dr. Ivan Yovitchévitch was Secretary General of the Council of State of Montenegro, "a statesman of high accomplishment and wide acquaintance" according to the magazine that published his views. There can be little doubt that much of what he reported was factual, but his prejudice, based on the history of the state, is also in evidence.

Montenegro is at the southern end of the Dinaric Alps and partially consists of the barren karst of Montenegro proper. On the west it is separated by the Zeta River and its plains from the higher Brda on the east. Here there are forest and pastures. Agriculture is almost nonexistent with people depending mostly on home industries for their livelihood. Transportation is poor, roads are bad and railroads are scarce. The Montenegrin people are Serbs who for 500 years, from the 14th to the 19th century, were involved in their principal activity—fighting the Turks who never entirely conquered their mountain stronghold.

The region constituting Montenegro was, in the 14th century, the virtually independent principality of Zeta in the Serbian empire. After Serbia was defeated by the Turks in the battle of Kossova (1389) Montenegro continued to resist and became a refuge for Servian nobles who fled the Turkish hordes.

Under Nicholas I (reigned 1860–1918) Montenegro was formally recognized as an independent state at the Congress of Berlin (1878) which vastly increased its territory and gave it a narrow outlet on the Adriatic. In 1910 Nicholas proclaimed himself king. He fought the Ottomans in the Balkan Wars and took Scutari in 1913, but was forced by the pressure of the European powers to evacuate it. Montenegro did, however, receive part of the territory claimed by newly independent Albania, and when the first World War broke out the Montenegrins invaded Albania. Montenegro declared war on Austria in August 1914, but late in 1915 it was overrun by Austrian-German forces. In November 1918 a national assembly declared Nicholas deposed and effected the union of Montenegro with Serbia. (The new constitution (1946) of Yugoslavia made Montenegro an autonomous people's republic and enlarged its territory by adding a section of Dalmation coast.)

The editors of the magazine felt that Dr. Yovitchévitch's plea for help deserved attention, and stated, "His appeal is worthy of response. Who will help the Montenegrins?"

In an authorized interview last summer I ventured to predict that war was imminent in Europe, and that the principal causes of war lay smouldering in the Balkans, which I had pictured as a slumbering volcano with three craters. My boldness in predicting the future appeared most presumptuous, perhaps the more so since the twentieth century is not an age of prophets.

Yet from my thorough knowledge of the situation in the Balkans I was practically certain that one of the craters would burst forth and inflame all Europe. I would be very happy if I had been mistaken.

Alas, my prophecy was fulfilled and the "second Balkan crater,"—that is to say—the ill feeling between Servia and Austria eventually cast the spark that set Europe on fire; and for many months the horrors of war have increased at a frightful rate, the number of the dead, the maimed, the widows and orphans receiving a daily increment. Ancient monuments lie in ruins; entire countries are ravaged by fire, and the armies, mad with blood lust have become such savages that they respect nothing that lies in their path. In the light of these horrible disasters one is obliged to conclude that there is but little difference between the warriors of today and the barbarian hordes of the Huns, who, under the leadership of their chief, Attila, sacked a part of southern Europe; it is this that has covered the twentieth century with shame.

Sad and impressive instances are the evil deeds of the German armies that hurled themselves like a plague upon unhappy Belgium. These armies committed such atrocities that the whole world was stupefied and dumbfounded. They burned towns and villages, massacring on their way men, women and children. The Austrian armies did the same thing in the countries that they occupied for a time; of this the poor Serb nation knows something. The armies of the other belligerents will do identically the same as soon as they arrive in the countries inhabited by the German race. Europe is, then, a hell, and its inhabitants are devils who kill one another like the lowest savages, the everlasting shame of our twentieth-century civilization.

How Long Will This Lamentable Situation Continue?

The duration of this war is a matter of world-wide concern. May I be permitted to express my opinion that the contest must continue for a long time and for this reason: A half-year has passed since the beginning of hostilities and the belligerents are at about the same point that they were at the outset, so far as victory is concerned. It is true that the losses are enormous, but who are the vanquished and who are the victors?

It is indisputable that this question remains unanswered up to this moment, and each belligerent is still animated with the firm resolve to conquer, and with the same hope that was cherished in the first days of hostilities. The second reason that makes me believe that this deplorable situation must last a long time is this: The two great giants, worthy combatants one of the other, for their strength, intrepidity and tactics, the Russian and the German, who are the preponderant factors in this monstrous struggle, do not seem to want to engage in a decisive combat. They are like two wrestlers who are afraid of each other and delay taking the hazard of a grapple; each, circling his adversary, hopes to conquer him when his strength is exhausted.

When these two big European antagonists, the Russian and the German, employ the tactics of two fear-struck wrestlers, it goes without saying that the European war will continue for a considerable period, granting that the two antagonists are equally matched in their economic and physical strength and in the matter of their *morale*.

It appears incontestable that the horrors of this war, which are without parallel, will continue for a lengthy period, and that the unfortunate people must endure more suffering and atrocities without number.

How Will the Terrible Struggle End?

The second question, not less interesting, is to know how the European war will end. When the hostilities began it was extremely difficult to give an opinion on either side, but one can say now that the chances of victory are on the side of Russia and her allies. One can say that the German plan has failed. This plan was to fall suddenly upon France and crush her completely before the concentration of the Russian armies could be accomplished, and then, thanks to her network of railroads, transport the German troops to the Russian frontier and defeat the armies of the Czar before their complete mobilization could be effected. But on one side the heroic resistance of the Belgians and on the other the quick mobilization of the Russians caused Germany to change her plans and transport a large part of her forces to East Prussia, which General Rennenkampf had penetrated with a Russian army. That saved Paris and perhaps the whole French army.

Austria-Hungary on her side was persuaded that Servia and Montenegro would be subdued in a short time and that, once in touch with Bulgaria and Turkey, she would force Rumania to join the two other states against Russia. However, the heroic resistance of the Serbs and the Montenegrins astonished the whole world, and because of the three above-mentioned facts, the plans of Germany and Austria-Hungary could not be carried out. And this plan, having failed at the beginning of the war, has no chance whatever of succeeding in the future.

Therefore it appears that the European war cannot be brought to an end by decisive battles, but only by the complete exhaustion of one of the parties, and as Germany and Austria-Hungary are comparatively in a state of blockade, one can say without fear of being mistaken that these two powers will be the more quickly exhausted; their adversaries being masters of the sea, they can without doubt resist longer from an economic point of view.

To conclude then, we can say with certainty that the Russians and their allies have the best of it, and that this terrible struggle will end in the complete defeat of Germany and Austria-Hungary.

The Probable Consequences

And what will be the result? The outcome of the present war may be conceived thus:

First: Russia will expand at the expense of Austria-Hungary, will annex Galicia, and will demand from Turkey the occupation of Constantinople and a part of Asia Minor.

Second: France will regain her two former provinces of Alsace and Lorraine.

Third: England will be benefited by gaining possession of the German colonies, as well as a part of Asia Minor.

Fourth: Belgium will receive as recompense for her stoic resistence the Duchy of Luxemburg.

Fifth: The two kindred kingdoms of Servia and Montenegro will receive as a reward for a struggle not less stoical, the two Austrian provinces peopled by the Serb race.

Sixth: Italy as a reward for her neutrality would receive the provinces of Austria-Hungary inhabited by Italians.

Seventh: Rumania for the same reason would receive Bukovina, an Austrian province peopled largely by Rumanians.

As to Turkey, which has been dragged into the war by German political intrigue, she will be erased from the map as an independent country. It will be the same with Albania; for her inhabitants, who are in a state of perpetual anarchy, cannot long exist as an independent people.

This, then, is my view of the conditions that will be imposed upon the conquered. Perhaps changes may be even greater; for it is possible that

Austria-Hungary, like Turkey, may cease to exist as an independent empire. Nor is it inconceivable that certain provinces might be snatched from Germany, as for example German Poland. But here you have in a few words my opinion of the actual situation now existing in Europe, and my predictions of the future.

PART II

THE POLITICS OF WAR

During the initial stages of the war, countries jockeyed for position, looking for the right partners with similar backgrounds and ambitions. Once united in combat, they announced the righteousness of their cause, and that eventual victory would be theirs. In the meantime, politicians formed cliques to pressure governments and made secret deals. In smoke-filled rooms, schemers plotted their profitable futures in new and more limited societies.

Are the German People Unanimously for the War?

William English Walling

THE OUTLOOK MAGAZINE, November 25, 1914

In the years before the war, despite the omnipresence of militarism, the periodic explosions of the ebullient, saber-rattling Kaiser, the militant indiscretions of the bumptious subaltern Crown Prince, the steady, remorseless expansion of the Army and Navy, the unconcealed and unconcealable preparations for Der Tag—*Germany was to all intents and purposes absorbed, like most of the world, in the arts of peaceful development. So wrote Frederic William Wile in his book* News Is Where You Find It *(The Bobbs-Merrill Co., 1939). A young reporter, just married, Walling took up his assignment in Berlin in 1901, as a representative of the Chicago* Daily News.

Speaking of the German citizenry he said, "Her people were genial and congenial. They were hearty, healthy, a race of intelligent, patriotic, tolerant, hospitable, home-loving, music-worshiping folk, who ate ravenously and sometimes audibly, and drank freely but capably.

"Their captains of industry—the Ballins, the Heineckes, the Stinnesses, the Thyssens, the Borsigs, the Lowewes, the Rathenaus, the Friedlander-Fulds, the Siemans-Halskes, the Stumms—did not dominate the social or political scene. That was still the preserve of the Junkers *and the military caste. Nevertheless, Germans, like ourselves, the British and the French, were mainly concerned, in the opening years of the new century, with their economic humanitarian and intellectual works and progress. War had no place in the average Teuton citizen's design for living.*

"In the field of business, especially industry and export, the United States was the Fatherland's model. Soon after I took up my post at Berlin, the Emperor dispatched Privy Commercial Councillor Ludwig Max Goldberger, an eminent Jewish captialist, on a special mission of investigation and discovery to our country. The result of his trip was a book called The Land of Unlimited Possibilities, *whose title added a popular idiom to the German language of the day. Before his departure for America, Herr Goldberger used to invite me to come to see him occasionally, to get a few pointers and to practice his English conversation. The* Geheimer Kommerzienrat, *a keen observer, came home, brimming with enthusiasm over everything seen and heard on our side of the Atlantic—from our* Wolkenkratzer *(cloud scratchers—German for skyscrapers) to mail chutes and ice water bubblers."*

Mr. Wile and his bride of less than three months, Bunny, knew nothing of the German language and depended upon the United States Consul General Frank H. Mason and Mrs. Mason for their advice—all the way from where to live to where to open an office.

The Consul General, an Ohioan, a former managing editor of the Cleveland Leader, *reserve Captain in the Union Army who saw service under General Grant at Vicksburg in 1863, entered the consular service under President Garfield, and for 33 years served until he retired in 1913.*

The Masons advised Wile and his wife to take a room in the West End until they were ready for housekeeping, and suggested that they establish the Chicago Daily News *office in the Equitable Building at Berlin's most prominent business center, the corner of Friedrich and Leipzigerstrassen, not only because it was the property of the Equitable Life Assurance Society of the United States but because it housed the Consulate-General. As an office neighbor, Mason hinted, he could keep an eye on him and steer him to many a story that originated in the consulate.*

One of the offices in the Equitable Gebaude was the German office of the American insurance company. In its managerial staff was a German named Wilhelm Schact who had spent some time in the United States and had a son, Hjalmer Horace Greeley Schact, the same Dr. Schact who became Reichsbank president in the early days of the republic. Dr. Schact tried to improve his English with free conversational lessons, and to that end, he spent many hours in the Daily News *bureau for a smoke and talks in the afternoons.*

When the reporter spent a brief honeymoon in London, he spent a weekend at the Thames-side country home of Colonel Hunsiker, the London representative of the United States Steel Corporation, who in turn introduced him to J. O'Hara Murray, European manager of the Worthington Pump and Machinery Corporation, and his wife Louise Nicholoson who had achieved artistic success as a singer in St. Petersburg and Moscow.

The Murrays invited the Wiles to stay with them in Berlin, and so the young couple moved out of the West End, and soon they met with the high social strata of the country.

Many of the United States news correspondents were seduced in this manner. Not knowing the language, following the advice of the Consul General, meeting the elite society and industrialists, it became difficult for the people back home to get the feeling of the average citizen in Germany.

The Outlook Magazine, *a weekly publication in the United States, went to an opposite extreme. Understanding that Socialism was sweeping Europe, the publication was concerned that European Socialists, who had always been ardent opponents of war, had, at least temporarily, given up their internationalism and were now patriotically supporting their national governments. The magazine approached a well-known American Socialist, William English Walling, who tried to show that the international movement had not broken down, but that one of the definite results of the European war would be a promotion in Europe of socialistic ideas and policies.*

In this war social differences have disappeared; even the Social Democrats stand behind us.—*Von Bethmann-Hollweg, Chancellor of the German Empire.*

It is one of the fundamental errors of American newspapers that this is a war of kings. Most emphatically it is a war of the German people. If any proof is needed for this statement, look at the attitude of the leaders of the German Social Democrats, who are loyally supporting the Emperor.—*Count von Bernstorff, German Ambassador to the United States.*

It is evident from these and many similar statements from the highest authorities that the German Government bases its case largely on the claim that the German people are unanimously behind it in this war.

Unfortunately, the German Government, which has failed to impress the public of the neutral countries with many of its arguments, has apparently succeeded in this instance. Hardly an important article, editorial, or opinion of the war fails to state or to assume that popular sentiment in Germany is, indeed, unanimous. Whatever doubts existed seem to have been entirely removed as it became generally known that on August 4, when the war was already going on in France, when Belgium was invaded, and the German people were aware of both these facts, the Social Democrats in the Reichstag allowed the socialist vote to be cast solidly for the war loan of five billion marks and permitted a declaration which said that they regarded the war as a purely defensive struggle against Russian despotism.

But if we look into the events leading up to this action of the 4th of August; if we look closely into the councils of the party during the first days of the war; and, above all, if we take note of the position of the party organ, "Vorwaerts," since the war began, we shall see indications that the German people are by no means unitedly for the war, and that the four million Socialists are split badly on the question. While admitting the undeniable fact that the Socialist *majority* did give its financial and moral support to the Kaiser, we shall discover that there is already a very large minority against the war.

Let us go back one year. In 1913 a large increase in military expenditures and in the size of the army was demanded. It was at that time that the German Socialist majority first surrendered to militarism. Of the 110 Socialist members of the Reichstag in the 1913 session, 51 were in favor of granting money for the army increase and 37 were against it, the rest being absent from the caucus or abstaining from the vote. The Socialist party, however, binds its minorities by a unit rule, so that the Socialists cast their 110 votes, as they did this year, solidly for the Government proposal.

Last year the official arguments of the majority were: that, since the rich and well-to-do, for the first time, were to pay the larger part of the new taxes, they would soon begin to oppose armaments and war; that to vote against this new taxation for military purposes would have only a moral value as the taxes would be passed anyway, in some form in spite of Socialist opposition; that if the Socialists did not vote for new military taxes to be levied against the rich, the other parties would vote for new military taxes to be levied against the poor; and, above all, that the precedent of graduated taxation, an innovation for the Empire, could be used later to raise money from the upper classes for the purposes of social reform.

Against this reasoning the Socialist minority pointed out that the rich and well-to-do would rather pay the taxes than forego the armaments of which they got the chief advantage, and that if they felt the burden shifting too rapidly onto their shoulders they would seek a solution by hastening the war to which so many of them looked forward. They argued that every minority must first offer an opposition that gives moral rather than practical results before it can hope to become a majority. They showed how the Government itself—largely for militaristic reasons—favored throwing the latest military burden on the shoulders of those best able to carry it without injuring the nation's industry. And they concluded that not all the social reform in the world could justify surrender to the arch-enemy of democracy, militarism.

But these anti-military arguments had no weight with the majority. For their real motive was not disclosed until the Socialist Congress was held several months after the vote in the Reichstag. A leading editorial of "Vorwaerts" pointed out that two of the most eminent leaders of the majority, Fischer and David, had publicly admitted that one of the majority's motives was the fear that if the Socialists did not vote for the military taxes their representation in the Reichstag would be reduced from 110 to 40.

Here, then, is their whole case. Militarism is highly popular among many classes in Germany. If the Socialists opposed it, the sixty or seventy Socialist Reichstag members of the majority faction would lose their seats. Only the forty-odd members of the minority, representing the most industrialized districts where live the working people (who now compose the majority of the population of Germany), could have been sure of being returned at a new election fought on the issue of militarism *versus* anti-militarism. For, because of Germany's unequal election districts, the rest of the Socialist members owe their election not to the anti-militarist laboring masses but to "progressive" votes given them for the most part at the second ballot. That is, they are dependent on the lower middle classes—small officials, clerks, and conservative artisans—who hold the political balance of power. These classes are either pro-militarist or very hesitant anti-militarists. By failing to satisfy such voters and losing their seats, the Socialist majority would at the same time lose, not only their careers (which may have influenced some of them), but also their power to advance those social and democratic reforms they have so much at heart (which doubtless influenced all). *In order to be in a position to win these reforms for the people of Germany, they were ready to support the Kaiser in his preparations for a possible war against the people of other countries.* That this was their position in 1913 will be clear to any one who takes the trouble to consult the proceedings of last year's Party Congress. That it is their position this year, in supporting the war itself, is evident from the statements of Scheidemann, Suedekum, and other leaders printed in the American Socialist press.

The division within the party is nearly the same now as it was last year. Karl Liebknecht, the leader of the minority, assures us that the meeting of the Socialist caucus on the 3rd of August witnessed a discussion "of a violence hitherto unknown" in the party's history; and he and sixteen other Socialist members of the Reichstag (a large number being absent) stood out to the end against the war. These are the members from the most populous election districts, and they are in the closest touch with their constituents. The representatives of at least a million German voters, then, stand as opponents to the war. There may be militarist minorities in their districts, but we can be sure that there are at least as great anti-militarist minorities in other constituencies.

"Vorwaerts" has always represented the main current of Socialist opinion, and it is highly probable that it represents the main current of Socialist opinion now—or certainly that of a very large faction. During the whole of the past year it has been conducting the liveliest kind of an anti-militarist agitation, which has frequently figured in cable despatches. In fact, this was its chief work for many months before the war. It was "Vorwaerts," for example, that published the Krupp scandal, as well as Karl Liebknecht's second revelation concerning the wholesale selling of titles. And in the weeks immediately preceding the war it was filled with the agitation of Rosa Luxemburg and others against the army. After the notorious Zabern affair she had said that cruelties committed by officers were an every-day affair in the barracks. The Government proceeded to prosecute her, and the Socialists responded by securing thirty-two thousand cases of recent acts of cruelty and over a thousand witnesses. "Vorwaerts" was still leading the campaign with the greatest bitterness in the middle of July.

As the war approached, about July 25, this anti-military agitation became even more intense, and finally turned into an anti-war demonstration of the first magnitude. Influenced, no doubt, by the radicalism of the Socialists of Greater Berlin, who furnish most of its readers, "Vorwaerts" took an especially fearless stand. Day after day it warned the Government, in thinly veiled terms, that a declaration of war might lead to defeat and to revolution. It put the chief blame for the impending war on Austria, and declared that the German Government knew that to support Austria's outrageous demands against Servia meant war. Even Russian mobilization, it showed, was a natural and unavoidable result of Austria's actions. As late as July 31 "Vorwaerts" declared that the French Government sincerely desired peace and that the Russian Government, "in spite of its mobilization," was ready for far-reaching concessions.

On July 29 the Socialists held gigantic war demonstrations throughout Germany. At one single meeting of the twenty-eight called by Berlin Socialists on this day, seventy thousand persons were present. In Berlin, Cologne, and elsewhere riots occurred, and it is claimed that the anti-militarists usually got the best of the "patriotic" mobs, except where the latter were aided by the police. In the Kingdom of Wurtemburg the Socialist party of that country, which was holding a Congress at the time, adopted a revolutionary resolution, proposed by Clara Zetkin, which clearly suggested a general strike.

Even since the declaration of war, under the very eyes of the military censor, and in the very presence of the terrors of martial law, "Vorwaerts" has cleverly managed to continue its anti-military agitation. Frequent cables have shown the general recognition of the value of its work, and its anti-war trend has been widely recognized. On Monday, August 3, when the Social Democratic group in the Reichstag decided to vote in favor of the war budget, "Vorwaerts" printed an article condemning German "patriotism" and the "patriots" who had suddenly become warriors fighting for "freedom against Czarism."

The article, which is entitled "War against Czarism" exposes the fallacy of this so-called Russian peril.

"Russia today is no longer a stronghold of reaction, but a land of revolution. The overthrow of the monarchy and of Czarism is now the aim of the Russian people in general, and of the Russian workers in particular."

The article points out that shortly before war was declared Russia was in the midst of a revolutionary blaze that was sweeping the country. The menacing general strike spread until stopped by the declaration of war. The Czarism had been strengthened then, not weakened by the declaration of war.

When Germany entered Belgium, "Vorwaerts" said, significantly: "Now when the war god reigns supreme, not only over the time but also over the press, we cannot say concerning the invasion of Belgium what we would like to say about it." On August 30 it had the courage to declare that the Belgian peasants ought not to be "punished," as they had been, for defending their homes without uniforms, since the German *Landsturm* was explicitly permitted to do the same thing according to the very words of the Prussian law. The real purpose of this editorial, as of many others, was to call the attention of the German soldiers to the fact that they were fighting a war of aggression. In Germany it raised a storm.

When it became a well-established fact that Italy had decided to break with the Triple Alliance, every "patriotic" German cried out against Germany's former ally. But "Vorwaerts," instead of condemning Italy, spoke enthusiastically in favor of its maintaining the position of neutrality.

When the Socialist leaders Guesde and Sembat, with the unanimous approval of their party, became members of the French Cabinet, "Vorwaerts" pointed out that this proved that the French proletariat regarded it as a people's war, and that Germany would be able to conquer only by conquering the French proletariat.

Guesde and Sembat, we are told, not only did rightly to enter the Cabinet, but are the finest types of Socialists. Guesde is described as "the old fighting companion of Marx and Engels, the founder and organizer of the Marxian tendency in France, the most uncompromising partisan of the idea of class struggle, the sworn enemy of every kind of opportunism." As to Sembat, "Vorwaerts" cites his speech of the 2nd of August, in which he defined the present war waged by France as one which was aimed neither at conquests nor at the destruction of German culture. This leads "Vorwaerts" to remark:

"The French nation is defending its existence, its unity, and its independence.

"Our comrades did not refuse the grave responsibility of this momentous hour. They felt that the independence and security of the nation are the first condition of its political and social emancipation, and they did not think it was possible for them to refuse their aid to that country in its struggle for life."

Could this be plainer? German territory and culture are not even attacked but France is struggling for existence. No wonder the "Vorwaerts" office was mobbed by "patriots" shortly after the printing of this editorial!

Surely this approval of the attitude of the French, Belgian, and Italian working people justified the indignation of the German anti-Socialist press, which rightly pointed out that such talk was no way to insure success in the war. But "Vorwaerts" ignored the attacks of its militarist enemies—which twice led to its suspension—and for two solid months continued to use every weapon in its journalistic arsenal against the supporters of the war.

Another editorial that must have infuriated the militarists was that of August 25, in which, ably avoiding every possible deadlock with the military authorities, the Socialist organ yet succeeded in pointing out that the supposed justification of the war, that it was a war of defense against Russia, had fallen away and that it had become a war of aggression.

If, after a series of defeats, the position of "Vorwaerts" becomes the position of the Socialists generally, and so of a large part of the German nation, the importance of this declaration cannot be overstated. Here are the two leading paragraphs:

"When the war broke out, the word went round, 'War against Czarism!' That was the cry that made the war seem inevitable even to those who were against it. . . . To military experts it appeared an unavoidable necessity that France must be first overcome, in order to advance with Austria against Russia. And to this necessity even those who mourn the frightful fate which drives two civilized peoples into this murderous struggle must resign themselves. . . . From the *military* point of view the first necessity is to overcome France. On the other hand, *politically*, the most urgent necessity is the overthrow and destruction of 'Czarism.' . . .

"If we should not succeed in overcoming 'Czarism,' if the strategic necessity should push the political necessity into the background, then, whatever the intentions of the rulers, the final result might lead to a return of the 'Holy Alliance,' in which 'Czarism' would once more hold the dominating influence, instead of a union of the civilized nations. . . . Then this war *would lose its justification.*" [Author's italics]

In other words, there is no moral justification for a war with France, and the Kaiser may soon find himself in another "holy" alliance with the Czar. This would scarcely surprise the readers of the Socialist press. For until the outbreak of the war the two monarchs, as their published correspondence shows, were on the terms of the greatest friendship, and German Socialist critics of the Czar were under prosecution this very year, precisely as if they had commited *lèse majesté* against the Kaiser himself. Socialists have been reminded of all this since the war.

A special full-page article of September 26, two days before the second suspension, celebrated the fiftieth anniversary of the foundation of the "International." In the course of the discussion of the main subject it recalls the fact that Bebel and Liebknecht had opposed the Franco-Prussian war to the very end, and it knows that these two names still carry more weight with the German masses than those of the Socialist leaders who are now with the Kaiser. Next, it reminds the reader that the French and Belgian Socialists have organized "an armed resistance against the invading enemies of their countries"—and the German reader knows that every Socialist discussion has reached the conclusion that the progress of Socialism requires that every invasion should be repelled. And finally, it concludes that the "Social Democrats of the rest of the world"—*i.e.* all those outside of Germany and Austria—see the war, before all else, as "the invasion of neutral Belgium and republican France." And "Vorwaerts," by an eloquent silence, indorses this opinion.

But it was only on the next day, September 27, that "Vorwaerts" reached the climax of its audacity.

The article that led to the second suspension of the paper began by referring to Germany's efforts "to make the truth known abroad," and to the fact that these efforts have not succeeded:

"The extent of these efforts show how difficult it is to create confidence in the German reports. . . .

"It is necessary to go back in times of peace to find the explanation.

For a long time a great measure of mistrust, suspicion, and antagonism to Germany has been heaping up abroad—even in the neutral countries—and we now see the effects of this."

In part, says "Vorwaerts," this was due to Germany's sudden rise in the economic world and to fear and suspicion on the part of the great capitalists.

But the jingoes abroad would hardly have had such success with their propaganda if another factor had not been present.

That land, which developed so mightily, was at the same time that land which made its workmen a present of an anti-socialist law, and which also, after the repeal of this law, instituted a police government of chicanery and allowed the equality of all citizens to exist only on the paper of the Prussian Constitution. . . .

Thus Germany appeared to the rest of the world, and even to the working classes, in the light of a Power whose rule meant militarism and political oppression. It was this that made it possible for the distrust and bitterness to arise which so greatly aided our bellicose opponents in the ruling classes, and which makes it possible for us to gain the sympathy of neutral countries only with the greatest effort.

This explains why regrettable pronouncements have come even from the laboring classes in these lands. These are regrettable above all because *they try to fasten upon the German folk as a whole the responsibility for the acts of a single class.* . . .

The comrades in foreign lands can be assured that the German working class disapproves to-day every piratical policy of state, just as it has always disapproved it, and that *it is disposed to resist the predatory subjugation of foreign peoples as strongly as the circumstances permit.*

The comrades in foreign lands can be assured that, though the German workmen also are protecting their father-land, they will nevertheless not forget that their interests are the same as those of proletariat in other countries, who, *like themselves, have been compelled to go to war against their will; indeed, even against their often repeated pronouncements in favor of peace.* [Author's italics]

Here we have the assurance of "Vorwaerts" that, in spite of the vote of the majority of the Socialist Reichstag members and the statements of such leaders as Scheidemann and Suedekum, the Socialists in the firing line are there against their will.

The reader must not get the impression that I have tried to give a complete idea of the work of "Vorwaerts" against the government and the military faction that now controls it. Hardly a day has passed when the cables have failed to mention one or another of its bold strokes, and a reference to the paper itself shows that it has neglected no opportunity. Repeatedly it has exposed the "lies" of the militarists. So-called "atrocities" against the German troops are shown to be either absurd in themselves, or crafty inventions or grossly exaggerated. German prisoners are *not* being mistreated in any of the foreign countries. In a word, the whole press campaign of the militarists is repudiated point by point. Always, of course, the point is emphasized that the people of the foreign countries are not hostile to the people of Germany. Not only does "Vorwaerts" reject the militarist case in detail, but it also rejects it as a whole—just as it did before the war. The fact that all of Germany's leading literateurs and scientists have defended the war merely supplies a subject of ridicule; one of the poets, formerly a democrat, is described as writing one patriotic poem every day and three on Sunday, which, we are reminded, makes nine a week. And when Maeterlinck and d'Annunzio are boycotted because they have turned anti-German, "Vorwaerts" ironically points out that the discovery has suddenly been made that they have no literary merit.

Yet for the first time since 1894 Socialist literature, including "Vorwaerts," has been admitted into the barracks, and on September 2 special arrangements were made by which it could even be sent into the camps on the firing line. So that the agitation I have described has not only reached the German people generally, but has been spread throughout the armies— probably the most momentous piece of propaganda ever accomplished by any agitation in all history. Evidently the reactionary Government made these extraordinary concessions from two motives. It recognized the military necessity of securing the enthusiastic loyalty of the millions of Socialists who compose a third of the German armies, and it assumed that the conservative Socialists, who had secured control of the Reichstag group on August 4, and those leaders who had been brought into the Government camp by the machinations of Bethmann-Hollweg at the secret conference of the previous day, represented the German Socialist movement as a whole. It forgot that the Reichstag members are often governed by political considerations which do not influence the Socialist masses; that the latter have put the control of the party, not into the hands of this group, but in an executive committee composed of a small number of its oldest and most trusted servants, including several revolutionists; and that "Vorwaerts" depends for its daily income upon the approval of the Socialist masses, especially those of Greater Berlin and central Germany. Instead of a tamed and loyal Socialism which is expected, "military necessity," then, has caused to circulate throughout the army literary material which, under the present circumstances, is of the most inflammatory character. For the Socialists, including a great proportion of revolutionists, are already there. All that was necessary was to remind them that all the vast anti-military and anti-monarchical agitation of recent years still holds good under present conditions, and to bring the agitation down to date.

Nor should the daily press, a part of it still more anti-military than "Vorwaerts," alone be mentioned. Now that Bebel is dead, the voice that represents the largest number of German Socialists is that of Karl Kautsky, who is generally acknowledged as the world's leading Marxist. As editor of the party's intellectual organ, "Die Neue Zeit," his influence in a country as devoted as Germany to intellectual authority is scarcely less than that of "Vorwaerts." Kautsky is a revolutionist, and in nearly every number manages to get by the censor with statements which none of his Socialist readers can fail to understand. For example, when he compares existing armies to the people's army of the French Revolution, it is scarcely necessary for him to go further and remind readers who have been thoroughly informed on this particular period that this revolutionary army over-threw monarch, aristocracy, and ruling classes generally. Yet, to make sure, he goes on to explain (in the number of September 25) that in the wars of the French Revolution "all respect for private property was cast aside, and all property was regarded as the property of the nation," adding that the present war may accomplish a great deal in this direction.

In the same article Kautsky speaks at length of the probability of a revolution in Russia, closing by a comparison with Germany and Austria which will suggest to every German reader that in reality he refers to those countries quite as much as to Russia:

"The war cannot be waged for any long period without concessions by the Czar, the granting of greater liberties, which perhaps are not meant very seriously, but which cannot be taken back after the war, unless glorious and brilliant victories occur, which certainly does not seem likely now.

"We must reckon with the possibility that a Russia will proceed from the war which, even if it is not a republic but only a constitutional monarchy, *will yet have greater liberties than its present enemies.* Along with America, Russia will be the chief gainer by the war. It only needs freedom in order to utilize its great natural resources and its enormous home market of 160 million inhabitants for a rapid economic development, provided, of course, that it is not hampered by increased armaments.

"Germany and Austria could not long avoid the effects of these changes." [Author's italics]

This must be read in connection with the commonplace among German Socialists already referred to, that a great European war which did not lead to victory is the most promising of all possible situations for a revolution and the establishment of a democratic republic. "Vorwaerts," too, is looking forward to German defeats, and is making the people ready for them by insisting with the most significant emphasis that unfavorable news must not be suppressed.

In the month of June, this year, at the last act of the last session of the Reichstag, fifty of the Socialist members proved their republicanism by forcing the whole Socialist group to remain seated and silent when the President called for standing cheers for the Kaiser. We may be certain that in the end the section of the party represented by "Vorwaerts" and these members of the Reichstag, in large part at least, will remain true to the republican and anti-militarist principles of the international Socialist move-ment. And we have every reason to hope that this army of half a million, enlarged to millions in the terrible hour of disillusionment and disaster that is drawing near, and taking advantage of the disorganization at the close of the war, may be able to overturn the military oligarchy that rules Ger-many, and set up in its place that democratic form of government which is the sole guarantee of international peace.

The German Constitutional Movement and the War

William Harbutt Dawson

THE AMERICAN REVIEW OF REVIEWS, January 1915

A new Germany was rising and as great as Bismarck had been, he could not grasp the new horizons. German life was evolving in a new fabric, a great commercial nation, a factory nation with resources in minerals and organization.

Germany's William II took control of the direction of the empire and looked to new conquests—new colonies to spread German product, language and culture.

William Harbutt Dawson worries in print that the German Parliament has turned into a club whose meetings no longer have any meaning. The Kaiser is in control of the destiny of Germany.

However the present great conflict may affect the political boundaries of Germany, it is hardly likely, writes William Harbutt Dawson in *The Contemporary Review*, to leave unchanged boundaries of its political liberty.

This English writer reviews the course of the German fight for constitutional liberty from the Napoleonic era to the present. The Prussian nation, he maintains, has no reason to look back with:

> feelings of either satisfaction or gratitude upon its long struggle with the Crown for liberties which are the birthright of the free nations of western Europe, for the fruits yielded have been scanty and unsubstantial.

The position of the sovereign in Prussia, he reminds us, is "supreme and unassailable," not only by tradition, but in constitutional body, he says:

> The predominant parliamentary form is a diet of two chambers, each possessed of equal power, but subject to an absolute veto on the part of the government, which means the Crown, since ministers are both appointed and removable by the sovereign, and neither of the legislative bodies can exercise directive control over them. For practical purposes a German Legislature is merely a discussion club, with the mortifying difference that though it may end its discussions by adopting

solemn resolutions, these resolutions cannot be executed unless graciously endorsed by a will outside its own. Below this exaggeration there is a foundation of truth, but if the words were literally accurate, it would not be very surprising. A German parliament achieves little on its own initiative, because it has no scope for the exercise of creative power, and is treated as a mere adjunct of the crown; it is accepted as a more or less necessary instrument for the execution of the royal will, but it is not expected to have a will of its own or allowed to assert one.

Prussia alone is responsible for this reactionary situation:

It is Prussia more than any other part of Germany, or all the rest of Germany together, which is responsible for the semi-absolutistic spirit in which that great country is still ruled, and by Prussia must be understood the Emperor-King with his absurd pretensions of divine right backed up by the military and bureaucratic caste and the Junker party from which that caste is chiefly drawn and which controls Government policy in both Houses of the National Diet. The Junkers have never frankly recognized the new order which came into being when, in 1849, King Frederick William IV capitulated to constitutionalism and they would subvert it today if they could. Moreover, the reactionary spirit which these irreconcilables display in the Parliament which they dominate and discredit they carry into the Parliament of the Empire, and endeavor to translate into the policy and legislation of the Imperial Government. It is not long since a typical Junker, one Herr von Oldenburg, declared, in the Imperial Diet, that "the Emperor should be in position at any moment to say to a lieutenant, 'Take ten men and shut up the Reichstag.' "

Recent German history, moreover, has shown repeatedly that:

the doctrine of ministerial responsibility, as interpreted by the German Emperor and his government, simply means that the former enjoys the privilege of making mischief by his indiscretions and of leaving his Chancellor to set things right. When such episodes occur the Reichstag debates vehemently; the press of all complexions storms as only a government-regulated press can storm when it momentarily slips the chain; and the nation, taking its cue from what it hears and reads, demands with entire sincerity that something shall be done; but as soon as passion has exhausted itself the matter ends with resolutions.

In conclusion, Mr. Harbutt Dawson has this to say:

Thoughtful Germans know well that one of the principal reasons why all past attempts to bring about a good understanding between their country and our own (the English) have failed has been the fact that the German government does not represent the German people, and that in the determination of national policy the nation has no effective voice. Nothing short of the substitution of genuine Parliamentary government for the present discredited personal regime will satisfy the aspirations of the modern democracy and give to the German nation the chance of striking at notorious evils which have now brought it to the verge of disaster, and have caused it to forfeit the sympathy of the entire civilized world.

What Italy Gains by Remaining Neutral

Staff and an Italian "Ex-Diplomat"

THE AMERICAN REVIEW OF REVIEWS, January 1915

The history of Italy during the period before and directly at the start of the war was marked by indecision.

King Victor Emanual, involved as a signatory to the Triple Alliance with Germany and Austria-Hungary still flirted with France and England seeking cordial relations.

The King attempted to stretch his neutrality into an asset on a continent that was choosing sides for the coming war. Apologists for the King's course of action published articles in his defense. The following was offered by a "nameless" diplomat.

There are dangers that would ensue if the impatience of the friends of one side or the other in the great conflict should be permitted to influence Italian policy so as to involve the country in the dreadful war now raging. Reciting the considerations favoring the government's determination not to change its present policy, [an Italian "ex-diplomat"] says:

> Our material interests and the lives of our countrymen are not risked in the bloody venture of battles, and we have reason to hope that the indispensible continuity of our nation labor will not be interrupted. Neither contracted obligations nor reasonable scruples prevent us, according to commonly accepted and respected rules, from prohibiting the expectation of the surplus of agricultural and industrial products over and above what must be guarded for the sustenance and defense of the peninsula, and trade, the basis of our economic activity, is being gradually resumed and may be expected to increase still further.
>
> We have no lack of laborers to raise and reap our crops, to till and sow our fertile fields; almost all our factories are still in operation and slowly but surely the delicate strands of credit, so rudely snapped asunder by the outbreak of the world war are being reknit.
>
> We cannot pretend that we should derive any profit from the present unfortunate situation which has enforced the return to their native land upon many thousands of Italians who had found work in foreign countries; we cannot cherish fond hopes of prosperity; we can only comfort ourselves with the thought that not all the currents of production are arrested, and that fields for Italian labor still remain open, and this conviction is strengthened by the current price of our national securities

as well as by the relatively moderate rate of exchange. Consoled by this knowledge, and aided by the efficient action of our government, the country is gradually recovering from the panic that overtook us at the end of last July, savings are flowing back to well-known institutions, and the supple genius of our people has sought and found a way to adapt our reserve energies to the new necessities. . . . Neutrality, therefore, has proved an effectual defense for our economic interests against greater and worse evils, and for a political standpoint it has procured for us the signal advantage of inducing many foreigners to justly estimate the worth of Italian friendship and of Italian power.

As to the extent of the obligation imposed upon Italy by the triple alliance, the writer lays stress on the fact that Austria's ultimatum to Servia, in its tenor and its requirements, exceeded the manner of Servia's direct responsibility for the dreadful crime of Serajevo. As a possible peaceful solution of the question had been proposed by Sir Edward Grey, through concerted action by the interested powers—Germany, France, Russia, and England—and this had not been absolutely refused by Germany at the outset, he insists that the war did not arise because of any necessity on the part of the members of the triple alliance to defend themselves from aggression. He continues:

> However, outside of the intrinsic arguments we must all take into consideration the extrinsic ones. It is inadmissable that a country should be forced to take so important a step as to participate in a war—even in one less vast and terrible than that now raging—simply because of a previous general engagement, when this is not subject to control and recognizable by all as indubitable, that is to say, without the attainment of an understanding reached through examination of the grounds leading to a common agreement.

> Now, not even this understanding which we must regard as fundamental, has been attained. The note sent to Servia, in which Russia was unquestionably an interested party, was not communicated to our government before it was transmitted to the telegraphic bureaus of information. Hence neither the scope of the treaty nor the considerations that determined the contest imposed upon us any obligation of solidarity. This fact has indeed been loyally recognized by the allied empires, as is shown by the statements of official journals and eminent statesmen, both German and Austro-Hungarian.

As to the considerations that might induce Italy to abandon her neutrality, this writer asserts that as yet there is no immediate prospect of such a change. While Von Bülow directs our attention solely to the Mediterranean, M. Pichon sees only the Adriatic, but Italy's interests are equally involved in both directions. In the meanwhile an armed neutrality assures to Italy protection from any unpleasant surprises, and may enable her to voice those sentiments of equity which alone can lead to a durable peace.

How the Turks Justify Their Entrance Into the War

Jeune-Turc

THE AMERICAN REVIEW OF REVIEWS, January 1915

Turkey's war with Italy (1911–1912) resulted in the loss of Libya. In the two successive Balkan Wars (1912–1913) Turkey lost nearly all its territory in Europe to Bulgaria, Serbia, Greece and to the newly independent Albania.

In 1913 the terroristic nationalism of the Young Turks, led by Enver Pasha, gained dictatorial power by a coup d'etat. These young revolutionaries were not of a nature to appease the remaining minorities of the empire.

The outbreak of the World War found Turkey solidly lined up with the Central Powers. Since the revolution of 1908, Germany increasingly influenced Ottoman affairs. Germany built the Baghdad Railway, and armed and trained Turkish forces. Much of the action and news from Turkey reflected the German propaganda line.

All the European belligerents, and the neutrals as well, agree that the fate of the Ottoman Empire will be finally settled by the war. The Turkish press is full of indignant attacks on the entente powers. According to the *Jeune-Turc*, the Turks feel that they are only defending themselves against "implacable enemies." As to the first acts of war, this journal says,

> The Turks claim that they were attacked first by a Russian fleet at the entrance of the Bosphorus, that the Dardanelles were practically blockaded by an Anglo-French fleet, that Akab was bombarded and a landing attempted there, the first two acts before any declaration of war by Russia or England and that only when they were thus provoked did they bombard Russian Black Sea ports.

Commenting on these claims, the *Jeune-Turc* remarks:

> We desired peace and tranquility, but it was impossible for us to consider the incidents in the Egean [sic] and Black Sea, the aggression on our oriental frontiers, as anything else than prearranged acts. . . . The Gauntlet has been thrown at us and we are lifting it up with courage and pride. . . . The great mistake of the allied powers was to believe that Turkey of 1914 was the Turkey of old, of despotism, trembling before the frowns and the threats of the great powers. The situation has changed completely, and no such surprise as in 1912 was possible.

A watchful government is ours that has not allowed itself to be coaxed by nice promises.

The text of the Sultan's manifesto to the Turkish army and navy is published in all the journals. It summarizes the reason for which Turkey regarded herself as justified in joining the Austro-German alliance against the Triple Entente. Referring to the historic enmity of Russia, and the growing hostility of Britain and France, the manifesto goes on to say:

> For three centuries Russia has brought about many territorial losses to our Empire and has always tried by war and thousands of ruses to destroy every promise of awakening and regeneration, tending to increase our national power and strength. The Russian, English and French governments, who make three hundred million Moslems groan under a tyrannic regime, have never ceased to harbor malignant intentions against our Caliphate, to which these Moslems are attached by religion and heart. Those states were the causes or the instigators of every misfortune and disaster which have befallen us. By the supreme struggle, which we undertake at present, we shall put an end, with the grace of the Almighty, to all the attacks which have at all times been directed against the prestige of our Caliphate on one side and our sovereign rights on the other.

War Opinion in England—Some Contrasts

Albert J. Beveridge
Former United States Senator from Indiana

THE AMERICAN REVIEW OF REVIEWS, July 1915

General military and political conditions in May 1915 led up to something like a British ministerial crisis, and resulted in the announcement that the cabinet would be entirely reconstructed and that the two great parties would share offices alike.

England had until now prosecuted the war with the Liberal party holding all the offices, except that Lord Kitchener, as a soldier and not a partisan, had been made Minister of War. Under existing law, a parliamentary election was to be held at least once in five years, but the House of Commons, chosen in 1910, found it inconvenient to hold a general election during the war years. The leaders of all parties agreed to postpone it. Under the circumstances, it became desirable to unify the country in the prosecution of the war by bringing the Unionist leaders into the cabinet, proceeding henceforth in total disregard to party lines.

In preceding numbers of The Review, *Senator Beveridge discussed certain conditions and aspects of national life and sentiment as he found them in Germany and France early in 1915. This article points out some marked contrasts between the state of the public mind in England and that of France or of Germany. Inasmuch as the relative discord and apathy that were apparent in March and April led up to the cabinet crisis and reconstruction of May, this memorandum of things noted in England had an especial timeliness.*

This reconstruction of the British cabinet surprised no one who had studied conditions in England by first hand investigation on the ground. It was plain even in March that this was certain to happen; for dissatisfaction was manifest at the extreme poles of political opinion, and sullenness reigned in the zones between. Some "war Liberals" said that power was making cabinet members too autocratic; and many "war Conservatives" declared, on the contrary, that the government showed weakness, indecision, and procrastination.

Also there were many who thought that Great Britain should not have gone to war; and these still smarted under the methods by which they declared that the nation had been led to take the fatal step. So while the great body of public sentiment upheld the war, yet there was bickering and discontent—the situation was startlingly unlike that in Germany and France.

Indeed, toward the close of the first phase of the combat of nations, the quick crossing of the Channel brought the student of peoples at war face to face with contrasts; conditions in England appeared to be the reverse of those in France and Germany.

A picturesque circumstance at once compelled sharp comparison. London swarmed with soldiers. For every soldier seen on the streets of Paris or Berlin, one might count at least a hundred in the British capital. No restaurant was without several military customers. Khaki-clad privates were seen strolling in all the public parks where the people of London take the air. The music halls were never without a bevy of officers.

Too much cannot be said in praise of the physical appearance of the majority of these British soldiers. Perhaps one-half of the thousands of these volunteers, personally studied, were superb examples of vigorous and robust manhood. The Scotch especially were magnificent specimens. Superior to all in their physical fitness, vitality, and bearing, were the soldiers and officers from Canada, although comparatively few of these were seen; most of them, it was said, were not at Aldershot or in London.

At a rough estimate, one would say that at least two-thirds, perhaps three-fourths, of all the soldiers and officers observed in England during March of 1915 were excellent military material—this includes the one-half of the whole who are exceptionally fine-looking men. The remainder were inferior in stature and all other evidences of physical strength.

It was frankly admitted by well-informed Englishmen deeply interested in the war that the officers were not well trained. "You couldn't expect anything else, could you?" said one of these. "They have not had six months's training. But," he added, with cheerful optimism, "you will find that they will turn out all right."

The heavy weight of British public opinion heartily supported the war. Thoughtful Englishmen of the highest consideration, like Lord Bryce, declared that "the British people are united more than they ever were united before" in support of the war.

Yet it was evident that there were not the compactness and unity of sentiment, or the utter devotion and unlimited resolve, that marked popular feeling in Germany and France. Such careful but outspoken conservatives as Lord Newton frankly asserted that "there are a large number who do not know what the war really means, and there are some who really say that they do not see what difference it would make to them even if the German Emperor ruled this country;" but Lord Newton said that "undoubtedly by far the greatest majority support the war."

Out of twenty-seven persons interviewed, belonging to the under strata of the "middle class" and ranging down to the "lower class," as the British term describes them, several had no clear idea of the reason for Great Britain's going to war.

"Why, sir, we went to war on Belgium's account," said one of these. "Belgium!" exclaimed another of the group. "We are fighting for ourselves. We can't afford to let Germany get to the Channel." The best-posted one of this class, a barber, thought that "England went into this war to keep Germany from being the first power of Europe—England couldn't permit that, sir, could she?"

All the others frankly confessed their total ignorance of the whole matter, or were either vague or absurd in their ideas of the cause of this greatest armed strife in human history. For example:

"That German Kaiser was going to come over here and rule England," said a cab driver. "You don't mean," exclaimed the questioner, "that the German Emperor meant to depose King George and ascend the British throne himself, do you?" "That's exactly what I mean," was the response.

The keeper of a little shop in the poorer quarters of London surmised that: "Money is at the bottom of it, sir." A small business man said that he had not been able to make up his mind why England went to war, but he was sure that she ought not to have done it and very emphatic in his "wish that the politicians would get through with it." There was much of such comment. Of the class referred to only the one quoted even mentioned Belgium.

The curious fact was generally admitted that the middle classes appeared to be unaroused and the so-called lower classes divided between those who are sullenly indifferent and those who are patriotically interested.

But the aristocracy were eager, united, and resolved. Never in history has the hereditary class shown its valor and patriotic devotion in a more heroic way than in the present crisis. Their courage amounts to recklessness. When one listens to undoubtedly true stories of these men's conduct in battle, one almost concludes that they regard it as a point of honor to get killed "like gentlemen." They are, of course, mostly officers; and it is said that the British private soldier does not take kindly to officers from his own class, but follows willingly only those from the ranks above him, and not even these unless they lead him with a death-inviting physical daring.

The military bustle and confused civilian opinion formed one of the many dissimilarities between war conditions in England and those in the two countries locked in deadly strife almost within sight of the British coast.

Perhaps the facts set forth in this article are the fruits of democracy, although this thought is modified by the reflection that France also is a democracy and the French even more democratic than the English. Or perhaps the conditions here reported flowed from British unpreparedness in land forces, due to her overpreparedness in sea forces; for Great Britain's mighty navy, greater than that of any other two nations combined, and the water-defended location of the United Kingdom, have justly given the British people a sense of security enjoyed by those of no other European country.

But whatever the cause, contrasts and surprises everywhere confronted one who stepped across the Channel from France and Germany to English soil, toward the close of the first period of the war, March of 1915. Antitheses were on every side; and fixed and settled ideas were driven from the mind by the lash of hard and remorseless facts.

Perhaps the labor and industrial situation was the most meaningful circumstance that challenged attention.

The first phase of Armageddon was drawing to its close. Great Britain was in the eighth month of the war. Although she had held but thirty miles of the almost four hundred miles of battle line in France, thousands of British soldiers had fallen and hundreds of her finest officers had laid down their lives. The larger part of her expeditionary force, comprising most of her disciplined troops and trained leaders, had been killed, captured, or disabled.

In answer to fervent exhortations and appealing advertisements hitherto unknown in warfare, it was said that 2,500,000 British volunteers had enlisted and were training—an immense number and yet only about half of the men with whom France now holds her battle lines or has, highly trained, waiting in reserve depots to join their comrades at the fighting front; just the same number who, according to informed Germans, although not called to the colors yet volunteered in Germany when hostilities opened; and perhaps one-third of the number that Germany has under arms or ready to take the field.

Yet popular discontent raised its many-headed visage in multitudes of places throughout the United Kingdom. The workers on the Clyde had struck. The dock laborers at Liverpool had either stopped work or threatened to do so. Here, there, and yonder, the protest of the toiler against conditions flamed up like a fire creeping beneath forest leaves and refusing to be extinguished. Bitter animosity arose.

The powerfully and ably edited London *Post* declared that:

> The behavior of some of our workmen just now would justify martial law. . . . Many of them only work half the week and idle away the rest of the time.

An article in the London *Times* from its special correspondent from Sunderland, entitled "Shipyard Shirkers," thus stated the situation:

> The pride of Sunderland (Clyde) is its claim to be the biggest shipbuilding town in the world; the shame of Sunderland is its large body of shirkers, and that shame is paraded openly and almost ostentatiously in the main street of the town. . . . It is a common thing for men to

be away three days each week. . . . Most employers and several working-men attribute the absenteeism to drink. . . . But absenteeism is not wholly, or indeed, largely due to intemperance. The shirkers who parade the steets are a remarkably sober-looking body of men.

The labor papers, on the contrary, tigerishly resented these attacks upon the workers. These journals saw in the assaults upon the British laboring man an effort to break down the whole trade-union system and exploitation of labor by the capitalistic classes. "This," declared *Justice*, an organ of the Social Democracy, in a signed article by a vigorous leader, "was the reason why Cabinet Ministers, shareholders, and capitalistic pressmen have commenced this campaign of calumny against a body of men who, but a short time before, they were united in praising. First it was the docker, who was lazy, now it is the engineer—whose turn will it be next? Not the shareholder, who calmly pockets his enhanced dividends, and then proceeds to abuse the men who made the dividends."

Another signed article in this labor paper concerning the strike of the engineers on the Clyde said:

"We find the engineering shops seething with discontent and it is difficult to say what may yet be the outcome."

These, out of scores of similar quotations on both sides of the labor controversy, give some idea of the sharpness of the economic strife in Great Britain.

So very grave did it finally become, and so acutely was the government embarrassed in conducting the war because of shortage of material and equipment, that toward the middle of March the most drastic and autocratic law ever passed by any legislative body in British history was enacted. Broadly speaking, the law gave the government absolute power to take over and conduct the whole or any part of the industry of Great Britain.

The factories were not turning out proper quantities of munitions. Shipbuilding firms were working on private contracts. There had been no general voluntary adjustment of manufacturing to changed conditions, as in Germany and France.

But, while employers were blamed for selfishness and profit hunger, the weightiest blows of censure fell upon the heads of British laborers. Thus the government armed itself with Czar-like powers of compulsion over British industry.

The government considered the revolutionary statute so necessary that Mr. Lloyd George, the Chancellor of the Exchequer, assured the House of Commons that "the success of the war depends upon it." Lord Kitchener, from his place in the House of Lords, told Parliament and the nation that military operations had "been seriously hampered by the failure to obtain skillful labor and by delays in the production of the necessary plants"; and complaining of labor indifference and trade-union's restrictions, he grimly declared that the Commandeering bill, as this extreme socialistic measure was popularly called, was "imperatively necessary."

The newspapers were swift to see and frank to state the profound change which this law wrought in British conditions, and justified it only upon the ground of deadly emergency. The *Daily Mail* said that the law established "a sort of industrial dictatorship."

The *Daily Express* asserted that "The new bill is, of course, State Socialism. That must not be accepted."

Because the debate disclosed remissness on the part of the manufacturers and the law gave autocratic control of them, the *Morning Post*, after a long comparison of the conduct of the workingmen and manufacturers, demanded that "If there are to be powers to deal with 'refractory manufacturers,' let us have powers also to deal with refractory workmen."

The *Star* stated that the "tremendous powers" of the Commandeering bill "make the government absolute dictators in the industrial field."

The *Daily Express*, in discussing another subject, announced that:

"Parliamentary government has temporarily come to an end in Great Britain."

At a large labor meeting personally attended, following the first debate in Parliament upon the Commandeering bill, bitter denunciations of the government were heard. The manufacturers, the ship-owners, the dealers in life's necessities, were, declared the speakers, using the war to squeeze blood-money from the people by an unconscionable raising of prices. One orator asserted that certain high members of the government were personally sharing these wicked profits.

At this particular labor meeting not one warm word was uttered in support of the war. But all demanded that the principles of the Commandeering bill should be applied to food and fuel in order to relieve the distress of the people. If the government, said they, is to take over factories and docks, and to compel labor to toil unreasonably in order that munitions of war shall be furnished, let the government also take over foodstuffs and compel dealers and carriers to sell reasonably for the provisioning of the poor.

Leaflets and pamphlets were distributed, filled with astounding figures showing the rise of prices and demanding government intervention. A pamphlet entitled "Why Starve?" showed that bread had risen since the outbreak of the war from five pence for a four-pound loaf to seven and one-half pence, and was still going up; and, while the price of all meat had risen sharply, that consumed by the common people had increased enormously.

The leaflet said that one result of the British Navy's clearing the seas of German shipping was that "ship-owners are thus free to increase freights 100, 200, 300, 400, and *even 500 percent*."; and demanded that "the government must take over the supply of food and fuel and the means of

transport, and must administer that supply for the benefit of the people."
The leaflet closed with an appeal for organization "to force the government
to act speedily in the interest of the whole people and to put a stop to this
robbery by a gang of profit-mongers trading on the necessities of the poor."

"Oh! they amount to nothing," said one of the most powerful men in
England when told of this labor meeting. On the contrary; "But you noticed
that the chairman was a member of Parliament, that the representative of
the British cooperative stores was one of the speakers, and that all of them
were trusted representatives of the working classes," remarked a studious
observer when told of this estimate of the insignificance of this labor
demonstration.

So familiar had one become, in Germany and France, with smooth-
working efficiency, solidarity of sentiment, contentment with economic
conditions, and steel-like resolve, that what was seen, heard, and read of
the labor and industrial situation across the channel startled and surprised.

Another, though a surface, example of the differences in the British
situation as compared with that existing in France and Germany: London
was literally plastered with striking posters, urgently appealing for
volunteers.

By the middle of March there were signs that such devices were palling
on the public; and the *Times*, in an earnest leader, asked, "What steps are
being taken to fill the places" of the killed and wounded? Referring to the
advertising devices for the securing of enlistments, this powerful leading
editorial declared that:

> We confess at once that we have not ourselves admired some of the
> expedients already employed. Sensational advertisements and indirect
> compulsion are not the methods by which a great people should raise
> their armies.

In France, on the contrary, no such flaming appeals to patriotism were
found. The only printed inducement to arms to be found in Paris was a
modest request to boys under military age, and their parents, to cooperate
with the Citizens' Military Committee, that they might be trained for future
emergencies. Even this was in plain black type and posted occasionally
and without ostentatious prominence on a wall here and there. And it was
answered liberally; unripe youth of France were drilling by the thousand.

In Germany appeared no entreaties of any kind for men to join the
colors or for women to support the war; and this was not because, as many
in America erroneously suppose, all German men are compelled to bear
arms. Hundreds of thousands of German soldiers then and now at the front
were and are volunteers.

And Belgium! The greatest surprise in store for the student of peoples
at war was the place Belgium occupied in British opinion as the cause of
Great Britain entering the conflict. For the American visitor supposed, of

course, that Germany's violation of Belgian neutrality was the one and only reason for Great Britain's drawing the sword.

Yet a remarkably bold and powerful editorial in the London *Times* of March 8, 1915 on Why We Are at War declared that:

> Our honor and our interest must have compelled us to join France and Russia, even if Germany had scrupulously respected the rights of her small neighbors. . . . Why did we guarantee the neutrality of Belgium? For an imperious reason of self-interest, for the reason which has always made us resist the establishment of any great power over against our East Coast. . . . We do not set up to be international Don Quixotes, ready at all times to redress wrongs which do us no hurt. . . . Even had Germany not invaded Belgium, honor and interest would have united us with France. We had refused, it is true, to give her or Russia any binding pledge up to the last moment. We had, however, for many years past led both to understand that, if they were unjustly attacked, they might rely upon our aid. This understanding had been the pivot of the European policy followed by the three powers. . . . We reverted to our historical policy of the balance of power for the reasons for which our forefathers adopted it. . . . When we subsidized every state in Germany, and practically all Europe, in the Great War, we did not lavish our gold from love of German or of Austrian liberty, or out of sheer altruism. No; we invested it for our own advantage. . . . England is fighting for exactly the same kind of reasons for which she fought Philip III, Louis XIV, and Napoleon. She is fighting the battle of the oppressed, it is true, in Belgium and in Serbia. . . . She is helping her great Allies to fight in defense of their soil and of their homes against the aggressor. . . . But she is not fighting primarily for Belgium or for Serbia, for France or for Russia. They fill a great place in her mind and in her heart. But they come in second. The first place belongs, and rightly belongs, to herself.

In a brilliant leader of March 17, the *Morning Post* asserted:

> This country did not go to war out of pure altruism as some people suppose, but because her very existence was threatened. A Germany supreme in France and the Netherlands must inevitably have destroyed the British Empire next. That is what really underlies 'the scrap of paper' and all the talk of "German militarism"!

Of several thoroughly informed and eminently thoughtful men belonging to the various political parties, whose names are well known in intellectual England, only one ventured to intimate that Great Britain would not have declared war if Germany had not violated Belgium's neutrality.

With this exception, every gentlemen conversed with said quite frankly that Great Britain would have entered the conflict regardless of Belgium, although all of them emphasized what they called "the Belgian outrage." A composite of the view of these gentlemen, Liberal and Conservative, was that Great Britain could not afford to see France crushed or to permit Germany to get a foothold on the Channel or to allow her to become strong enough to contest, or even quetion, Great Britain's mastery of the seas; or to upset Europe's balance of power, which, it was asserted, Germany's growing strength was overturning.

And every one of them said that if Germany is not beaten now, "it will be our turn next." Just as in France it was agreed that if France had let Germany defeat Russia, "it would have been our turn next," so in England the common expression among supporters of the war was that if England had let Germany defeat Russia and France, "it would have been our turn next." In both England and France it seemed to be taken for granted that Germany could beat any one of the allies, or any two of them combined, and that the safety of each required the united effort of all.

The consensus of competent opinion was that the British Government would have plunged into the maelstrom of blood even though Belgium had gone untouched by German hands.

So, while those sincere and powerful men and consummate politicians, Mr. Asquith and Mr. Lloyd George, in their public appeals during the first months of the war, gave the Belgian violation as the one reason for Great Britain's plunging into Armageddon, yet in March, 1915, few could be found who were willing to say that this was the sole cause of Great Britain's action.

Most of the press was decidedly warlike and whetted to a keen edge of bitterness. "The Huns" was the term commonly applied to the Germans, and this, too, by respectable and important newspapers. One favorite description of the Germans was "The Pirates." An influential journal called Germany "Europe's kitchen-wench decked in her mistress's clothes and trespassing in the drawing-room." Yet even the most belligerent papers occasionally lashed out in criticism of the government and bewailed conditions—much more so than American newspapers do.

While moderate-minded men who heartily support the war frowned upon extravagant epithets, it seemed probable that they express the feelings of great numbers of ultra-warlike people. *John Bull*, a penny weekly said to have immense circulation, voiced this militant view in sledge-hammer fashion. It said that the "Kaiser is a lunatic;" it called him "The Butcher of Berlin," "that mongrel Attila," who "will be known to infamy forever as 'William the Damned,' " and asserted that "no principle of equity would be outraged if he were blown from the cannon's mouth."

This popular war weekly assumed, of course, that the Allies would soon overwhelm Germany—nothing else was thinkable; and *John Bull* thus editorially sketched for the British eye "The Glory That Shall Be:"

> This war is the precursor of a new era for the British race and Empire. . . . The German fleet must be swept from the face of the seas.

. . . No false notions of humanity or of economy must be permitted to hinder the work of destruction. . . . From the close of this war Germany shall use the waterways of the world by the courtesy of Britain. And, when it comes to peace, we must assert ourselves as the predominant partner. . . . For the Huns there can be no readmission to the free commonwealth of Europe. . . . Britain shall recover her challenged supremacy in the western fraternity of nations. . . . *We shall not disarm.*

In an editorial entitled "Not a Vestige of the German Empire to Be Left," *John Bull* declared that Germany "must be wiped off the map of Europe." In still another editorial it described the doom of Germany and the destiny of Great Britain according to the divine plan:

"God moves in a mysterious way His wonders to perform," and the wonder He is now performing is the riddance of Europe, and mankind, of the Teutonic menace to His scheme of things. That scheme, as clearly as human intelligence can comprehend anything, was and is that, for good or ill, He has placed the destiny of the earth in hands of the Anglo-Saxon race, with the Latins as their natural allies. All else is accidental, or caprice; it cannot affect the final order of the world.

In March, 1915, there was in England no such solid and unbroken certainty of victory as was found in either France or Germany. Still, the bulk of British opinion was sure and undoubting. "So far as the result is concerned, the war is over now," said one of the most influential men in the Empire [on March 11, 1915].

On the contrary, in an uncommonly thoughtful and frank leader the London *Post* analyzed the situation and, while concluding that the Allies will be victorious, said:

But we admit that Fate hangs upon a fine edge, and there is no certainty in the matter; there is only hope and determination. . . . We have just barely held our own. . . . It must be a long pull, a strong pull, and a pull all together if the enemy is to be hoisted across the border.

While such expressions were frequent, yet it is believed that they did not reflect the general feeling; most people in England had sturdy faith in the success of the Allies. But is was undeniable that doubt did exist in some minds and the weariness of the war was affecting many who were its stanch supporters.

Mr. Bryan's Position

George F. Milton

THE AMERICAN REVIEW OF REVIEWS, August 1915

George Fort Milton was one of the best representatives of the vigorous Southern journalism of his day. Editor and publisher of the Chattanooga (Tennessee) News, *he was one of the leading figures in the Democratic party of his state. He had been a delegate to several national Democratic conventions, and voted for Wilson on every ballot in the Baltimore convention of 1912. He was an officer in the Spanish American War, was interested in educational affairs, and wrote much about World War I for his own newspaper. He had, undoubtedly, a wide understanding of public opinion in the South and portions of the West.*

Mr. Bryan's resignation from the office of Secretary of State, like many other incidents of his remarkable career, furnished the signal for a chorus of newspaper attacks on him. Probably nine-tenths of these showed lamentable lack of appreciation of his reasons and ignorance of the international situation. Many editors discovered in the incident an opportunity to belabor a political leader whom they had been fighting since he first appeared in politics, and even in a grave crisis such as the country faced they could not resist the temptation to wreak petty political revenge on their adversary, who they thought at last had been discomfited.

But even some of Mr. Bryan's best friends also jumped to unwarrantable conclusions and wore sorrowful countenances, such as are observed at political funerals.

Now, however, that more than a month has elapsed it is more easily possible to reach a viewpoint from which a correct perspective of the incident may be secured.

Indeed caution may always be properly exercised before pronouncing adversely on acts of Mr. Bryan, for so often those at first catalogued as mistakes have proven otherwise.

For instance, the quantitative theory of money which he defended in 1896 is written into the currency law of 1914.

His campaign against imperialism in 1900 is bearing fruit in the pledge of the present administration for the independence of the Philippines.

In 1908 he advocated railroad rate regulation, but predicted that government ownership of railroad and telegraph lines probably would be necessary. It is likely this frankness lost him the Presidency, but the Government now is building a railroad in Alaska and also favors the purchase of telegraph and telephone lines.

Against intense opposition he secured the adoption of constitutional amendments for the income tax and for popular election of Senators.

Incident to his course at the Baltimore National Democratic Convention he was denounced as unwise, a party disorganizer, and general nuisance. This was because he opposed Judge Parker for chairman, favored a resolution directed against Ryan, Belmont, and Murphy and insisted that Tammany should not control the nomination of a candidate. Feeling ran high against him, but when the country had been heard from the delegates fell into line for what Mr. Bryan favored and a golden era of progressive Democracy became possible.

So experience has very clearly shown that it will not do hastily to class one of Mr. Bryan's often surprising and sometimes radical acts as that of an unsafe leader. Although at times he has been in error, more often he has been proved right and his courage and leadership for new things have been of incalculable value.

No one, in fact, experienced greater change of view regarding Mr. Bryan than the President himself. Once he wished him "knocked into a cocked hat." As time went on, however, the views of the two men approached more closely and each came to have appreciation of the services the other was rendering. Unquestionably, the Nebraskan, more than any other public leader, produced the great political revolution in the country which found its expression finally in the Baltimore platform. There were strong reactionary elements in both parties and at Chicago they controlled, but at the Democratic gathering they were completely beaten. Mr. Wilson was nominated not only on account of his worth, but also because he had declined to permit "the interests" to finance his campaign and shared Mr. Bryan's views as to the impropriety of selecting Judge Parker for chairman. The Democratic party will go to the country next year for its verdict of approval or disapproval, depending on the record made in accordance with platform pledges, and that the record is good is due to a large extent to the loyal assistance given Mr. Bryan while the President's premier. The two men evidently were sincere in their expressions of mutual esteem when they parted and no more severe blow could be struck the Democratic party than that marplots should succeed in producing a breach between them.

From personal acquaintance with Mr. Bryan and study of his life and character I venture to assign as the principal reasons for his resignation the following:

Our country had established in the thirty treaties negotiated with foreign countries the principle which in his opinion should govern in our affairs with Germany—that is, that there should be a period of delay and investigation before final action. Germany had accepted the principle as embodied in the thirty treaties and suggested arbitration. We would have been compelled to follow this course if the representations had been with Great Britain, which country had ratified one of the treaties.

But despite the difference of opinion with his chief I am nevertheless inclined to the belief that Mr. Bryan would have found some way to conciliate these differences, as undoubtedly he did with the first note, but for the fact that he felt the press of the country was rapidly rushing us into war and that, therefore, it was necessary for him to meet this menace and by obtaining the ear of the nation offset the influence of this jingo publicity. In the July number of this *Review* the editor discusses intelligently and none too harshly the sensational manner in which the newspapers, especially the metropolitan press, at that time were promoting their war propaganda. The record makes an ugly page in the history of American journalism.

Before leaving the cabinet, Mr. Bryan secured considerable modification of the second note. But we are still traveling the ultimatum route and there was a bellicose feeling apparent in both countries. He could see but one result. If the people were not in some way reached and their sentiments for peace aroused and expressed there would be war. He determined, therefore, at whatever cost to throw himself into the breach. The result was anti-climax. Probably Mr. Bryan himself did not forsee just what would be the immediate effect. What did happen was this: Immediately Mr. Bryan became the target, instead of the Kaiser. There was another head to hit. They hit it. As many shillalahs were raised as at the famed Donnybrook Fair. Also our German-American friends were given pause. They were astounded that any father-in-law of a British officer could be neutral. They began to apologize, saying they might have been mistaken as to the President also. Their kinsmen across the water also became more polite. Soon it was evident that a peaceful solution of the *Lusitania* incident was likely.

Following Germany's reply to our second note there was a slight flare-up of the jingo spirit in the press; but a number of very influential papers were more conservative than in the case of the first note and even the most immoderate, with not many exceptions, calmed down in a few days. The astonishing news was carried under a Washington date line shortly afterward that the new Secretary of State and the German Ambassador were considering mediation—Mr. Bryan's views prevailing again.

As a private citizen, Mr. Bryan occupies the position in which he always has been and now again is of greater service to the country. His immediate work before the nation and the world is to make something more than "scraps of paper" of the treaties he has negotiated, and on which history will judge his career as Secretary of State. There must be a sentiment behind these treaties or in case of any incident affecting the national honor in public opinion the prediction of Mr. Roosevelt will come true and no attention will be paid to them. It is true we had no such treaty with Germany, but that country had accepted the principle, and again proposed to abide by it. If we are bound by solemn treaties to arbitrate with any one of thirty countries of the world, how may we consistently refuse similar peaceful conciliation between a friendly country and ourselves, even if no treaty actually has been signed?

Destroying a Nation

E. M. Chadwick

THE WORLD'S WORK, April 1918

Dissatisfied with its failure to secure a major part of Macedonia in the first Balkan War (1912–1913), Serbia turned against its former ally, Bulgaria, in 1913 (the second Balkan War) and defeated that country, making Serbia the foremost slavic power in the Balkans. The Austrian annexation of Bosnia and Hercegovina (1908) led to increased Austro-Serbian tension which culminated in the direct cause of World War I: the assassination of Archduke Francis Ferdinand (June 28, 1914) at Sarajevo by a Serbian nationalist.

The Serbian army at first held back the Austro-Hungarian forces, but in 1915 when the Austrians were reinforced by the Germans, Serbia was quickly overrun.

After all the years of hostility and hatred, there began an effort of exterminating the Serbian people by the Austrians and Bulgarians that reached the proportions of the calamity the Turks visited upon the Armenians.

By this time Turkey's periodic persecution of the Armenians surprises no one. It is recognized frankly for what it is; an effort to exterminate a whole race. But even three years of war as practised by the Central Powers have not accustomed the civilized world to the spectacle of professedly Christian nations employing the same policy of actual extermination.

That is why it is difficult to make the average man understand what is going on in the Balkans at the present moment.

Austria and Bulgaria are together carrying out a perfectly definite and well organized scheme for wiping the Serbian people off the face of the earth. It is not possible to explain what is going on in Serbia on the ground of even the Teutonic conception of "military necessity." Military necessity has nothing whatever to do with it. No military purpose can possibly be served by the measures now in force in Serbia, unless, indeed, one is also prepared to recognize as military operations the performances of Burmese thugs, or to accept as permissible to Christian peoples the way of Israel with the Amalekites.

Austria and Bulgaria have divided Serbia between them, Bulgaria getting about two-thirds and Austria the remaining third; and they are working hand in hand toward the complete elimination of the Serb element in the Balkan Peninsula. While wholesale murder and general practice of "atrocities" form a large item in the programme, the occupying Powers by no means confine themselves to such crude and inadequate weapons. They are nothing if not thorough. The two nations must be classed together in this matter, because, while in the execution of each detail of the scheme Bulgaria has proved herself somewhat more ruthless—or shall we merely say more efficient than her Ally—the scheme itself gives evidence of such perfect teamwork that its organizers must be held jointly responsible for the results.

Deportation naturally plays a large part in the programme. Germany has demonstrated its uses in Teutonic war-fare, but she has much to learn from her allies.

An official Serbian report states that, directly after the taking of Belgrade by the Austrians, about five thousand residents of the city (men, women, and children) were deported to Doboj in Bosnia, where already large numbers of other prisoners were interned. As to the conditions in Doboj, here is a brief extract from a speech made in the Vienna House of Parliament on October 19, 1917. As a hostage the Dalmatian poet, Dr. Tresić-Pavičić, had himself suffered the rigors of the Austrian detention camps, and after his release resumed his seat in the Reichsrat in order to make what was probably the most terrible indictment ever brought by a subject against the Government under which he lived.

At Doboj," said Dr. Tresić-Pavičić, "it was still worse. On December 27, 1915, there arrived the first batch of Serbian and Montenegrin prisoners, accompanied by a crowd of people from Bosnia, forced to leave their homes near the frontier. Women, old men, and children had to travel in open cattle-trucks, exposed to cold, rain, wind, hunger, and lack of sleep. . . . They were shut up in huts which had once served as a veterinary hospital and which, infected with all kinds of horses' diseases and full of manure, had never been cleaned out. Soon exanthematic typhus, small-pox, and cholera broke out. Every kind of vermin abounded.

"A confidential order from the military in Sarajevo enjoined upon the warders the most drastic treatment of the prisoners, and all was done to send them as quickly as possible to the other world. The most convenient and paying method was starvation. Women with four or five children were given only one loaf every five days. . . . Often the mother was already dead when the child tried to wake her crying for bread.

"At first 15 to 20 of these people died daily. On the 5th of April, 1916, 92 died. The bodies were driven through the streets of Doboj in open daylight. According to reliable persons more than 8,000 innocent victims died there.

At the great detention camp at Braunau it is estimated that there are (or were) at least 35,000 prisoners. At this place the Austrians are holding a large number of Serbian children. The Vienna *Reichspost* of December

6, 1916, speaks of 800 boys between 9 and 19 years of age being confined at Braunau; but according to Servian official information the number has reached at least 2,000.

Many of the Austrian detention camps are situated in the most malarial districts of the Danube Valley, veritable hotbeds of disease, where fever and neglect save the authorities the trouble of otherwise disposing of their victims. An epidemic of dysentery at Braunau almost wiped out the children confined there at the time; and the cruel rigor of the treatment to which they are subjected—to say nothing of the bad food—is destroying the vitality of those who managed to survive. An exchanged Serbian officer, Lieutenant Vidak Koprivitza, of the 2nd Regiment of the Combined Serbian Division, who was confined in a camp where soldiers and civilians of both sexes were mixed together, reported having seen boys and girls hunting in the drain-courses for scraps of food.

Bulgaria, as usual, has outdone her ally in the matter of deportation. She has carried off from the districts under her control all the remaining members of the Serbian Parliament, all the priests and teachers, all the physicians—in fact, all the leading men. Not content with this, she has deported the *entire population* of certain districts chiefly in Serbian Macedonia and New Serbia generally. At Prizren and Prishtina, after most of the leading men had been killed, practically every Serbian family was carried away. From Poretch and Prilip all the male population from 15 to 70 years was ordered to be deported. These deportations have been carried out with even greater brutality than those organized by Austria, the Bulgar soldiers driving the wretched people along the roads like cattle.

The deportations carried out by Bulgaria are followed by the confiscation of all the properties of the deported people, so that the proceeding amounts to complete obliteration of the population.

Most atrocious of all Bulgaria's crimes in this direction has been the carrying off of young girls. M. Pachitch, the Servian Premier, stated in London last September that eight thousand young Serbian girls have been sent to Constantinople and two thousand to Asia Minor. These were children chiefly of ten to fourteen years of age.

"These deportations," said M. Pachitch, "have been going on since February 1916, but the number was very limited till a few weeks ago. Now it has been systematized under Bulgarian controllers and it is impossible to tell how far it will go. . . . Prisoners whom we have taken on the Saloniki front tell us that the traffic in our girlhood had grown to be a byword in Bulgaria and Turkey. The girls are kidnapped and taken away secretly. . . . Dozens of small towns have been quite denuded of their young female population. . . . The girls are too young to be of any use for laboring purposes; besides neither Turkey nor Bulgaria is seriously handicapped for labor, and in Turkey the use of young women for outdoor work is practically unknown."

A pitiful letter, written and somehow smuggled out from the Serbian mountains by a man who took part in the heroic insurrection of the Serbs against the Bulgars last spring, throws a sidelight on this traffic.

"On the 25th of April," says this writer, "they embarked on trains at Belotintze 8,000 children of twelve to fifteen years—destination: Constantinople. Many of these children threw themselves from the moving cars and thus found death."

One is afraid to ask what has been the fate of the others.

Added to every other horror of this situation is the unspeakable bitterness for Serbia of seeing her children handed over to her ancient enemy the Turk, who in all his five hundred years of tyranny over her was never able to undermine the heroic purity of Serbian womanhood.

There is one phase of Bulgaria's proceedings, however, for which no parallel can be found even in the blackened records of her allies. She has called up for active service in her own army the male population of the invaded districts of Serbia. The Bulgarian papers refer constantly and with the utmost frankness to this recruiting. During last year, on September 26, the *Preporetz* announced that the recruiting commissions had commenced their work in all the "new liberated lands;" on October 6 the *Dnevnik* stated that all the male residents of Tetovatz between the ages of 15 and 50 have been ordered to appear before the recruiting commission: On October 17 the *Mir* announced the sending to Sofia of 3,000 recruits from the districts of Ochrid, Debar, and Struga.

The Allied Armies on the Saloniki front have actually captured Serbs from these districts who had been forced into the Bulgarian Army; and the endless reports from deserters which are constantly coming to the Serbian Government furnish ample confirmation of the facts.

Since it is hardly practicable to carry off or kill every single Serb in Serbia, the deportations are being supplemented by the systematic denationalization of the remaining population.

The first step toward denationalization is always the suppression of the language.

Austria has forbidden the employment of the Cyrillic characters, in use in Serbia since the earliest times; and has even abolished the Julian calendar. She has prohibited the publication or sale of books which are distinctively Serbian. All volumes of the wonderful traditional poetry (the greatest treasure of Serbian culture) have been confiscated. Works of modern Serbian poets, such as Radichevitch and Jovan Jovanovitch, have been forbidden; and even a pedagogic study by Dr. Bakitch on "National Education" has been condemned on the strength of its title alone.

German and Magyar have been substituted for Serbian in the schools under Austrian control. Moreover, these Orthodox children are being educated as Roman Catholics. They are obliged to wear uniforms similar to those of Austrian soldiers, and are in general being brought up as "loyal

Austrians." Since vast numbers of these children are orphans, it is proportionately easier to rob them of their national heritage than if they had parents at home who could counteract the poison that is being poured into their minds.

Bulgaria, not content with trying to wipe out Serbian national literature, has ordered the destruction of all books printed or written in the Serbian language. Even priceless old manuscripts in the monasteries and ancient archives which represented all the records Serbia had brought with her out of her five centuries of bondage, have been destroyed.

By the way of general compensation for the destruction of the literary heritage of Serbia, Bulgaria is offering complimentary copies of the works of modern Bulgarian authors, a proceeding which has not been without some measure of comic relief in the shape of violent jealousies on the part of Bulgar authors not thus honored by their Government.

Bulgaria has laid the entire Serbian Church under an interdict. She has replaced the Serb priests deported to Sofia, Philipponopolis, and Ril, by Bulgar priests who offer the people the services of the Bulgarian Church— a Church which was founded by a Sultan of Turkey in 1871, and has always been regarded by the ancient Orthodox Catholic Churches (Russian, Serbian, and Greek) as schismatic. The Serbs have even been forbidden to celebrate in memory of their patron saint, St. Sava.

The great historic Serbian monasteries (those at Ravanitza and Masanija in particular), shrines respected even by the Turks, have been devastated by the Bulgars. All sculptural inscriptions, memorials of ancient Serbian rulers, have been destroyed by hammer and axe. Not only in churches, but even on old Macedonian bridges, have such inscriptions been erased.

Bulgaria has followed the same course as her ally in the matter of education; and, as usual, has gone a few steps farther. She has sent so many Bulgar teachers into Serbia that there are not enough left in Bulgaria to serve the schools there.

Both allies have changed street names in cities under their control into German, Magyar, or Bulgarian; but it was reserved for Bulgaria alone to force the Serbs to change the termination of their surnames from the typical Serbian "ić" and "ović" to the Bulgar "off" (Savić—Savoff, Ivanić—Ivanoff, etc.).

It is comprehensible that in such a programme as this the economic exploitation of Serbia should play a large part. It has, in fact, been carried out with a thoroughness that might be termed Prussian, were it not so typically Austro-Bulgarian.

There is not space enough here to give details of the ways in which Austria has manipulated the Serbian taxation laws to her own advantage and the destruction of Serbian trade. Bulgaria has not even observed the formality of a theoretical adherence to Serbian law, but has discarded it completely and imposed arbitrary taxation as she pleased.

Under Austrian administration Serbian money has been forcibly depreciated fifty per cent. Serbian currency is being gradually withdrawn from circulation and replaced by Austrian money and War Notes. The excuses given for this proceeding, viz., that there was not a metal basis in the country to cover the notes in circulation, and that there was reason to fear the Serbian Government would place in circulation new bank notes of which the proportion would not correspond to the metal basis, are neither of them tenable. Firstly, the Serbian National Bank had ample reserve to cover the notes in circulation in the occupied territory. Secondly, since leaving Serbian territory the Serbian Government has had to make all its payments in foreign money, and would consequently have no interest in increasing the supply of Serbian notes.

According to reliable information received by the Serbian Government, the Austrian authorities have taken Serbian money by force from private individuals, replacing it with Austrian money at a rate of less than fifty per cent of its nominal value. This amounts to direct confiscation of private property—or to wholesale theft, according as one prefers to call a spade a spade, or an instrument for delving.

Bulgaria has simply removed Serbian money from circulation altogether. Not only does she not recognize it as legal tender, but she inflicts severe punishment on any person found in possession of Serbian currency. The effect of such measures on the condition of the population is too obvious to require comment.

The Austrians have followed in Serbia the example of their German colleagues in Belgium and northern France as regards robbery. The museums at Belgrade, the Royal Palace, and private houses whose owners are absent, have all been systematically looted.

Bulgaria's views on looting are entirely original. She has declared all property whose owners are absent to be in fact "ownerless." The following extracts from Bulgarian journals speak for themselves:

> The King has confirmed the decision taken for the fourth time by the Government to hand over to the State the properties of those who, having abandoned their country, have not yet returned to it. (*Dnevnik,* March 17, 1916)

> There will arrive here in a few days 1,000 kilos of wool belonging to nobody; it will be sold together with 13,000 kilos of coffee. The sale will take place in small quantities, so that the smaller tradespeople can lay in a provision of these articles. (*Narodni Prava,* June 16, 1916)

> A wagon-load of tombstones from Old Serbia has arrived at the railway station at Sofia. (*Dnevnik,* February 24, 1916)

> On the 24th inst., there will be sold in the State Warehouse, among other ownerless objects collected by the Administration in Serbia, a number of lots of perfume, pomade, eau de Cologne, all at exceptional prices. (*Narodni Prava*)

Practically nothing is being done by the occupying Powers to feed the population in Serbia. The situation is naturally worst in the towns. For some time before the United States entered the war, the Mission of the American Red Cross in Serbia, headed by Mr. Edward Stuart, did admirable work, not only in relieving to some extent the appalling distress, but in bringing to the stricken people that sympathy and kindliness of which their lives were otherwise so pitifully empty. Moreover, the presence of neutral observers serves in some measure to check at any rate, the worst abuses. Since the Red Cross Mission was obliged to leave Serbia, it is hard to know what is being done for the people. The indications are that nothing whatever is being done. A Swiss Committee for some time did valiant work; but under existing arrangements Switzerland is no longer able to export any food, even for relief work; so that at present no food is being sent into Serbia from outside, and the people are entirely dependent on the tender mercies of the enemy.

So much for the civilian population. Of the condition of Serbian prisoners of war in enemy hands something has been learned from exchanged invalid prisoners, escaped prisoners, and from neutral observers. There seems little likelihood that many of these men will live to return to their country if the war goes on much longer. The chances of their returning in good enough physical condition for the ordinary occupations of life are very slight indeed.

Last November the Serbian Legation in Washington issued a verbatim report of a declaration made to the Serbian Legation in Berne by Colonel Nikola Tomashevitch, who was exchanged and transported to Switzerland from an Austrian prison camp. The statement is too long to reproduce *in extenso*, but the following extract is typical of the whole:

> The prisoners are dying continually of hunger because the food given them is not only insufficient but harmful. . . . We often saw them searching the refuse heaps for bones or scraps of food. They just rubbed the bones a little before beginning to gnaw them. Sometimes we would see them pulling up grass for food. . . . According to the statement of the doctors, any nursing of the sick is useless . . . because the soldiers are slowly dying of starvation. It is not only the sick, but also those suffering from no actual malady. . . . The morning often finds them dead or frozen. So far, there are in Austria-Hungary at least 50,000 graves of Serbian soldiers.

On September 22, 1917, the Paris paper *Le Temps* published the result of a long and careful investigation made by its special correspondent in Zurich, Switzerland, who interrogated a large number of exchanged and escaped prisoners (not only Serbian, but French, British, and Russian) in addition to many trustworthy neutral witnesses. Here are a few brief extracts from his report:

The fate of the Serbian prisoners at Mauthausen (in Austria) was the most terrible of all.

In 1916 spotted typhus began to ravage the Serbian prisoners' camps. Instead of rendering assistance to the prisoners, the military authorities caused the barracks to be closed, and not until a week had passed was a regimental surgeon dispatched, who had the barracks re-opened and succeeded in localizing the disease. But already 9,000 Serbian prisoners had perished. The camp had become one vast Serbian grave. In order to conceal this crime the dead were buried by the hundreds in one grave. Then the earth was levelled, an Orthodox chapel erected on the site and the inscription put up:

"Here are buried Serbian soldiers who died of wounds received in the Austro-Hungaro-Serbian War provoked by Serbia."

The *Temps* correspondent is further responsible for the statement that "according to the account of an Austrian medical man, there are concentrated at Krizevci, in Croatia, more than 3,000 Serbs, prisoners of war and deported persons, who have become insane. The statistics recently published by the Austrian and German authorities prove that this information is correct."

Bulgaria has put herself beyond the pale of humanity by refusing all information regarding her prisoners and forbidding all correspondence between them and their families. It is consequently very difficult to get accurate information regarding prisoners in Bulgarian hands; but an eye-witness who saw fifty or sixty Serbian officer prisoners in Philippopolis reported:

They all look ill. Their clothes are torn and terribly filthy. They never take a bath, because they have no facilities for taking one. The only food they receive is smoked goat flesh. They have no money, because they receive none from anywhere. Even today I shudder when their image rises before my eyes.

Contrast this with the behavior of the Serbian soldiers who on the terrible retreat before the triple invasion in 1915, shared to the last their infinitesimal rations with the Austrian prisoners who marched with them; or with the luxurious comfort that surrounds the German prisoners held in England at Donnington Hall and the other beautiful country houses taken over by the British Government for the housing of enemy officers.

It is difficult to estimate with even approximate correctness Serbia's actual loss of life since the war began. On May 5, 1917, the *Vossische Zeitung* stated that the total number of Serbian prisoners of war in the hands of the Central Powers up to February 1, 1917, was 154,630, distributed as follows:

	Officers	Men	Total
In Germany	. . .	25,879	25,879
In Austria-Hungary	709	96,363	97,072
In Bulgaria	187	31,942	31,679
			(sic.)

At the outbreak of the war the Serbian Army numbered 465,000. The strength of the army now fighting on the Saloniki front was in August, 1917, about 100,000 (about 65,000 fighting men). If this figure, together with the 154,630 nominally surviving as prisoners, is deducted from the original 465,000, Serbia's loss in killed and incapacitated would seem to amount to 210,370 (about 45 per cent of her army), even assuming that all prisoners are eventually returned, which we know is out of the question.

There are probably between 50,000 and 60,000 Serbian civilians interned in Austria-Hungary; and it is known that Bulgaria has deported more than 10,000 *families*, to say nothing of the great numbers of individuals carried off; but it is impossible to get at reasonably exact figures. In view of the conditions in the camps it is idle to hope for the survival and eventual return home of any large proportion of the deported people. Those sent to Asia Minor by Bulgaria, for instance, are as likely to recover their freedom as the Armenians driven there by Turkey. It is known, moreover, that more than 20,000 persons perished in the ill-fated insurrection in Serbia last spring; and the toll of murder, summary execution, and death from hunger and maltreatment must be appalling.

Serbian officials place the total loss (civilians and army) at probably a million, up to the present, or more than 20 per cent of the entire population.

It may be said that it is not fair to impute, even to such enemies as those whom we are fighting now, so atrocious an intention as the actual destruction of a race, unless one is able to show unmistakably the motives for it.

Bulgaria's motives in this scheme are too clear to require much elucidation. She wants to own the Balkans; and since history has proved that the Serbs are not the kind of people to allow any other nation to own their land in peace, Bulgaria's only course, as she sees it, is to eliminate them, by killing as many as possible and nationalizing the rest. She appears also to imagine that by removing the Serb population and all traces of Serbian occupation and culture, she may, even in the event of an Entente peace, be able to retain possession of the conquered territories on the score of apparent nationality. Add to this the fact that she is enjoying an unrivalled opportunity for avenging the humiliations of the Second Balkan War; and, further, that in the Bulgar the Mongol ancestry is frequently more in evidence than the Slav; and Bulgaria's whole conduct of the war becomes intelligible.

Austria's treatment of Serbia is only part of a larger policy. Quite apart from any question of interest in the Berlin-Bagdad scheme, the Austro-Hungarian tendency, even since Sadowa and the Compromise of 1867 which established the Dualist principle, has been toward the suppression of all races within the Monarchy except the German and Magyar. The two ruling peoples, who are not even in a numerical majority, have sought by every means in their power to cripple the others; and their hand has lain with crushing weight on the Southern Slavs.

The speech of Dr. Tresić-Pavičić in the Reichsrat is a sufficient testimony to Austrian methods; and more significant than the speech itself is the fact that its accusations have never been denied. Here is a passage from his description:

> The most notable and best educated among the population were taken as hostages. Only very few of these contrived to play their part to the end and to save their lives. As a rule they were, by the order of some officer, taken from the casemates to the courtyard, where each of them was handed over to two Moslems armed to the teeth. The officer then proceeded in a loud voice to instruct the guards for half an hour, pointing out all the cases in which they must kill the hostage. "At the slightest sound plunge the bayonet in his heart. If you hear the crack of a rifle in the woods, blow out his brains. If he should turn to the left shoot him; if he makes a movement to the right cut him in pieces." And the Moslem guards did not stand in need of encouragement.
>
> The hostages were selected at night. The loathsome face of Scholier the gaoler, set in a frame of bayonets that gleamed like mortuary candles, entered silently, as, like a tiger, he sought out and pounced on his victims. The hair of more than one was blanched in a single night with terror. One day he carried off boys in the prime of youth, the next, old men bowed with age. Such as desired to prolong their miserable life for a few days indicated by gestures how many banknotes they were prepared to sacrifice. To be taken as hostage was equal to a sentence of death. Hundreds perished in this way. . . .

It must be remembered that the victims to whom Dr. Tresić-Pavičić referred were subjects of Austria-Hungary, not of an enemy state. In view of the whole situation, in the Southern Slav territories of Austria-Hungary as in Serbia, it does not seem possible to regard the joint campaign as other than an effort to destroy this whole people.

But if nothing is left of the Serbian people but the magnificent remnant of an Army at Saloniki and the 30,000 refugees scattered through Europe, the duty of the Entente Powers toward this, the most heroic and faithful of their allies, can only be made thereby greater, not less. Civilization can never repay Serbia for what she has sacrificed for it.

Ambassador Morgenthau's Story

Henry Morgenthau
Formerly American Ambassador to Turkey

THE WORLD'S WORK, June 1918

The magazine, The World's Work, *divided Henry Morgenthau's Turkish memoirs into three parts, running them consecutively, from May through July 1918. He recorded his experiences and emotions as he watched the war begin and spread through Asia Minor and southeastern Europe. He later put his experiences in a book, "Ambassador Morgenthau's Story" (1918), and followed that with another, "All In a Lifetime" (1922).*

In August 1914 he witnessed an event that eventually led to the downfall of Russia and pulled Turkey into the war on the side of Germany.

Two German battle cruisers, the Goeben *and the* Breslau, *chased by the British and French navies, sought and received haven from Turkey's government by being allowed to pass through the Dardanelles. The treaty of Paris signed in 1856 provided that warships should not use the Dardanelles except on the special permission of the Sultan, which permission could be granted only in time of peace. In practice the government had seldom given this permission except for ceremonial occasions. In the existing conditions it would have amounted to virtually an unfriendly act for the Sultan to have removed the ban against war vessels in the Dardanelles, and to permit the German cruisers to remain in Turkish waters for more than twenty-four hours would have practically been a declaration of war.*

Germany's wily Ambassador Wangenheim circumvented the treaty of Paris by "selling" the cruisers and their German crew to Turkey. Now the treaty was not violated, and Germany tightened its noose about Russia by closing off the Dardanelles to all commercial shipping.

Ambassador Morgenthau excused this oversight by the British admiralty saying, "Depending as usual upon the sanctity of international regulations, the British Navy had shut off every point through which these German ships could have escaped to safety—except the entrance to the Dardanelles. Had England rushed a powerful squadron to this vital spot, it would have changed the shape of the war." In truth, it was a costly oversight that contributed to the extension of the war and the fall of Russia by cutting off its outlet to the Mediterranean. Wheat exports were stopped, seriously affecting Russia's economy, and the import of arms was curtailed thereby destroying the effectiveness of its army.

The following excerpt from Ambassador Morgenthau's second report records his experience as Germany tightened its grip on that part of the world in the early days of the war (when Germany and its allies looked forward to a rapid victory) and the reshaping of the face of Europe and Africa.

In reading the August newspapers which described the mobilizations in Europe, I was particularly struck with the emphasis which they laid upon the splendid spirit that was overnight changing the civilian populations into armies. At that time Turkey also was mobilizing—not for definite hostilities but merely as a precautionary measure; yet the daily scenes which I witnessed in Constantinople bore few resemblances to those which were taking place in Europe. The martial patriotism of men and the sublime patience and sacrifice of women may sometimes give war an heroic aspect; in Turkey, however, the prospect was one of general listlessness and misery. Day by day the miscellaneous Ottoman hordes passed through the streets; Arabs, bootless and shoeless, dressed in their most gaily colored garments, with long linen bags, containing five days' rations, thrown over their shoulders, shambling in their gait and bewildered in their manner, touched shoulders with equally dispirited Bedouins, evidently suddenly snatched from the desert. A motley aggregation of Turks, Circassians, Greeks, Kurds, Armenians, and Jews showing signs of having been summarily taken from their farms and shops, constantly jostled one another. Most were ragged, many looked half-starved, everything about them suggested hopelessness and a cattle-like submission to a fate which they knew that they could not avoid. There was no joy of approaching battle, no feeling that they were sacrificing themselves for a mighty cause; day by day they passed, the unwilling children of a tatter-demalion empire that was making one last despairing attempt to gird itself for action.

These wretched marchers little realized what was the power that was dragging them from the four corners of their country. Even we of the diplomatic group had not then clearly grasped the real situation. The signal for this mobilization had not come originally from Enver or Talaat or the Turkish Cabinet; the General Staff in Berlin and its representatives in Constantinople, Liman von Sanders and Brounsart were really directing the variegated operation. . . .

Misery and starvation soon began to afflict the land. Out of 4,000,000 adult male population more than 1,500,000 were ultimately enlisted; about a million families were left without breadwinners, all of them in a condition of extreme destitution. The Turkish Government paid its soldiers 25 cents a month, and gave the families a separation allowance of $1.20 a month. As a result thousands were dying from lack of food and many more were enfeebled by malnutrition; I believe that the Empire has lost a quarter of its Turkish population since the war started. I asked Enver why he permitted his people to be destroyed in this way. But sufferings like these did not distress him. He was much impressed by his success in raising a large army with practically no money—something, he boasted, which no other nation had ever done before. In order to accomplish this, Enver had issued orders which imposed the death penalty for evading military service, and also adopted a scheme by which any Ottoman could obtain exemption by the payment of about $190. Still Enver regarded his accomplishment as a notable one. It was really his first taste of unlimited power and he enjoyed the experience greatly.

That the Germans directed this mobilization is not a matter of opinion but of proof. I need only instance that the Germans were requisitioning materials in their own name for their own uses. I have a photographic copy of such a requisition made by Humann, the German naval attache, for a shipload of oil cake. This document is dated September 29, 1914—about a month before Turkey had declared war. "The lot by the steamship *Derindje* which you mentioned in your letter of the 26th," this paper read, "has been requisitioned by me for the German Government." While the Germans were thus exercising the powers of sovereignty at Constantinople, the ambassadors of the other powers stood aside. The cards had been stacked against them. . . .

I have already mentioned that the German Ambassador left for Berlin soon after the assassination of the Grand Duke, and he now revealed the cause of his sudden disappearance. The Kaiser, he told me, had summoned him to Berlin for an imperial conference. This meeting took place at Potsdam on July 5th. The Kaiser presided; nearly all the ambassadors attended; Wangenheim came to tell of Turkey and enlighten his associates on the situation in Constantinople. Moltke, then Chief of Staff, was there representing the army, and Admiral von Tirpitz spoke for the navy. The great bankers, railroad directors, and the captains of German industry, all of whom were as necessary to German war preparations as the army itself, also attended.

Wangenheim now told me that the Kaiser solemnly put the question to each man in turn. Was he ready for war? All replied "Yes" except the financiers. They said they must have two weeks to sell their foreign securities and to make loans. At that time few people looked upon the Sarajevo tragedy as something that was likely to cause war. The conference took all precautions that no such suspicion should be aroused. It decided to give the bankers time to readjust their finances for the coming war, and then several members went quietly back to their work or started on vacations.

In telling me about this conference, Wangenheim, of course, admitted that Germany had precipitated the war. I think that he was rather proud of the whole performance; proud that Germany had gone about the matter in so methodical and far-seeing a way; especially proud that he himself had been invited to participate in so momentous a gathering. The several

blue, red, and yellow books which flooded Europe the few months following the outbreak, and the hundreds of documents which were issued by
German propaganda attempting to establish Germany's innocence, never
made any impression on me. For my conclusions as to the responsibility
are not based on suspicions or belief or the study of circumstantial data.
I do not have to reason or argue about the matter. I know. The conspiracy
that has caused this greatest of human tragedies was hatched by the Kaiser
and his imperial crew at this Potsdam conference of July 5, 1914. One of
the chief participants, flushed with his triumphs at the apparent success of
the plot, told me the details with his own mouth. Whenever I hear people
arguing about the responsibility for this war or read the clumsy and lying
excuses put forth by Germany, I simply recall the burly figure of Wangenheim as he appeared that August afternoon, puffing away at a huge
black cigar, and giving me his account of this historic meeting. Why waste
any time discussing the matter after that?

The Imperial Conference took place July 5th; the Serbian ultimatum
was sent on July 22nd. That is just about the two weeks interval which the
financiers had demanded to complete their plans. All the great stock ex-
changes of the world show that the German bankers profitably used this
interval. Their records reveal that stocks were being sold in large quantities
and that prices declined rapidly. At that time the markets were somewhat
puzzled at this movement; Wangenheim's explanation clears up any doubts
that may still remain. Germany was changing her securities into cash, for
war purposes. If any one wishes to verify Wangenheim, I would suggest
that he examine the quotations of the New York stock market for these
two historic weeks. He will find that there were astonishing slumps in
quotations, especially on the stocks that had an international market. Between July 5th and July 22nd, Union Pacific dropped from 155½ to 127½,
Baltimore and Ohio from 91½ to 81, United States Steel from 61 to 50½,
Canadian Pacific from 194 to 185½ and Northern Pacific from 111⅜ to
108. At that time the high protectionists were blaming the Simmons-
Underwood tariff act as responsible for this fall in values; other critics of
the Administration attributed it to the Federal Reserve Act—which had
not yet been passed. How little the Wall Street brokers and the financial
experts realized that an Imperial Conference held in Potsdam, presided
over by the Kaiser, was the real force that was then depressing the market!

Wangenheim not only gave me the details of this Potsdam conference,
but he disclosed the same secret to the Marquis Garroni, the Italian Ambassador at Constantinople. Italy was at that time technically Germany's
ally.

The Austrian Ambassador, the Marquis Pallavicini, also practically
admitted that the Central Powers had precipitated the war. On August
18th, Francis Joseph's birthday, I made the usual ambassadorial visit of
congratulation. Quite naturally the conversation turned upon the Emperor,

who had that day passed his 84th year. Pallavicini spoke about him with the utmost pride and veneration. He told me how keen-minded and clear-headed the aged Emperor was; how he had the most complete understanding of international affairs, and gave everything his personal supervision. To illustrate the Austrian Kaiser's grasp of public events, Pallavicini instanced the present war. The previous May, Pallavicini had had an audience with Francis Joseph in Vienna. At that time, Pallavicini told me, the Emperor had said that a European war was unavoidable. The Central Powers would not accept the Treaty of Bucharest as a settlement of the Balkan question, and only a general war, the Emperor had told Pallavicini, could ever settle that problem. The Treaty of Bucharest, I may recall, was the settlement that ended the second Balkan war. This divided the European dominions of the Balkan states, excepting Constantinople and a small piece of adjoining territory, among the Balkan nations, chiefly Serbia and Greece. That treaty strengthened Serbia greatly, so much did it increase Serbia's resources, indeed, that Austria feared that it had laid the beginning of a new European state that might grow sufficiently strong to resist her own plans of aggrandizement. Austria held a large Serbian population under her yoke in Bosnia and Herzegovina; these Serbians desired, above everything else, annexation to their own country. Moreover, the Pan-German plans in the East necessitated the destruction of Serbia, the state, which, so long as it stood intact, blocked the Germanic road to the East. It had been the Austro-German expectation that the Balkan War would destroy Serbia as a nation—that Turkey would simply annihilate King Peter's forces. This was precisely what the Germanic plans demanded, and for this reason Austria and Germany did nothing to prevent the Balkan wars. But the result was exactly the reverse; out of the conflict arose a stronger Serbia than ever, standing firm like a breakwater against the Germanic path. Most historians agree that the Treaty of Bucharest made inevitable this war. I have the Marquis Pallavicini's evidence that this was likewise the opinion of Francis Joseph himself. The audience at which the Emperor made this statement was held in May, more than a month before the assassination of the Grand Duke. Clearly, therefore, the war would have come irrespective of the calamity at Sarajevo. That merely served as the convenient pretext for the war upon which the Central Empires had already decided. . . .

It is quite evident that the battle of the Marne saved Paris from the fate of Louvain.

So confidently did Wagenheim expect an immediate victory that he began to discuss the terms of peace. Germany would demand of France, he said, after defeating her armies, that she completely demobilize and pay an indemnity. "France now," said Wangenheim, "can settle for $5,000,000,000; but if she persists in continuing the war, she will have to pay $20,000,000,000."

He told me that Germany would demand harbors and coaling stations "everywhere." At that time, judging from Wangenheim's statements, Germany was not looking so much for new territory as for great commercial advantages. She was determined to be the great merchant nation; and for this she must have free harbors, the Bagdad railroad, and extensive rights in South America and Africa. Wangenheim said that Germany did not desire any more territory in which the populations did not speak German; they had had all of that kind of trouble they wanted in Alsace-Lorraine, Poland, and other non-German countries. This statement certainly sounds interesting now in view of recent happenings in Russia. He did not mention England in speaking of Germany's demand for coaling stations and harbors; he must have had England in mind, however, for what other nation could have given them to Germany "everywhere"?

If England attempted to starve Germany, said Wangenheim, Germany's response would be a simple one: She would starve France. At that time, we must remember, Germany expected to have Paris within a week; and she believed that this would ultimately give her control of the whole country. It was evidently the German plan, as understood by Wangenheim, to hold this nation as a pawn for England's behavior, a kind of hostage on a gigantic scale, and, should England gain any military or naval advantage, Germany would attempt to counterattack by torturing the whole French people. At that moment German soldiers were murdering innocent Belgians in return for the alleged misbehavior of other Belgians, and evidently Germany had planned to apply this principle to whole nations as well as to individuals.

All through this and other talks, Wangenheim showed the greatest animosity to Russia.

"We've got our foot on Russia's corn," he said, "and we propose to keep it there." By this he must have meant that Germany had sent the *Goeben* and the *Breslau* to the Dardanelles and so controlled the situation in Constantinople. The old Byzantine capital, said Wangenheim, was the prize which a victorious Russia would demand, and her lack of an all-the-year-round port in warm waters was Russia's tender spot —her "corn." At this time Wangenheim boasted that Germany had 174 German gunners at the Dardanelles, that the strait could be closed in less than thirty minutes, and that Souchon, the German admiral, had informed him that the straits were impregnable. "We shall not close the Dardanelles, however," he said, "unless England attacks them." Even then, two months before Turkey had entered the war, Germany had prepared the fortifications for the naval attack that England ultimately made. "The Dardanelles are defended as effectively as Cuxhaven," said Wangenheim.

At that time England, although she had declared war on Germany, had played no conspicuous part in the military operations; her "contemptible little army" was making its heroic retreat from Mons. Wangenheim entirely discounted England as an enemy. It was the German intention, he said, to place their big guns at Calais, and throw their shells across the English Channel to the English coast towns; that Germany would not have Calais within the next ten days did not occur to him as a possibility. In this and other conversations at about the same time Wangenheim laughed at the idea that England could create a large independent army. "The idea is preposterous," he said. "It takes generations of militarism to produce anything like the German army. We have been building it up for two hundred years. It takes thirty years of constant training to produce such generals as we have. Our army will always maintain its organization. We have 500,000 recruits reaching military age every year and we cannot possibly lose that number, so that our army will be kept intact."

A few weeks later civilization was outraged by the German bombardment of English coast towns, such as Scarborough and Hartlepool. This was no sudden German inspiration; it was part of their carefully considered plans. Wangenheim told me, on September 6th, 1914, that Germany intended to bombard all English harbors, so as to stop the food supply. It is also apparent that German ruthlessness against American sea trade was no sudden decision of Von Tirpitz, for, on this same date, the German Ambassador to Constantinople told me that it would be very dangerous for the United States to send ships to England.

In those August and September days Germany had no intention of precipitating Turkey immediately into the war. As I had a deep interest in the welfare of the Turkish people and in maintaining peace, I telegraphed Washington asking if I might use my influence to keep Turkey neutral. I received a reply that I might do this provided that I made my representations unofficially and purely upon humanitarian grounds. As the English and the French ambassadors were exerting all their effort to keep Turkey neutral, I knew that my intervention in the same interest would not displease the British Government. Germany, however, might regard any interference on my part as an unneutral act, and I asked Wangenheim if there could be any objection from that source. His reply somewhat surprised me, though I saw through it soon afterward. "Not at all," he said, "Germany desires, above all, that Turkey shall remain neutral." Unfortunately Turkey's policy at that moment precisely fitted in with German plans. Wangenheim was every day increasing his ascendency over the Turkish Cabinet, and Turkey was then pursuing the course that best served the German aims. Her policy was keeping the Entente on tenterhooks; it never knew from day to day where Turkey stood, whether she would remain neutral or enter the war on Germany's side. Because Turkey's attitude was so uncertain Russia was compelled to keep large forces on the Caucasus, England was obliged to strengthen her forces in Egypt and India, and to maintain a considerable fleet at the mouth of the Dardanelles. All this worked in beautifully with Germany's plans, for these detached forces just so much weakened England and Russia on the European battle front. I am now speaking of the period just before the Marne, when Germany expected to defeat France and Russia with the aid of her ally, Austria, and thus obtain a victory that would have enabled her to dictate the future of Europe. Should Turkey at that time be actually engaged in military operations, she could do no more toward bringing about this victory than she was doing now, by keeping idle and useless considerable Russian and English forces. But should Germany win this easy victory with Turkey's aid, she might find her new ally an embarrassment. Turkey could demand compensation—probably the return of Egypt, perhaps the recession of Balkan territories. Such readjustments would have interfered with the Kaiser's plans, and he wanted Turkey as an active ally, only in case he did not win his speedily anticipated triumph. If Russia should make great progress against Austria, then Turkey's active alliance would have great military value, especially if her entry should be so timed as to bring in Bulgaria and Rumania. Meanwhile Wangenheim was playing a waiting game, making Turkey a potential German ally, strengthening her army and navy, and preparing to use her whenever the moment arrived for using her to the best advantage. If Germany could not win the war without Turkey's aid, Germany was prepared to take her in as an ally; if she could win without Turkey, then she would not have to pay the Turk for his cooperation. Meanwhile the sensible course was to keep her prepared in case the Turkish forces became essential to German success.

The duel that now took place between Germany and the Entente for Turkey's favor was a most unequal one. Germany had won the victory when she smuggled the *Goeben* and the *Breslau* into the sea of Marmora. The English, French and Russian ambassadors well understood this, and they knew that they could not make Turkey an active ally of the Entente. They probably had no desire to do so; however, they did hope that they could keep her neutral. To this end they now directed all their efforts. "You have had enough of war," they would tell Talaat and Enver. "You have fought three wars in the last four years; you will ruin your country absolutely if you get involved in this one." On condition that Turkey should remain neutral they offered to guarantee the integrity of the Ottoman Empire. So greatly did the Entente ambassadors desire to keep Turkey out of the war, they did not press to the limit their case against the *Breslau* and the *Goeben*. It is true that they repeatedly protested against the continued presence of these ships, but every time the Turkish officials maintained that they were Turkish vessels.

"If that is so," Sir Louis Mallet would urge, and his argument was unassailable, "why don't you remove the German officers and crew?" That was the intention, the Grand Vizier would answer; the Turkish crews that had been sent to man the ships built in England, he would say, were returning to Turkey and would be put on board the *Goeben* and the *Breslau* as soon as they reached Constantinople. But days and weeks went by; these crews came home; and still Germany manned and officered the cruisers. These backing and fillings naturally did not deceive the British and French foreign offices. The presence of the *Goeben* and the *Breslau* was a standing *casus belli*; but the Entente ambassadors did not demand their passports, for such an act would have precipitated the very crisis which they were seeking to delay, and if possible, to avoid—Turkey's entrance as Germany's ally. Unhappily the Entente's promise to guarantee Turkey's integrity did not win Turkey to their side.

"They promised that we should not be dismembered after the Balkan wars," Talaat would tell me, "and see what happened to European Turkey, then."

Wangenheim constantly harped upon this fact. "You can't trust anything they say," he would tell Talaat and Enver, "didn't they all go back on you a year ago?" And then with great cleverness he would play upon the only emotion which really actuates the Turk. The descendants of Osman hardly resemble any people I have ever known. They do not hate, they do not love; they have no lasting animosities or affections. They only fear. And naturally they attribute to others the motives which regulate their own conduct. "How stupid you are," Wangenheim would tell Talaat and Enver, discussing the English attitude. "Don't you see why the English want you to keep out? It is because they fear you. Don't you see that, with the help of Germany, you have again become a great military power? No wonder England doesn't want to fight you!" He dinned this so continually in their ears that they finally believed it, for this argument not only completely explained the attitude of the Entente, but it flattered Turkish pride.

Whatever may have been the attitude of Enver and Talaat, I think that England and France were more popular with all classes in Turkey than was Germany. The Sultan was opposed to war; the heir apparent, Youssouff Izzadin, was openly pro-ally; the Grand Vizier, Said Halim, favored England rather than Germany; Djemal, the third member of the ruling triumvirate, had the reputation of being a Francophile—he had recently returned from Paris, where the reception he had received had greatly flattered him; a majority of the cabinet had no enthusiasm for Germany; and public opinion, so far as public opinion existed in Turkey, regarded England, not Germany, as Turkey's historic friend. Wangenheim, therefore, had much opposition to overcome and the methods which he took to break it down form a classic illustration of German propaganda. He started a lavish publicity campaign against England, France, and Russia. I have described the feelings of the Turks at losing their ships in

England.* Wangenheim's agents now filled columns of purchased space in the newspapers with bitter attacks on England for taking over these vessels. The whole Turkish press rapidly passed under the control of Germany. Wangenheim purchased the *Ikdam*, one of the largest Turkish newspapers, which immediately began to sing the praises of Germany and to abuse the Entente. The *Osmanischer Lloyd*, published in French and German, became an organ of the German Embassy. Although the Turkish Constitution guaranteed a free press, a censorship was established in the interest of the Central powers. All Turkish editors were ordered to write in Germany's favor and they obeyed instructions. The *Jeune Turc*, a pro-Entente newspaper, printed in French, was suppressed. The Turkish papers exaggerated German victories and completely manufactured others; they were constantly printing the news of Entente defeats, most of them wholly imaginary. In the evening Wangenheim and Pallavicini would show me official telegrams giving the details of military operations, but when, in the morning I would look in the newspapers I would find that this news had been twisted or falsified in Germany's favor. A certain Baron Oppenheim traveled all over Turkey manufacturing public opinion against England and France. Ostensibly he was an archaeologist, while in reality he opened offices everywhere, from which issued streams of slanders against the Entente. Huge maps were pasted on walls, showing all the territory which Turkey had lost in the course of a century. Russia was portrayed as the nation chiefly responsible for these "robberies" and attention was drawn to the fact that England had now become Russia's ally. Pictures were published, showing the grasping powers of the Entente as rapacious animals, snatching away at poor Turkey. Enver was advertised as the "hero" who had recovered Adrianople; Germany was pictured as Turkey's friend; the Kaiser suddenly became "Hadji Wilhelm," the great protector of Islam; stories were even printed that he had become a convert to Mohammedanism. The Turkish populace was informed that the Moslems of India and of Egypt were about to revolt and throw off their English "tyrants." The Turkish man-on-the-street was taught to say *Gott Strafe England* and all the time the motive power of the infamous campaign was German money.

---

* Turkey had two dreadnaughts under construction in England when the war broke out. These ships were not exclusively governmental enterprises; they represented a great popular movement of the Turkish people. They were to be the agencies through which Turkey was to attack Greece to win back the islands of the Aegean, and in a burst of patriotism the Turkish people had raised the money to build them by popular subscription. Agents went from house to house, painfully collecting these small subscriptions; there had been entertainments and fairs; in their eagerness for the cause Turkish women sold their hair for the benefit of the common fund. These two vessels thus represented a spectacular outburst of patriotism that was unusual in Turkey, so unusual that many detected signs that the government had stimulated it. At the very moment when the war began, Turkey made her last payment to the English shipyards and the Turkish crews had arrived in England prepared to take the finished vessels home. Then very soon before the time set to deliver them, the British Government stepped in and commandeered these dreadnaughts for the British Navy.

But Germany was doing more than poisoning the Turkish mind; she was appropriating Turkey's military resources. I have already described how, in January, 1914, the Kaiser had taken over the Turkish Army and rehabilitated it in preparation for the European war. He now proceeded to do the same thing with the Turkish Navy. In August Wangenheim boasted to me that, "We now control both the Turkish army and navy." At that time the *Goeben* and *Breslau* arrived, an English mission, headed by Admiral Limpus, was hard at work restoring the Turkish Navy. Soon afterward Limpus and his associates were unceremoniously dismissed; not the most ordinary courtesies were shown them. The English naval officers quietly and unobservedly left Constantinople for England—all except the Admiral himself, who had to remain longer because of his daughter's illness.

Night after night whole carloads of Germans landed at Constantinople from Berlin; there were finally 3,800 men, most of them sent to man the Turkish Navy and to manufacture ammunition. They filled the cafes every night, and they paraded the streets of Constantinople in the small hours of the morning, howling and singing German patriotic songs. Many of them were skilled mechanics, who immediately got to work repairing the destroyers and other ships and putting them in shape for war. The British firm of Armstrong & Vickers had a splendid dock in Constantinople, and this the Germans now appropriated. All day and night we could hear this work going on and we could hardly sleep because of the hubub of riveting and hammering. Wangenheim now found another opportunity for instilling more poison into the minds of Enver, Talaat, and Djemal. The German workers, he declared, had found that the Turkish ships were in a desperate state of disrepair, and for this he naturally blamed the English naval mission. He said that England had deliberately let the Turkish Navy go to decay; this was all part of England's plot to ruin Turkey! "Look!" he would exclaim, "see what we Germans have done for the Turkish Army, and see what the English have done for your ships!" As a matter of fact, all this was untrue: Admiral Limpus had worked hard and conscientiously to improve the Navy and had accomplished excellent results in that direction.

All this time the Germans were strengthening the fortifications at the Dardanelles. As September lengthened into October, the Sublime Porte practically ceased to be the headquarters of the Ottoman Empire. I really think that the most powerful seat of authority at that time was a German merchant ship, the *General*. It was moored in the Golden Horn, near the Galata Bridge, and a permanent stairway had been built, leading to its deck. I knew well one of the most frequent visitors to this ship; he used to come to the embassy and entertain me with stories of what was going on.

The *General* was practically a German Club or Hotel. The officers of the *Goeben* and the *Breslau* and other German officers who had been sent to command the Turkish ships ate and slept on board. Admiral Souchon, who had brought the German cruisers to Constantinople, presided over these gatherings. Souchon was a man of French Huguenot extraction; he was a short, dapper, clean-cut sailor, very energetic and alert; to the German passion for command and thoroughness he added much of the Gallic geniality and buoyancy. Naturally he gave much liveliness to the evening parties on the *General*, and the beer and champagne which were liberally dispensed on these occasions loosened the tongues of his fellow officers. Their conversation showed that they entertained no illusions as to who really controlled the Turkish Navy. Night after night their impatience for action grew; they kept declaring that, if Turkey did not presently attack the Russians, they would force her to do so. They would relate how they had sent German ships into the Black Sea, in the hope of provoking the Russian fleet to some action that would make war inevitable. Toward the end of October my friend told me that hostilities could not much longer be avoided; the Turkish fleet had been fitted for action, everything was ready, and the impetuosity of these hot-headed German officers could not much longer be restrained. "They are just like a lot of boys with chips on their shoulders!" he said.

On September 27th, Sir Louis Mallet, the British Ambassador, entered my office in a considerably disturbed state of mind. The Khedive of Egypt had just left, and I began to talk to Sir Louis about Egyptian matters.

"Let's discuss that some other time," he said. "I have something far more important to tell you. They have closed the Dardanelles."

By "they" he meant, of course, not the Turkish Government, the only power which had the legal right to take this drastic step, but the actual ruling powers in Turkey, the Germans. Sir Louis had good reason for bringing me this piece of news, for this was an outrage against the United States as well as against the Allies. He asked me to go with him and make a joint protest. I suggested, however, that it would be better for us to act separately and immediately I started for the House of the Grand Vizier.

When I arrived a Cabinet conference was in session, and, as I sat in the ante-room, I could hear several voices in excited discussion. I could distinctly distinguish Talaat, Enver, Djavid, and other familiar members of the government. It was quite plain, from the tone of the proceedings, that these nominal rulers of Turkey were almost as worked up over the closing as were Sir Louis Mallet and myself.

The Grand Vizier came out in answer to my request. He presented a pitiable sight. His face was blanched and he was trembling from head to foot. When I asked him whether the news was true he stammered out that it was.

"You know this means war," I said, and I protested as strongly as I could in the name of the United States.

All the time that we were talking I could hear the loud tones of Talaat and his associates in the interior apartment. The Grand Vizier excused himself and went back into the room. He then sent out Djavid, the Minister of Finance, to discuss the matter with me.

"It's all a surprise to us," were Djavid's first words—this statement being a complete admission that the cabinet had had nothing to do with it. I repeated that the United States would not submit to closing the Dardanelles; that Turkey was at peace; that she had no legal right to shut the straits to merchant ships except in case of war. I said that an American ship laden with supplies and stores for the American Embassy was outside waiting to come in. Djavid suggested that I have this vessel unload her cargo at Smyrna and that the Turkish Government would pay the cost of transporting it overland to Constantinople. The proposal, of course, was a ridiculous evasion of the issue and I brushed it aside.

Djavid then said that the cabinet proposed to investigate the matter; in fact they were discussing the situation at that moment. He told me how it had happened. A Turkish torpedo boat had passed through the Dardanelles and attempted to enter the Aegean. The British warships stationed outside hailed the ship, examined it and found that there were German sailors on board. The English Admiral at once ordered the vessel to go back; this, under the circumstances, he had a right to do. Weber Pasha, the German general who was then in charge of the fortifications, did not consult the Turks; he immediately gave orders to close the straits. Wangenheim had already boasted to me, as I have said, that the Dardanelles could be closed in thirty minutes and the Germans now made good his words. Down went the mines and the nets; the lights in the lighthouses were extinguished; signals were put up, notifying all ships that there was "no thoroughfare" and the deed, the most highhanded which the Germans had yet committed was done. And here I found these Turkish statesmen, who alone had the authority over this indispensable strip of water, trembling and stammering with fear, running hither and yon like a lot of frightened rabbits, appalled at the enormity of the German act, yet apparently powerless to take any decisive action. I certainly had a graphic picture of the extremities to which Teutonic bullying had reduced the proud descendants of Osman. And at the same moment before my mind rose the figure of the Sultan, whose signature was essential to close legally these waters, quietly dozing at his palace entirely oblivious of the whole transaction.

Though Djavid informed me that the Cabinet might decide to reopen the Dardanelles, it never did so. This great passage way has remained closed from September 27, 1914 to the present time. I saw, of course, precisely what this action signified. That last month of September had been a disillusioning one for the Germans. The French had beaten back the invasion and driven the German armies to entrenchments along the Aisne. The Russians were sweeping triumphantly through Galicia; they had captured Lemburg and it seemed not improbably that they would soon cross the Carpathians into Austria-Hungry. In those days Pallavicini, the Austrian Ambassador, was a discouraged, lamentable figure; he confided to me his fears for the future. The German programme of a short, decisive war had clearly failed; it was now quite evident that Germany could only win, said Pallavicini, after a protracted struggle. I have described how Wangenheim, while preparing the Turkish army and navy for any eventualities, was simply holding Turkey in hand, intending actively to use her forces only in case Germany failed to crush France and Russia in the first campaign. The time had now come to transform Turkey from a passive into an active ally, and the closing of the Dardanelles was the first step in this direction. Few Americans realize, even today what an overwhelming influence this act had upon future military operations. I may almost say that the effect was decisive. The map disclosed that enormous Russia has just four ways of reaching the seas. One is by way of the Baltic, and this the German fleet had already closed. Another is Archangel, on the Arctic Ocean, a port that is frozen over several months in the year, and which connects with the heart of Russia only by a long, single-track railroad. Another is the Pacific port of Vladivostok, also ice bound for three months, and reaching Russia only by the thin line of the Siberian railway, 5,000 miles long. The fourth passage was that of the Dardanelles; in fact, this was the only practicable one. This was the narrow gate through which the surplus products of 175,000,000 people reached Europe, and nine-tenths of all Russian exports and imports had gone this way for years. By suddenly closing it, Germany destroyed Russia both as an economic and a military power. By shutting off the exports of Russian grain, she deprived Russia of the financial power essential to successful warfare. What was perhaps even more fatal, she prevented England and France from getting munitions to the Russian battle front in sufficient quantity to stem the German onslaught. As soon as the Dardanelles was closed, Russia had to fall back on Archangel and Vladivostok for such supplies as she could get from these ports. The cause of the military collapse of Russia in 1915 is now well known; the soldiers simply had no ammunition with which to fight. In the last few months Germany has attempted desperately to drive a "wedge" between the English and French armies—an enterprise which up to the present writing has failed. When Germany, however, closed the Dardanelles in late September, 1914, she drove such a "wedge" between Russia and her allies.

In the days following this bottling up of Russia, the Bosphorus began to look like a harbor suddenly stricken with the plague. Hundreds of ships from Russia, Rumania, and Bulgaria, loaded with grain, lumber and other products, arrived only to discover that they could go no further. There were not docks enough to berth them, and they had to swing out into the stream, drop anchor, and await developments. The waters were a cluster of masts and smoke stacks; the crowded vessels became so dense that a motor boat had difficulty in picking its way through the tangled forest. The Turks held out hopes that they might reopen the water way, and for this reason these vessels, constantly increasing in number, waited patiently for a month or so. Then one by one they turned around, pointed their noses toward the Black Sea and lugubriously started for their home ports. In a few weeks the Bosphorus and adjoining waters had become a desolate waste. What for years had been one of the most animated shipping points in the world was now ruffled only by an occasional launch or a tiny Turkish caique. And for an accurate idea of what this meant from a military stand-point, we need only call to mind the Russian battle front in the next year. There the peasants were fighting German artillery with their unprotected bodies, having no rifles and no heavy guns, while mountains of useless ammunition were piling up in their distant Arctic and Pacific ports, with no railroads to send them to the field of action.

We were all there in a highly nervous state because we knew that Germany was working hard to produce a *casus belli*. Souchon frequently sent the *Goeben* and the *Breslau* to maneuver in the Black Sea, hoping that the Russian fleet would attack. There were several pending situations that might end in war. Turkish and Russian troops were having occasional skirmishes on the Persian and Caucasian frontier. On October 29th, Be-douin troops crossed the Egyptian border and had a little collision with British soldiers. On October 29th I had a long talk with Talaat. I called in the interest of the British Ambassador, to tell him about the Bedouins crossing into Egypt. "I suppose," Sir Louis wrote me, "that this means war; you might mention this news to Talaat and impress upon him the possible results of this mad act." Already Sir Louis had had difficulties with Turkey over this matter. When he had protested to the Grand Vizier over Turkish troops near the Egyptian frontier, the Turkish statesman had pointedly replied that Turkey recognized no such thing as an Egyptian frontier. By this he meant, of course, that Egypt itself was Turkish territory and that the English occupation was a temporary usurpation. When I brought this Egyptian situation to Talaat's attention he said that no Ot-toman Bedouins had crossed into Egypt. The Turks had been building wells on the Sinai peninsula to use in case war broke out with England; England was destroying these wells and the Bedouins, said Talaat, had interfered to stop the destruction. At this meeting Talaat frankly told me that Turkey had decided to side with the Germans and to sink or swim with them. He went over the familiar grounds, and added that if Germany won—and Talaat said that he was convinced that Germany would win— the Kaiser would get his revenge of Turkey if Turkey had not helped him to obtain this victory. Talaat frankly admitted that fear—the motive, which, as I have said, is the one that chiefly inspires Turkish acts—was driving Turkey into a German alliance. He analyzed the whole situation most dispassionately; he said that nations could not afford such emotions as gratitude or hate, or affection; the only guide to action should be cold-blooded policy. "At this moment," said Talaat, "it is for our interest to side with Germany; if a month from now it is to our interest to embrace France and England, we shall do that just as readily."

"Russia is our greatest enemy," he continued, "and we are afraid of her. If now, while Germany is attacking Russia, we can give her a good strong kick, and so make her powerless to injure us for some time, it is Turkey's duty to administer that kick!"

And then turning to me with a half melancholy, half defiant smile, he summed up the whole situation.

"*Ich mit die Deutschen*, he said in his broken German.

Because the cabinet was so divided, however, the Germans themselves had to push Turkey over the precipice. The evening following my talk with Talaat, most fateful news came from Russia. Three Turkish torpedo boats had entered the harbor of Odessa, sunk the Russian gunboat *Donetz*, killing a part of the crew, and damaged two Russian dreadnaughts. They also sank the French ship *Portugal*, killing two of the crew and wounding two others. They then turned their shells on the town and destroyed a sugar factory, with some loss of life. German officers commanded these Turkish vessels; there were very few Turks on board, as the Turkish crew had been given a holiday for the Turkish religious festival of *Bairam*. The act was simply a wanton and unprovoked one; the Germans raided the town deliberately, simply to make war inevitable. The German officers on the *General*, as my friend had told me, were constantly threatening to commit some such act if Turkey did not do so; well, now they had done it. When the news reached Constantinople, Djemal was playing cards at the Cercle d'Orient. As Djemal was Minister of Marine, this attack, had it been an official act of Turkey, could have been made only on his orders. When someone called him from the card table to tell him the news, Djemal was much excited. "I know nothing about it," he replied. "It has not been done by my orders." On the evening of the 20th I had another talk with Talaat. He told me that he had known nothing of this attack beforehand, that the whole responsibility rested with the German, Admiral Souchon.

Whether Djemal and Talaat were telling the truth in thus pleading ignorance I do not know; my opinion is that they were expecting some such outrage as this. There is no question that the Grand Vizier Said Halim was genuinely grieved. When Monsieur Bompard and Sir Louis Mallet called on him and demanded their passports, he burst into tears. He begged them to delay; he was sure that the matter could be adjusted. The Grand Vizier was the only member of the cabinet whom Enver and Talaat particularly wished to placate. As a prince of the royal house of Egypt and as an extremely rich nobleman, his presence in the cabinet gave it a popular standing. This probably explains the message which I now received. Talaat asked me to call upon the Russian Ambassador and ask what amends

Turkey could make that would satisfy the Czar. There is little likelihood that Talaat sincerely wished me to patch up the difficulties; he merely wished to show the Grand Vizier that he was attempting to meet his wishes, and, in this way, to keep him in the cabinet. I saw M. Giers, but found him in no submissive mood. He said that Turkey could make amends only by dismissing all the German officers in the Turkish army and navy, he had his instructions to leave at once and should do so. However, he would wait long enough in Bulgaria to receive their reply; if they accepted his terms, he would come back.

"Russia, herself, will guarantee that the Turkish fleet does not again come into the Black Sea," said M. Gier, grimly. Talaat called on me in the afternoon, saying that he had just had lunch with Wangenheim. The cabinet had the Russian reply under consideration, he said; the Grand Vizier wished to have M. Gier's terms put in writing, would I attempt to get it? By this time Garroni, the Italian Ambassador, had taken charge of Russian affairs, and I told Talaat that such negotiations were out of my hands and that any further negotiations must be conducted through him.

"Why don't you drop your mask as messenger boy of the Grand Vizier and talk to me as Talaat?" I asked.

He laughed and said, "Well, Wangenheim, Enver, and I prefer that the war shall come now."

Bustány, Oskan, Majomoud, and Djavid at once carried out their threats and resigned from the cabinet, thus leaving the Government in the hands of Moslem Turks. The Grand Vizier, although he had threatened to resign, did not do so; he was exceedingly pompous and vain, and enjoyed the dignities of his office so much that, when he came to the final decision, he could not surrender them. The Party of Union and Progress now controlled the Government in practically all its departments.

One final picture I have of these exciting days: On the evening of the 30th I called at the British Embassy. British residents were already streaming in large numbers to my office for protection, and fears of ill treatment, even the massacre of foreigners, filled everybody's mind. Amid all this tension I found one imperturbable figure. Sir Louis was sitting in the chancery, before a huge fireplace, with large piles of documents heaped about him in a semi-circle. Secretaries and clerks were constantly entering, their arms full of papers, which they added to the accumulations already surrounding the Ambassador. Sir Louis would take up document after document, glance through it, and almost invariably drop it into the fire. These papers contained the Embassy records for probably a hundred years. In them were written the great achievements of a long line of distinguished ambassadors. There appeared the story of all the diplomatic triumphs in Turkey of Stratford de Redcliffe, the "Great Elchi," as the Turks called him, who, for the greater part of almost fifty years, from 1810 to 1858, practically ruled the Turkish Empire in the interest of England. The records of other great British Ambassadors at the Sublime Porte now went, one by one, into Sir Louis Mallet's fire. The long story of British ascendency in Turkey had reached its close. The twenty years' campaign of the Kaiser to destroy England's influence and to become England's successor had finally triumphed, and the blaze in Sir Louis's chancery was really the funeral pyre of England's vanished power in Turkey. As I looked upon this dignified and yet somewhat pensive diplomat, sitting there amid all the splendors of the British Embassy, I naturally thought of how once the Sultans had bowed with fear and awe before the majesty of England, in the days when Prussia and Germany were little more than names. Yet the British Ambassador as is usually the case with British diplomatic and military figures, was quiet and self-possessed. We sat there before his fire and discussed the details of his departure. He gave me a list of the English residents who were to leave and those who were to stay, and I made final arrangements with Sir Louis for taking over British interests. Distressing in many ways as was this collapse of British influence in Turkey, the honor of Great Britain and her Ambassador was still secure. Sir Louis had not purchased Turkish officials with money, as had Wangenheim; he had not corrupted the Turkish press, trampled on every remaining vestige of international law, fraternized with a gang of political desperadoes, and conducted a ceaseless campaign of misrepresentations and lies against his enemy. The diplomatic game that had ended in England's defeat was one which English statesmen were not qualified to play. It called for talents such as only a Wangenheim possessed.

Dignity Demanded

Editorial

UNION TOWNSHIP DISPATCH, January 1918

Even after the United States was in the war six months, arguments still continued as to the purpose of entering the conflict. Some claimed it was to make the world safe for democracy, others claimed that autocracy had to be crushed or no democracy could survive. Then there were others who agreed with (Col.) George Harvey.

George Harvey was no shrinking violet. He was loud and his language was sharp. A man of extreme wealth with friends highly placed in politics as well as commerce, he purchased a monthly publication, The North American Review. *He used the magazine as a lance, tilting it at politicians, businessmen, and when he thought it necessary, at the American people.*

When George Harvey talked, people listened. Newspapers ran editorials on his essays. With his disenchantment of President Wilson, he produced strong editorials that newspapers nationally commented upon. Here is one of them.

Colonel George Harvey, who rendered the civilized world a great service when he unearthed Woodrow Wilson at Princeton ten years ago and brought him forth as a presidential possibility, is still working might and main to undo his great service.

His latest grievance against the President is the sending of Colonel House to Europe to participate in the great Allied conference as the representative of President Wilson. Colonel Harvey does not feel that Colonel House measures up to the importance of the conference, and the Camden *Courier*, one of those typically partisan Republican newspapers of South Jersey, agrees thoroughly.

According to the *Courier*, it seems that the fact that President Wilson and Colonel House are chums disqualifies the latter for the important mission upon which he has been sent. While Colonel Harvey proved himself to be a good picker when he saw presidential timber in the former Princeton chief, President Wilson had had a good deal of experience as a picker himself in recent years.

There are bigger men and more experienced statesmen in America than Colonel House, but he is evidently a man who is better able to grasp the

Wilson viewpoint than some others, and the man who can carry out a Wilson plan is a more serviceable man than some who might suit Colonel Harvey. When Mr. Wilson chose Elihu Root to head the mission to Russia he showed that his selections were not controlled either by personal friendship or partisanship.

The country, and the entire world, should appreciate Colonel Harvey's great service in bringing Woodrow Wilson to the attention of his country at the time when the world needed just such a man, but, having done that, he should not permit personal grievances and disappointments to interfere with a full appreciation of what the President is doing. He should be big enough to make the best of it, and at least act with dignity.

We Must Kill to Save

George C. Harvey

NORTH AMERICAN REVIEW, February 1918

George Harvey's pointed editorial in the February 1918 issue of the North American Review *told Americans in no uncertain terms what he thought they should be fighting for. He spelled out the war aim in the tone of a father speaking to a reluctant child. The editorial was titled* We Must Kill to Save.

For three years and a half Europe has been drenched in blood. For three years and a half the manhood of Europe—youth in the glory of its gallantry, in the splendor of its promise—has been fed to the furnace of war. Europe is a temple of sorrow, and Rachel mourns for her children because they are not.

Soon, all too soon, France, hitherto the playground of the western world, will be sacred soil to Americans. There our dead will rest. Rude wooden crosses will dot the shell-scarred battlefields, each simple cross marking the grave of an American soldier who died in France in defence of the America he loved and those dear to him. America has yet to suffer her spiritual agony, but she cannot be spared. She, like Europe, must toil painfully the weary road to Calvary.

Has not the time come for America to take stock, to ask itself if it knows the meaning of this war, to face facts instead of feeding on illusion? Millions of men have been slaughtered, more millions have gone forth in the pride of their strength to come back broken. Shall America swell the ever mounting toll, giving and yet giving the youth on whom its future centres, or shall the guiding hand of America lead the world to peace?

Rhetoric is a spiritual stimulant, and like its grosser counterpart often valuable when a sudden burst of moral or physical energy is required, but after the effect wears off there comes reaction, exaltation gives way to depression, reality takes the place of imagination, and truth is grim. It is unfortunate that the American people entered this war with two alluring rhetorical phrases ringing in their ears—unfortunate because it has obscured the real meaning of the war and diminished its importance to them.

We were told that we went to war to make the world safe for Democracy. If this were all there is of it, clearly in the long catalogue of immoral and wanton wars that blackens the page of history there would be no war more immoral or more wanton than this. We believe in Democracy, we know its blessings, in the strength of our conviction we see that through Democracy the world marches to progress, but if we should try by force of arms to make people embrace Democracy who are wedded to autocracy, morally we should be as guilty as Louis XVI, who slew his thousands in the name of the gentle Christ who taught charity and love. It is what every bigot and zealot has done. Believing with sincerity that there was only one way to gain salvation, that every other way led to eternal damnation, with clear conscience and the frenzy of the fanatic he consigned to the rack and the stake the misguided, because better for them death or torture than torment without end. Our boasted civilization is back in the middle ages if in this enlightened day we are willing to make war to spread the political system of which we approve.

But, as we have said over and over again, what we are fighting for is not to make the world safe for Democracy but to make the world safe for us. Forced into war by Germany, who violated our rights as ruthlessly as she did those of Belgium, we are fighting a war of self defense. We are today in peril. To avert that peril we have taken up arms. We are fighting to defend our wives and children from the defiling hand of the German. We are fighting to protect our homes from a beast who knows no mercy, a beast whose lust is destruction; we are fighting to preserve the institutions we love, the liberty we cherish, the freedom dear to us. We are fighting in France because it is there we can strike the enemy, but if we are defeated in France, we shall be conquered in America; no longer shall we be freemen but the slaves of the most merciless and brutal taskmaster the world has known. Our danger is great, and only our courage and our determination can avert it.

Nor is it true, rhetoric again to the contrary, that we are fighting not the German people but only the German Emperor and the German Government, and for the German people we have no feeling of hate. You can no more separate the German Government from the German people than you can separate the bite of the mad dog from his blood. The wickedness and infamy of the German people is in their blood; it is the corruption and poison of their blood that have made the German people—not a small class or caste, not their rulers alone, but the whole people—a nation of savages. Nor is it true that the Prussian alone is guilty. The brutality of the Prussian cannot be exceeded, for that were impossible, by Bavarian or Saxon, but in the refinement of their cruelty, their beastliness, their inhumanity, between North and South German there is little choice.

Our duty is to kill Germans. To the killing of Germans we must bend all our energies. We must think in terms of German dead, killed by rifles in American hands, by bombs thrown by American youths, by shells fired by American gunners. The more Germans we kill, the less danger to our wives and daughters; the more Germans we kill, the sooner we shall welcome home our gallant lads. Nothing else now counts. There is no thought other than this, no activity apart from the duty forced upon us by Germany. The most highly civilized nations are united as they never were before, actuated by the same impulse. In England, France and Italy, among the English speaking peoples of the new world, under the southern cross and on the torrid plains, they like us see their duty clear. It is, we repeat, to kill Germans.

We have no apologies to make, no excuses to offer, no regret for having unclothed the masquerade of rhetoric and put the case in stark and naked words. Doubtless we shall offend the over nice sensibilities of those well meaning but unbalanced persons who waste their sympathies over the sufferings of the lobster as his complexion turns from dirty blue into delicate pink while they are unmoved by the knowledge of the misery and distress of the poor and unfortunate. We hope so. We are endeavoring to arouse the millions of easy going, complacent Americans, unctuously flattering themselves they are good Christians because they feel no hate, to whom the war has as yet no meaning, to a realization of what this war means, not only to them but also to their men; that it is the lives of their men against the lives of Germans.

We do not know how many Germans we have yet to kill, whether it is 500,000 or 5,000,000, but we do know that when the necessary number has been killed, when the German people lose heart and rebel against being led to the slaughter, this war will end, but that is the only way it will end. We may play at war and pay the cost in the toll of blood, or we can make war with courage, resolution and intelligence and our reward shall be fewer of those pathetic crosses on the wayside of France.

Recognizing the bravery of our Allies—and in all history there has been nothing more superb than the heroism of that "contemptible little British Army" fighting with bare hands against the onrushing German legions armed with machine guns and heavy artillery, who day after day were forced back and fiercely contested every foot with never a thought of surrender and then at last turned and defeated the enemy; or the French fighting and feinting until they were in position to stop Kluck and save Paris from the barbarian; or the Italians inch by inch scaling the snow-capped mountains; or the Russians mowed down by thousands stolidly waiting to take from the dead a rifle, in the end to be betrayed by their leaders—knowing what they have suffered, the sacrifices they have made, the misery they have endured; knowing what we have yet to know in this country, the devotion of their women, who have offered their lives and sacrificed their health and abandoned their comfort as generously as their men, we are forced to ask ourselves, in view of this will to win among the peoples of the Allied nations, and the resolution with which that will has made itself felt, why it is that the war has not yet been won, and why after three and a half years of sanguinary warfare no decision has been reached.

For now with half of the fourth year of combat spent not only have the

Allies not won but, surveying the great theater of war as a whole, we are no nearer victory than we were in the first month of hostilities; and, what is more disheartening, Germany is today the victor. Unwelcome as it is to be forced to make that admission we should be guilty of the same crass folly against which we have warned our readers were we to blink the truth and find comfort in the delusion of fatuous optimism. At the beginning of the new year Germany is stronger than she was twelve months earlier. Then, encircled by her enemies, she was fighting on two fronts, today the ring is broken and only one front has to be defended. Russia has ceased to be a menace to Germany, and the vast Russian grain supplies will flow into Germany as soon as her engineers put the railways in service. Germany has conquered Belgium and Northern France; she has her foot firmly planted on Italian soil; she has destroyed Serbia and Rumania; she has reduced Austria and Bulgaria and Turkey to the status of vassal States. Against this we (we link ourselves with the men who have braved danger while America has stood idle, because while we have not yet fought, in spirit we are their brothers in arms) have wrested from Germany her colonies, great spaces on the map but which she would gladly sacrifice for the gain of that little strip of Belgium coast she holds so tenaciously; and we occupy Jerusalem. The success of the Palestine campaign, Mr. Lloyd George told the House of Commons a few days ago, would have a permanent effect on the history of the world. We are willing to believe this, but that will not win the war. The war will be won in France and Flanders; it is only when the Germans are driven out of France and their hold on Belgium is broken that Germany will be defeated and compelled to accept the terms we shall impose. Everything else is merely a side-show.

The war ought to have been won by Germany before the close of the year 1914. While France was hastily organizing and England was recruiting, Germany, organized as no nation has ever been, recruited to the last man, swept forward. Those first months were the crucial period of the war. Had the French wavered or the English faltered, had the Germans possessed a little greater military skill or a trifle more resolution—so evenly did fate poise the scale—Germany would have won. She did not. Unable to win then she cannot win now; but she has not yet been defeated. Can we win?

When we speak of winning the war we do not mean a stalemate peace. We can have peace tomorrow on the basis of the map of August 1, 1914, but that would be no real peace, it would be simply a temporary truce; it would be a breathing spell to enable the exhausted belligerents to recuperate and feverishly prepare for a renewal of hostilities on an even greater scale; and in reality it would be a German victory. Peace, a perdurable peace, will come only when the fangs of the mad beast of Europe have been drawn, when the military power of Germany is broken; when the German people are under the harrow, sweating to pay the indemnity that is the price of their crime, in their poverty and suffering made to realize the suffering they have brought to the world.

The Vice of Secret Diplomacy

A. Maurice Low

THE NORTH AMERICAN REVIEW, February 1918

An article by A. Maurice Low, described by Col. Harvey as "a journalist of distinction," calls for a halt to secret treaties between governments. Mr. Low's writing style, it will be noted, strongly parallels George Harvey's. This may be due to extensive editing or sheer coincidence. Mr. Low delivered pointed arguments that are obviously directed at the people who will eventually sit at the peace table, whenever that would be.

No greater contribution to political morality and national security has ever been made than that of the framers of the Constitution of the United States when they wrote the Sixth Article in these words:

"This Constitution, and the laws of the United States which shall be made in pursuance thereof; and all Treaties made, or which shall be made, under the authority of the United States, shall be the supreme Law of the land."

It was a blow struck at that mass of intrigue, deceit and dishonesty which for centuries the world had known as secret diplomacy, the most vicious, immoral and dangerous power seized by a ruler in defiance of the rights of his subjects. Diplomacy was the royal prerogative. It was one of the divine attributes of kings. They it was who made war, contracted alliances, bartered territory, sacrificed liberty for a whim or superstitious fear. Even when the people began to exert their power, to assert their right to some control over their own affairs, to raise taxes and to determine how they should be spent, the king was still the sole authority in foreign relations. Diplomacy was supposed to be beyond the comprehension of the common mortal. It had to be conducted with much mystery and always great secrecy. The people knew nothing until they were plunged into war because in the exercise of his royal prerogative their sovereign had made a secret alliance, and the nation was committed to a costly campaign involving great sacrifices.

The framers of the Constitution determined this should be impossible in America. When they wrote into the compact of the States that treaties should have the same force as laws, they deprived a weak, ambitious or unscrupulous President of the power to contract a secret alliance. A law to be observed must be made public, for no man can know what the law is unless it has been published. As a treaty was placed on the same footing as the law and had the same force and effect as a law, like the law it must be made public for its terms to be respected.

We have seen within the last few years the evils of secret diplomacy, that is the power of sovereigns to enter into agreements without the knowledge or acquiescence of their subjects; and the history of Europe from the time that its history first began to assume concrete form and diplomacy was established as a principle, is largely the record of this unrestrained power. It is responsible for the endless intrigue and cabal so dear to the Minister without conscience or willing to barter his honor for gain. The people, the victims of the system, who had to pay for it, were always in a state of fear, never knowing when they were next to be dragged into the army and forced to fight for a shadowy cause about which they were ignorant and cared nothing. Yet while the world has seen nothing so disastrous as secret diplomacy, it has seen nothing so foolish, more befitting the idle moments of schoolboys, then the serious work of statesmen to whom the world ascribes genius.

Every nation in turn has sought to secure advantage by means of a secret alliance, and every treaty of alliance solemnly entered into, declaring on the faith of kings that it would be loyally observed, invoking the name of the Most High or the Trinity, in the stilted language of diplomacy as witness to the sincerity of the high contracting parties, has been merely a scrap of paper, made for the advantage of the moment and broken without a qualm of conscience when a greater advantage was to be obtained. That is the stupendous folly of this diplomacy. Similar to the Bourbons who learned nothing and forgot nothing, the necromancers who practiced the black art of secret diplomacy forgot everything and profited nothing by experience, otherwise how can one explain that king succeeded king, and minister followed minister, and yet this wretched farce went on, not for a period, not for years, but for centuries, and the tradition has been handed down to our own times; for have we not seen the Autocrat of Prussia and the Autocrat of all the Russias writing to each other in the language of schoolboys and secretly intriguing against the peace of their neighbors?

Bismarck, the most cynical but also the most astute man of his times, defended his immorality by asserting that when he entered into a secret agreement intended to nullify a public convention he was simply taking out a policy of reinsurance. The phrase was his, but the principle was as old as diplomacy itself, and as mistaken. Instead of the secret treaty being a policy of reinsurance, that is a measure of protection, it was, on the contrary, always a measure of danger. Sovereigns were too well versed in the dishonesty of kings to put faith in the royal promise, and while treaties might be kept secret from their subjects they became known to the governments against whom they were directed, who on their part took out a policy of reinsurance against the treachery of a nominal ally by making a counter alliance. That has been one of the evils of the vice of secret diplomacy. It has never protected, it has never prevented war, it has never curbed the ambition of a conscienceless ruler, but it has provoked other and more dangerous combinations, and the allies confident of their strength have treacherously forced war or struck at the security of nations at peace.

It would require too much space merely to catalogue the long list of secret alliances and their consequences, but a few taken at random may be offered to show they never exercised the slightest restraint upon their signatories, and they were shamelessly broken almost as soon as they were concluded.

In 1516 Henry VIII of England entered into negotiations with Charles V of Spain directed against Francis I of France, whereupon Charles made a secret treaty with Francis. Later when both were rivals they sought the support of the King of England, and both bribed his chancellor, Cardinal Wolsey.

In 1668 England and the Netherlands made a secret treaty to force Louis XIV of France to make peace with Spain, but he heard the news with indifference. The forehanded Louis had already made a secret treaty with the Emperor of Austria by which they were to divide the Spanish dominions on the death of the then king.

Charles II of England, who was chronically hard up, secretly sold Dunkirk to France.

Richelieu was always making and breaking secret agreements.

The secret family compact of the Bourbons, France and Spain, in 1733, was one of the causes of the French and English war in America.

Napoleon III, walking in the footsteps of his illustrious uncle, secretly proposed to Bismarck that France should be given Belgium and Luxemburg as the price of his friendship to the new German Confederation.

In the discussion of secret diplomacy a confusion exists between negotiation and consummation. Secret negotiation is not only proper, but, in many cases, absolutely essential; it is so necessary that if negotiations were not kept secret few treaties could be concluded and the negotiators would always be hampered. If the political or commercial interests of the United States require it to obtain a strip of territory to construct a canal, or a group of islands having strategic value, it would be unwise in the extreme for the United States to publicly proclaim what it was after. It might get it, but it would be forced to pay an extravagant price, it might even fail because of the opposition of a rival. The essence of a good bargain—and a treaty, it must always be remembered, is only another name for a bargain—is secrecy and a certain skill in affecting indifference.

Secrecy, therefore, in the early stages of negotiation is perfectly proper and was so recognized by the men who made the Constitution, and they were good judges of how far it was wise to entrust authority. In explanation of the power given to the President to negotiate treaties, but not to conclude them, Jay* wrote:

"It seldom happens in the negotiation of treaties, of whatever nature, but that perfect *secrecy* and immediate *dispatch* are sometimes requisite. There are cases where the most useful intelligence may be obtained, if the persons possessing it can be relieved from the apprehension of discovery." He adds, "there are many persons who would rely on the secrecy of the President, but who would not confide in that of the Senate," therefore, "the convention has done well" in so arranging that although the President must act by the advice and consent of the Senate, "yet he will be able to manage the business of intelligence in such a manner as prudence may suggest."

This is an arrangement as nearly perfect as human intelligence can devise. It combines the prime requisites of secrecy in negotiation, which is all essential; counsel after the negotiations have been concluded; and publicity when the Council of State, the Senate, has assented. The United States is the one great nation that has written into its Constitution the equality of laws and treaties, but the example set by the United States, its morality and advantages, is beginning to make the peoples of other countries ask whether it would not be wiser for them to have a share in the making of treaties instead of surrendering their authority to a few persons; the sovereign in an autocratic government; in a democratic monarchy, as in England, where by a legal fiction the treaty runs in the name of the king, actually it is the Prime Minister and his Cabinet, the real Government of England, that negotiates and concludes. Recently Mr. Balfour, the Secretary of State for Foreign Affairs, found it necessary to attempt to stem the growing demand for the democratization of European diplomacy: "I think there is in the public mind a profound illusion as to this so-called secret diplomacy," he told the House of Commons. Governments, he said, could no more conduct their affairs in the open than individuals reveal their domestic difficulties, so the business of diplomacy had to be conducted in secret, and the less light that was let in on "the mysterious intricacies of foreign diplomacy," the better it was for the peace of mind of all concerned. A member suggested that the creation of a Parliamentary Foreign Relations Committee, to have practically the same functions as those of the Foreign Relations Committee of the Senate, would be an improvement. Mr. Balfour did not agree with him. The present system worked well enough, and "to reveal from day to day what is ultimately revealed with all due precaution in the Blue Book would really be insanity."

No sane man proposes that the day to day conversations between the

---

* George Washington named Chief Justice John Jay as envoy extraordinary for the negotiation of a treaty with Great Britain in April 1794 to settle difficulties arising mainly out of violations of the Treaty of Paris of 1783.

minister and an Ambassador shall be revealed, but between that reticence and the unlimited power to commit the nation to a policy that involves thousands of lives and millions of treasure is quite another thing. What was the arrangement existing between Germany and Austria in the closing days of July 1914? No one knew, for that was a secret between the two Emperors. How far was Germany prepared to go in the support of Austria in reducing Serbia to terms? Again that question remains unanswered, because while the two emperors knew their subjects did not. What understanding existed between England and France? The British people did not know, the British Parliament did not know, neither the German Emperor nor the Austrian Emperor knew. Sir Edward Grey, the then Foreign Secretary, converted a somewhat loose entente, the terms of which even to this day no one knows, into a formal alliance, and then went down to the House of Commons and told what he had done. Parliament naturally had to stand behind the Government, what other course was possible?, but it simply ratified an executive act, after the act was committed, instead of delegating to the Executive authority to act, as the American Congress does thanks to the foresight of the Fathers.

"Diplomacy with its shoes of felt" clings to secrecy because even in an age of progress diplomacy remains faithful to tradition. It resists innovation, and it stands triumphant as the one perfect institution devised by the perverted ingenuity of man. The professional diplomatic service of Europe is a trade union, very jealous of its membership, but, similar to other trade unions, while the members quarrel and intrigue against each other, they are always ready to forget their differences when in danger from outside attack. A Foreign Minister may know of the incompetence of his Ambassador, but the code of professional ethics and loyalty to the trade union stay his dismissal because that would be a reflection upon the service. The interests of a nation may be put in jeopardy, but the feelings of a diplomat must never be hurt.

In the speech I have quoted, Mr. Balfour said the business of a diplomat "is entirely directed not to making quarrels, but to healing quarrels; not to creating difficulty but to preventing difficulty; not to provoking war but to stopping war;" but when a member of the House of Commons suggests that if the House had been taken into the confidence of the Government, the war would not have burst upon the country as an unexpected thunderbolt, Mr. Balfour said, "I do not believe that the Government, in June, 1914, had the slightest notion that there was any danger ahead." It was a cynic who described a doctor as saying to a patient, "I haven't as yet made the diagnosis, but do not alarm yourself needlessly, for we will be able to discover everything at the autopsy"; and Mr. Balfour's admission that sixty days before the greatest war the world has known the British Government had no suspicion of what was coming, suggests the happy indifference of the physician, who atones for his lack of diagnostic skill by his ability in

making the post mortem, which satisfied the laudable curiosity of the prac-
titioner but does not exactly compensate the patient. If it were not for the
coroner, fewer medical mistakes would go unrecognized, and the diplomat,
shrouded from public gaze, can blunder until war or history, usually written
long after the event, reveals his ineptitude, and then it is too late for the
damage to be repaired. Lord Salisbury traded Heligoland for a shadowy
German claim in Africa. Imagine the amiable Mr. Bryan, with his deep
love of humanity and his horror of war by virtue of his office as Secretary
of State, offering to Germany Key West in consideration of Germany
signing an arbitration treaty, convinced that Key West was of little value
to the United States but its transfer to Germany would forever render
impossible any danger of war between Germany and the United States,
and then when the treaty was duly sealed, signed and delivered calmly
announcing to the country his latest diplomatic triumph!

That brilliant Frenchman, Andre Chéradame, says:

> The typical professional diplomat lives in a world of his own. Either
> his information comes from the office or it is second-hand; it rarely is
> reached by direct observation of people or facts. The secretaries of the
> Embassies divide their time between office work, copying documents
> in copper plate hand, or social functions, pleasant enough but confined
> to a particular and narrow set. Few of the secretaries know the language
> of the country in which they reside, fewer still travel in the interior of
> the land in order to study it.

"It is necessary," he adds, "to dispel the false notion the man in the
street has of diplomacy. He fondly thinks that diplomats, while preparing
clever and mysterious combinations, fashion history, but experience shows
that they merely chronicle history and do not make it; "diplomats are
history's attorney," is his epigrammatic description. "Unfortunately," he
points out, "it does not seem that fortune has endowed any of our Allied
countries, either before or since the war, with a head capable of leading,
on grand lines, the diplomatic affairs of the Entente. The latter therefore
has been only served by those diplomats who are mere officials, and who
as such await instructions from higher quarters, and these instructions are
very often found wanting."

No one, I think, will question the fairness of these observations. This
war has torn away a lot of the tarnished trappings of conventional civilization, but nothing stands so thoroughly discredited as professional diplomacy, "folly in a coat that looks like sagacity." Between the assassination
of the Archduke Francis Ferdinand and the Austrian ultimatum to Serbia
twenty-five days elapsed. In those twenty-five days the world's fate was
being decided, yet not a single Entente Ambassador nor a single Minister
for Foreign Affairs had the slightest knowledge of what was going on and
so little was the gravity of the crisis appreciated that at the time of the

delivery of the ultimatum some of the Ambassadors of the Great Powers were away from their posts on holiday. In London, Paris, Rome, and elsewhere Excellencies with high sounding titles and numerous decorations, sat, in Crabbe's phrase, "dexterously writing despatches, and having the honor to be," but knowing nothing; blind themselves blissfully leading the blind, and looking forward with certitude to their invaluable services being rewarded with another Grand Cordon. The diplomacy developed by the war, and the diplomats who have made reputations are those of the United States, which an Englishman may say without being accused of undue partiality. Gerard, Herrick, Francis Van Dyke, Brand Whitlock, Maurice Egan, Penfield, and the two Pages, with no professional training and only the most perfunctory instruction, lawyers, bankers, men of letters, passing from their customary vocations to their new posts, have done extraordinarily well; in trying situations they have kept their heads and shown the same shrewdness, grasp of affairs and quick comprehension that won them their place in law, commerce and literature. . . .

European diplomacy is a survival for which there is little justification at the present time. It is an attempt to link the stage coach with the telephone, an unworkable combination; and it is about as sensible as it would be were our khaki clad girls to drive an ambulance in the crinolines of their Victorian grandmothers. Three or four hundred years ago the Ambassador really was the personal representative of his sovereign, in Sir Henry Wotton's classical phrase he was "an honest man sent abroad to lie for the good of his country;" and it was a seventeenth century commentator who advised that no matter what his religion, it was an Ambassador's duty to invent falsehoods and to go about making society believe them. In short, as Paschalius suggested, while an Ambassador should study to speak the truth, he was not debarred from the "official lie," and, on occasion, he should be *splendide mendax*. He was naturally deep in the confidence of his king, he was compelled to act almost entirely on his own judgment and initiative, because communication was slow and uncertain, and the great game in which sovereigns were engaged could be so easily upset by an Ambassador more adroit, whose wits were more nimble or who was more unscrupulous, who knew the right minister to bribe or the woman to make love to; and it was an Empress of Russia who advised Frederick of Prussia to replace his elderly Ambassador with a young and handsome man having a good complexion. In those days a youth, looks and a good complexion counted for much, and if in addition the royal representative was rich, a grand seigneur, able to turn a neat phrase, well versed in the classics, careful in his religious observances and yet sufficiently immoral to excite a flutter in the breasts of dowagers and anticipation in the hearts of the reigning beauties, then this Admirable Crichton would be a success as an Ambassador and either win for his master an empire or lose him his crown.

But we have changed all that, and the pulchritude of an Ambassador is no longer considered when he is about to be appointed, nor is it necessary that his complexion shall be the envy of a boarding school miss. He need not necessarily be old, but he will certainly not be young, for wisdom and not fascination is his recommendation and yet how terribly unwise so many Ambassadors have proved themselves to be. He still remains that fictional character, the personal representative of royalty; actually he is the agent of the Foreign Office, which keeps a very tight rein on him. In modern times, no Ambassador has latitude of action or is given a free hand, and every move he makes must be immediately reported to the Foreign Office. . . .

Some time, one hopes that time may be near but dreads to think it may yet be far, but some time the greatest war mankind has known must be brought to a close by the signatures of the plenipotentiaries to the most momentous treaty of peace in the world's history. That treaty will, it can be safely assumed, contain many radical and startling articles as befitting the climax to the titanic struggle, and may not America again serve the world by ridding it of secret diplomacy? By insisting that there shall be written in the treaty an article that in every country treaties shall like laws constitute the supreme law of the land, and must be ratified by Parliaments, the immorality of the secret agreement would no longer be possible. It would appeal to the democracies of England, France, Italy and Russia, and it would be championed by the enlightened republics of South America, whose constitutions have been so closely modelled on that of the United States. It would do more to keep the world safe for democracy than any one other thing. It would be a greater protection against a repetition of the horrors of the last three years than paper disarmaments, theoretical freedom of the seas, leagues of peace, or economic alliances. It would not bring Utopia, but it would make diplomacy honest, straightforward, clean; it would make almost impossible the chicanery, fraud, intrigue that for centuries have deluged Europe in blood and brought misery to its people, and there would be little further opportunity for a Hohenzollern or a Hapsburg, a Ferdinand or a Constantine, to make alliances for war unless with the authority and consent of their subjects.

A Short History of the Great War

William L. McPherson

G. P. PUTNAM'S SONS, 1920

In September 1919 William L. McPherson, military critic of the New York Tribune *delivered his manuscript, "A Short History of the Great War" for publication. It dealt with the military and diplomatic aspects of the war and the part played in it by the United States.*

In this book he discussed the purely strategic phases of the war only so far as it was necessary to establish the true relation of battles and campaigns to one another and the ultimate result. He admits that at the time of writing, military details were lacking and many of his impressions will undoubtedly be corrected after the archives of the belligerent nations begin to be published. At the time of the book's release, few German war records were available, but the list of researched material offered is impressive.

The following excerpt represents what was available to the reading public in 1920 as the details of the conflict were being pieced together.

No state ever showed more moderation under provocation than Serbia did. But the Austrian programme had been determined on in advance. Baron Giesl, the diplomatic representative of the Dual Monarchy stationed at Belgrade, received the Serbian reply at 5:45 P.M. on July 25th. Within a few minutes notice was given to Premier Pasitch that the communication was unsatisfactory. At 6:30 P.M. the Austrian Legation Staff left Belgrade. The Minister had not taken the trouble to wire the note to Vienna and await instructions. Hostilities began on July 26th. Austria-Hungary formally declared war on July 28th.

The vital question from the beginning had been how far Russia would go to protect Serbia. Russia's course was open and straightforward. Her people had recovered from the depression following the Japanese War. Defeat in the East had led the government to turn its attention again to the Balkans. The Balkan wars had helped Russia while injuring Austria Hungary. Popular feeling in the Empire demanded a demonstration of some sort on Serbia's behalf. Otherwise Russian prestige in the Balkans would be shattered.

About the middle of July, Sazonoff, the Russian Minister of Foreign Affairs, had told the British Ambassador to Russia that "anything in the shape of an Austrian ultimatum to Belgrade could not leave Russia indifferent and she might be forced to take some precautionary military measures." With the Austro-Hungarian Ambassador, who delivered a copy of the ultimatum on July 24th, he was equally outspoken. Count Szapary reported to Vienna that Sazonoff's "attitude was throughout unaccommodating and hostile." Count Pourtales, the German Ambassador to St. Petersburg, reported to Berlin that on the same day Sazonoff declared to him "most positively that Russia could not permit under any circumstances that the Serbo-Austrian difficulty should be settled between the parties concerned alone." But the latter was the only sort of settlement which Berlin and Vienna were willing to tolerate.

Diplomatic efforts between July 26th and August 1st to head off war by some sort of joint European mediation were predestined to failure. So far as the two Teuton Powers were concerned, they were a by-play intended chiefly to mystify the British Government. France and Russia both distrusted German intentions. Sir Edward Grey was more optimistic and his illusions were furthered by the fact that the German Ambassador at London, Prince Lichnowsky, an honest and high-minded diplomat, had been kept in ignorance of what was actually going on in Berlin.

On July 26th Austria-Hungary mobilized twelve of her first line army corps—eight completely and four partially. On July 29th Russia mobilized in the military districts of Odessa, Kiev, Moscow, and Kazan. Berlin had been informed in advance of this move, with a notice that there was no intention in it of aggression against Germany. On the same day Count Pourtales served notice on Sazonoff that "any further development of Russian military preparations would compel us to take countermeasures, and that meant war."

Since Russia could not mobilize effectively against Austria-Hungary without calling out the troops in the Poland district, which faced Germany as well as Austria-Hungary, a completer mobilization was ordered on July 30th. Germany intended to make this an excuse for a mobilization against both Russia and France. On July 31st she sent an ultimatum requiring Russia to stop within twelve hours "every measure of war against us and against Austria-Hungary." The next day Germany declared war on Russia.

The Berlin-Vienna plot had been carried out to the last detail. It is interesting to note that, at the last moment, Austria-Hungary showed signs of weakening. These may have been intended merely as a climax in deception. If they were genuine, they reflected the eleventh-hour realization of the Austrian General Staff that it was hardly prepared to fight Serbia on one front and Russia on another. At any rate, Vienna, under Entente pressure, began to admit that some discussion of the terms of the Serbian note was possible and also that Russian mobilization need not be interpreted as involving war. But by this time—late on July 31st—the German Government had clinched war by declaring practically that Russian mobilization against either Germany or Austria-Hungary constituted a *casus belli*.

It didn't suit the German General Staff to mobilize against Russia alone. France must be attacked and destroyed first. Berlin could never have imagined that France would fail to live up to her obligations to Russia. Nevertheless, it was desirable to draw France in at once. So the German Ambassador at Paris was instructed to inform the French Government, if it exhibited a desire to remain neutral, that neutrality could be purchased by the surrender to Germany, for the period of the war, of the frontier fortresses of Verdun and Toul.

France did not desire to remain neutral. She mobilized on August 1st, but neither declared war nor committed any hostile act. The German Government was, therefore, forced to invent some fictitious acts of aggression, and use them as the basis for a declaration of war against France. This declaration was made on August 3d. Thereafter, Germany was free to develop her long elaborated plans for an invasion of France.

Great Britain's attitude was still undefined. Sir Edward Grey had been the most sanguine supporter of the futile diplomacy of mediation. On August 1st he still had some faith in Germany's willingness to forego war. After Berlin had taken the final step, he began to have questionings as to the extent of Great Britain's obligations to France and Russia, particularly to France. Self-interest and self-preservation both required Great Britain to draw the sword against Germany. But the Asquith government had strongly pacifist tendencies. It had kept Great Britain unready for war, and now shrank from facing the consequences of unreadiness.

Fortunately Germany herself resolved British hesitations. The German General staff had decided to attack France through Belgium. On August 2d the German Government demanded free passage across Belgian territory for the German armies. The Belgian Government refused this unwarranted demand. On August 3d Berlin issued an ultimatum to Belgium and followed it by violating the Belgian border.

Sir Edward Grey had now a reason for siding with Germany's enemies which could not be challenged. Great Britain had guaranteed the territorial integrity and neutrality of Belgium. Germany—succeeding to the diplomatic contracts of Prussia—was a co-guarantor. Great Britain was morally bound to defend Belgium. It was also to her obvious interest to do so. Having once assumed that attitude, war with Germany was sure to follow.

Great Britain protested against the violation of Belgian neutrality and asked for assurances that Germany would not persist in it. Germany had no idea of giving such assurances. The British demand hardened on August 4th into an ultimatum, expiring at midnight. No assurances having been received from Berlin, Great Britain formally declared war against Germany on August 5th.

When on the evening of August 4, 1914, Sir Edward Goschen, the British Ambassador in Berlin, called on Bethmann-Hollweg, he found the latter in a tremendous state of excitement. The Chancellor expressed the greatest astonishment that Great Britain should think of going to war just for a "scrap of paper"—meaning her engagement to uphold Belgian neutrality. He accused Great Britain of "striking a man from behind while he was fighting for his life against two assailants." And he added with a sneer: "At what price will that compact (the Belgian treaty) have been kept? Has the British Government thought of that?"

Bethmann-Hollweg, being only a civilian and living in the unreal atmosphere of Continental diplomacy, may have been startled by the idea that German policy had driven Great Britain into full partnership in the Entente. But the German military leaders could have had no illustions as to the effect of their adventure in Belgium. They had counted the cost. They were willing to fight Great Britain rather than forego the advantages of access through Belgium to the open plain of Northern France.

At first glance it seemed as if Germany had recklessly plunged into a war in which the odds were enormously against her. She had created an enemy coalition comprising three Great Powers—France, Great Britain, and Russia—and three smaller states—Belgium, Serbia, and Montenegro (for Montenegro was certain to act with Serbia). Portugal had a military alliance with Great Britain. So had Japan. These two countries were to be added to Germany's enemies. Austria-Hungary was the only ally Berlin had in sight. Italy was uncertain and might not remain "benevolently neutral" as the Triple Alliance treaty required her to do in case either or both her associates engaged in a war of aggression. Rumania, formerly a satellite of the Teuton Powers, had drifted away from them in recent years almost as far as Italy had.

The two Teuton empires were greatly outnumbered at the start, and remained outnumbered. Turkey joined them in the fall of 1914. But Italy joined the Entente in May 1915. Bulgaria sided with them in October, 1915. Rumania sided with the Entente in August 1916, and Greece in the summer of 1917. When Russia dropped out of the war the United States came in.

At the beginning of the war the man-power equation, based on population returns for the years immediately preceding, was:

THE TEUTON POWERS		THE ENTENTE POWERS	
Germany	68,000,000	France (without her colonies)	
Austria-Hungary	52,000,000		39,600,000
		The United Kingdom	46,000,000
Total	120,000,000	Canada, Australia,	
		New Zealand	
		and South Africa	20,000,000
		Belgium	7,500,000
		Serbia and Montenegro	3,500,000
		Portugal	6,000,000
		Russia	178,000,000
		Total	300,600,000

Japan entered the war on August 23, 1914. But her man power is not included in the Entente total, because she confined her operations to Asia. She sent no troops to Europe and only a few of the smaller units of her navy to the Mediterranean. On the other hand, Great Britain was able to recruit more than one million men in her Indian possessions. These were used chiefly in Mesopotamia and Palestine (many of them in the noncombatant services). A few East Indian divisions fought in France in the fall of 1914, but the climate was too severe for them. France drew on her African colonies for more than five hundred thousand first line troops and auxiliaries. The best of these were employed regularly on the Western Front.

In 1915 the numerical equation stood:

QUADRUPLE ALLIANCE		ENTENTE	
Germany and		Members in 1914	300,600,000
Austria-Hungary	120,000,000	Italy	35,000,000
Turkey	21,000,000		
Bulgaria	4,750,000	Total	335,600,000
Total	145,750,000		

Germany and her associates were always outnumbered more than two to one. The defection of Russia did not lower the ratio, numerically, in view of the accession of the United States, Rumania, and Greece and the steadily increasing supply of British and French colonials.

Yet the German General Staff had foreseen an enemy preponderance in crude man power, and had frankly discounted it. The Germans knew that there were other factors in modern war more important than unorganized numbers. Numbers could count little against superior military organization, unified leadership, better trained troops, heavier guns, and completer technical equipment. Germany was thoroughly prepared for war. No one of the Entente belligerents, except France, was even moderately well prepared for it.

The German General Staff counted on a relatively short war. For a European war lasting three years—and against the enemies in sight at the beginning of it—Germany and Austria-Hungary had ample man power. Their strength could be fully developed within twelve months. On the other side only France's could be. Great Britain could not be ready to fight on a large scale until summer of 1916. Russia, owing to her isolated position and her backward condition industrially, would never be able to make effective use of her vast numbers. Italy, after she entered the war, would be held down to the defensive or to ineffectual offensives, because of military difficulties she faced on her modern frontier.

Having her military resources well in hand, Germany also expected to fight a war of elimination. She tried to crush France in 1914, and failed.

But she extinguished Belgium. She overran Serbia and Montenegro in 1915 and Rumania in 1916. She put Russia out of the lists in 1917. Had she not unnecessarily dragged the United States into the war at the same time, she might have carried the struggle against France, Great Britain, and Italy to a draw (which would have meant a substantial victory for her) before her military strength had been exhausted.

Her advantages in the way of geographical position, rapidity of mobilization, centralized command, possession of the strategic offensive, larger munitions supplies, and superiority in heavy artillery and machine guns, more than offset the Allied advantage in potential man power. Bethmann-Hollweg ludicrously distorted the facts when he pictured Germany in 1914 as a man being stabbed in the back by Great Britain while he was fighting for his life with two other assailants—Russia and France. There was never any serious shortage of German troops on the Western Front until September, 1918. And Germany always possessed a decided military superiority on the Eastern Front.

The general strategic objectives of the two groups of combatants were simple enough, in the broader sense. It was Germany's plan to dispose of France first and then to turn east and crush Russia. France was not disposed of in the great onrush which ended with the First Battle of the Marne. But she was pinned down for four years to an uncomfortable defensive on her own soil.

After 1914, it was Germany's natural policy to fight a holding battle in the West, to destroy Russia, and to bring into being that Mittel-Europa of which the Pan-Germans had dreamed. She did create in 1915 and 1916 a German Empire extending from the Gulf of Riga, on the Baltic, to the mouths of the Danube and thence to the Caucasus, the lower Tigris, and the Sinai Desert. After the Russian collapse she added to it Finland, Estonia, Livonia, Lithuania, the Ukraine, the Crimea, and Trans-Caucasia. The way was opened for German penetration to the Urals, to Bokhara and Herat.

But the German military leaders kept turning back to the original conception of a war of conquest in the West. They could not renounce the idea of capturing Paris and bringing Great Britain to her knees. So, after finishing Russia, they set out to conquer the world. It was a vain and foolish quest. For the submarine war against Great Britain forced the United States in as a belligerent and made a military decision against Germany (which before had been extremely doubtful) a practical certainty. Overwhelming ambition and unsound strategy cost Germany the war.

As to the Entente, its primary strategic aim was to connect the Western Front with the Eastern Front. This was never accomplished. And failure to accomplish it led to the downfall and elimination of Russia. The original Franco-Russian plan was to defeat Germany by a concerted Eastern and Western offensive. But Russia was never equal to an offensive against

Germany. And the French offensive didn't really get going until July 1918.

The Allies fought the war disjointedly. Without unity of command they could hardly hope to get anywhere. But it took nearly four years of failures and disappointments to achieve unity. The Western Allied powers held on, each fighting for itself, while their Eastern associates went down singly to disaster. But France, Great Britain, and Italy maintained themselves until America could arrive. And that was long enough.

PART III
PROPAGANDA

Once the war machines began plowing their ways through fields of death and destruction, nations began to mobilize and tried to control the minds of their people to encourage them to double and then redouble their efforts toward victory. Even in many professed democracies the freedom of citizens was sharply curtailed, and lies, masquerading as truth, fought their own battles in the war.

How We Advertised America

George Creel

HARPER AND BROTHERS, 1920

A nation at war must mobilize its manpower, prepare them to mentally accept regimentation, hardships, separation from loved ones, mutilation, pain and death. It must prepare its men, who have all their lives been inculcated to live peacefully by law and religion, to suddenly learn to kill or be killed. And a government must convince families to give their men up for a year, two, or forever.

The fight for the minds of all citizens of every country is as vital in wartime as the fights on the battlegrounds.

The war of ideas is advanced on the silent winds of censorship power that gradually creates waves of patriotic hysteria. At the beginning of World War I, American resistance to repressive measures was not great, and still an unknown quantity was how much military dictatorship Americans would allow to intrude upon their civil life.

Dr. Harold Lasswell, in his book, Propaganda Techniques in the World War, *wrote, "In the Great Society it is no longer possible to fuse the waywardness of individuals in the furnace of the war dance; a new and subtler instrument must weld thousands and even millions of human beings into one amalgamated mass of hate and will and hope. A new flame must burn out the canker of dissent and temper the steel of bellicose enthusiasm. The name of this new hammer and anvil of social solidarity is propaganda. Talk must take the place of drill; print must supplant the dance. War dances live in literature and at the fringes of the modern earth; war propaganda breathes and fumes in the capitals and provinces of the world."*

And in describing the specific objectives of war propaganda, Dr. Lasswell gives this list:

1. *To mobilize hatred against the enemy.*
2. *To preserve the friendship of allies.*
3. *To preserve the friendship and, if possible, to procure the cooperation of neutrals.*
4. *To demoralize the enemy.*

The Committee on Public Information (CPI) set up by President Wilson under the leadership of George Creel arrived at this formula early, almost upon its inception, thus making the record of its activity a significant chapter in American history.

The Committee on Public Information fanned the flames of censorship, and Congress passed wartime laws against espionage and sedition. Heavy penalties were levied at those who criticised the government, the Constitution, the flag, the uniforms of the army and navy, any allied nation or for obstructing the sale of United States War Bonds. Under these laws an offender could be fined $10,000 and/or receive 20 years in prison for saying anything "disloyal, profane, scurrilous or abusive" about any aspect of the government or the war effort.

In 1917 there were more than 2 million Americans of actual German birth and millions more of German descent living in the United States. As the war progressed and outrage against German spies mounted, treason charges were hurled at them as well as recent immigrants from countries governed by the Central Powers.

The United States government requested employers to investigate the national origin of employees. Those with German sounding names were usually terminated.

The fever touched everyday items such as hamburgers, which found a new name, "Liberty Steak." Sauerkraut became "Liberty Cabbage," and dachshunds became "Liberty Pups."

At an informal dinner given to honor George Creel, the Secretary of War, Mr. Newton D. Baker gave a speech containing the following excerpts on November 29, 1918.

. . . When you are near the trenches the biggest thing in the world is the man in the trenches, and he is a very big thing in the world while the war is on. Our minds are fascinated by the presence of Americans in France. We see stretching over France the products of our mills and our factories; we see the boys we have taken from field and workshop and factory and office and school manufactured overnight into an altogether unsuspected stature of heroism and capacity for sacrifice in the field. We see the trained and veteran armies of the countries which have long maintained a great military policy caught up with by our own recruits, hastily trained; we see the ocean, filled with new and difficult perils, carrying larger numbers of American soldiers than have ever been transported in the history of mankind. Perhaps the greatest foreign army that ever crossed a sea in the history of the world prior to the present war was the Persian army of a million men, which bridged and crossed the Hellespont, and here the American army has sent two millions of men across the Atlantic. We see workshops and factories in America transferred from civilian occupations and learning new and difficult arts, accustoming their tools to the manufacture of war supplies, and we see American labor learning new skills, new mechanical inventions brought into quantity production among us.

So we think of the physical things accomplished because we are close to them and because they are visible to the senses. Our minds naturally dwell chiefly upon the physical things that have been done. . . .

These things form our imagination; it is our disposition to think of the war as a great conflict of physical forces in which the best mechanic won, and in which the nation that was strongest in material things, which had the largest accumulation of wealth and the greatest power of concentrating its industrial factors, was the victorious nation. Yet, as I said at the outset, I suspect the future historian will find under all these physical manifestations their mental cause, and will find that the thing which ultimately brought about the victory of the Allied forces on the western front was not wholly the strength of the arm of the soldier, not wholly the number of guns of the Allied nations; but it was rather the mental forces that were at work nerving those arms, and producing those guns, and producing in the civil populations and military populations alike of those countries that unconquerable determination that this war should have but one end, a righteous end. . . .

The question which still remains as a part of winning the war is gathering up the results of that war and extracting the real fruits. Of course, we should all be happy over the military victory, but the things in the victory that will make for our happiness of our children twenty years from now, and our grandchildren forty years from now, are the real winnings of the war; these are the things that will count most both for our enduring happiness and the profit of our children and grandchildren, the things that will make most for the truth and the freedom and liberty of mankind always; and these are the things that are to be won out of this war, not by our way of fighting, but by what we fought for, and what other people believe we fought for. . . .

Wars are sometimes fought for land, sometimes for dynastic aspiration, and sometimes for ideas and ideals. We were fighting for ideas and ideals, and somebody who realized that, and knew it, had to say it and keep on saying it until it was believed. That was a part of the function of the Committee on Public Information. . . .

The mobilization of America, superb as it was, was a mobilization not of men alone, nor of money, nor of industry or labor, but a mobilization of true appreciation of the rights of man. It was a democratic movement which made this great result possible, and in that mobilization of ideas the Committee on Public Information played a part of great distinction and value. . . . The land forces, for which I speak especially, recognize with gratitude the debt which they owe for making their victory possible, and also making it worthwhile.

One year after the Committee on Public Information was dissolved, George Creel wrote his memoirs of the period of his administration, setting forth his aims and some of his accomplishments. The following are some of his remembrances concerning the history of the committee.

Back of the firing-line, back of armies and navies, back of the great supply-depots, another struggle waged with the same intensity and with almost equal significance attaching to its victories and defeats. It was the fight for the *minds* of men, for the "conquest of their convictions," and the battle-line ran through every home in every country.

It was in this recognition of Public Opinion as a major force that the Great War differed most essentially from all previous conflicts. The trial of strength was not only between massed bodies of armed men, but between opposed ideals, and moral verdicts took on all the value of military decisions. Other wars went no deeper than the physical aspects, but German *Kultur* raised issues that had to be fought out in the hearts and minds of people as well as on the actual firing-line. The approval of the world meant the steady flow of inspiration into the trenches; it meant the strengthened resolve and the renewed determination of the civilian population that is a nation's second line. The condemnation of the world meant the destruction of morale and the surrender of that conviction of justice which is the very heart of courage.

The Committee on Public Information was called into existence to make this fight for the "verdict of mankind," the voice created to plead the justice of America's cause before the jury of Public Opinion. The fantastic legend that associated gags and muzzles with its work may be likened only to those trees which are evolved out of the air by Hindu magicians and which rise, grow, and flourish in gay disregard of such usual necessities as roots, sap, and sustenance. *In no degree was the Committee an agency of censorship, a machinery of concealment or repression. Its emphasis throughout was on the open and the positive. At no point did it seek or exercise authorities under those war laws that limited the freedom of speech and press.* In all things, from first to last, without halt or change, it was a plain publicity proposition, a vast enterprise in salesmanship, the world's greatest adventure in advertising.

Under the pressure of tremendous necessities an organization grew that not only reached deep into every American community, but that carried to every corner of the civilized globe the full message of America's idealism, unselfishness, and indomitable purpose. We fought prejudice, indifference, and disaffection at home and we fought ignorance and falsehood abroad. We strove for the maintenance of our own morale and the Allied morale by every process of stimulation; every possible expedient was employed to break through the barrage of lies that kept the people of the Central Powers in darkness and delusion; we sought the friendship and support of the neutral nations by continuous presentation of facts. We did not call it propaganda, for that word, in German hands, had come to be associated with deceit and corruption. Our effort was educational and informative throughout, for we had such confidence in our case as to feel that no other argument was needed than the simple, straightforward presentation of facts.

There was no part of the great war machinery that we did not touch, no medium of appeal that we did not employ. The printed word, the spoken word, the motion picture, the telegraph, the cable, the wireless, the poster, the sign-board—all these were used in our campaign to make our own people and other peoples understand the causes that compelled America to take arms. All that was fine and ardent in the civilian population came at our call until more than one hundred and fifty thousand men and women were devoting highly specialized abilities to the work of the Committee, as faithful and devoted in their service as though they wore the khaki.

While America's summons was answered without question by the citizenship as a whole, it is to be remembered that during the three and a half years of our neutrality the land had been torn by a thousand divisive prejudices, stunned by the voices of anger and confusion and muddled by the pull and haul of opposed interests. These were conditions that could not be permitted to endure. What we had to have was no mere surface unity, but a passionate belief in the justice of America's cause that should weld the people of the United States into one white-hot mass instinct with fraternity, devotion, courage, and deathless determination. The *war-will*, the will-to-win, of a democracy depends upon the degree to which each one of all the people of that democracy can concentrate and consecrate body and soul and spirit in the supreme effort of service and sacrifice. What had to be driven home was that all business was the nation's business, and every task a common task for a single purpose.

Starting with the initial conviction that the war was not the war of an administration, but the war of one hundred million people, and believing that public support was a matter of public understanding, we opened up the activities of government to the inspection of the citizenship. A voluntary censorship agreement safeguarded military information of obvious value to the enemy, but in all else the rights of the press were recognized and furthered. Trained men, at the center of effort in every one of the war-making branches of government, reported on progress and achievement, and in no other belligerent nation was there such absolute frankness with respect to every detail of the national war endeavor.

As swiftly as might be, there were put into pamphlet form America's reasons for entering the war, the meaning of America, the nature of our free institutions, our war aims, likewise analyses of the Prussian system, the purposes of the imperial German government, and full exposure of the enemy's misrepresentations, aggressions, and barbarities. Written by the country's foremost publicists, scholars, and historians, and distinguished for their conciseness, accuracy, and simplicity, these pamphlets blew as a great wind against the clouds of confusion and misrepresentation. Money could not have purchased the volunteer aid that was given freely, the various universities lending their best men and the National Board of Historical Service placing its three thousand members at the complete disposal of the Committee. Some thirty-odd booklets covering every phase of America's ideals, purposes, and aims were printed in many languages other than English. Seventy-five million reached the people of America, and other millions went to every corner of the world, carrying our defense and our attack.

The importance of the spoken word was not underestimated. A speaking division toured great groups like the Blue Devils, Pershing's Veterans, and the Belgians, arranged mass-meetings in the communities, conducted forty-five war conferences from coast to coast, co-ordinated the entire speaking activities of the nation, and assured consideration to the crossroads hamlet as well as to the city.

The Four Minute Men, an organization that will live in history by reason of its originality and effectiveness, commanded the volunteer services of 75,000 speakers, operating in 5,200 communities and making a total of 755,190 speeches, every one having the carry of shrapnel.

With the aid of a volunteer staff of several hundred translators, the Committee kept in direct touch with the foreign-language press, supplying selected articles designed to combat ignorance and disaffection. It organized and directed twenty-three societies and leagues designed to appeal to certain classes and particular foreign-language groups, each body carrying a specific message of unity and enthusiasm to its section of America's adopted peoples.

It planned war exhibits for the state fairs of the United States, also a great series of interallied war expositions that brought home to our millions the exact nature of the struggle that was being waged in France. In Chicago alone two million people attended in two weeks, and in nineteen cities the receipts aggregated $1,432,261.36.

The Committee mobilized the advertising forces of the country—press, periodical, car and outdoor—for the patriotic campaign that gave millions of dollars' worth of free space to the national service.

It assembled the artists of America on a volunteer basis for the production of posters, window-cards, and similar material of pictorial publicity for the use of various government departments and patriotic societies. A total of 1,438 drawings was used.

It issued an official daily newspaper, serving every department of government, with a circulation of one hundred thousand copies a day. For official use only, its value was such that private citizens ignored the supposedly prohibitive subscription price, subscribing to the amount of $77,622.58.

It organized a bureau of information for all persons who sought direction in volunteer war-work, in acquiring knowledge of any administrative activities, or in approaching business dealings with the government. In the ten months of its existence it gave answers to eighty-six thousand requests for specific information.

It gathered together the leading novelists, essayists, and publicists of the land, and these men and women, without payment, worked faithfully in the production of brilliant, comprehensive articles that went to the press as syndicate features.

One division paid particular attention to the rural press and the plate-matter service. Others looked after the specialized needs of the labor press, the religious press, and the periodical press. The Division of Women's War Work prepared and issued the information of peculiar interest to the women of the United States, also aiding in the task of organizing and directing.

Through the medium of the motion picture, America's war progress, as well as the meanings and purposes of democracy, were carried to every community in the United States and to every corner of the world. "Pershing's Crusaders," "America's Answer," and "Under Four Flags" were types of feature films by which we drove home America's resources and determinations, while other pictures, showing our social and industrial life, made our free institutions vivid to foreign peoples. From the domestic showings alone, under a fair plan of distribution, the sum of $878,215 was gained, which went to support the cost of the campaigns in foreign countries where the exhibitions were necessarily free.

Another division prepared and distributed still photographs and ster-eopticon slides to the press and public. Over two hundred thousand of the latter were issued at cost. The division also conceived the idea of the "permit system," that opened up our military and naval activities to civilian camera men, and operated it successfully. It handled, also, the voluntary censorship of still and motion pictures in order that there might be no disclosure of information valuable to the enemy. The number of pictures reviewed averaged seven hundred a day.

Turning away from the United States to the world beyond our borders, a triple task confronted us. First, there were the peoples of the Allied nations that had to be fired by the magnitude of the American effort and the certainty of speedy and effective aid, in order to relieve the war-weariness of the civilian population and also to fan the enthusiasm of the firing-line to a new flame. Second, we had to carry the truth to the neutral nations, poisoned by German lies; and third, we had to get the ideals of America, the determination of America, and the invincibility of America into the Central Powers.

Unlike other countries, the United States had no subsidized press service with which to meet the emergency. As a matter of bitter fact, we had few direct news contacts of our own with the outside world, owing to a scheme of contracts that turned the foreign distribution of American news over to European agencies. The volume of information that went out from our shores was small, and, what was worse, it was concerned only with the violent and unusual in our national life. It was news of strikes and lynchings, riot, murder cases, graft prosecutions, sensational divorces, the bizarre extravagance of "sudden millionaires." Naturally enough, we were looked upon as a race of dollar-mad materialists, a land of cruel monopolists, our real rulers the corporations and our democracy a "fake."

Looking about for some way in which to remedy this evil situation, we saw the government wireless lying comparatively idle, and through the close and generous cooperation of the navy we worked out a news machinery that soon began to pour a steady stream of American information into international channels of communication. Opening an office in every capital of the world outside the Central Powers, a daily service went out from Tuckerton to the Eiffel Tower for use in France and then for relay to our representatives in Berne, Rome, Madrid and Lisbon. From Tuckerton the service flashed to England, and from England there was relay to Holland, the Scandinavian countries, and Russia. We went into Mexico by cable and land wires; from Darien we sent a service in Spanish to Central and South American countries for distribution by our representatives; the Orient was served by telegraph from New York to San Diego, and by wireless leaps to Cavite and Shanghai. From Shanghai the news went to Tokyo and Peking, and from Peking on to Vladivostok for Siberia. Australia, India, Egypt, and the Balkans were also reached, completing the world chain.

For the first time in history the speeches of a national executive were given universal circulation. The official addresses of President Wilson, setting forth the position of America, were put on the wireless always at the very moment of their delivery, and within twenty-four hours were in every country in the world. Carried in the newspapers initially, they were also printed by the Committee's agents on native presses and circulated by the millions. The swift rush of our war progress, the tremendous resources of the United States, the Acts of Congress, our official deeds and utterances, the laws that showed our devotion to justice, instances of our enthusiasm and unity—all were put on the wireless for information of the world, Teheran and Tokyo getting them as completely as Paris or Rome or London or Madrid.

Through the press of Switzerland, Denmark, and Holland we filtered an enormous amount of truth to the German people, and from our headquarters in Paris went out a direct attack upon Hun censorship. Mortarguns, loaded with "paper bullets," and airplanes, carrying pamphlet matter, bombarded the German front, and at the time of the armistice balloons with a cruising radius of five hundred miles were ready to reach far into the Central Powers with America's message. . . .

To our representatives in foreign capitals went, also, the feature films that showed our military effort—cantonments, shipyards, training-stations, warships, and marching thousands—together with other motion pictures expressing our social and industrial progress, all to be retitled in the language of the land, and shown either in theaters, public squares, or open fields. Likewise we supplied pamphlets for translation and distribution, and sent speakers, selected in the United States from among our foreign-born, to lecture in the universities and schools, or else to go about among the farmers, to the labor unions, to the merchants, etc. Every conceivable means was used to reach the foreign mind with America's message. . . .

Before the flood of publicity the German misrepresentations were swept away in Switzerland, the Scandinavian countries, Italy, Spain, the Far East, Mexico, and Central and South America. From being the most misunderstood nation, America became the most popular. A world that was either inimical, contemptuous, or indifferent was changed into a world of friends and well-wishers. Our policies, America's unselfish aims in the war, the services by which these policies were explained and these aims supported, and the flood of news items and articles about our normal life and our commonplace activities—these combined to give a true picture of the United States to foreign eyes. It is a picture that will be of incalculable value in our future dealings with the world, political and commercial. It was a bit of press-agenting that money could not buy, done out of patriotism by men and women whose services no money could have bought. . . .

The initial disadvantages and persistent misunderstandings that did so much to cloud public estimation of the Committee had their origin in the almost instant antagonism of the metropolitan press. At the time of my appointment a censorship bill was before Congress, and the newspapers, choosing to ignore the broad sweep of the Committee's functions, proceeded upon the exclusive assumption that I was to be "the censor." As a result of press attack and Senate discussion, the idea became general and fixed that the Committee was a machinery of secrecy and repression organized solely to crush free speech and a free press.

As a matter of fact, I was strongly opposed to the censorship bill, and delayed acceptance of office until the President had considered approvingly the written statement of my views on the subject. It was not that I denied the need of some sort of censorship, but deep in my heart was the feeling that the desired results could be obtained without paying the price that a formal law would have demanded. Aside from the physical difficulties of enforcement, the enormous cost, and the overwhelming irritation involved, I had the conviction that our hope must lie in the aroused patriotism of the newspaper men of America. . . .

Censorship laws, too, even though they protest that the protection of military secrets is their one original object, have a way of slipping over into the field of opinion, for arbitrary power grows by what it feeds on. "Information of value to the enemy" is an elastic phrase and, when occasion requires, can be stretched to cover the whole field of independent discussion. Nothing, it seemed to me, was more dangerous, for people did not need less criticism in time of war, but more. Incompetence and corruption, bad enough in peace, took on an added menace when the nation was in arms. One had a right to hope that the criticism would be honest, just, and constructive, but even a blackguard's voice was preferable to the dead silence of an iron suppression.

My proposition, in lieu of the proposed law, was a voluntary agreement that would make every paper in the land its own censor, putting it up to the patriotism and common sense of the individual editor to protect purely military information of tangible value to the enemy. The plan was approved and, without further thought of the pending bill, we proceeded to prepare a statement to the press of America that would make clear the necessities of the war-machine even while removing doubts and distrusts. . . .

What the Government Asks of the Press

The desires of the government with respect to the concealment from the enemy of military policies, plans, and movements are set forth in the following specific requests. They go to the press of the United States directly from the Secretary of War and the Secretary of the Navy and represent the thought and advice of their technical advisers. They do not apply to news despatches censored by military authority with the expeditionary forces or in those cases where the government itself, in the form of official statements, may find it necessary or expedient to make public information covered by these requests.

For the protection of our military and naval forces and of merchant shipping it is requested that secrecy be observed in all matters of:

1. Advance information of the routes and schedules of troop movements. (See Par. 5.)

2. Information tending to disclose the number of troops in the expeditionary forces abroad.

3. Information calculated to disclose the location of the permanent base or bases abroad.

4. Information that would disclose the location of American units or the eventual position of the American forces at the front.

5. Information tending to disclose an eventual or actual port of embarkation; or information of the movement of military forces toward seaports or of the assembling of military forces at seaports from which inference might be drawn of any intention to embark them for service abroad; and information of the assembling of transports or convoys; and information of the embarkation itself.

6. Information of the arrival at any European port of American war-vessels, transports, or any portion of any expeditionary force, combatant or non-combatant.

7. Information of the time of departure of merchant ships from American or European ports, or information of the ports from which they sailed, or information of their cargoes.

8. Information indicating the port of arrival of incoming ships from European ports or after their arrival indicating, or hinting at, the port at which the ship arrived.

9. Information as to convoys and as to the sighting of friendly or enemy ships, whether naval or merchant.

10. Information of the locality, number, or identity of vessels belonging to our own navy or to the navies of any country at war with Germany.

11. Information of the coast or anti-aircraft defenses of the United States. Any information of their very existence as well as the number, nature, or position of their guns, is dangerous.

12. Information of the laying of mines or mine-fields or of any harbor defenses.

13. Information of the aircraft and appurtenances used at government aviation-schools for experimental tests under military authority, and information of contracts and production of air material, and information tending to disclose the numbers and organization of the air division, excepting when authorized by the Committee on Public Information.

14. Information of all government devises and experiments in war material, excepting when authorized by the Committee on Public Information.

15. Information of secret notices issued to mariners or other confidential instructions issued by the navy or the Department of Commerce relating to lights, lightships, buoys, or other guides to navigation.

16. Information as to the number, size, character, or location of ships of the navy ordered laid down at any port or shipyard, or in actual process of construction; or information that they are launched or in commission.

17. Information of the train or boat schedules of traveling official missions in transit through the United States.

18. Information of the transportation of munitions or of war material.

Photographs—Photographs conveying the information specified above should not be published.

These requests to the press are without larger authority than the necessities of the war-making branches. Their enforcement is a matter for the press itself. To the overwhelming proportion of newspapers who have given unselfish, patriotic adherence to the voluntary agreement the government extends its gratitude and high appreciation.

Committee on Public Information,
By George Creel, *Chairman.*

Our European comrades in arms viewed the experiment with amazement, not unmixed with anxiety, for in every other belligerent country censorship laws established iron rules, rigid suppressions, and drastic prohibitions carrying severe penalties. Yet the American idea *worked.* And it worked *better* than any European law. Troop-trains moved, transports sailed, ships arrived and departed, inventions were protected, and military plans advanced, all behind a wall of concealment built upon the honor of the press and the faith of the individual editor. Yet while the thing itself was done there was no joy and pride in the doing. Never at any time was it possible to persuade the whole body of Washington correspondents to think of the voluntary censorship in terms of human life and national hopes. . . .

Long training had developed the conviction that nothing in the world was as important as a "story" and not even the grim fact of war could remove this obsession. . . .

"Pershing's Crusaders," "America's Answer," and "Under Four Flags" are feature films that will live long in the memory of the world, for they reached every country, and were not only the last word in photographic art, but epitomized in thrilling, dramatic sequence the war effort of America. Yet these pictures, important as they were, represented only a small portion of the work of the Division of Films, a work that played a vital part in the world-fight for public opinion. A steady output ranging from one-reel subjects to seven-reel features, and covering every detail of American life, endeavor, and purpose, carried the call of the country to every community in the land, and then, captioned in all the various languages, went over the seas to inform and enthuse the peoples of Allied and neutral nations. . . .

Our first hope was to avoid all appearance of competition with the commercial producers, and as a consequence the bulk of material was distributed fairly and at a nominal price among the film-news weeklies. Experts were then engaged to put the remainder into feature form, and these pictures were handed over to the State Councils of Defense and to the various patriotic societies. They were not shown in motion-picture theaters, nor was admission charged except in the case of benefits for a particular purpose. . . .

Our first feature-film was "Pershing's Crusaders," and at intervals of six weeks we produced "America's Answer" and "Under Four Flags." The policy decided upon was this: first, direct exhibition of the feature by the Committee itself in the larger cities in order to establish value and create demand; second, sale, lease or rental of the feature to the local exhibitors. This activity was placed in the hands of Mr. George Bowles, an experienced theatrical and motion-picture manager, who had made a name for himself in exploiting "The Birth of a Nation." Mr. Bowles operated as many as eight road companies in different sections of the country at one time, each with its own advertising, advance sales, and business management. The utmost care was taken with these "official showings," for what we sought was an impressiveness that would lift them out of the class of ordinary motion-picture productions in the minds of the public. L. S. Rothapfel, of the Rialto and Rivoli theaters in New York City, gave us his own aid and that of his experts in the matter of scenic accessories, orchestra, and incidental music, while for "America's Answer" Frank C. Yohn painted a great canvas, so much a thing of beauty and inspiration that it thrilled audiences into enthusiasm for the motion pictures that followed. . . .

With the tremendous advertising gained from these governmental showings in the principal cities we were then able to go direct to the exhibitor in the certainty of his keen interest. Our aim was to secure the widest possible distribution of the government films in the shortest possible time. To this end every effort was made to eliminate the competitive idea from the minds of exhibitors, and wherever possible to secure simultaneous showings in houses which ordinarily competed for pictures.

Mr. Denis Sullivan and his assistant, Mr. George Meeker, who were in charge of domestic distribution through motion-picture houses, inaugurated a proportionate selling plan whereby the rental charged every house was based on the average income derived from that particular house. By this method the small house as well as the large one could afford to run the government films. The result of these efforts to obtain the widest possible showing for government films was amazingly successful, and the showing of "America's Answer" broke all records for range of distribution of any feature of any description ever marketed. . . .

The films were loaned to army and navy stations, educational and patriotic institutions, without charge except transportation. Other organizations and individuals were usually charged one dollar per reel for each day used. When it is considered that the average reel costs forty dollars for raw stock and printing, and that the average life of a reel is about two hundred runs, it can be readily seen that this charge of one dollar per reel barely covered cost. For the purpose of comparison the leading motion-picture houses in New York pay as high as three thousand dollars for the use of one picture for one week's run.

On June 1, 1918, the Division of Films formed a scenario department to experiment with an interesting theory. The departments at Washington had been in the habit of contracting for the production of films on propaganda subjects and then making additional contracts to secure a more or less limited circulation of the pictures when produced. The general attitude of motion-picture exhibitors was that propaganda pictures were uninteresting to audiences and could have no regular place in their theaters. The theory of the Division of Films was that the fault lay in the fact that propaganda pictures had never been properly made, and that if skill and care were employed in the preparation of the scenarios the resultant pictures could secure place in regular motion-picture programs. Producers were at first skeptical, but in the end they agreed to undertake the production of one-reel pictures for which the division was to supply the scenario, the list of locations, and permits for filming the same, and to give every possible co-operation, all without charge. The finished picture became the sole property of the producer, who obligated himself merely to give it the widest possible circulation after it had been approved by the Division of Films. Mr. Rufus Steele was given charge of the new venture, and while many difficulties had to be overcome, the theory proved sound. . . .

Late in the summer of 1918, our system of production through outside concerns having worked out satisfactorily, it was decided to undertake production on our own account. . . .

A second series of six two-reel pictures had been laid out and the filming was about to proceed when the armistice caused the division to suspend all new undertakings. . . .

Even had I not been an ardent suffragist, we could not have ignored the importance of women in connection with the war or failed to see the necessity of reaching them with our activities. There was a Woman's Committee of the Council of National Defense, however, headed by such brilliant personalities as Dr. Anna Howard Shaw, Mrs. Carrie Chaman Catt, and Miss Ida Tarbell, and it seemed a certainty that it would meet every need. What soon developed, unfortunately, was that the Woman's Committee had no money and was also expected to confine itself to "advising" the business of initiation having been placed in other hands.

By way of assistance, and at the request of Miss Tarbell, I attached Mrs. Clara Sears Taylor to the News Division and assigned her to the Woman's Committee as its general reporter. Lack of money and lack of authority joined to slacken effort very materially, and because an important work that *had* to be done was *not* being done I fell in with Mrs. Taylor's suggestion to form a Division of Women's War-work in the Committee on Public Information. Not only was Mrs. Taylor a person of tremendous energy and rare ability, but she had the gift of attracting women of similar type, and it was not long until a staff of twenty-two, many of them volunteers, were in full and effective swing.

What women were doing to help win the war was the one theme, and not only did they fill the women's pages in the daily press, as well as earning large space in magazine sections, but they fought their way to a place in the sun in the news columns. They went into the colleges where girls studied, into clubs of every kind, into ghettoes and foreign colonies, among the colored women of the country, giving information and arousing enthusiasm. Added to this, the division was a "question and answer" bureau that handled thousands of letters daily from women in every corner of the United States.

During the nine months of its existence, 2,305 stories were sent to 19,471 newspapers and women's publications. These releases included a wire and mail service, and were made up of news stories and feature articles. They were sent daily to 2,861 papers in seven columns a week, containing from twelve to twenty stories each. More than 10,000 cards were indexed on women's work, including the personnel of both organizations and individuals, and a collation of material of immense value to magazine and newspaper writers. Two hundred and ninety-two pictures were furnished newspapers, showing women actively engaged in war-work.

Weekly columns sent to newspapers and magazines included, first, war-work being done in national organizations; second, in governmental departments; third, in decentralized organizations throughout the United States; fourth, in schools and colleges; fifth, in churches; sixth, foreigh co-operation; seventh, work being done by organizations of colored women.

Close co-operation was formed with the colleges, through representatives sent out by the collegiate alumni, and with fraternal organizations through representatives co-operating with the governmental departments through their international associations. The news for the foreign column was received by means of co-operation with the foreign embassies, legations, high commissions, and committees and committees in foreign countries at war with Germany.

Mrs. Mary Holland Kinkaid, well-known magazine and newspaper editor and writer of New York, edited the columns of news which created an interchange in thought between the women war-workers of the world, culling from letters and other forms of communication the facts, figures, hopes, and ambitions that were woven into "stories." She handled also the copy brought in by trained reporters who had the governmental departments and national organizations in Washington for their "beats."

These reporters included women from many states and representing as many points of view. The War Department, with its thousands of women war-workers, was "covered" by Mrs. William A. Mundell (pen name Caroline Singer), a newspaper writer of San Francisco. News of the Woman's Committee of the Council of National Defense, which operated under the War Department, was collected by means of their own machinery, and prepared by them, and then distributed by the Committee on Public Information.

The State and Navy Departments' picturesque tales of the yeomanettes, women finger-print experts, etc., were gathered and written into magazine and newspaper stories by Miss Margaret Moses, who came to the division with recommendations from *The New York Times*, Columbia University, and Barnard College.

Miss Mildred Morris, of Denver and Chicago newspaper experience, invaded the Department of Labor, and from its statistical shelves and important war investigations and reports made available for the press much extremely valuable information. The labor-supply, depleted by the cutting off of immigration and by the military draft, necessitated calling into industrial services many women who had never before been wage-earners. The distribution of this information was extremely helpful in aiding to solve the problems which automatically arose from the advent of these women into industrial life. A clever feature-writer of Washington, Miss Helen

Randall, assisted in this labor field, writing stories from the Agricultural Department.

Miss Dorothy Lewis Kitchen of Kansas City, Mo., a young woman who had been active in settlement and civic work and in the Consumers' League, had charge of the Interior Department, writing articles about teachers, librarians, and the many phases of work done in the Department of the Interior. Miss Kitchen compiled two brochures on "War-work of Women in Colleges." The issuance of these brochures was commenced in February, 1917, when the smaller colleges were more or less at sea as to the nature of the war-work best suited for them, and when the larger colleges were just establishing definite programs for more intensive work. The brochures were sent to colleges, schools, newspapers, magazines, women's organizations, and government officials. The effect was amazing. Every college in the country took advantage of the suggestive reports of every other college, and a vast amount of patriotic energy was utilized in a most effective manner. The news of this activity was immensely stimulating to other war-workers. An edition of twenty-five thousand copies was exhausted in a very short time, and thousands more were sent in response to requests from libraries, college officials, and individuals.

There was an appendix to this pamphlet called "Opportunities in War-work for Women, which was used so widely that it was later revised, and was just ready for the printer when the work of the division ceased. It contained a list of the chairmen of the Woman's Committee in each state, a list of civil service commissions of farm-help specialists under the Department of Agriculture, and of the fourteen Red Cross divisions, besides definite ideas for war-work for trained and untrained college girls, for educated and uneducated—in fact, for every class of woman.

The Department of Agriculture, with all the war bodies associated with it, and with the women's organizations which functioned through it, was combed each day for news of women's war-work by Miss Constance Marguerite McGowan, now Mrs. C. B. Savage of New York. Mrs. Savage came from Lindenwood College, where she was dean of journalism.

The Treasury, with its great Liberty-loan work by women, the Post Office, and the Department of Justice were reported by Mrs. Susan Hunter Walker, an able writer of wide experience.

Mrs. Florence Normile of New York Public Library was given the Department of Commerce, the Fosdick Commission, and the Young Women's Christian Association.

This information, having been collected and written, was mimeographed and "placed on the table" for distribution among the nine hundred and odd correspondents then in Washington. The number, of course, included the correspondents of the big press associations, so that every paper in the United States was reached. When the matter was not "spot" news— that is, when it was not of sufficient news importance to be carried by telegraph—the material was worked up into feature and special stories for news syndicates, or else was sent out in clip sheets. Many of the papers carried these columns in full, showing the interest felt all over the country in what was being done by women. . . .

The various departments in Washington and many Senators and Congressmen also got in the habit of sending women's letters to the Division of Women's War-work for answer. Thus the division, besides being a centralized medium of communication between writers, publicity bureaus, organization heads, and the government, soon became an important factor in the strengthening of the morale of women in America.

Miss Ellen Harvey, and later Mrs. Laura Miller of St. Louis, handled the bulk of this work, although Mrs. Taylor considered it of such great importance in sustaining the high morale of the work of the home that she gave it her personal attention, and insisted on the warm cooperation of every member of the staff in finding definite, accurate answers to the many questions asked.

These letters were the expressions of the very heart of American womanhood. The wording of an answer had power to determine whether or not a discontented and unhappy writer should form a center of agitation against the war. Some of these letters were addressed to the President, and many to the Secretary of War. The method employed was to answer the queries, and then to get the writer in touch with the group of women doing war-work in the vicinity of her home. In case of want, home-service workers were interested in the case. Often glowing expressions of patriotism followed a fiery protest against "sending my husband to war," or letters showing a new interest in life followed a suicide threat—"because you took my only son." Always the idea was to interest these unhappy women in something real and vital.

All this ended suddenly and even tragically. In June, 1918, I went before Congress for my appropriation. When it came to the Division of Women's War-work, Congress refused funds on the ground that we were trespassing upon a field "already occupied by the Women's Committee of the Council of National Defense." Plain proof that this was not the case failed to secure a reversal of the decision, and Mrs. Taylor and her heartbroken associates were compelled to quit a great work that was just coming to the peak of its importance.

The Press as Affected by the War

Oswald Garrison Villard

THE AMERICAN REVIEW OF REVIEWS, January 1915

Getting information from the fighting fronts has always been difficult, but during World War I censorship came down very heavily on all news pertaining to the armed forces. Generals, admirals and national leaders were as concerned in protecting themselves and covering their mistakes as divulging military intelligence. Under the guise of protecting the country and its fighting men, the news was politically doctored to convey the brilliance of leadership.

Publishers of newspapers and periodicals, faced with rising costs and an audience thirsting for war news, felt a terrible frustration. Oswald Garrison Villard, the president of the New York Evening Post, *discusses the hardship of producing a daily newspaper in a war-torn world.*

For one thing this war has made it impossible to revive to any extent the old charge that the newspapers brought it on. Unquestionably, the Austrian press had much to do with preparing the public mind for the ultimatum to Servia, the sensational murder of the Archduke giving it the excuse for every sort of accusation and hostile attack upon their small but, to them, pestiferous neighbor, Servia. In England the London *Times*, during the critical days from July 28 to August 3, printed a series of despatches from St. Petersburg of which it will not be maintained that they made for anything else than bad blood, though they must have given immense satisfaction in the Czar's capital.

Other British newspapers of jingo type, Conservative and Liberal, eagerly upheld the Foreign Minister, for whom Bernard Shaw hopes a reduction at least to the rank of Prime Minister as a result of this national crisis, so that he may not have the power to involve England in war all by himself. But the time was so short between the first alarm and the actual beginning of hostilities that the Hessians of the press were not able really to bring their batteries into action, particularly in Germany, where early appreciation of the overwhelming magnitude of the danger added sobriety to their first-page leaders.

By and large, the press was as much surprised by the suddenness with which the tornado burst as anyone else. There was no time given prior to hostilities for the mobilization of correspondents and scouts. Veteran war reporters, usually able to scent trouble from afar, and ready for the first shots, were caught unprepared and far from the scene of action. The paralyzing of ocean traffic made it all the more difficult to reach the front, and when the correspondents did finally arrive there, never was a military front so coldly inhospitable.

For another thing, if this war lasts as long as Lord Kitchener prophesies, it ought effectually to dispose of the familiar popular fallacy that war is a good thing for the press. Newspaper men have put up with no more trying person than the friend who slaps them on the back and says, "Well, old man, this war may be bad for some kinds of business, but it's fine for yours." Nothing could be further from the truth. Newspapers, for some devilish reason or another, may incite to war, as did some of our "yellows" in 1898, and the London *Times* prior to the Boer war, but they pay a pretty price for it even when it does not bring with it a national industrial and financial depression. There is nothing that a business manager or managing editor dreads as much as war, for nothing so quickly sends up the budget. There are special correspondents and their expenses, the costly pictures to illustrate their articles; the staff photographers, when such are permitted; the cost of extra news services and of the reports of such star syndicate writers as Richard Harding Davis.

The cable tolls go up with such rapidity that one great New York daily has sent an expert editor to London merely to take out the needless words from cable messages, and he is understood to be much more than covering his salary by the savings he makes. Thus far the Associated Press, which serves 900 American newspapers, has met the enormously increased cost of cabling by cutting down on its domestic news and drawing on its surplus.

Not in the lifetime of men of fifty has so little news about the rest of the country appeared in the Eastern press as in these last few months. On one day in September two of the leading New York newspapers contained five and six pages of cable news from Europe while one newspaper printed three. The other four papers didn't carry any news from any domestic points outside of New York, excepting Washington. Not until election time came was there a substantial change in this situation. Thus, among the curious effects of the war has been a temporary news isolation of the West, South, and North from the East.

Then there are the extra editions. They involve heavy expense, not only in composition and paper, but in actual handling. There are extra trips to be made by wagons and bundle-carriers, while the cost of expressing and mailing of bundles to suburbs and nearby cities has to be met. But, says the layman, you are selling more newspapers and so making plenty of money. Unfortunately for the newspaper publisher, this is not true, particularly for the newspapers sold at one cent. The proceeds from the sale of copies of the newspaper never meet the cost of the paper upon which they are printed unless the issue is held down to twelve pages, so that increased circulation, unless accompanied by increased advertising, is a loss. In fact, the average publisher regards a large circulation as undesirable in itself, but as a means to an end. He wants a large output so that he may influence the advertiser to pay him for announcing his goods, for, as few laymen can seem to understand, it is the advertising which supports our journals and gives them their profit.

But, the reader may ask, if you obtain an increase in advertising with an increase in circulation, does not a war largely add to a newspapers advertising revenues? To this the answer is that a war checks advertising fully as effectively, if not perhaps more quickly, than a financial panic, and this applies to magazines as well as dailies. This is particularly true of the present struggle. *T. P.'s Weekly*, the well-known London publication, declared soon after the outbreak of the war that if hostilities lasted a year a handful only of the strongest English dailies would escape bankruptcy. A superficial perusal of the London *Times* and the Manchester *Guardian* is sufficient to convince anybody that this is not a wild prophecy. The cessation of certain lines of advertising is complete; the loss as compared with conditions a year ago is staggering.

It is reliably reported in newspaper circles that the London *Times'* advertising revenue from America alone dropped $10,000 in a single month. Already some of the weaker British publications have begun to go down. One important church publication, laboriously built up, has had to curtail its appearance, and a reform organ, just reaching the point where it could show a satisfactory balance sheet, has been wiped out. When one picks up a London evening newspaper like the *Westminster Gazette* and sees the almost total dearth of advertising, it is easy to forsee plenty of journalistic wrecks along the Strand unless there are sufficient rich men found to foot the deficit for personal or political reasons.

In this country, too, the war has had a grave effect upon newspaper advertising income. All financial and steamship advertising has practically ceased. Publishers find a market chiefly for war books and are advertising less than usual. And so it goes. The three strongest advertising mediums in New York lost, between August 1 and December 1, 1,089, 1,488, and 2,926 columns of advertising, respectively, as contrasted with their showing for the same months in 1913. If we assume, very conservatively, that they usually receive on an average of $80 a column, this represents a falling off in income of $87,120, $115,840, and $234,080, respectively.

When to this are added the enormously increased costs due to the gathering of war news, even the layman can understand why it is that newspapers are reducing the number of their reporters and editors, cutting off all special domestic despatches, and striving in every way to decrease expenses. If this results in cutting out some unnecessary waste and the devising of more economical methods, the gain is none the less comparatively slight. The reader can appreciate in short, why it is that from the point of view of their own exchequer newspapers ought to be the chief advocates of peace.

It is quite possible—even a journalist must admit—that if a number of newspaper wrecks should occur with a resultant decrease in our journalistic output, the thinking American public might regard this not as one of the horrors but as one of the pitifully few blessings that come out of such a horrible strife as we are now witnessing. The trouble is, as the English experience has shown, that some valuable journals of small means may go down, while richer and less desirable survive.

If we turn from the embattled counting rooms to the editorial departments, we find the editors also grappling with war problems of the utmost difficulty, intensified by the fact that the great bulk of the war news must come through London and is subjected to British censorship. London has always been, besides the greatest financial mart, the world's chief exchange and clearinghouse for news. When, therefore, the British cut the German cables to this country they took a step which has done much to intensify the bitter feeling against Great Britain that now pervades all Germany to such an extent as to leave comparatively little room for animosity against the other Allies.

If the Germans are manifestly wrong in attributing to the cutting of the cables their failure to win American public opinion to their side, they undeniably have a just grievance against the British censor and so has the American press. To those conversant with the facts as to the stupidity, the one-sidedness, and the political bent of the British censorship, this war has given a severe shock; it will be hard for them to believe again in the good sportsmanship of Englishmen.

The London censorship has been a disgrace to England primarily because of its folly. Thus, dozens of German official despatches were not permitted to pass over the cables, although they were being received in New York by wireless via Sayville at the same time. As if there were no mails from Italy, the London censor suppressed the late Pope's call to Catholics to pray for peace, on the ground, so it is believed in some quarters, that it would not be to England's advantage for the United States, being a great Catholic country, to pray for peace!

Another stupid half-pay colonel twice gave out important news items to the Central News or the Hearst News service, because, he said, they served only a few newspapers, perhaps fifty, and denied it to the Associated Press because it supplied news to 900 newspapers! Not content with suppression, these same half-pay colonels next edited an important utterance by President Poincare, of France, changing it to suit their taste because they did not like some of the things he said and did not wish the English public to know them. This was a typical case, but by no means the only one of alteration of despatches.

The censors have not stopped there, however; they have censored or suppressed their own Prime Minister's speeches and those of the Foreign Minister on the ground that they would create an unfavorable impression abroad. They have laid heavy hands on the King's messages to India and the Dominions, and even the outgivings of their own press bureau.

Although Winston Churchill solemnly promised at the beginning of the war that every naval loss would be promptly reported to the House of Commons, the sinking of the *Audacious* was carefully suppressed both at home and abroad. They have so completely concealed all news of the military movements and progress that at the censors' doors are laid the responsibility for the slump in recruiting which so frightened the British Ministry until the story of the gallant retreat of Sir John French's army was made known through the publication of the narrative of the eloquent official reporter, Col. E. D. Swinton. It is generally believed in newspaper circles that the responsibility for this rigid censorship rests with Lord Kitchener, whose dislike for correspondents is notorious. The late Lord Roberts, on the other hand, was much more favorably disposed; indeed, he owed not a little of his great reputation with the English public to such brilliant correspondents as Archibald Forbes and Bennet Burleigh. No one could accuse men of this type of doing mischief. Besides keeping the British informed of the progress of their various small wars, they more than once enriched literature.

With the suppression of the news of military movements there can be no quarrel; the concealment of the news of the loss of a ship is, of course, legitimate from the military point of view. Indeed, with an efficient military censorship no one can justly find fault.

But what the American press is complaining about is that the British censorship is turning from a military into a political one. American journalists have the right to assert that it is beyond the functions of a foreign censor to say whether Americans shall or shall not receive news of a Papal letter; whether they shall be given a falsified account of a speech by the President of France, and whether there is any news from Germany which British censors have a right to suppress. Wars are not won this way, particularly when the mails are open and German letters and newspapers arrive with amazing regularity by way of Holland and Italy.

The favorable opinion of the United States is being courted as never before in its history, but that public opinion is not to be won by falsifications on either side. And there have been misrepresentations on the German side, too. Indeed, if the Associated Press had carried out a recent plan to expose at length the London suppression and mishandling of the news, public sentiment as to England in this country would have been unfavorably affected to a considerable extent.

The difficulties of the situation are, if anything, intensified by the semi-official character of at least two of the foreign agencies, the Agence Havas and the Wolff Agency. Reuter's, with headquarters in London, is responsible for the news of all of the great English over-sea dominions, except Canada, and for Great Britain as well. The Havas Agency, with headquarters in Paris, is responsible for the Latin countries, Spain, Portugal, France, Belgium, and Switzerland. The Wolff Bureau covers, in peace times, Germany, Austria, Turkey in Europe, Russia, the Balkan States, Scandinavia, and the German colonies. All of them work in cooperation with the officials from whom they draw their governmental and political news, even Reuter being subject to pressure from them. It is easy to understand the difficulties that this creates for the Associated Press, which stands aloof from all officialdom, and it makes it the more difficult to obtain news for the United States during this conflict which is unbiased and uncolored.

Plainly, there are two markedly different theories as to the reporting of military operations—that which controlled in our Civil War and the modern policy of having, if possible, no correspondent within a hundred miles of the front. From 1861 to 1865 correspondents accompanied our armies and were free not only to describe battles and marches, but to criticize operations, generals, and admirals. That much harm resulted from this is indisputable. Military information of value was gathered by both sides through the exchange of newspapers at the picketlines. But the chief injury done, some think, was through the criticism of plans of campaigns and of generals, and the rousing thereby of animosities within the armies and the starting up of political movements or of unwise public demands for action or non-action.

By contrast the extreme military view to-day is that nothing shall appear save a brief daily official despatch. This is the case in Germany today. Even there, however, military experts may interpret these despatches to the public after approval of the censorship, and certain selected correspondents have been allowed to do descriptive writing in the rear of the armies. Criticism is, of course, forbidden, as is to be expected in an autocracy. At first the company of foreign correspondents, like that of foreign military observers, was everywhere declined with thanks. Now, however, they are being welcomed in some degree; indeed, the charges of misconduct by German soldiers and of unnecessary harshness in waging war have apparently made the Germans regret that they did not from the first ask a number of correspondents from neutral lands to accompany their armies. At least they have used to the fullest extent the favorable reports of Messrs. Irvin Cobb, John T. McCutcheon, and the other American reporters who fell into their hands in Belgium.

The writer's father, who reported the operations of the Federal armies and fleets from the first battle of Bull Run through the Wilderness campaign, and reached Austria in 1866, in time to describe the wreck of the Austrian armies and the aftermath of the Prussian success, was fond of saying that were he a general he would allow no correspondents at the front. The mischief his own fraternity did in 1861–65 seemed to him to outweigh the good. But in a republic, at least, there are other conditions to be considered than the purely military.

The public cannot be left in all but total ignorance of a campaign; it must be informed in some detail as to what is going on if the war spirit is to be kept up, and, since it may be called upon to change its rulers in the middle of a war, as it had to choose between Lincoln and McClellan in 1864, it is entitled to the true facts upon which to form its judgment. Again, if the good opinion of the rest of the neutral world is desired, something more than official despatches is needed to win it: certainly all the German official bulletins thus far issued have not overcome the unfavorable judgments caused by non-official reports of the happenings in Belgium. On the other hand, even in war-time there is genuine danger in giving to military men complete control of a situation.

Besides the present illustration of this in England, we had a perfect example of it during our early warfare in the Philippines. There was an ideal situation for the working of a military censorship; there was but one cable and no correspondent could penetrate into the interior save with an army column.

The net result was not creditable to those in charge; the censorship, to say the least, was partisan. It speedily became political. Nothing unfavorable to the contentions of the McKinley government was allowed to come out. Constant charges that Mr. Bryan's speeches were encouraging the Filipinos were cabled, as well as other reflections upon Democrats and Democratic policies. Just as the censors today, whether they be in London, Paris, or Petrograd, conceal all bad news or gloss over defeats with euphemisms, only good news came out of Manila. So frankly political, so intolerable did this censorship become, that some influential journalists called upon the Secretary of War and were successful by threat of exposure in bringing about a change, not, however, until the American public had received an erroneous impression as to what was going on in the archipelago. It is needless to say that no news of the soldier wrong-doing in the Philippines, such as the use of the abominably inhuman water-cure, to which a stop was finally put by a vigorous order by President Roosevelt, could get by the censor. In this case the army needed to be saved by publicity from the effects of its own wrongdoing.

This is nothing more than saying that frail human nature, even at its best, suffers when given arbitrary power over others, particularly if those whom it controls are objects of race prejudice, or of national hatreds. If the press is necessary in peace times in every country, republic or absolute monarchy, to prevent the abuse of power by those holding office, it is in the long run equally necessary that it should have some voice in war-time to present all the vital facts and to reflect to the commanding generals the temper of the people whose battles they are fighting. We come perilously close to despotism when a few men, whatever the emergency, concentrate all power in their own hands, and then by an impenetrable cloak of silence effectively veil their actions. What may happen in those circumstances is forever on record in the history of the fall of the French Government in 1870 and of the Commune, which quite naturally followed the German victories and the exposure of the campaign of lies and misinformation with which the military men of Napoleon III deluded the people.

It would seem, therefore, as if a well controlled system of field correspondents were necessary; indeed, the amount of news sent in by special representatives of American newspapers shows that, despite European military autocrats, the American reporter has been able to get to the front and to mail uncensored stories to this country to delight his managing editor. The writer is inclined to believe, as already indicated, that as the war progresses the restrictions will be loosened rather than tightened, as they have been in Germany; that the military leaders will feel the need of the moral support that comes from an enlightened and intelligent public opinion; that they will realize that the only basis for genuine mutual confidence between the military and the public is absolute truth-telling, whether it be favorable or unfavorable, by those who control the news; the public and army are interwoven in their best interests.

A powerful factor in bringing about this change should be a realization of how the several belligerent countries are being hurt by the false information, the cruel and misleading rumors that appear about them abroad, which can, in the long run, best be overcome by full and frank statements, both from official and unofficial sources. That any censorship will ever work to complete satisfaction may well be doubted, since it is at best founded on suppression, deceit, and concealment, however justifiable that may be in war-time.

From the viewpoint of humanity one may well ask, too, whether the censorship in war-times does not work against the coming of universal peace. How may we best rouse the moral sentiment of the world against war? Surely not by suppressing the horrors of the battlefield by failing to portray to people everywhere the wickedness of taking human life on a grand scale.

American journalists, it would seem, cannot have any more patriotic duty in this hour than to portray truthfully the breakdown of militarism as taught and practiced by the nations of Europe.

How Stories of Atrocities Are Invented

Staff

THE AMERICAN REVIEW OF REVIEWS, February 1915

Emotions run high during wartime, and it is one of the chores of government to keep hatred for the enemy whipped to a white heat. In the effort to convince the citizenry of all countries that the Germans were "beasts," the Allies tied them to Attila and his barbarous acts by calling them "Huns." This was to convince the world of German savagery. Stories were released "illustrating" the brutality and malevolence of the advancing German forces.

In Volume 2 of the History of the World War *(Doubleday, Page & Company, 1918) the following claim was made:*

> The records of more than a thousand individual atrocities rest in the archives of France against the day of reckoning. There are countless letters and diaries taken from the bodies of dead German soldiers. Out of the large number, note the following:
>
> Notebook of Private Max Thomas: *Our soldiers are so excited, we are like wild beasts. To-day, destroyed eight houses with their inmates. Bayoneted two men and their wives and a girl of eighteen. The little one almost unnerved me, so innocent was her expression.*
>
> Diary of Eitel Anders: *In Vendre all the inhabitants without exception were brought out and shot. This shooting was heartbreaking as they all knelt down and prayed. It is real sport, yet it was terrible to watch. At Haecht I saw the dead body of a young girl nailed to the outside door of a cottage, by her hands. She was about fourteen or sixteen years old.*
>
> *In retreating from Malines eight drunken soldiers were marching through the street. A little child of two years came out and a soldier skewered the child on his bayonet and carried it away while his comrades sang.*
>
> *Withdrawing from Hofstade, in addition to other atrocities, the Germans cut off both hands of a boy of sixteen. At the inquest affidavits were taken from twenty-five witnesses, who saw the boy before he died or just afterward.*

Atrocity stories were seldom, if ever, checked out, but always widely spread. Newspapers loved them. It made good copy and sold well. When an attempt was made to track down some of these tales, the "facts" slowly melted away and the investigator learned there really was no atrocity. The

American Review of Reviews *thought enough of these monstrous stories to print a short piece on the subject.*

One of the lessons taught by the war is the general unreliability of newspaper accounts of atrocities committed by soldiers. As a rule they have been proved to be purely imaginative creations, part of that output which is the special contribution of war to literature. They are the product not only of war correspondents, but of all sorts of fiction writers and poets. It is a species of inventiveness of which no country can claim a monopoly, a pretty even balance of power being maintained among all the belligerent nations.

Sometimes the stories come from the neutral countries. The Berlin *Vorwaerts* records an interesting tale of terror which was hatched in our own New York. At the outbreak of the war a German poet, Hans Heinz Ewers, happened to be visiting New York. Though far from the scene of hostilities, he was immediately inspired by the war muse and wrote a poem entitled "My Mother's House," which was published in German in a Berlin newspaper and in English in *The Fatherland*. The poem gives a touching picture of the way in which his mother's house has been converted into a hospital. In one room lies a youthful soldier amidst beautiful little bits of artistic objects collected from every part of the world. Alas! the youth cannot enjoy the beauty of his surroundings. The Belgians in Loucin, near Liège, have gouged out his eyes. Four other soldiers are in the dining room, one of whom will never recover, having been struck by a dum-dum bullet. There are sixteen wounded soldiers in the house of the poet's mother; every room is a chamber of horrors.

Upon reading the poem the editor of the Berlin *Vorwaerts* wrote to the correspondent of his paper in Düsseldorf, where Ewers' mother lives, to investigate the story. The following is the correspondent's report as translated by J. E. Koettgen in the New York *Call*:

> In accordance with your request I have been to the house of Hans Heinz Ewers' mother, and am in a position to state that the old lady never had one or several soldiers in her home to care for, and especially none whose eyes had been gouged out. Ewers' mother is a kindly but frail old lady, full of motherly pride in her poet son. She explained to me that in consequence of the poem (I had not mentioned the poem to her) she had had many inquiries already, especially from Berlin. But the poem was merely a production of her son's imagination. It is true that she had written to her son about her visits to wounded soldiers in the hospitals, but not a word about gouged-out eyes. She herself knew of no such case from personal experience, and as to caring for wounded soldiers in her own home, to do that she had neither the physical strength, nor was she materially in a position to undertake such work.

It was really touching to hear the old lady read the poem, which she did with such feeling and confidence as only a mother can who loves her son above everything else. I should therefore be very sorry for the little old lady if her son were punished in public for his unconscionable atrocity stories, as he really deserves.

He has not been punished, however, Koettgen adds. On the contrary, he is reported to have been appointed court poet and decorated with the Iron Cross of the first class.

On the other hand, we are told that the stories against the German soldiers rest upon an equally flimsy foundation. Houston Stewart Chamberlain, in an article called "Deutschland," scouts the idea that German soldiers are capable of committing atrocities.

What other nation, he asks, has expert authorities on art accompanying the armies to see to it that when a city is occupied its art treasures are properly taken care of? When Rheims fell these experts took the German soldiers through the cathedral, and the soldiers all crowded around them, eager to learn and to see. Could such men commit outrages on human beings or wantonly destroy works of art? The present charges against the German soldiers are as baseless as those that were current in the war of 1870, which, in the matter of spreading false reports, furnishes an exact parallel to what is taking place now. Concerning the conditions in that war, Chamberlain says, he can speak from the fulness of his experience, because he had lived in France before and immediately after the war.

It was everywhere the same story. I never met a single Frenchman who even intimated that he himself had suffered any cruelty, or even unnecessary harsh treatment from the Germans. The residents of Versailles assured me that the German soldiery did not dare to misbehave there because it was the chief headquarters and the residence of the King. But in Normandy, they said, the Germans acted like fierce barbarians. It happened that I was connected with certain peasant families in Normandy. I inquired, and was informed that there were no atrocities there. They were fortunate. The army, operating under Manteuffel, were a splendid lot of men, so perfectly disciplined that they did not dare to steal an egg. But in Alsace, I was told, the conditions must have been terrible. I happened to become acquainted with an Alsatian pastor, a rabid Germanophobe, but no liar. When I put the same question to him, he took out a sketch-book from a drawer and showed me a German infantry soldier of giant stature peeling potatoes in his kitchen; an Uhlan sitting on a stone bench in front of the door and with awkward tenderness feeding the bottle to an infant; and other idyls of a similar nature. *"Quelle bonne pate d'hommes!"* he exclaimed almost with pathos. "What kindhearted men!" And then came the ususal remark: "We were lucky. But in Orleannais it was terrible."

> # Thrilling Stories of the World's Greatest War:
> ## Sinking of the Lusitania and Other Atrocities
>
> ### Thomas H. Russell, A.M., LL.D

THE BRADLEY-GARRETSON CO., LTD., 1915

In this strangely titled book (what could be thrilling about atrocities?), a young woman tells of her "experience" at the hands of the advancing German army in Belgium. Does her story stand up under careful scrutiny? You be the judge.

Here is the story of Marguerite Vyttebroeck who lived through the sacking of Louvain and reached London September 11 en route to the town where she was born—Assumption, Illinois—the youngest child of a family numbering nine.

Marguerite, aged 19, was sure that only her aged mother, who was with her, was alive. Three weeks before all her brothers and sisters were together with their parents in a farmhouse on the outskirts of Louvain.

"My mother and father," the girl began, "went to the United States from Belgium twenty-five years ago and settled at Assumption. We farmed there, but a year ago we all moved back to Louvain, where father bought a farm outside the city and renewed old acquaintances.

"There was fighting beyond Louvain the whole day and night before the Belgian soldiers began to run through the town with the Germans hot on the trail. We all hid at first and watched the pursuit between the shutters, but when the first scare was over we sat on the doorsteps and saw the parade of the German soldiers with their bands playing and their good order.

Nobody had an idea they would harm us, and it was almost like going to a theater to see them march by. They didn't pay any attention to us for a time, but when the soldiers were dismissed they began getting drunk. Then things became bad.

"I was at a friend's house in the city, and the first thing I knew the house next door was on fire.

"When we tried to rush out into the street bullets came against the door like hail. My girl friend's father and mother were killed in their own vestibule. We turned around and ran upstairs to the attic and stayed there until flames began coming through the walls. Then we got on to the roof and climbed along over other roofs to the end of the street, got down through the house and out into the back garden over the wall, and began to run through the fields toward my house.

"It was dark. We ran almost into two Uhlans. One of them had an electric torch. He flashed it in my face and asked me where I was going.

"When I told him in English that I was going to my house, he asked if I was English. I told him I was an American, but he only laughed. He was going to dismount when his horse took fright at something, pitched him on the ground and stunned him. I fled while the other Uhlan was caring for his comrade.

"When I reached my house I found the Germans had taken father and my four brothers prisoners, and had taken them away—where, mother did not know.

"As we were trying to decide what to do another company of German soldiers came along, rode over the fence, and set fire to the house and barns. My two sisters told the soldiers what they thought of such wickedness and the last I saw of them they were being carried off by half a dozen soldiers, and never came back.

"While the fire was burning fiercely I suddenly remembered a piece of paper a priest gave my mother in Assumption, Illinois, when I was born. It was in my room and was my only proof that I was an American.

"So I ran around the house, climbed up over the trellis, and got into my room, already full of smoke. I took the paper, and then, with my mother, got back to the city and put her in a friend's house.

"I started looking for my father, brothers, and sisters. My hunt lasted five days and nights, and during that time I saw many terrible sights.

"On the sixth day it was announced that trains would take us to Germany, and when the soldiers came they told some old men to line up and march to the station. They obeyed gladly. When they got to the station they were lined up against a wall and shot.

"If the Belgian commission wants eyewitness proof of atrocities in Louvain I can tell them the names of women I saw outraged and thrown into a fire, and other things even worse."

The girl, with her mother, sailed for New York September 12th on the Megantic.

The young lady's story was followed by an "official communication of the German general staff" intended to show that the military admitted to firing upon civilians, and the spirit exhibited by the civilian population in not giving in to the enemy. But the report, if true, simply illustrates the horror of war. If you do not surrender, you are subject to the general terror of battle whether or not you wear a uniform. . . .

An official communication of the German general staff on the occur-
rences at Louvain, Belgium, dated August 30th and made public September
19, 1914, was as follows:

"The city of Loewen (Louvain) had surrendered and was given over
to us by the Belgian authorities. On Monday, August 24th, some of our
troops were shipped there and intercourse with the inhabitants was developing quite friendly.

"On Tuesday afternoon, August 25th, our troops, hearing about an
imminent Belgian sortie from Antwerp, left in that direction, the commanding general ahead in a motor car, leaving behind only a colonel with
soldiers (landsturm battalion 'Neuss') to protect the railroad. As the rest
of the commanding general's staff with the horses was going to follow and
was collected on the market place, suddenly rifle fire opened from all the
surrounding houses, all the horses being killed and five officers wounded,
one of them seriously.

"Simultaneously fire opened at about ten different places in town, also
on some of our troops just arrived and waiting on the square in front of
the station and on incoming military trains. A designed cooperation with
the Belgian sortie from Antwerp was established beyond a doubt.

"Two priests caught in handing out ammunition to the people were
shot at once in front of the station.

"The fight lasted till Wednesday, the 26th, in the afternoon (twenty-
four hours), when stronger forces, arrived in the meantime, succeeded in
getting the upper hand. The town and northern suburb were burning at
different places and by this time have probably burned down altogether.

"On the part of the Belgian Government a general rising of the population against the enemy had been organized for a long time. Depots of
arms were found, where to each gun was attached the name of the citizen
to be armed.

"A spontaneous rising of the people has been recognized at the request
of the smaller states at the Hague conference as being within the law of
nations, as far as weapons are carried openly and the laws of civilized
warfare are being observed; but such rising was only admitted in order to
fight the attacking enemy.

"In the case of Loewen the town already had surrendered without any
resistance, the town being occupied by our troops. Nevertheless, the population attacked on all sides and with a murderous fire the occupying forces
and newly arriving troops, which came in trains and automobiles, knowing
the hitherto peaceful attitude of the population.

"Therefore, there can be no question of means of defense allowed by
the law of nations, nor a warlike *guetapens* (ambush), but only of a treach-
erous attempt of the civil population all along the line, and all the more
to be condemned as it was apparently planned long beforehand with a
simultaneous attack from Antwerp, as arms were not carried openly, and

women and young girls took part in the fight and blinded our wounded, sticking their eyes out.

"The barbarous attitude of the Belgian population in all parts occupied by our troops has not only justified our severest measures, but forced them on us for the sake of self-preservation. The intensity of the resistance of the population is shown by the fact that in Loewen twenty-four hours were necessary to break down their attack.

"We ourselves, regret deeply that during these fights the town of Loewen has been destroyed to a great extent. Needless to say that these consequences are not intentional on our part, but cannot be avoided in this infamous franctireur war being led against us.

"Whoever knows the good-natured character of our troops cannot seriously pretend that they are inclined to needless or frivolous destruction.

"The entire responsibility for these events rests with the Belgian Government, which with criminal frivolity has given to the Belgian people instructions contrary to the law of nations and incited their resistance, and which, in spite of repeated warnings, even after the fall of Luettich (Liège), have done nothing to induce them to a peaceful attitude."

The third section of the Belgian commission appointed to inquire into alleged breaches of international law by the Germans was published September 20th and denied the German allegation that the inhabitants of Louvain brought on the destruction of the town by firing on the Germans. It follows in part:

"The inhabitants of Louvain took no part in the fighting. Moreover, the destruction of the town came eleven days after the last Belgian troops had evacuated the district. Witnesses declare that the first shots were fired by intoxicated German soldiers at their own officers. Another fact established is as follows:

"A crowd of 6,000 to 8,000 men, women and children were taken by the One Hundred and Sixty-second Regiment of German Infantry August 28th to the Louvain Riding School, where they spent the night. The place of confinement was so small that all had to remain standing. The sufferings were so great that several children died in their mothers' arms and a number of women lost their reason."

From the German standpoint, the invasion of Belgium as part of the planned march to Paris, though it met with unexpected resistance, was successful. The first round of the great international conflict ended with the honors on the German side, though the round was not decisive. The Anglo-French allies met with several serious reverses and the power and mobility of the German military machine was demonstrated. Though halted and perhaps seriously delayed at Liège and Namur, it "rolled back the allies' defense from Switzerland to the North Sea." The Belgian army, with French aid, kept the Germans from entering Brussels until August 20th and then retired behind the forts at Antwerp. The Kaiser's troops then overran practically all of Belgium, took Namur, fought back the British at Mons, forced the Allies south over the border at several points and finally succeeded in occupying Lille, Roubaix and Valenciennes on the first line of French defense against invasion from the north. Simultaneously the French towns of Longwy and Luneville, to the east, were gained after severe fighting, while the French invasion of Alsace-Lorraine, at first successful, was speedily checked.

Thus when the first month of war ended, the Germans had made good with their plan of seizing Belgium as a base of operations against France and had arrived in full force at the first line of French defenses, well on the way to coveted goal, Paris.

But poor little Belgium, the "cockpit of Europe," ran red with blood.

PART IV

RECRUITMENT AND CAMP LIFE

With the declaration of war, the ranks of the armed forces needed immediate expansion. Young men volunteered or were selectively drafted to become soldiers or sailors. Professional men, plucked from lucrative private practice, were plunged into the rough and dangerous existence along with the farmers and city sophisticates. They all trained side by side, and they were all taught the fine art of killing.

English Conscription and Our Civil War Draft

Staff

THE AMERICAN REVIEW OF REVIEWS, March 1915

England's first expeditionary force landed at Oostende, Calais and Dun-kirk on August 7th, 1914. The Central Powers were not impressed with Britain's armed forces, and the German General Staff promptly dubbed it "England's contemptible little army." That name was seized upon by En-gland to spur volunteering. It brought to the surface national pride and a fierce determination to compel Germany to reckon with the "contemptible little army."

The British expeditionary force was almost immediately swept up in a rear-guard action, fighting and retreating along with the French. They at-tempted to make a stand at Ypres, and the British force was practically exterminated.

General Rawlinson commanded the 7th Division, Sir Douglas Haig com-manded the 1st Army Corps and General Allenby was to assist them with his cavalry.

The battle of Ypres began on October 20th and finally ended November 11th, 1914. When the smoke cleared, the 7th Division alone lost 356 out of 400 officers, and of its 12,000 men, 9,664 were killed or wounded. British total losses at Ypres were 60% of its army killed, captured, or wounded. While heavy losses were inflicted upon the enemy, England found its army almost destroyed at the time Germany was tightening its submarine blockade of the British Isles.

The Allies needed land victories to relieve the pressure of the blockade, but instead they suffered heavy losses in men and material. Getting experi-enced troops to fill the ever increasing vacancies on the firing line presented a tremendous problem. In addition the news of the first gas attack in April 1915 destroyed nearly one-third of the Canadian contingent in Europe. As all this information filtered back to the mainland, army volunteers faded away. Since England's recruitment system depended wholly upon volunteers, there was much concern in the government regarding army replacements, and the concern was echoed in the British press.

The memory of the draft riots in New York City during the American Civil War was still fresh in the minds of Britains rulers. With that war barely fifty years old, England wondered aloud how its own civilian population would respond to a conscription of all able-bodied men.

Two summaries appeared in American magazines of articles that were published in British publications and discussed the advisability of a draft to replenish Britain's armed forces.

It is interesting to note that in the arguments now being brought forward in England to justify compulsory military service, or conscription, resort is frequently had to American experience during the Civil War. In the London *Spectator*, for example, attention has been directed to the attitude of President Lincoln on the subject of the draft. An editorial article in that journal declares that Lincoln went through all the stages that England is now going through in the matter of raising troops, except that the voluntary system in America gave results which numerically and in proportion to the population were below those which the voluntary system has given England in the first few months of the war.

Contrary to the general assumption that volunteering in Great Britain has not been as good as it was in the North before the draft was put in force, the *Spectator* declares that it has been very much better. It is assumed, however, that sooner or later, the voluntary system will prove not to be giving as many men as are wanted and that recourse to compulsion will be necessary. In that event the *Spectator* holds that the government should make it quite clear to the nation that the excellent pay and allowances now given to England's soldiers cannot be extended to men taken into the ranks by compulsion. The man who comes forward voluntarily should have better terms than he who waits to be compelled. In the case of compulsion the service rendered will not be voluntary service, but will be in the nature of a tax which men are compelled to pay in the interests of the state. The first step of the government, in the *Spectator*'s view, should be to draw up a muster roll. The exact number of men within the military age should be ascertained and they should be classified in every recruiting area in the country, or in such area as may be determined.

Having ascertained the number of men of military age in the country not employed (1) by the state; (2) in carrying out government contracts; (3) in transportation, the government should calculate how many more men in their opinion will be required. Let us, for the purpose of argument, say two million more. Then they should calculate what will be the quota required to be taken from every Parliamentary area—*i.e.*, constituency—or such other area as may be determined upon. The next step will be to make an appeal in that area for men to supply its particular quota. If the quota is obtained voluntarily, well and good. If it is not, there must be a ballot amongst the men on the muster-roll—the men of military age—in order that the call of the government for so many men from such and such a place may be answered.

In this connection the *Spectator* refers to Lincoln's appeal to the country in support of the draft, which because of circumstances was not published at the time, and, in fact, was first given to the world in the authorized life of Lincoln by Nicolay and Hay. The *Spectator* characterizes Lincoln as "a liberal and a democrat and an upholder of popular rights if ever there was one in the world. Yet, strange as it may seem to our Radical friends, he was from the very beginning a strong advocate of compulsory service, or, as he called it, conscription, as the fairest and best way of raising troops for a great national emergency."

This appeal to the people in defense of the draft which Lincoln wrote at the critical juncture is pronounced by the *Spectator* "one of the greatest state papers ever produced in the English language." Lincoln's refusal to publish the document was based not on any lack of confidence in his arguments, but on the the fact that after the draft was put in operation it proved to be less unpopular than had been expected, and it was feared that the strength of the language used by Lincoln might possibly have irritated certain men who were rapidly becoming reconciled to the measure. Among the striking passages in Lincoln's address which have been marked by the *Spectator* as peculiarly applicable by the present situation in Great Britain are the following, which the editor commends to his English readers:

> At the beginning of the war, and ever since, a variety of motives, pressing, some in one direction and some in the other, would be presented to the mind of each man physically fit for a soldier, upon the combined effect of which motives he would, or would not, voluntarily enter the service. Among these motives would be patriotism, political bias, ambition, personal courage, love of adventure, want of employment, and convenience, or the opposite of some of these. We already have, and have had, in the service as appears, substantially all that can be obtained upon this voluntary weighing of motives. And yet we must somehow obtain more, or relinquish the original object of the contest, together with all the blood and treasure already expended in the effort to secure it.
>
> To meet this necessity the law for the draft has been enacted. You who do not wish to be soldiers do not like this law. This is natural; nor does it imply want of patriotism. Nothing can be so just and necessary as to make us like it if it is disagreeable to us. We are prone, too, to find false arguments with which to excuse ourselves for opposing such disagreeable things. In this case, those who desire the rebellion to succeed, and others who seek reward in a different way, are very active in accomodating us with this class of arguments. . . . There can be no army without men. Men can be had only voluntarily or involuntarily. We have ceased to obtain them voluntarily, and to obtain them involuntarily is the draft—the conscription. If you dispute the fact, and declare that men can still be had voluntarily in sufficient numbers, prove

the assertion by yourselves volunteering in such numbers, and I shall gladly give up the draft. Or if not a sufficient number, but any one of you will volunteer, he for his single self will escape all the horrors of the draft, and will thereby do only what each one of at least a million of his manly brethren have already done. Their toil and blood have been given as much for you as for themselves. Shall it all be lost rather than that you, too, will bear your part?

I do not say that all who would avoid serving in the war are unpatriotic; but I do think every patriot should willingly take his chance under a law, made with great care, in order to secure entire fairness. . . . The principle of draft, which simply is involuntary or enforced service, is not new. It has been practiced in all ages of the world. . . . Shall we shrink from the necessary means to maintain our free government, which our grandfathers employed to establish it and our own fathers have already employed once to maintain it? Are we degenerate? Has the manhood of our race run out? . . . With these views, and on these principles, I feel bound to tell you it is my purpose to see the draft law faithfully executed.

Recruiting in England

Apropos of the strenuous efforts now being made throughout Great Britain to enlist soldiers for service in the great war, there have been several frank expressions of opinion in the English reviews. In the *Fortnightly*, for example, a member of Parliament, Mr. L.G. Money, does not hesitate to criticise the methods employed by his government to induce volunteering.

Mr. Money complains that accurate knowledge as to the progress of recruiting and the results of the government's recruiting machinery is denied even to members of Parliament. But taking into account the facts that lie on the surface and are better known to all men, this writer finds that "an enormous amount of money is being spent in issuing the most extraordinary series of advertisements ever issued by a government. In every newspaper and on every wall, there appear variegated appeals not only to men of military age, but to the wives, mothers, sisters, employers, friends, and acquaintances of men of military age. Some of these appeals are so extravagant that a visitor from Mars might be pardoned for believing them to be the handiwork of desperate men in whom rhetoric had got the better of reason. Many of them are apparently intended to create a feeling of shame in the minds of unrecruited young men."

One of these advertisements in which the writer addresses "four questions to the women of England" reads in part as follows:

> Do you realize that the one word "Go" from YOU may send another man to fight for our King and Country?
> When the War is over and your husband or son is asked, "What did you do in the great War?"—is he to hang his head because YOU would not let him go?

To this was added:

"Women of England, do your duty! Send your men to-day to join our glorious army. God save the King!"

Mr. Money cannot refrain from raising the question whether a "volunteer" who would be shamed into going to war by such an appeal as the above would be a really valuable soldier. The main suggestion, however, made by these and other costly advertisements is that recruiting cannot be altogether satisfactory if it is thought necessary to resort to appeals of such character.

Alluding to the government's boast that 72,000 railroad men have been recruited for the war—an achievement that was described by the Prime Minister as "magnificent"—Mr. Money is tempted to say that it may be magnificent, but it is not necessarily war. His point is that when a nation is organized for war its railroads become an integral part of its military operations, and if you send to the fighting line a single man who ought to be at his post helping to operate a railroad system a serious error is committed. The same thing is true in regard to men in other forms of necessary industrial employment.

As a result of the English recruiting system it seems clear that certain trades which are essential to the proper organization of the nation for war are being depleted, while many men whose services are of a different sort and who can much better be spared for the fighting-line are still unrecruited. It is asserted that many married men are taken while there are still an enormous number of unmarried men available.

It is Mr. Money's contention that in order to obtain a maximum of military and economic strength from the nation, promiscuous recruiting must be stopped at once. That every man of military age, whatever his rank or station, must be considered in relation to the national problem, and such part of that manhood as can be utilized for military purposes with the least loss of economic strength be taken. In this way there would be retained for the production of wealth, and especially for such commodities as are required for war material, that part of the country's labor forces that can best supply its needs.

While admitting that in this war the middle classes in England have played a better part than ever before, Mr. Money is still convinced that the proportion of recruiting from the middle classes has been much smaller than from the working classes. He regards it as unfortunate for the nation "that a vigorous young man of the middle classes should stop at home while a railroad man or miner goes to war, and the nation ought to see to it that such a double loss does not occur as that we should keep those we can spare and send those away whom we need at home."

An American observer, Mr. William C. Edgar, editor of the *Bellman* (Minneapolis), noted the use of the brass band as a supplemental agency in a recruiting campaign in progress in London. Troops marched through the streets, he says, to the sound of lively music. Some of the glamor of war was restored and the possible recruit was moved to action through not only his mind, but his imagination as well.

Mr. Edgar was impressed, however, by the posters, placards, and labels seen everywhere in London and throughout the United Kingdom as interesting and graphic evidences of a vigorous attempt being made to rouse the people to the national danger to the end that they may volunteer for service.

> Lethargy and self-complacency, a feeling that the war is being conducted on foreign soil and therefore does not directly and immediately affect the individual Briton, retards recruiting to some degree; hence it is necessary to stir up the public to the gravity of the situation by every possible means.

The trouble in England, as Mr. Edgar sees it, is not from lack of confidence in the outcome nor from want of courage, but from a prevailing sentiment, especially among the less intelligent, that the Allies are sure to win anyhow and that there is no necessity for enlisting, at least for the present.

In a remarkable editorial published immediately after Lord Kitchener's call in May for 300,000 more recruits, the London *Spectator* declares:

> If he had asked for a million, or even two million, more men we should not have been surprised, though even then, taking the Army and Navy together, we should not be doing, per head of population, more than, or even as much as the French, and should be doing a very great deal less than the Germans. At such a juncture as this to ask for only three hundred thousand men literally makes one's brain reel. It would seem to show one of two things: either Lord Kitchener during the ten months that have elapsed since the beginning of the war has obtained far more men than the nation has any idea of—which, of course is a perfectly incredible, ridiculous, and and impossible supposition—or else Lord Kitchener is not aware of the wastage of war, and is under the delusion that the cadres of his fighting force can be kept up to strength (the absolutely essential condition for an efficient army) without a huge reserve.
>
> A very little consideration will show that the notion of such a miscalculation on the part of so great a soldier as Lord Kitchener must be dismissed. We must not make any calculations as to the exact numbers of the men who are at this moment outside England fighting our enemies. Let us assume, however, purely for the sake of argument, that, taking into consideration not only the army in Flanders, but our forces at the Dardanelles, on the Persian Gulf, and in other parts of the world, we shall soon have a million men in the field. But when our men are fighting as they are bound to fight this summer, for the summer is the soldier's season, if we average the war wastage of the great battle months, such as May has proved, with that of the quiet months, it will

at the very least be 10 per cent per month. (It may of course prove to be much more.) This means an immediate wastage of one hundred thousand a month to be made good. It means that unless one hundred thousand fresh men are raised every month, the armies in the field will begin to wither away. Of course up to now there has been no such wastage. We are speaking of the future—of the period when the New Army will be at the front.

If no new men are raised, an army of a million would in ten months cease to exist. Therefore Lord Kitchener's new army of three hundred thousand, if he got them by June 1st, would have disappeared by September 1st.

Admitting that Lord Kitchener has other great supplies of men for drafting purposes and could keep 1,000,000 men in the field for a year without using these extra 300,000, the *Spectator* regards it as still probable that England will want to have ultimately not 1,000,000 men but a million and a half in the field and a million and a half at home to feed them. The *Spectator*'s only suggestion to explain Lord Kitchener's policy is that he intends to make successive calls at short intervals for additional enlistment. This policy the *Spectator* regards as wholly unsatisfactory, and ventures to predict that within a few months there will be an imperative need for supplying drafts to the British army at the front and that the voluntary system will prove inadequate to supply them. Then the government will be compelled to adopt a policy of compulsion, or what in this country was known as the draft in the Civil War.

Making Officers for Our New Army

William Menkel

THE AMERICAN REVIEW OF REVIEWS, July 1917

When the United States declared war on the Central Powers it had a standing army of 30,000 men. The majority of the handful of trained officers was immediately scattered among the training camps to whip what officer material that was available into shape for the expanding army. A Students Army Training Corps was created encompassing 359 American colleges and universities where 150 thousand men entered these institutions for the purpose of becoming trained soldiers. After a few months they might be sent to an officer's training camp, or to some technical school or in a regular army cantonment with troops as a private according to the degree of aptitude shown on the college campus.

The men received uniforms, rifles, equipment and 20¢ a day for housing, and 80¢ a day for subsistence This was based on the regular per diem tuition charge of the institution in the year 1917–1918.

The hunt was on for men who were ready to assume command. The government gave the problem of turning out officers capable of leading the armed forces in battle one of its highest priorities in 1917.

There has never been much question about the ability of Uncle Sam to raise a million men for war purposes, either by the volunteer method or by conscription. The chief anxiety has been to secure officers to train the million after they had been raised. The Regular Army needs all its own officers, and, when recruited to its recently authorized strength, will need more. The National Guard is in the same position. Apart from the comparatively few officers in the Reserve Corps, there were practically no officers available to take charge of the proposed new draft army that will have more than half a million men at the start.

With the declaration of war and the decision to conscript a large fighting force, the War Department immediately set about (under Section 54 of the National Defense act of June 3, 1916), to secure the necessary officers. The plan adopted was a modification, suited to war conditions, of the Federal Training Camps for Civilians, which had become popular throughout the country as the Plattsburg Idea, and had attained a high degree of success. The principle of these camps was a short period of intensive military training for men physically and mentally fit.

Accordingly sixteen officers' training camps were projected last April, and the lists thrown open for applications. In spite of rigid requirements as to health, mental equipment, and experience, more than the desired number of men were easily obtained.

These camps were open to Reserve officers of the line and engineers, members of the Officers' Reserve Corps Training Unit, duly authorized members of the National Guard, graduates of military schools, and civilians with or without military experience, provided they were college graduates or otherwise educated, and had clearly demonstrated their ability in business or other activities. Also they were required to be men of good moral character and sound physical condition.

The only obligations were that the candidates must enlist for a period of three months and agree to accept such appointment in the Officers' Reserve Corps of the United States Army as the Secretary of War should tender to them at the close of the training period. Generally considered, the Government provisions for the camp attendants were liberal. Transportation, uniforms, books, subsistence, and equipment were furnished, and in addition each man was allowed $100 a month pay. Those who had already, been commissioned in the Officers' Reserve Corps received the regular pay of their rank.

The sixteen camps were located at Plattsburg Barracks (N.Y.), Madison Barracks (Sackett's Harbor, N.Y.), Fort Niagra (N.Y.), Fort Myer (Virginia), Fort Oglethorpe (Georgia), Fort McPherson (Georgia), Fort Benjamin Harrison (Indiana), Fort Sheridan (Illinois), Fort Logan H. Roots (Arkansas), Fort Snelling (Minnesota), Fort Riley (Kansas), Leon Springs (Texas), and the Presidio of San Francisco.

With the exception of the "double" camps, like that of Plattsburg, which accommodates over 5,000 men, each camp was organized as one provisional training regiment, with a maximum attendance of twenty-five hundred men. The object of each regiment was to train officers for one full division of troops and one additional cavalry regiment. From the total of 40,000 men in training it was planned to select ten thousand to officer the first army increment of 500,000 men which Congress was expected to authorize, with commissions for many more for service elsewhere, or in the Reserve Corps.

Over seventy-five per cent of the officer material attending the camps is extremely good. The ages of the men run from 21 years to 45. College graduates, professional men and men of large business affairs predominate. Many have left lucrative positions or made other personal sacrifices to attend the camps.

The course of training, while in a measure similar to that of previous training camps, lasts three months instead of one, and includes more subjects than could be packed into a month's course. Also the working hours are longer and the discipline more severe. This was, of course, natural. The former camps were held while we were still at peace. They partook somewhat of the nature of propaganda, and no obligation went with attendance. The training was excellent and the experience valuable, but when the camp was over the men were through and went back to civil life. Now we are at war, and these camps are for actual war purposes. The men attending them are on the first lap of the road to France. Officers are to be made under high pressure, to command men who will engage in actual fighting. When their too brief time of training is up they will almost immediately take charge of raw troops that will be ready for them by that time and will try to pass on to them a good part of the training they have received.

It is by no means considered that the men will be finished officers when the camps close. But they will have been given a good start. They can be expected to go ahead afterward by themselves. With their own previous equipment and this added three months' intensive training, they will be able to keep well in advance of the men they are to teach, learning and re-learning as they go along.

The period of training in these camps began on May 15 and will end on August 11. It is divided into two terms. During the first term of one month all attendants were put through a uniform course of instruction in infantry work and the duties common to officers of all arms. On the completion of this period, the men were separated according to the various branches they had chosen, and then began their special training for two months in those particular branches. Infantrymen, who continued on in that line of work, have remained generally at the original camps. But engineers, artillerymen and aviation students have been detached and concentrated in other camps given over wholly to their particular branch.

The camp day, lasting from reveille at 5:45 A.M. to taps at 9:45 P.M., is based on a ten-hour schedule of actual work—five in the morning, three in the afternoon, and a two-hour study period at night. This night studying is not done individually as the men may please, lying in bunks or any other convenient place and subject to all sorts of interruptions. They are marched off by companies to their classrooms immediately after supper, and sit down in a body for a solid period of two hours in silent study. In addition to the field work, there is a conference period of an hour and a half each morning and afternoon at which the candidates for commissions are quizzed by their instructors on the lessons studied the evening before. While there are short rests during the day, the only free time of any length is Saturday afternoon and Sunday, with the possibility of Saturday afternoon being filled with "catching up" work later on.

The first month's infantry course consisted of the usual drill in close and open order, manual of arms, musketry training, physical drill, semaphore and flag signaling, and bayonet and saber drill. In addition to the books covering these subjects, the men also studied the "Manual of Court-Martial," "Small Problems for Infantry" and "Manual of Interior Guard Duty." The care of equipment, organization of the regiment, and other branches of the military art were taken up in the morning and evening conference. In the second period of training, all the phases of actual warfare in Europe will be realistically taken up. Conditions of trench warfare will be accurately reproduced, the men taking their turns in dugouts and on firing lines, and learning all about grenade and gas attacks, both offensive and defensive, barbed wire entanglements, machine-gun work, night attacks, and trench raids, to the accompaniment of star shells and all the other paraphernalia of modern warfare, with a three-day period of war maneuvers to finish up.

The courses are designed to develop the men as instructors, managers and leaders. They are subjected to the same drills and individual training that they will be called on to give as officers, and must submit to the same discipline and rigid attention to detail that they will have to exact in turn from those under them. They are living the same mode of life that their future subordinates will have to live, with added instruction in the proper method of supplying, messing, administering, and disciplining organizations, and caring for the welfare and comfort of their men. Leadership is being developed by giving every man by turns an opportunity to command various company units in field work.

The camps are a kind of hot-house West Point, minus the academic work and its theoretical training—plus some very practical up-to-date war lessons. The training is not too arduous. Neither is it easy. It cannot well be under the circumstances. The men have a lot to learn in an all too brief time. So it is a fairly steady grind, with no time for loafing, and everything going with vim and snap. But the men are standing up well under it. The selective process by which they were originally chosen resulted in securing material able to absorb rapidly an intensive course of this kind.

The instruction contemplates a thorough grounding in the fundamental work of the soldier—the necessary general knowledge which will help the new officers to meet special situations as they arise. This is a highly important point. It was overlooked in training some of the English and Canadian forces who were drilled exclusively in certain special phases of the new warfare. And when conditions changed these men were at a loss to meet them. Nevertheless, while profiting by the mistakes of our allies, we are also benefiting by their advice and instructions. The experience of foreign armies during the past three years is being freely drawn upon for lessons of the latest developments in modern warfare. Thoroughness and precision are being emphasized.

Lack of equipment has handicapped the work to a certain extent, and there is a decided shortage of officer instructors. At a certain school in Canada 300 men are supplied with a teaching staff of 30 officers—one instructor to each ten men. At the double camp at Plattsburg there are 55 officer instructors (not counting the medical staff) to over 5,500 men—one to every 100.

Camp officials have, however, expressed themselves as well satisfied with the progress made. More than 60 per cent of the men will probably earn commissions. Even this would indicate some severe weeding out. The process of elimination has, in fact, been going on ever since the camps opened. In addition to the physical examination on acceptance of the candidate's application, a further physical test was applied at the camps, resulting in many rejections. Other men have dropped out for business or personal reasons. Some, recognizing their own unfitness as the work progressed, have voluntarily discontinued the course. A few have been dismissed for the good of the service. Those who are not successful in securing commissions in the drafted forces or in the Regular Army may be invited to attend a later camp for further training. Examinations and the result of day-by-day observation on the part of officers will largely determine the fitness of the men to receive commissions.

Failure to be chosen for a commission will not necessarily reflect on the individual candidate. All men are not cut out to be military officers. Temperament, the ability to handle men, and the talent to impart instruction—prime requisites in a good officer—are not possessed by all. But every man is being given an absolutely fair show and equal treatment. Individual students have freely acknowledged that if they fail it will be due to their own fault.

The men are working hard and submitting cheerfully to rigid discipline. The strictest supervision is being constantly maintained over their conduct both inside and outside the camps. Provost officers and assistants are utilized for this purpose. Gross violations of discipline mean prompt discharge from the camp, while all the little things that show carelessness or imperfections in habits or character are carefully set down and will score against the candidate in the final judgment. During the first month rank was not observed as between the men in training, many of whom had already received their commissions as lieutenants, captains, and majors in the Reserve Corps; but after this period these men had to be duly saluted by the uncommissioned privates.

Health and moral conditions are being well guarded in and about these officers' training camps. The War Department has made strict regulations to this end, and the camp authorities are carrying out instructions to the letter. Two regulations have a direct bearing along these lines. The first is that the men are required to wear their uniform in public all the time. The second regulation forbids any man in uniform from entering a drinking-place or a house of prostitution. In New York State also a new law was secured prohibiting the sale of liquor within a quarter of a mile of any army reservation, and many rum shops promptly went by the board.

It may be said for the men that they are not anxious to break the regulations. Of excellent character to begin with, the majority of them could doubtless get along very well without restrictions on their conduct. Housed by companies in rough wooden shacks, eating plain food with physical work out of doors most of the day, and regular hours, the men are living clean and healthy lives. They realize the task looming up before them, and are seriously intent on making good. The Y.M.C.A. as usual is standing by at the camps in various useful ways. It assists materially in the oversight of recreation, supplies personal conveniences, and conducts religious services. Church attendance—at the big double camp at Plattsburg, for example—is exceptionally good. An average of a thousand men appear at the morning and evening services at this camp, while hundreds of others go to the various churches in the city.

Altogether it is an interesting experiment for us to make our army officers in this way. It is revolutionary, this method of selecting officers in time of war by the competitive process instead of by personal or political influence. The democracy of it is appropriate to the democratic character of our conscript army.

Training Colored Officers

Lucy France Pierce

THE AMERICAN REVIEW OF REVIEWS, December 1917

When the declaration of war with Germany was proclaimed it was just a little more than fifty years that the Civil War in the United States had come to an end and blacks had become free people.

All through the South blacks lived in segregated ghetto neighborhoods and attended all-black schools; and public toilets and public drinking fountains were plainly marked "white" or "colored." Jim Crow laws were enacted and enforced.

Black troops fighting in the Civil War were assigned to all-black battalions. The army carried this tradition forward in World War I.

With War Department General Order No. 109, the First Provisional Infantry Regiment (colored), later designated as the 371st Infantry, was organized at Camp Jackson, Columbia, South Carolina. This regiment was to be composed of blacks from the first draft and was to be commanded by white officers. Ninety per cent of those officers were from the states of North Carolina, South Carolina and Tennessee and were graduates of the first Officers' Training Camps.

It was becoming increasingly obvious that if blacks were to be drafted in large numbers, black officers would be necessary to lead them. A belated Officers' Training Camp for them was opened without fanfare. The writer of the following piece was given much less space for her story than the white Officers' Training camp received. It will be noted that the article, reflecting the period, is both patronizing and racist.

At a special reserve officer's training camp established at Fort Des Moines, Iowa, exclusively for negro citizens, 625 men of the colored race have been commissioned as officers in the National Army. Of this number, 105 were made captains; the remainder were awarded the rank of first- and second-lieutenant. These especially trained colored officers will be assigned to duty with the full division of drafted colored troops about to be mobilized in the various cantonments throughout the country. For the first time in the history of the United States Army, colored officers will lead colored troops. This the War Department deems a matter of justice in view of the splendid record of the black citizen as a fighting man.

The training camp at Fort Des Moines was opened on June 18, under the command of Brigadier-General C. C. Ballou, with Colonel Charles W. Castle as second in command and head of a staff of twelve West Point instructors. Twelve hundred and fifty men were enrolled for training, a picked body of colored citizens, representing every State in the Union, many colleges, and every profession in which the colored man has distinguished himself. Many lawyers, physicians, clergymen, college instructors, and successful business men were among the number. Tuskegee Institute alone furnished sixty men. Two hundred and fifty men from the four colored regiments of the regular army were accepted as candidates.

To the original three-month's period of intensive training was added on an additional month and commissions were awarded on October 15, when just one-half of the original total enrollment received the cachet of military rank. The additional month of training devoted to drill and war games was granted not because the black men were found to be deficient in grasping techniques of military science or less adaptable to military training than white men, but because it was not found expedient to mobilize drafted colored troops until November 1, and the newly made officers were not required for duty until that time. Under the able tutelege of Colonel Castle, an officer who has seen twenty years of grueling service in the Philippines and on the Mexican border, over one hundred captains have been turned out whom the commandant, Brigadier-General Ballou, views as most promising material for distinguished leadership.

The character of the training at Fort Des Moines has been identical with that arranged for the reserve officers' training camps for white men. The candidates were housed in regular barracks of the post, which is one of the most modern in the country. They were furnished with transportation, uniforms, equipment, rations, and $100 a month during the period of training. The units of the division of colored troops will be organized at those cantonments where the number of such troops is sufficient to organize a divisional unit. Only when ordered to France for duty will this body of troops be mobilized as a division, and it will then be the largest fighting unit of negro troops ever called to the colors.

PART V
NAVIES AT WAR

For hundreds of years the seas were used mainly as the highways for commerce of all nations. However, with the coming of the modern era the oceans were, more and more, battle areas; the control of the high seas had become vital for victory. A new and devastating weapon was introduced into this fight, a weapon that brought a chill to the hearts and minds of the allies—the submarine.

Newspaper Editorials, 8 and 9 May 1915

Editors

THE NEW YORK HERALD, THE NEW YORK WORLD, BALTIMORE
SUN, ST. LOUIS REPUBLIC, RICHMOND (VA.) TIMES-DISPATCH,
MEMPHIS COMMERCIAL APPEAL

> *The Statue of Liberty now*
> *Has a tear in her eye*
> *I think it's a shame*
> *Someone is to blame*
> *All we can do is just sigh*
> *Some of us lost a true sweetheart*
> *Some of us lost a dear Dad*
> *Some lost their mothers, their sisters and brothers*
> *Some lost the best friends they've had*
> *It's time they were stopping this warfare*
> *That women and children must die*
> *—Many brave hearts went to sleep in the deep . . .*
> *When the* Lusitania *went down.*
>
> *Song of 1915*

The one incident that brought the United States close to war with Germany in 1915 was the sinking by submarine of the British luxury liner, the Lusitania.

The opulent ship, launched on 7 June 1906, almost fifteen months after the laying of the keel, was more than a floating palace. It was described as a beautiful town on water.

The decorative and architectural features compared favorably to the finest hotels in the world. It boasted elevators, scores of telephones, 1,200 curtained windows, and more than 5,000 electric lights in rooms and hallways. There were domed ceilings, painted and fashioned by well-known artists and artisans, and rich tapestries, rugs and draperies. The first class dining room was dazzling in white and gold, the predominating color was vieux rose. The sideboard was a polished mahogany with gilt metal ornaments. The lounge decorations were of the late Georgian period, and beneath the beautifully modelled dome ceiling there were exquisite inlaid mahogany panels. A carved onyx fireplace that reached from floor to ceiling was centered against the wall. An elaborate and harmonious chamber served as a library, writing and smoke room. Private accomodations listed Regal Suites which were composed of a dining room, drawing room, two bedrooms, bath and toilet rooms with an adjoining maid's room.

Second class passengers also enjoyed posh surroundings with special public rooms that included the dining room, smoke room, library and lounge. Third class passangers too found themselves in plush accomodations.

All of it went down in 60 fathoms of water in a brief 18 minutes after being hit by only one torpedo.

On 1 May 1915 the giant ocean liner left New York City for Liverpool with an impressive passenger list despite an advertisement appearing in New York newspapers warning travelers that one sailed on British ships at one's own risk. Before the Lusitania sailing, 20 telegrams were sent to prominent passengers aboard ship urging them not to sail. "The Lusitania was doomed to be torpedoed." The signatures on the telegrams were not recognized by the recipients, and not one of them transferred their sailing to another ocean liner.

The Lusitania was sunk on the sunny afternoon of Friday, May 7th, eight miles from land off the south east cost of Ireland near the entrance of St. George's channel at 2:23 o'clock by the German submarine, U-20. There were 1,916 aboard the liner, 1,251 were passengers of which 782 were lost at sea, including 128 Americans and 63 children. The crew of 665 lost 348 men and women.

The sympathy of the American people had been split between Britain and Germany until the "Lusitania Massacre" and then sentiment swung widely, almost unanimously to the side of the English.

President Wilson did his utmost to keep America neutral, but at this point the sentiment of the people was such that the United States was ready and willing to become an arsenal for the Allies, and to prepare for a war they were sure would come. The attitude sparked a sudden prosperity that affected one million unemployed men and one hundred thousand starving citizens. Americans were stimulated morally and financially as they went back to work, and the hatred for all things German increased.

The world shouted "atrocity" at the Germans, but the Kaiser rejected the accusation. He claimed the Lusitania carried contraband and because of that was fair game for the submarines ringing the British Isles.

With the passing years, more and more information surfaces in regard to the sinking of the Lusitania. A mist of mystery shrouds the incident and this premise presents itself: did Winston Churchill with or without the knowledge of the British Admiralty stage the atrocity? Did he (or they) bait the Germans with this million dollar decoy, loaded with munitions, floating slowly through submarine infested waters? If the German navy behaved in its usual manner, the world would be provided with a shocking act, and the prize would be the United States! Sympathy, now equally divided, would swing to Britain and if the Americans should go to war, it would be as allies of the British and French forces. What a cheap and effective means to gain so great an advantage!

Consider this sequence of events:

1. Contrary to public opinion that the Lusitania *was unarmed, the ship was prepared to receive armament on 12 May 1913. Cunard announced that the liner was being taken temporarily out of service to have the latest design of turbines installed. But the* New York Tribune *reported that the* Lusitania *was being equipped with high power rifles.*

The Tribune *made an error in that the high power rifles were not installed, though orders for them had been placed. What actually was done (documented in the Cunard archives) were alterations to accept the guns. The entire length of the ship between the shelter deck and below the upper deck was double plated and hydraulically riveted. The stringer plate of the shelter deck was doubled. The reserve coal bunker forward of No. 1 boiler room was converted to hold special shell racking, so that shells rested against the bulkheads. Handling elevators were installed. A second magazine was carved out of part of the mail rooms at the stern, and revolving gun rings were mounted on the forecastle and afterdeck. Each deck could mount two 6– inch quick-firing guns. The shelter deck was adapted to take four 6–inch guns on either side, making a total complement of twelve guns or a broadside of six guns. On 8 August the* Lusitania *was moved into the Canada drydock on Merseyside and was equipped with guns. The armament was completely installed by September and the* Lusitania *was entered in the Admiralty fleet register as an armed auxiliary cruiser.*

2. The cargo manifests were constantly tampered with in regard to British shipping. (There were four different manifests for the Lusitania's *last trip.) Shrapnel, fuses, and ammunition were carried in the hold of the large ocean liner. Her fuel supply was cut to accomodate the oversized load of war materials, and the lack of coal was one of the excuses given for the fastest ship of its time to cut its usual speed of 24 knots to 18 on her last crossing. Speed was the* Lusitania's *greatest defense against submarines, but it was denied to her on her final trip.*

3. On the evening of 6 May Captain Turner, on board the Lusitania, *received a wireless message warning him there was a U-boat in the South Ireland channel, but the Captain carried strict orders forbidding him to go around the North of Ireland. He had no choice but to continue on course, directly in the path of the marauding submarine, and hope to meet a protective naval force.*

4. Although there had been three sinkings in two days in the area the Lusitania *was now crossing, no special measures were taken to protect the ocean liner. Cruisers and torpedo boats remained in harbor at Queenstown, and harbor patrol boats were instructed to resume their normal duties. And approximately 35 miles away, the* Lusitania *found its final resting place.*

By this one act, the face of World War I was changed; it was the beginning of the end for the Kaiser and his cronies.

The New York Herald

The Slaughter of Neutrals and Non-combatants   The civilized world stands appalled at the torpedoing of the Lusitania with the terrible loss of life—non-combatants, many of them citizens of neutral countries.

If ever wholesale murder was premeditated this slaughter on the high seas was. By official proclamation of an intention to disregard all rules of blockade and all international law, Germany declared that her submarines would sink every ship that sought to enter or leave the ports of the United Kingdom and France. By official advertisement signed by the imperial German Embassy at Washington, all passengers were warned not to take passage on British ships from the United States for England. By letter and telegram passengers were warned not to go by the Lusitania. The ship had been marked for slaughter. The warnings were disregarded, but she was doomed from the minute she passed out of the three mile limit.

There may be a thousand dead, there maybe 1,500. The extent of the disaster matters little in an international crisis. One American life lost makes another case against Germany similar to that of the *Gulflight.** But undoubtedly hundreds of Americans have been sent swirling to eternity by the German pirates.

Henceforth is international anarchy to be the controlling factor in marine warfare? Henceforth is piracy on the high seas to be recognized and go unprotected and unpunished? Henceforth is the wanton murder of neutrals and non-combatant passengers to be treated as regrettable incidents and go at that?

It is for the neutral countries, and above all the United States, to answer these questions. It is a time of gravity in American history unmarked since the civil war.

This cold-blooded premeditated outrage on a colossal scale will cause such a blinding white light of indignation throughout the neutral portion of the world, unhappily growing smaller and smaller, that there can not conceivably be in Washington any thoughts of turning back from the note to Germany, sent February 10.

In the note the United States informed Germany that it viewed the possibilities with great concern and requested Germany to consider the critical situation which might arise were the German naval forces in carrying out the policy foreshadowed to destroy any merchant vessels of the nation or cause the death of American citizens.

"Or cause the death of American citizens!"
Again in this communication the State Department informs the German

---

* *Gulflight* was an American steamer sunk May 1, 1915 by torpedo off Sicilly Isles. Three lives were lost.

Government that if German commanders should destroy on the high seas an American vessel or the lives of American citizens, it would be difficult to view the act in any other light than as an indefensible violation of neutral rights.

"Or the lives of American citizens!"

The *Lusitania* was a British ship, but this fact does not mitigate the crime of the Kaiser's navy against this republic in killing peaceful American passengers. Nor does the fact that warnings were given mitigate the crime. It rather increases its enormity. Americans had the right to go by any steamship they chose. They had the right to protection by this Government. No Government can long last that does not protect its own citizens.

The grave crisis which was precipitated by the torpedoing of the *Gulflight* grows greater each hour as the tidings from Queenstown swell the list of the dead.

The New York World

The Sinking of the Lusitania   Morally, the sinking of the *Lusitania* was no worse than the sinking of the *Falaba*.*

In each case a passenger ship carrying neutrals and non-combatants was destroyed by a German submarine, and hundreds of helpless men, women and children left to float or drown as luck decreed. The destruction of the *Lusitania* makes a more dramatic appeal to the human imagination then did the destruction of the *Falaba*, but both were crimes against civilization in equal degree.

It is no fault of the German Government that anybody escaped from either ship. It is no fault of the German Government that every American on board the *Lusitania* is not lying at the bottom of the sea.

The German authorities claim in extenuation that fair warning was given to Americans by the German Embassy at Washington that the *Lusitania* was to be torpedoed. The fact that A formally announces his intention to murder B at 3 o'clock tomorrow afternoon does not make the subsequent murder of B an innocent or justifiable act.

What Germany expects to gain by her policy is something we cannot guess. What advantage will it be to her to be left without a friend or a well wisher in the world? The war can not last forever. Peace will eventually come, if only through exhaustion. What will be the attitude of other nations toward Germany when the conflict is finished? How many decades must pass before Germany can live down the criminal record that she is writing for herself in the annals of history?

* The British passenger steamer, *Falaba*, was sunk off Wales March 27, 1915 by a German submarine. 111 lives were lost including one American. 113 were saved.

Baltimore Sun

One thing should not be forgotten in considering this latest "German triumph." It strikes a far more dangerous blow at Germany than at England.

St. Louis Republic

For the moment there is no law of nations. Brute force rules. The more inexcusable the outrages of the present war, the surer the reaction.

Richmond (Va.) Times-Dispatch

Germany surely must have gone mad. The torpedoing and sinking of the *Lusitania* evinces a disregard of the opinions of the world in general and of this country in particular—only compatible with the assumption that blood lust has toppled reason from its throne.

Memphis Commercial Appeal

The United States should notify Germany that the loss of American life and passenger ships by torpedoing without taking off passengers will be regarded as an act of war and demand an answer. If an answer is not satisfactory Congress should be called in extra session to consider a declaration of war.

German Opinion on the Case of the Lusitania

Editorial, Frankfurter Zeitung

THE AMERICAN REVIEW OF REVIEWS, July 1915

An editorial in the Frankfürter Zeitung *of May 21 discusses the points of President Wilson's first note to Germany demanding the cessation of submarine warfare endangering the lives of passengers and crews of undefended merchant ships.*

Referring to the fact that a number of days elapsed after the receipt of the note at Berlin before the German government made a reply, this article accepts the delay as proof that the matter was carefully weighed before an official answer was given, and that the policy once announced by Germany would be maintained with firmness.

The article suggests that the American note, on the other hand, had perhaps not been prepared with equally careful deliberation. "It is visibly written under the influence of the excitement that was evoked in the United States through the death of the many American citizens that went down with the Lusitania, *including some of the wealthiest men of America. This reflection of the popular resentment may work for the popularity of the note in America itself. If some of the expressions in it may seem very drastic to us in view of the intended diplomatic results, there is nevertheless in Germany an understanding of the conditions of a government that must reckon with the sentiments of great, strongly incited, and little enlightened masses."*

The article takes issue with the President's note chiefly on the point of the character of the Lusitania *and her cargo. The main argument under this head is embodied in the following paragraphs.*

The *Lusitania* was an English auxiliary cruiser, drew as such very large money subsidies from the English Government, was built under the supervision of the English Admiralty, appeared quite regularly in the English Navy lists with a heavy armament. Now, whether or not the ship on its last voyage carried the armament that had been provided for it is a matter of utter indifference in the pending dispute.

In the first place, the German Government cannot possibly know whether English warships just happen to have their cannon with them; in the second place, the *Lusitania*, upon completion of its voyage, would again have been equipped with arms in England and then used as a warship against Germany. A soldier who has lost his gun might just as well pose as a harmless noncombatant.

But, even taking it for granted that the United States should not admit this view of the case, which, to be sure, places a heavy neglect of duty upon them, the English Government and the Cunard Line, there remains nevertheless the fact, officially communicated through the English Embassy at Bern, that the *Lusitania* carried in her hold munitions of war, and that, too, in enormous quantities. The rapid sinking of the ship was caused precisely by the explosion of these combustibles, since only a single German torpedo was fired.

If the reasoning of the note on the propriety and humanity of torpedoing merchant ships were to be followed, says this writer, "Germany would have to allow every English ship, filled to the rail with bombs for the mass destruction of our German soldiers, to sail into every English port, so long as any 'neutral' American finds it to his liking to travel to Europe upon it."

The editorial declares that in view of the warnings given by the German Embassy in Washington, the United States Government should itself have prevented the departure of the *Lusitania*. "In order to save its own citizens, it should have held back the ship in any event, no matter how much it was otherwise of the opinion that the principles of the German methods of warfare on the sea were contrary to law."

In its concluding paragraph the editorial offers some hope for an understanding between the two powers. "in spite of all that has been done to us from over there and is still being done, we do not desire a serious sharpening of this conflict. But the supreme consideration for us now remains the energetic and purposeful waging of the war, and all other considerations recede into the background behind this."

In connection with its comment on the first American note the *Hamburger Nachrichten* makes the following plea in defense of German submarine warfare:

> The German submarine is only one fruit, the latest, of the science of shipbuilding and the use of explosives. When gunpowder was invented the entire system of warfare and of safety had to undergo a change. At that time, in the beginning of this development, many persons remonstrated against the use of such changed means of warfare, and Ludovico Ariosto* speaks in glowing verses his curse against the gun as an implement of warfare. The human spirit of invention did not suffer itself to be arrested, and humanity reconciled itself to the innovations and the changed conduct.

---

* One of Italy's great poets (1474–1533). His epic treatment of the Roland story, theoretically a sequel to the unfinished masterpiece of Boiardo, is perhaps the greatest of Renaissance poems. Roland was Charlemagne's prefect of the Breton march; he was one of those killed when Basques cut off in a pass in the Pyrenees the rear guard of the army returning from the Spanish invasion of 778.

One result of the invention of gunpowder was the construction of steel ships with their mighty guns, and a still further development was the German submarine, with their wide radius of activity. Humanity must accustom itself to the one as well as to the other, even as, in fact, it has accustomed itself to the battle with explosives, even to airships and aeroplanes that throw bombs. Yes, even to the French stink bombs. Only when the German troops brought still more effective asphyxiating gases to bear upon the French did the clamor of woe begin to resound. We cannot assume that the Government at Washington, in the friendship which it emphasizes in its note, wishes to appropriate to itself the pharisaical French indignation simply because it is a German means of warfare.

The submarines are warships as well as any others, only they are new and bring with them new concomitant phenomena. Whereas cruisers that sail on the sea give warning by their mere appearance, other means of warning are furnished for the submarines. We have applied them.

The general tenor of German press comment on President Wilson's first note is indicated by the following paragraph from the *Vossische-Zeitung*:

If America succeeds in bringing it about that British merchant vessels shall no longer sail under false flags, that England shall cease arming merchant vessels, and that contraband cargoes shall no longer be protected by American passengers, then the United States will find Germany on her side in an endeavor to lead submarine war into more humane channels.

If America fails to influence Great Britain thus, the United States will have to put up with submarine war as at present waged. She must take care that her citizens enter as little into the naval war zone as they would into the firing line near Arras, Lille, or Przemysl.

In the *Deutsche Tages Zeitung* Count Reventlow, writing on the possibilities of war between America and Germany, said:

Trade between Germany and America has shrunk to microscopic dimensions. What they receive from us is more valuable and necessary than what we receive from them. The complete cutting off of negotiations would leave us where we are. America would only be able to damage us by confiscating the ships left in her harbors and much other German property. Further dangerous deeds of war from America are not to be feared because they are not possible. Also we do not forget certain interior difficulties in America. That is another side of the business. On the other hand, any stopping of the submarine war, if only for the time, would have most important results. Any orders to submarine commanders to conform to any formal conditions laid down by international law would mean hindering their actions and making the submarine war an empty farce, a kind of screen behind which one would have obediently to withdraw with apologies.

The German undersea war is no improvisation of sudden caprice, but a well-considered measure on a great scale. On a great scale, therefore, must be the practical carrying out of the measure if it is to be an apparatus of great value. When the German Empire, in this great struggle for existence, decides to take such steps, then there is no drawing back.

After the receipt at Berlin of the second note from President Wilson there was a marked change in the tone of German newspaper comment on the issue between the two countries. Thus the general director of the *Lokal Anzeiger*, Eugen Zimmermann, said in his journal on June 13:

President Wilson desires nothing more and nothing less than an understanding between Germany and England concerning the forms of maritime warfare, which at the same time will ensure the safety of American passengers. The task is not light, considering the development of naval war, but it can be solved if all interests display goodwill.

Herr Zimmermann proposed, as a new basis of naval operations, that passengers on ships with special identification marks and sailing under the government guarantee that they are unarmed should receive proper consideration at the hands of submarine commanders. Such a compromise, however, would also involve the withdrawal of the British Admiralty's instruction to merchantmen to attack and ram submarines on sight.

The *Tageblatt*, edited by Theodor Wolff, advocates the creation of an advisory council to the German Foreign Office in which former Ministers and Secretaries of Foreign Affairs, Ambassadors, and leading members of the Reichstag shall have seats. This, he thinks, would be a suitable method for giving German diplomacy adequate authority and prestige at home, and would result in the avoidance of new conflicts.

Referring to President Wilson's demand that the Allies and non-combatants shall not be endangered by submarine warfare, the *Kreuzzeitung* says that the mild form of the President's note cannot conceal the gravity of the situation and that it reveals that President Wilson has not the slightest comprehension of the German standpoint nor the situation which has compelled Germany to act as she has done:

Americans who want to visit England can do so without appreciable danger on American ships that have pledged themselves to carry no contraband, a pledge that can easily be verified by German consular officials.

Under the present circumstances, however, as long as travelers use ships which carry contraband and possibly are armed and, in conformity with the orders of the British Admiralty, attempt to ram submarines, this demand of the note it is impossible to fulfil. If we are to give in to the demands of the note, Great Britain first would have to make serious changes in its previous practices and guarantee the changes satisfactorily. President Wilson must busy himself about this next. He must be able to comprehend that we are not going to let submarine warfare out of our hand as a weapon in order that American travelers may cross without danger to Europe on British ships, perhaps with the intention of insuring the freightage of ammunition and other war materials for our enemies.

The *Frankfürter Nachrichten* proposes, as a method for modifying the hardships of submarine warfare, that the United States Government consent to the stationing of German commissioners in American ports to examine ships sailing for Europe, so that those which carry no armaments, munitions or troops may be exempt from attack by German submarines.

As a precedent for such action the *Nachrichten* cites the fact that similar commissioners are maintained by the British Government in various neutral countries to examine and certify with regards to cargoes bound to neutral ports.

Writing in the *Vossische Zeitung*, George Bernhard says that not one of the essential differences between Germany and the United States has been removed by the exchange of notes:

America told us she would take the initiative in preventing England from a future misuse of naval warfare. This we greeted thankfully. If America's representations are unsuccessful, she may repeat them. Whether the German submarine warfare can be moderated depends solely on the attitude of England.

Germany's Submarines

H. T. Wade

THE AMERICAN REVIEW OF REVIEWS, June 1915

Shipbuilders were faced with the problem of making ships torpedo-proof. Failing that, new ideas were needed to keep ocean liners afloat long enough so that they could be evacuated with safety.

It took the Titanic *four hours to sink after striking an iceberg, but the* Lusitania *hit the ocean floor twenty minutes after being struck by a torpedo. Some unification in building ships was obviously necessary, and as the shipbuilders floundered, the underwater threat grew. The submarine began to play a greater role as a deadly war weapon.*

Public interest increased rapidly as the underwater crafts showed the potential for creating a German victory.

The sinking of the Lusitania, one of the largest and fastest of the transatlantic liners, by a German submarine, must be considered not only as a great marine disaster, but as marking an epoch in the military use of underwater craft. Whatever opinion may be held as to the ethics of the use of the submarine, or as to the questions of international law, morals, or humanity involved in sinking without a direct warning a passenger steamer carrying non-combatants, women and children, the fact still remains that the aspect of war at sea and the activity of the merchant marine of both combatant and neutral nations have been materially changed by the advent of the submarine. In this Germany has stood preëminent and when it is recalled that in the adoption of submarines she followed rather than led other European powers, it is worth considering how this arm has been developed and used with such striking efficiency and grim success.

Not only have submarine torpedoes carrying up to 420 pounds of the most powerful explosives been used, but German submarines, armed with special guns brought out by the Krupps, rising suddenly to the surface, have halted merchant ships with one or more shots and have destroyed them either by gun-fire or by charges of high explosives placed aboard rather than by torpedoing.

When one considers that this present war on its naval side so far has not been characterized by tactical evolutions as much as by naval raids, then it can be appreciated how much the submarines have accomplished.

Even the smaller and older craft have shown a surface radius of action of some 1,200 miles at 9 knots, which has been found more than adequate to enable them to harry British commerce, while there is every indication that the Germans have made tactical use of the submarine in groups according to previously arranged plans. Thus naval professional opinion has been expressed that the sinking of the *Lusitania* was not the result of a chance meeting along the liner's route, but rather the outcome of a tactical plan whereby a group of submarines, a dozen or less, were strung across the probable path of the steamship so that at least one would be within sinking distance, just as in the North Sea the Germans are reported to have used a fishing boat or other surface craft as a decoy, pretending that it was a mine-layer.

As regards actual operation as well as design and construction, the whole submarine situation is shrouded in the deepest secrecy. Not only details but even the number of craft in service and under construction are known to few. While the British blockade has bottled up German battle-ships and cruisers, the submarines have been almost free to pass out into the open sea and wreak destruction on warship and merchantman alike. But the Germans have not operated with impunity. Sinking or capture has been the fate of more than one submarine, but in the main manifest injury has been inflicted on the foe. It has been the submarine that has enforced the German decree of blockade which became effective on February 18, under the terms of which belligerent ships, or those of neutrals carrying contraband, might be sunk on sight. How effective this has been may be recalled by the fact that in the interval from February 18 to May 7, when the *Lusitania* was struck, 91 merchant vessels were sunk by German sub-marines or mines, with a loss of some 1,450 lives.

Germany's first submarine *U 1*—all German submarines being known by the letter "U" for *Unterseeboote* and a number—commenced in 1903, was launched at the Krupp Germania Works, adjacent to the great naval dockyard at Kiel, on August 30, 1905, not entering service, however, until February, 1907. The *U 1* was an imitation of the French submarines of the *Aigrette* type of 1902, and had a surface displacement of 185 tons, which was increased to 240 tons when running submerged. The *U 1* had a length of 128 feet 3 inches. Its internal combustion engines for surface operation were of 400 B.H.P., affording a speed of 11 knots, while the electric motors were of 240 B.H.P., and could drive the vessel submerged at a speed of 8 knots. For armament there was one torpedo-tube and three 17.7–inch torpedoes.

In 1906–7 seven more submarines were commenced, and in the 1907 budget, the sum of $1,250,000 figured for submarine construction, and this really opened the era of such craft in Germany. The *U 2* to *U 8* vessels were larger, with a displacement of 237 tons at surface and 300 tons sub-merged, 141 feet 8 inches in length, and had more powerful motors, so that they were capable of greater speed, while their surface radius of action was stated at 1,200 miles at 9 knots, and submerged 50 miles at the same speed. The single torpedo-tube was replaced by two, and four torpedoes were carried.

In 1908, *U 9, U 10, U 11,* and *U 12* were commenced, all slightly larger than the *U 2* class, but of the same general type. Of these the *U 9* was responsible for the destruction of three British cruisers early in the war. This group was succeeded by eight still larger submarines resembling the *Pluviose* class in the French Navy, and begun in 1909 and 1910. The displacement was 450 tons on the surface and 550 tons submerged, with correspondingly increased speed, and armament, a third torpedo-tube, two extra torpedoes and a 1.456–inch gun being added.

By this time the item for submarines in the annual naval budget had reached $3,750,000 and in 1913 it rose to $5,000,000, and was fixed at $4,500,000 in 1914, the German naval program calling for 72 boats by 1917. In 1911 and 1912 a new group, *U 21* to *U 32,* was put under construction, with a surface displacement of 650 tons, submerged displacement of 800 tons, 213 feet 3 inches length. Their engines were of 1,800 brake-horse-power, giving 16 knots on the surface, while the motors were of 800 B.H.P., affording a speed submerged of 10 knots. These submarines had a radius of 1,500 miles at 12 knots, and 70 miles at 6 knots submerged. By this time four torpedo-tubes and eight torpedoes 19.6 inches in diameter were carried, as well as two 3.464-inch guns.

In January 1914, Germany's submarine strength consisted of twenty-four submarines ready and fourteen in construction, eight completed and available at the outbreak of the war, while the remainder, which represented the class begun in 1913, *U 33* to *U 38,* were of 675 tons displacement on the surface and 835 tons displacement submerged, and engines of 2,500 B.H.P., giving a speed on the top of the water of 17 knots.

Germany, at the end of 1914 was reported to have under construction twenty new submarines, each with a length of 214 feet 1¾ inches, beam 20 feet, surface displacement 750 tons, submerged 900 tons, surface speed 20 knots, submerged speed 10 knots, 4,000 brake-horsepower and twin screws. Rumors received in this country indicate that the German boats are being rushed and new craft constantly being launched.

The Greatest Naval Battle in History

Francis A. March, Ph. D.
Richard J. Beamish

"HISTORY OF THE WORLD WAR"
THE UNITED PUBLISHERS OF THE UNITED STATES AND CANADA,
1919

Ever since the English navy defeated the Spanish Armada in *1588*, Britannia ruled the high seas. Despite the French naval buildup in the *18th* and early *19th*, centuries, England continued to be the uncontested major naval power in the world.

The recognition that the British Empire depended on naval might even more than had the Roman Empire, made other expanding powers undertake to develop their own navies, notably Germany and Japan.

Britain's success in bottling up the German fleet during World War I convinced the major powers of the importance of a large, well-trained navy, and spurred the naval build-up in all nations after World War I.

The Battle Of Jutland was the only major engagement of the British and German fleets in World War I. In Germany it was known as the Battle of the Skagerrak. It was fought on *31 May 1916* about 60 miles west of the coast of Jutland. The main engagement began at 6 P.M. and ended late in the night, when the Germans, under the cover of darkness and fog, made their escape to their home base. In this battle the Germans displayed a brilliant knowledge of naval tactics. The two official statements of losses by each government at the time is as follows:

British Losses

	Tons		Officers & Men
Queen Mary	27,000	Battle Cruiser	1,000
Indefatigable	18,750	Battle Cruiser	790
Invincible	17,250	Battle Cruiser	780
Defence	14,600	Armoured Cruiser	850
Black Prince	13,550	Armoured Cruiser	750
Warrior	13,550	Armoured Cruiser	750
Tipperary	1,430	Destroyer	160

Ardent	*935*	*Destroyer*	*100*
Fortune	*935*	*Destroyer*	*100*
Shark	*935*	*Destroyer*	*100*
Sparrowhawk	*935*	*Destroyer*	*100*
Nestor	*1,000*	*Destroyer*	*100*
Nomad	*1,000*	*Destroyer*	*100*
Turbulent	*1,430*	*Destroyer*	*150*
	113,300		*5,830*

German Losses

	Tons		Officers & Men
Lützow	*26,600*	*Battle Cruiser*	*1,200*
Pommern	*13,200*	*Battleship*	*729*
Wiesbaden	*5,600*	*Light Cruiser*	*450*
Frauenlob	*2,715*	*Light Cruiser*	*264*
Elbing	*5,000*	*Light Cruiser*	*450*
Rostock	*4,900*	*Light Cruiser*	*373*
Five Destroyers	*5,000*		*500*
	63,015		*3,966*

The official estimate by Sir John Jellicoe of German losses was two dreadnoughts, one Deutschland, one battle cruiser, five light cruisers, six torpedo-boat destroyers, and one submarine; in all 119,200 tons, or 6,000 tons more than the British loss, with a correspondingly larger loss in personnel.

The Germans gained no advantage from the battle, and their whole fleet remained bottled up in harbor for the rest of the war. Increased German submarine activity was the result. The Battle of Jutland was, as far as tonnage was concerned, the greatest naval battle the world had until then known.

What follows are the British and German versions of the great naval clash.

Germany's ambition for conquest at sea had been nursed and carefully fostered for twenty years. During the decade immediately preceding the declaration of war, it had embarked upon a policy of naval upbuilding that brought it into direct conflict with England's sea policy. Thereafter it became a race in naval construction, England piling up a huge debt in its determination to construct two tons of naval shipping to every one ton built by Germany.

Notwithstanding Great Britain's efforts in this direction, Germany's naval experts, with the ruthless von Tirpitz at their head, maintained that, given a fair seaway with ideal weather conditions favoring the low visibility tactics of the German sea command, a victory for the Teutonic ships would follow. It was this belief that drew the ships of the German cruiser squadron and High Seas Fleet of the coast of Jutland and Horn Reef into the great battle that decided the supremacy of the sea.

The 31st of May, 1916, will go down in history as the date of this titanic conflict. The British light cruiser *Galatea* on patrol duty near Horn Reef reported at 2:20 o'clock on the afternoon of that day that it had sighted smoke plumes denoting the advance of enemy vessels from the direction of Helgoland Bight. Fifteen minutes later the smoke plumes were in such number and volume that the advance of a considerable force to the northward and eastward was indicated. It was reasoned by Vice-Admiral Beatty, to whom the *Galatea* had sent the news by radio, that the enemy in rounding Horn Reef would inevitably be brought into action. The first ships of the enemy were sighted at 3:31 o'clock. These were the battle screen of fast light cruisers. Back of these were five modern battle cruisers of the highest power and armament.

The report of the battle, by an eye-witness, that was issued upon semiofficial authority of the British Government follows:

First phase, 3:30 P.M., May 31st. Beatty's battle cruisers, consisting of the *Lion*, *Princess Royal*, *Queen Mary*, *Tiger*, *Inflexible*, *Indomitable*, *Invincible*, *Indefatigable*, and *New Zealand*, were on a southeasterly course, followed at about two miles distance by the four battleships of the class known as Queen Elizabeth.

Enemy light cruisers were sighted and shortly afterward the head of the German battle cruiser squadron, consisting of the new cruiser *Hindenburg*, the *Seydlitz*, *Derfflinger*, *Lützow*, *Moltke*, and possibly the *Salamis*.

Beatty at once began firing at a range of about 20,000 yards (twelve miles) which shortened to 16,000 yards (nine miles) as the fleets closed. The Germans could see the British distinctly outlined against the light yellow sky. The Germans, covered by a haze, could be very indistinctly made out by the British gunners.

The Queen Elizabeths opened fire on one after another as they came within range. The German battle cruisers turned to port and drew away to about 20,000 yards.

Second Phase, 4:40 P.M. A destroyer screen then appeared beyond the German battle cruisers. The whole German High Seas Fleet could be seen approaching on the northeastern horizon in three divisions, coming to the support of their battle cruisers.

The German battle cruisers now turned right around 16 points and took station in front of the battleships of the High Fleet.

Beatty, with his battle cruisers and supporting battleships, therefore, had before him the whole of the German battle fleet, and Jellicoe was still some distance away.

The opposing fleets were now moving parallel to one another in opposite directions, and but for a master maneuver on the part of Beatty the British advance ships would have been cut off from Jellicoe's Grand Fleet. In order to avoid this and at the same time prepare the way so that Jellicoe might envelope his adversary, Beatty immediately also turned right around 16 points, so as to bring his ships parallel to the German battle cruisers and facing the same direction.

As soon as he was around he increased to full speed to get ahead of the Germans and take up a tactical position in advance of their line. He was able to do this owing to the superior speed of the British battle cruisers.

Just before the turning point was reached the *Indefatigable* sank, and the *Queen Mary* and the *Invincible* also were lost at the turning point, where, of course, the High Seas Fleet concentrated their fire.

A little earlier, as the German battle cruisers were turning, the Queen Elizabeths had in similar manner concentrated their fire on the turning point and destroyed a new German battle cruiser, believed to be the Hindenburg.

Beatty had now got around and headed away with the loss of three ships, racing parallel to the German battle cruisers. The Queen Elizabeths followed behind engaging the main High Seas Fleet.

Third Phase, 5 P.M. The Queen Elizabeths now turned about to port 16 points in order to follow Beatty. The *Warspite* jammed her steering gear, failed to get around, and drew the fire of six of the enemy, who closed in upon her.

The Germans claimed her as a loss, since on paper she ought to have been lost, but, as a matter of fact, though repeatedly straddled by shell fire with the water boiling up all around her, she was not seriously hit, and was able to sink one of her opponents. Her Captain recovered control of the vessel, brought her around, and followed her consorts.

In the meantime the *Barham*, *Valiant* and *Malaya* turned short so as to avoid the danger spot where the *Queen Mary* and the *Invincible* had been lost, and for an hour, until Jellicoe arrived, fought a delaying action against the High Seas Fleet.

The *Warspite* joined them at about 5:15 o'clock, and all four ships were so successfully maneuvered in order to upset the spotting corrections of their opponents that no hits of a seriously disabling character were suffered. They had the speed over their opponents by fully four knots, and were able to draw away from part of the long line of German battleships, which almost filled up the horizon.

At this time the Queen Elizabeths were steadily firing on at the flashes of German guns at a range which varied between 12,000 and 15,000 yards, especially against those ships which were nearest them. The Germans were enveloped in a mist and only smoke and flashes were visible.

By 5:45 half of the High Seas Fleet had been left out of range, and the Queen Elizabeths were steaming fast to join hands with Jellicoe.

To return to Beatty's battle cruisers, they had succeeded in outflanking the German battle cruisers, which were therefore obliged to turn a full right angle to starboard to avoid being headed.

Heavy fighting was renewed between the opposing battle cruiser squadrons, during which the *Derfflinger* was sunk; but toward 6 o'clock the German fire slackened very considerably, showing that Beatty's battle cruisers and the Queen Elizabeths had inflicted serious damage on their immediate opponents.

Fourth Phase, 6 P.M. The Grand Fleet was now in sight, and, coming up fast in three directions, the Queen Elizabeths altered their course four points to the starboard and drew in toward the enemy to allow Jellicoe room to deploy into line.

The Grand Fleet was perfectly maneuvered and the very difficult operation of deploying between the battle cruisers and the Queen Elizabeths was perfectly timed.

Jellicoe came up, fell in behind Beatty's cruisers and, followed by the damaged but still serviceable Queen Elizabeths, steamed right across the head of the German fleet.

The first of the ships to come into action were the *Revenue* and the *Royal Oak* with their fifteen-inch guns, and the *Agincourt*, which fired from her seven turrets with the speed almost of a Maxim gun.

The whole British fleet had now become concentrated. They had been perfectly maneuvered, so as to "cross the T" of the High Seas Fleet, and, indeed, only decent light was necessary to complete their work of destroying the Germans in detail. The light did improve for a few minutes, and the conditions were favorable to the British fleet, which was now in line approximately north and south across the head of the Germans.

During the few minutes of good light Jellicoe smashed up the first three German ships, but the mist came down, visibility suddenly failed, and the defeated High Seas Fleet was able to draw off in ragged divisions.

Fifth Phase, Night. The Germans were followed by the British, who still had them enveloped between Jellicoe on the west, Beatty on the north, and Evan Thomas with his three Queen Elizabeths on the south. The *Warspite* had been sent back to her base.

During the night the torpedo boat destroyers heavily attacked the German ships, and, although they lost seriously themselves, succeeded in sinking two of the enemy.

Coordination of the units of the fleet was practically impossible to keep up, and the Germans discovered by the rays of their searchlights the three Queen Elizabeths, not more than 4,000 yards away. Unfortunately they were then able to escape between the battleships and Jellicoe, since the British gunners were not able to fire, as the destroyers were in the way.

So ended the Jutland battle, which was fought as had been planned and very nearly a great success. It was spoiled by the unfavorable weather conditions, especially at the critical moment, when the whole British fleet was concentrated and engaged in crushing the head of the German line.

At daylight on the 1st of June the British battle fleet, being southward of Horn Reef, turned northward in search of the enemy vessels. The visibility early on the first of June was three to four miles less than on May 31st, and the torpedo-boat destroyers, being out of visual touch, did not rejoin the fleet until 9 A.M. The British fleet remained in the proximity of the battlefield and near the line of approach to the German ports until 11 A.M., in spite of the disadvantage of long distances from fleet bases and the danger incurred in waters adjacent to the enemy's coasts from submarines and torpedo craft.

The enemy, however made no sign, and the admiral was reluctantly compelled to the conclusion that the High Sea Fleet had returned into port. Subsequent events proved this assumption to have been correct. The British position must have been known to the enemy, as at 4 A.M. the fleet engaged a zepplin about five minutes, during which time she had ample opportunity to note and subsequently report the position and course of the British fleet.

The German official report makes the best presentation of the German case. It follows in full:

The High Sea Fleet, consisting of three battleship squadrons, five battle cruisers, and a large number of small cruisers, with several destroyer flotillas, was cruising in the Skagerrak on May 31st for the purpose, as on earlier occasions, of offering battle to the British fleet. The vanguard of small cruisers at 4:30 o'clock in the afternoon (German time) suddenly encountered, ninety miles west of Hanstholm (a cape on the northwest coast of Jutland), a group of eight of the newest cruisers of the Calliope class and fifteen or twenty of the most modern destroyers.

While the German light forces and the first cruiser squadron under Vice-Admiral Hipper were following the British, who were retiring northwestward, the German battle cruisers sighted to the westward Vice-Admiral Beatty's battle squadron of six ships, including four of the Lion type and two of the Indefatigable type. Beatty's squadron developed a battle line on a southeasterly course and Vice-Admiral Hipper formed his line ahead on the same general course and aproached for a running fight. He opened fire at 5:40 o'clock in the afternoon with heavy artillery at a range of 13,000 meters against the superior enemy. The weather was clear and light, and the sea was light with a northwest wind.

After about a quarter of an hour a violent explosion occurred on the last cruiser of the Indefatigable type. It was caused by a heavy shell, and destroyed the vessel.

About 6:20 o'clock in the afternoon five warships of the Queen Elizabeth type came from the west and joined the British battle cruiser line, powerfully reinforcing with their fifteen-inch guns the five British battle cruisers remaining after 6:20 o'clock. To equalize this superiority Vice-Admiral Hipper ordered the destroyers to attack the enemy. The British destroyers and small cruisers interposed, and a bitter engagement at close range ensued, in the course of which a light cruiser participated.

The Germans lost two torpedo boats, the crews of which were rescued by sister ships under a heavy fire. Two British destroyers were sunk by artillery, and two others—the *Nestor* and *Nomad*—remained on the scene in a crippled condition. These later were destroyed by the main fleet after German torpedo boats had rescued all the survivors.

While this engagement was in progress a mighty explosion, caused by a big shell, broke the *Queen Mary*, the third ship in line, asunder at 6:30 o'clock.

Soon thereafter the German main battleship fleet was sighted to the southward, steering north. The hostile fastsquadrons [sic] thereupon turned northward, closing the first part of the fight, which lasted about an hour.

The British retired at high speed before the German fleet, which followed closely. The German battle cruisers continued the artillery combat with increasing intensity, particularly with the division of the vessels of the Queen Elizabeth type, and in this the leading German battleship division participated intermittently. The hostile ships showed a desire to run in a flat curve ahead of the point of our line and to cross it.

At 7:45 o'clock in the evening British small crusiers and destroyers launched an attack against our battle cruisers, who avoided the torpedoes by maneuvering, while the British battle cruisers retired from the engagement, in which they did not participate further as can be established. Shortly thereafter a German reconnoitering group, which was parrying the destroyer attack, received an attack from the northeast. The cruiser *Wiesbaden* was soon put out of action in this attack. The German torpedo flotillas immediately attacked the heavy ships.

Appearing shadow-like from the haze bank to the northeast was made out a long line of at least twenty-five battleships, which at first sought a junction with the British battle cruisers and those of the Queen Elizabeth type on a northwesterly to westerly course, and then turned on an easterly to southeasterly course.

With the advent of the British main fleet, whose center consisted of three squadrons of eight battleships each, with a fast division of three battle cruisers of the Invincible type on the northern end, and three of the newest vessels of the Royal Sovereign class, armed with fifteen-inch guns, at the southern end, there began about 8 o'clock in the evening the third section of the engagement, embracing the combat between the main fleets.

Vice-Admiral Scheer determined to attack the British main fleet, which he now recognized was completely assembled and about double superior. The German battleship squadron, headed by battle cruisers, steered first toward the extensive haze bank to the northeast, where the crippled cruiser *Wiesbaden* was still receiving a heavy fire. Around the *Wiesbaden* stubborn individual fights now occurred.

The light enemy forces, supported by an armored cruiser squadron of five ships of the Minatour, Achilles, and Duke of Edinburgh classes coming from the northeast, were encountered and apparently surprised on account of the decreasing visibility of our battle cruisers and leading battleship division. The squadron came under a violent and heavy fire, by which the small cruisers Defense and Black Prince were sunk. The cruiser Warrior regained its own line a wreck and later sank. Another small cruiser was damaged severely.

Two destroyers had fallen victims to the attack of German torpedo boats against the leading British battleships and a small cruiser and two destroyers were damaged. The German battle cruisers and leading battleship division had in these engagements come under increased fire of the enemy's battleship squadron, which, shortly after 8 o'clock, could be made out in the haze turning to the northeastward and finally to the east. Germans observed, amid the artillery combat and shelling of great intensity, signs of the effect of good shooting between 8:20 and 8:30 o'clock particularly. Several officers on German ships observed that a battleship of the Queen Elizabeth class blew up under conditions similar to that of the Queen Mary. The Invincible sank after being hit severely. A ship of the Iron Duke class had earlier received a torpedo hit, and one of the Queen Elizabeth class was running around in a circle, its steering apparatus apparently having been hit.

The Lützow was hit by at least fifteen heavy shells and was unable to maintain its place in line. Vice-Admiral Hipper, therefore, transshipped to the Moltke on a torpedo boat and under a heavy fire. The Derfflinger meantime took the lead temporarily. Parts of the German torpedo flotilla attacked the enemy's main fleet and heard detonations. In the action the Germans lost a torpedo boat. An enemy destroyer was seen in a sinking condition, having been hit by a torpedo.

After the first violet onslaught into the mass of the superior enemy the opponents lost sight of each other in the smoke by powder clouds. After a short cessation in the artillery combat Vice Admiral Scheer ordered a new attack by all the available forces.

German battle cruisers, which with several light cruisers and torpedo boats again headed the line, encountered the enemy soon after 9 o'clock and renewed the heavy fire, which was answered by them from the mist, and then by the leading division of the main fleet. Armored cruisers now flung themselves in a reckless onset, at extreme speed against the enemy line in order to cover the attack of the torpedo boats. They approached the enemy line, although covered with shot from 6,000 meters distance. Several German torpedo flotillas dashed forward to attack, delivered torpedoes, and returned despite the most severe counterfire, with the loss of only one boat. The bitter artillery fight was again interrupted, after this second violent onslaught, by the smoke from guns and funnels.

Several torpedo flotillas, which were ordered to attack somewhat later, found, after penetrating the smoke cloud, that the enemy fleet was no longer before them; nor, when the fleet commander again brought the German squadrons upon the southerly and southwesterly course where the enemy was last seen, could our opponents be found. Only once more—shortly before 10:30 o'clock—did the battle flare up. For a short time in the late twilight German battle cruisers sighted four enemy capital ships to seaward and opened fire immediately. As the two German battleship squadrons attacked, the enemy turned and vanished in the darkness. Older German light cruisers of the fourth reconnoissance group also were engaged with the older enemy armored cruisers in a short fight. This ended the day battle.

The German divisions, which, after losing sight of the enemy, began a night cruise in a southerly direction, were attacked until dawn by enemy light force in rapid succession.

The attacks were favored by the general strategic situation and the particularly dark night.

The cruiser Frauenlob was injured severely during the engagement of the fourth reconnoissance group with a superior cruiser force, and was lost from sight.

One armored cruiser of the Cressy class suddenly appeared close to a German battleship and was shot into fire after forty seconds, and sank in four minutes.

The Florent (?) Destroyer 60, (the names were hard to decipher in the darkness and therefore were uncertainly established) and four destroyers— 3, 78, 06, and 27—were destroyed by our fire. One destroyer was cut in two by the ram of a German battleship. Seven destroyers, including the G-30, were hit and severely damaged. These, including the Tipperary and Turbulent, which after saving survivors, were left behind in a sinking condition, drifted past our line, some of them burning at the bow or stern.

The tracks of countless torpedoes were sighted by the German ships, but only the Pommern (a battleship) fell an immediate victim to a torpedo. The cruiser Rostock was hit, but remained afloat. The cruiser Elbing was damaged by a German battleship during an unavoidable maneuver. After vain endeavors to keep the ship afloat the Elbing was blown up, but only after her crew had embarked on torpedo boats. A post torpedo boat was struck by a mine laid by the enemy.

Solving the Problem of the Submarine
Burton J. Hendrick

HARPER'S MAGAZINE, October 1918

Before the outbreak of the war many Germans had foreseen the value of the submarine as a weapon. Had Germany embarked on a program of constructing submarines in the pre-war years instead of capital ships they might have won the war in the first three years—before the British navy learned to cope with this new form of sea war.

It wasn't until after the battle of Jutland that the Germans concentrated their energies upon the construction of submarines and began to produce not less than three a week. When the Germans resumed their unrestricted sinkings in February 1917, they were able, thanks to new construction, to mount a stunning sea campaign, and contrary to all reports of that period, their loss was inconsiderable.

Against this campaign the British navy had neither fortified itself by the construction of destroyers (the only type of craft at the time that could deal with the submarine), nor had it formed any plans against such an emergency.

The British destroyers were engaged in protecting the Grand Fleet. The few that were left for sea patrol were so inadequate as to make the task assigned to them a hopeless one.

Nor had the British government foreseen the coming crisis, and provisioned the British Isles in advance. In April 1917 the Germans sank a million tons of shipping, when Britain had six weeks of foodstuffs on hand. A continued rate of sinkings equal to that April would have made a British surrender by 1 November inevitable.

The gravity of the crisis was long hidden from the people in the Allied countries as the following article indicates. In all her history Great Britain had never been so near to ultimate ruin. The submarine campaign affected domestic morale, military fronts weakened, the fainthearted began their cries of "peace at any price," and treason flourished.

In desperation new techniques were devised to meet the submarine menace. An article published one month before the Armistice gave the origin and development of the underwater craft, and noted its passing as a tool that could win the war for the Germans.

Just before the outbreak of the European war the outlook for the British navy, because of the development of submarine fleets, seemed to be very dark. The prevailing pessimism found expression in the famous words of Sir Percy Scott, one of the greatest experts in the British navy.

"The introduction of vessels that swim under the water," he said, "has entirely done away with the utility of ships that sail on top of the water. Money spent on dreadnaughts is just so much money thrown into the sea."

The war had hardly been going on a month when the German navy apparently made good Sir Percy's prophecy.

The failure of the German submarine has an importance that extends far beyond the present war. That it has failed to stop the food-supply of the Allies and the transportation of troops and war materials from the United States to Europe is the great fact that will inevitably cause Germany's defeat. But the sorry showing of the submarine means even more than this, for, had the Germans succeeded in their ambitious naval program, England would have disappeared as a naval power, not only temporarily, but for all time. She would have become, to use Disraeli's phrase, merely a "Belgium at sea."

German submarines crept up to three English cruisers, the *Aboukir*, the *Hogue* and the *Cressy*, and sent them to the bottom in short order. The whole world went faint with horror when this news was received; the submarine was apparently accomplishing the task for which it had been preparing for more than a century. Under these stealthy attacks it seemed inevitable that the British navy should either retire to its harbors or, if the ships ventured out, that they should suffer the fate of these cruisers.

This dramatic event took place more than four years ago. Yet those three war-ships are almost the only ones that the British navy has lost from submarine attack. British war-ships now sail the seas as uninterruptedly as ever, and the vessels of all the Allied fleets go freely to all parts of the world, and even penetrate the waters which are thickly strewn with German submarines. Apparently the fears which disturbed the sleep of British naval experts for a hundred years had no foundation, and Sir Percy Scott, great naval authority that he is, has proved to have been a sadly mistaken prophet.

Lord St. Vincent and William Pitt said one hundred years ago, "The submarine is useless to a strong naval power, and is useful only to a weak naval power," and, as I have shown, this dictum represented the opinion of all naval experts from their day up to the outbreak of the present war. But all these authorities have been absolutely wrong. What these great statesmen should have said is the exact reverse. "The submarine is somewhat useful to the nation that commands the seas, but it is absolutely valueless in the hands of a weak naval power." The present conflict has established an entirely new principle of naval warfare. That principle is this: *a nation that controls the surface of the sea also controls the subsurface.* That is, only a navy that commands the top of the water can successfully operate its submarines.

Perhaps the greatest shortcoming of the submarine is that, after all, it is not a submarine. A war-ship that could sail continuously under the water, leaving no trace of its presence, and able at the same time to keep the surface under constant observation, would promptly put an end to all the surface navies. But that is precisely what the present submarine cannot accomplish. One of its greatest handicaps is that, when submerged, it has to depend exclusively upon electricity for motive force; it cannot use a gas-engine, an oil-engine, or a steam-engine, because these mechanisms would quickly exhaust the precious oxygen which is so essential to the existence of its crew. With an electric engine, however, the batteries need frequently to be charged, and this charging can be done only on the surface. According to Vice-Admiral Sims, the submarine can sail continuously under the surface for only forty, or fifty, or sixty miles, according to its size; after making this distance it has to rise to the top and renew its store of electric fluid. The business of charging its batteries takes about five hours, during all of which period the vessel is the prey of its enemies that are scouring the surface. Even when sailing under the surface this craft usually reveals its presence by several signs which now the experienced sailor can easily detect. The most obvious, of course, is the periscope; but, even when the periscope is not visible, the submarine, however deeply it may be submerged causes a disturbance, a kind of wake, which, even though it may be very slight, betrays its presence to the keen eye of the practised observer. A watcher on the bridge of a war-ship can usually detect this disturbance, while to a watcher in a hydroplane or other aerial craft it stands out glaringly. Because of these limitations, the submarine actually spends the larger part of its time upon the surface. It cruises around until it sights its prey, discharges its torpedo, and then dives to make its escape. The so-called submarine might thus accurately be described as a surface war-ship whose chief defensive quality is its ability to submerge.

These two facts—that it must spend a great part of its existence upon the surface, and that, even when in the depths of the sea, it cannot absolutely conceal its presence, are what have made the anti-submarine warfare so successful. For it is no longer true that there is no "answer" to this little adder of the seas. About twenty-five years ago a new type of fighting-craft appeared which caused almost as much consternation among naval men as did the submarine at the beginning of the present war. That was the torpedo-boat. This was a little reptile-like vessel, which was capable of great speed, and whose main weapon of offense, as is the case with the submarine, was the automobile torpedo. It was the function of the torpedo-boat to creep up to a fleet, especially in the night-time, discharge its explosive and then scamper away to safety. The torpedo-boat, that is, was intended to perform about the same part in warfare as has the submarine, its one great difference being that it had to make its escape on the surface, since it could not submerge. Yet at one time it was generally prophesied that the torpedo-boat had rendered the battleship useless, and there were great naval authorities, just like Sir Percy Scott in more recent times, who declared that money spent on these great fighting-ships was simply money thrown away. Yet the torpedo-boat enjoyed a very brief career; many years ago, indeed all navies ceased to build them. For, in response to this need a new type of craft arose, whose purpose was sufficiently described by its name, "torpedo-boat destroyer." Against this agile war-ship the torpedo-boat fought helplessly, for its chief weapon, the torpedo, was utterly useless against the destroyer. The chief reason for this was that the torpedo, in order to make a straight course, had to sail about fifteen feet under the surface, whereas the draft of the destroyer was only eight or nine. These ugly mechanisms, that is, almost invariably passed harmlessly under the keel. This left the torpedo-boat nothing but a very light gun with which to oppose its suddenly discovered enemy. But the destroyer was much larger than the torpedo-boat; it made even greater speed, it carried much heavier guns, and it could thus demolish it almost on sight. In a short time it had so completely rid the sea of the much feared little craft that the "torpedo-boat destroyer" lost the first part of its name and went upon all naval lists as "destroyer." There were no more torpedo-boats to destroy, and it was not worth while to to continue building them.

Thus, when the war began, the "destroyer" had one complete and splendid victory to its credit. And this war had not gone far when it appeared that it was likely to have a second victory. The successful attack by submarines on the *Cressy, Hogue*, and *Aboukir* so shocked the world that it gave an altogether false emphasis to the submarine in naval warfare. What has not made so great an impression is the more significant fact that, after these first few months, the German submarines sank practically no more Allied war-ships. Since this first great naval tragedy most of the spectacular torpedoings of war-vessels have been made by the Allied fleets—on the Turks in the Dardanelles, on the Austrians in the Adriatic, and so on. For more than four years the Grand Fleet of Great Britain has been absolutely immune to submarine attacks. How little the popular mind understands the situation is explained by the fact that most of us picture the British dreadnaughts as anchored in landlocked harbors, protected by nets, booms, and other similar obstructions. The idea that the Grand Fleet has spent four years anchored more or less continuously behind such shore protections is ridiculously false. If this popular conception represented the true situation it would simply mean that Germany had long since won the war. The fact is, however, that the British fleet, in the last four years, has had constant access to the high seas and has actually spent more than half its time cruising in the waters about the British Isles, including the areas which are supposed to be dominated by Germany. This fleet is not only master of the seven seas, but it has the utmost freedom of action. The famous policy of "attrition," by which the British dreadnaughts were to be reduced by a slow and agonizing process, has utterly failed. Instead of disappearing, unit by unit, under the attacks of German submarines, the British fleet, as Sir Eric Geddes has publicly announced, is 160 per cent more powerful than in 1914. Yet all this time the German submarines have had these magnificent targets cruising in the open sea! Why have they not disposed of them?

The fact is that the "destroyer" has practically eliminated the submarine from naval warfare, precisely as it had already eliminated the torpedo-boat. And for the same reasons. As already explained, the submarine, for the larger part of its career, travels upon the surface. But if it happens to come to the surface anywhere near a destroyer, it almost immediately meets destruction. It cannot fight the destroyer with the torpedo, for the reasons already given. If the submarine attempts the combat with her guns, the odds are again altogether against her, for the destroyer usually carries a more powerful armament than the submarine, and has the great advantage of shooting down from a high platform, whereas the submarine must shoot upward. Moreover, the destroyer is so swift—some of our new boats are making forty knots—and the submarine is so clumsy and so slow, that the latter ship always runs the danger of being rammed. Even though the submarine submerges, it still stands little chance of escaping. The destroyer can usually tell its approximate neighborhood by the disturbance on the surface, and then a depth bomb ends its career. The destroyer also knows that, once submerged, the submarine must come to the surface somewhere within a radius of fifty or sixty miles. It can therefore wireless to all surface craft within this area that a submarine is in the neighborhood, and one or more of these ships, by keeping a watchful patrol, are usually on hand when the harried underwater vessel cautiously rises to the top. These are the reasons why the British fleet is almost as safe on the open sea as in the protective harbors which have figured so largely in discussions of modern naval warfare. This armada always sails surrounded by two circles of destroyers about ten miles from the fighting ships. Between these two lines are a large number of other swift and light surface craft. Only one German submarine has ever succeeded in penetrating that screen; it did this by diving under the boats and coming up on the other side, where it was promptly rammed and sunk by a battleship.

In the early part of 1915 the German Admiralty discovered that its submarines could make no headway against a fleet which was so impenetrably screened by destroyers. It openly confessed the failure of its submarine flotillas against vessels of war by turning them against merchantships. Instead of attacking war-ships like the *Hogue*, the *Cressy*, and the *Aboukir*, the submarine now proceeds to assault the *Falaba*, the *Lusitania*, the *Arabic*, and hundreds of other vessels, and once more Germany boasted that she had found the solution of her naval program. Yet, as subsequent events have disclosed, she has not found such a solution at all. It needs no elaborate argument to show that the destroyer can screen from submarine attack a convoy of merchant-vessels quite as successfully as it can screen a fleet of war-ships. Yet Germany for a time did have a great success in sinking merchant-ships, but this success was purely fortuitous and could have had no permanent effect upon the ending of the war. Her submarines won this temporary and questionable triumph only because the Allies did not have enough destroyers to provide this screen. Great Britain began this war with 240 destroyers, and France had an entirely negligible number. The Allies needed all these destroyers to protect the Grand Fleet and to safeguard communications with France across the English Channel. If the Admiralty in 1915 had had a sufficient number of destroyers to provide an escort for the *Lusitania*, that vessel would probably never have fallen prey to submarines. But the *Lusitania* was sunk simply because the strategy of war demanded that Great Britain would send a great army to France as rapidly as possible and that the great dreadnaught fleet upon which the whole cause of the Allies hung should be held intact. England has transported millions of soldiers and millions of tons of supplies to France because these have all been protected by destroyers, and the British fleet has cruised with the utmost security because it has always been surrounded by an adequate destroyer screen. The *Lusitania* and hundreds of other ships have gone down simply because there have been no destroyers to protect them. But merely to state the case shows that Germany's cowardly success was necessarily only temporary. She could sink merchant-vessels just as long as there were no destroyers to act as convoys, and no longer. England's obvious answer was to build destroyers on the largest possible scale, and that is what she immediately began to do. In 1916 British shipyards turned out far less merchant tonnage than in peacetimes: the explanation was that they were devoting all their time to building war ships, particularly destroyers. American shipyards are now building these and kindred types on a tremendous scale; indeed, we are probably surpassing our British allies in this construction. We all remember the enthusiasm with which the British public acclaimed that fleet of fifty or sixty American destroyers which appeared in England about a month after Congress had declared war. The cause of this enthusiasm was that destroyers were the particular munition of war that was most needed just then—each one was worth more, in actual fighting value at that moment, than a dreadnaught or a battle-cruiser.

At the present time more German submarines are being sunk than are being built, and the amount of merchant shipping which is submarined is growing smaller every month. The great increase in the production of Allied destroyers is the explanation. The submarine proved useless against warships because the Allies, in the early days, had destroyers enough to interfere with their activities, and it is likewise becoming useless now against merchant-ships because the Allies, enormously helped by American shipyards, are rapidly building enough to protect these vessels also. From the beginning of the war destroyers have been convoying the Allied ships of war, and now they are with equal success convoying our transports and our merchant marine. In a year the lanes of travel will be simply swarming with destroyers and kindred craft. But perhaps one doubt still lingers in the mind. Is it not possible that Germany can build submarines faster than we can build destroyers? This question again involves great misconception. The present situation on the sea is not a race between the construction of submarines and destroyers. Germany cannot restore the equilibrium and perhaps gain the upper hand by turning out submarines on an enormous scale. Her great difficulty is that the fundamentals in this contest are working against her. A flotilla of destroyers, such as furnish a convoy for merchant-ships or transports, can sink a dozen submarines almost as easily as it can sink a solitary one. As already described, a submarine simply cannot fight a destroyer on anything that approaches equal terms, whereas the destroyer can most efficiently fight a submarine. If a single destroyer meets three or four submarines, it can lay around in comparative security and pick off one after another; it can send all to the bottom almost as easily as it can send one; its enemies can only escape destruction by running away and submerging, and, as already described, the latter process also involves great perils. Thus we may say, as a general principle, that it makes little difference how many submarines Germany possesses, provided we have destroyers enough to convoy our war-ships and our merchant marine.

Does all this mean that the submarine is valueless in warfare and is destined to disappear, like the torpedo-boat? Not necessarily, though it does mean that it has a much more restricted use than we believed four years ago. It also means, as I have already indicated, that the submarine is the weapon of the strong naval power, and not, as the British statesmen and naval experts contended for nearly a century, of the weak naval power. The last four years have proved that it is only the nation that controls the surface of the sea which can operate its submarines in any way that can make them permanently effective. Destroyers can annihilate submarines wherever they show their heads, but destroyers themselves cannot operate unless the fleet of which they are a part controls the surface of the water. Before Germany can make her underwater boats the determining factor in the war she must first succeed in driving the Allied destroyers off the sea. In order to do this she must have a stronger surface fleet than that of the Allies—that is, she must herself control the seas. In other words, the basis of British sea-power is to-day precisely what it has always been—a great preponderance in battleships. The destroyers operate to eliminate the submarine only because back of them stands a mighty force of dreadnaughts. At first this principle apparently eliminates the submarine, for the fleet that commands the surface has already done what this new type of craft was expected to accomplish; it has driven the enemy fleet into its ports and chased its mercantile ships off the seas. But it is the opinion of our greatest naval experts, such as Admiral Sims, that large sea-going submarines, attached to the Grand Fleet, could accomplish very destructive results in a sea battle. But in such an engagement they would be useful only to the navy that had strength enough to protect them against their natural enemies, the destroyers. Thus we reach this new principle of naval warfare, that the nation which controls the surface also controls the sub-surface; in other words, that the navy which rules the surface need stand in no particular fear of submarines. Isolated sinkings there may be, but these will not affect this basic principle. The position of the submarine, which has haunted naval strategists for a century, is definitely determined.

All this has a great bearing upon the problem of defending the American coast. There are still many who believe that a large force of submarines, based on Atlantic and Pacific ports, could prevent the bombardment of our large cities and the landing of an invading army. But whether they could do this or not would depend upon one point and one point only— whether we or the enemy fleet controlled the surface of the sea. If the invading nation were more powerful in dreadnaughts than we, a thousand submarines could not interfere with its operations. For such a fleet would approach our seacoast screened by rows of destroyers, which would readily dispose of any number of submarines that we could send against them. Then the enemy fleet could leisurely spend its time picking up any mines that interfered with its progress, and afterward bombard our cities and land an army. If, however, our fleet of capital ships succeeded in maintaining a more than equal combat against the enemy, and in sinking or rendering harmless its destroyer screen, then a flotilla of large sea-going submarines would have the utmost freedom of action and could probably inflict great damage. And so we can come back to the point that, despite all the modern improvements of war, the underlying principles have changed very little. The battleship, just as in the days of Drake and Nelson, still determines the issue at sea. For the United States to stop building great fighting surface ships and to depend upon submarines for coast defense would be merely to extend an invitation to an invading fleet.

PART VI

WAR BY THE PARTICIPANTS

Air Force pilots were the elite corps. They slept in beds, had hot meals, fine uniforms, and generally fought only in good weather. The sailor, if he could withstand the rolling seas, was also generally afforded hot food, clean clothes and fought in short engagements. But the infantry man, facing death daily in battles that lasted for weeks at a time, lived in muddy trenches, had cold meals when food was available, was attacked by rats and lice, and wore a wool uniform that constantly itched. He was expected to capture land, hold it, and march on to final victory.

One Man's War:
The Diary of a Leatherneck

Corporal J. E. Rendinell
George Pattullo

J. H. SEARS AND CO., INC., 1928

Getting the United States, a sprawling, unorganized country, on a war footing in 1917 was a monumental task. It was scarcely fifty years since the end of the American Civil War when Germany decided to strike, and America, with wounds still healing, was trying to forget the crippling attempt at division. When the United States declared war on the Central Powers, it had but a small standing army and navy, and a sluggish preparedness program. There wasn't even an inventory of arms or heavy weapons, nor were there any contingency plans for raising an armed force.

In Europe, where nations were bounded by strong antagonists, the young men were organized in their early childhood, and military training was mandatory. Established mobilization centers were always prepared for action. Factories and farmers knew what was expected of them in time of war, and the entire country's population was expected to work as a team under the leadership of the commander-in-chief.

France was one of the best examples of the well-organized-for-war country. The army was made up of three classes. The first line contained the youngest men who were expected to withstand the brunt of the heaviest fighting. This group was constantly under arms, undergoing active training in time of peace, and received a military education. The next class was called the reserve, composed of men aged 27 to 37 years of age. The third class contained men over 37 who were to protect railroads, bridges, and factories. At the start of World War I it took France only 16 days to mobilize the entire country, put the country on a war footing, organize all industries to supply the sinews of war, and start the trains loaded with troops rushing to the war front.

The German army was organized in a similar manner, their men separated by age in classes. When young men came of age, they had to undergo military training or hold themselves in readiness for such duty. The country was divided into districts for military purposes and from each district an army unit was raised in time of peace. The districts, each with its particular function to perform, were organized on a basis called an army corps. Little armies in themselves, they had all the branches of the military services in them—artillery, infantry, cavalry, engineers, air force and supply trains. When mobilized and ready for conflict, they contained 400,000 men aged 18 through 27. During war time, several of these corps were grouped together to form the fighting force.

Once these troops left home, other military organizations took their places and continued training courses. The recruits moved out of these new training companies as replacements to the original fighting units at the front.

When the war began the Germans had each of their army corps districts fully mobilized and ready to fight, with sufficient equipment on hand to turn out not one army corps from each district, but four!

Each year recruits were called up to serve two to three years according to the requirements of their type of service, then they were placed on the reserve list. In Germany only about 55% of the total number of men available each year was called on for military service; the balance was used in industry. But everyone was listed. When the call came, instead of 25 army corps taking the field (which is the number of army corps districts Germany had), each army corps formed three more in its district, and one hundred army corps were put into the field within a short time after the war began. This was the surprise that Germany sprung on the Allies. It required 200,000 men for the field organizations out of approximately 400,000 men in each army corps district and that left behind a reserve of 100%! This was a total of about 10,000,000 young men who could be used for active military service, with more than half of them thoroughly trained! The German High Command believed that a nation so prepared and mobilized could carve out victory after victory and end the war before any nation could train its men sufficiently to check the teutonic rush.

Americans rallied as the country galvanized into action. Men, women and children got behind the war effort working in shops, the fields and hospitals, putting up with sacrifices of food rationing, higher prices, lightless nights, gasolineless Sundays, and diminished railway and trolley services. The country even approved new taxation which it had bitterly rejected in the past.

The young American men with a brashness born of the ignorance of war's brutality rushed to enlist in the armed forces. There was a fever in the air to get into uniform, teach the Hun a lesson, punish him for the atrocities he had committed. They exuded invincibility and exhibited their intense belief in their own immortality. They would go "over there," kill the Kaiser, and make the world safe for democracy. The song, "I Didn't Raise My Boy To Be A Soldier," so popular before the sinking of the Lusitania, *gave way to songs like "Over There" and "Goodbye Broadway—Hello France."*

The young American soldiers felt themselves superior to their counterparts in the Allied forces. They respected them for what they had done, but now the Yanks would wrap up the war for them, hand them the victory they fought for so long, but could never obtain. Now America would win the war, destroy the Hun and end war for all time. This was to be the war to end all wars.

In six months the innocence of the American youth was shattered by shellfire and poison gas.

In the spring of 1917 I was working in the steel mills as an electrician and wondering when U. S. would declare war. I could not do my work for thinking about it and how I would love to go. A dear friend of mine, Dave Felch, and I talked war a lot. Gee, why don't the U. S. wake up?

We were eating dinner when we got word the U. S. had declared war with Germany. I went home to break the good news to my mother, but she couldn't see it that way. Then I went down to the Navy Recruiting Station. Sgt. in charge was being bombarded with questions as to how soon U. S. would send troops over. We signed up and was told to wait until we were called for examination. That would be as soon as they received word from Washington.

I went home for supper but could not eat much. I bought all the newspapers and read about the war. Mother and Dad came into my room and I read the papers to them. Mother asked me if I was going to enlist and leave her and Dad alone. Of a family of eight, three girls—two married and away from home—five boys—three married with homes of their own. My other brother was away working. So there was my youngest sister and myself staying home.

Poor mother how she prayed that war would end. She asked me to wait a while & stay at home. That night there was very little sleep in me. Mother called me next morning to go to work. Oh how I hated the steel mills then. Weeks and weeks I worked. Mother felt better. She thought I had given up the idea of enlisting, but she didn't know what I was planning. I told all my friends I would enlist in the Navy.

June 1st. I quit my job and went to see Mr. George Hainey, chief electrician, and Mr. Elliot Lewis, asst chief electrician, and I told them I was enlisting in the Navy. They wished me good luck and assured me my job would be waiting for me when I got back & I thanked them. Shook hands with the boys. I was the first from the line gang to enlist. Next morning I went to Cleveland and stayed for three days to get away from home until Mother stopped her crying.

June 5th. I went and registered to be drafted. Some of my friends were there and I asked them to come with me and join the Navy, but none wanted to so I went alone.

The first man I met was a U. S. Marine. He sure looked fine, too. He showed me the Marines' posters, first to fight on land or sea & I was so impressed that I signed. He was a fast worker alright. I passed the examination & then the Dr.'s examination. I was fit. I reported back to the recruiting station & he had me ready to ship to Cleveland that same night. I asked for 2 days before I could leave & he said Sure. I told him I would report in Cleveland June 7th, 1917. O.K. with him.

In the meantime my boy friends seen Dave Felch and told him I went and enlisted in the Navy. He went to town and enlisted in the Navy. I got back home and told Mother and Dad that I had enlisted and nobody was going to stop me. It was like a funeral around home.

That night I went to say goodbye to my friends. They told me what Dave Felch had done and I looked all over for him. Early next morning, June 6th, I got Dave out of bed & told him I had enlisted in the Marines & was leaving next morning. He dressed and he and I went to where he worked, quit his job, and I took him over to the Marine recruiting station and told the Sgt. what he had done. The Sgt. said he would fix it up O.K. So Dave enlisted in the Marines, but was five pounds underweight.

I asked Sgt. Fuller to let him go with me but he said "Between now and time you go to Cleveland, eat all the bananas you can hold and drink all the milk and water you can get down so you will be able to pass the examination in Cleveland." We got our orders to be at Erie station 8:30 A.M. We certainly were a happy pair of boys. . . .

June 7th.   There were fourteen Marine recruits leaving Cleveland that day. We got a dollar traveling expenses for the day. Arriving at Columbus, another party of Marine recruits joined us. The same at Cincinnatti. One of the boys got a quart of whiskey with his dollar. We nicknamed him Pork Chop. He sure was funny.

The conductor gave us a coach to ourselves. Pork Chop took a colored boy along with him who could play the banjo. The kid knew that below the Mason-Dixon line all colored & white folks separated, but not with Pork Chop. "He is riding with us, see, or we Marines will wreck the coach."

What fun we had that night. Nobody could sleep. Conductor locked us in our coach, but he forgot the windows could be broken & they were, too. Arrived at Atlanta, GA, at 9 A.M.

June 9th.   A Marine escort took us in charge, and with a report from the railroad Co. for damages done to windows. We paraded in Atlanta to boost for more recruits. We put up at the Kimble House that night, left next morning for Augusta, Ga, with another Marine escort. There was 93 in our party now & some party it was. Poker games, craps, was the order of the day. Every time the train would stop we were out, yelling and taking things from station. In one town in Ga. when the train stopped, we saw one of those old-fashion horse cars. The gang got off & started to go for a ride over the protest of the owner. We almost missed our train. Pork Chop got a bottle of corn and passed out.

We arrived at a little town and had to change trains. We saw a Marine Sgt. talking to our escort & then this Marine took charge but didn't say a thing till we started to raise a rough house & Oh, Boy, from then on we sure knew we were in the Marine Corps. He sure was tough. Offered to lick any guy in the car. He had us sitting in our seats like school boys. That .45 he had looked too big, anyhow.

Rode all afternoon. The train stopped and he yelled "Everybody out, and make it snappy." There were Marines everywhere. Dave and I wondered what place it was & one of the Marines said Port Royal. What a place! I looked around and saw a few old houses and a barge. No ocean liners. I could not believe my eyes. Thousands of boys that came after us felt the same way about it. A gov't tug come along side and our tough sgt marched us on two by two.

Dave and I were buddies, bound for Paris Island, one hour's sail from that Port Royal. We were both sore. He blamed me for getting him into such a place. Later on we had lots of fun about Paris Island.

We finally arrived at Paris Island with all the palm trees & brick barracks. There were thousands of Marines there, and the remarks they passed! "Join the Marines & see the world." "Join the world & see the marines." "Pull in your ears, low bridge. Oh, look at the guy with the face."

They knocked my hat off & pulled my shirt out. "What will you take for your shoes?" They would trip you & down you go. Well, I wasn't the only one, the other 92 got theirs too. A form of initiation. Those that came after us got theirs, too, so it's all even.

Our tough Sgt marched us three miles from main barracks to quarantine station—the little Red House without no lights & the bunks close together in one big room. It was here we stopped & was given mess kits & cups.

"All right, boys, those of you that want chow fall in line and make it snappy."

I went along with the rest. The first fellow passed out bread, the next slum. It looked as though it was made of beef stew, boiled potatoes, hash, dish rags, and a few old shoes mixed together, as close as I could figure.

I stepped up to the next guy, he spilt coffee. Spilt is right. I held out my cup & he poured hot coffee all over my hand & it certainly was hot. To make a long story short I did not have any supper, that dam fool burnt my hand & I dropped everything. I was sore. What I told him was plenty.

The rest of the boys passed up the coffee, ate, & those who didn't were on my side. No supper. I didn't bother to pick up my mess kit. Oh, what a dull place this quarantine camp is.

May 30th, 1918. Decoration Day. I was transferred to Battalion Intelligence under Lt. Marshall. At 6 P.M. orders to pack double quick and marched to Serans. Bivouacked all night out in open fields & boarded camions in morning for a rush to the front lines. The Germans have broke through and are headed for Paris. Everybody excited. At last we will have a chance to do some real fighting.

The long caravan of camions took a route that brought us close to Paris. The people in these small villages ran out & yelled "The Americans are coming." Most of these people never seen American marines & soldiers in great numbers as there were now, miles & miles of camions all loaded with American soldiers. We were kidding & joking with them as if we were on a picnic. Children were yelling "Vive l'Amerique."

On the edge of Meaux we seen refugees. The roads were crowded with them. A steady stream of carts with them. A steady stream of carts with the few belongings they could take along. Some of the peasants pulled their carts themselves because they did not have any cattle. Old women & young women with babies at their breasts. Children hung on to their skirts & and they all looked tired & were crying. Hundreds of them knelt on the side of the the road when they seen us go by & prayed for us. It sure was a pathetic scene. We were not laughing now like we were before. This was the saddest procession I ever seen.

We were on the road in camions about 33 hrs. We reached a little town & left our camions and bivouacked for the night. We could hear the artillery booming away in the distance & Boche aeroplanes was dropping bombs somewheres near.

The French were retreating. Thousands of them passed us & only the French rear guard were checking the Germans till the main body could beat it. As they went by they shook their heads & said Good bye to dear Paree. They felt sure it was all over now. The situation was mighty bad, at that. A few more miles and the Boches could shell Paris. We were ordered to move & support position in back of French.

June 2nd.   The Germans made another attack on the French, who were forced back through our lines.

June 4th.   On June third, about 5 o'clock, the enemy attacked again & then we were ordered to open fire. "Make every shot count, men. Pass the word on down the line. Do not waste ammunition."

It was machine-gun & rifle fire. How we raked the German ranks. We all took careful aim before every shot. My gun got so hot I could not touch it, so I crawled over & took one of my buddies rifles for he was done for and I used both guns, alternating as they got too hot.

The Germans kept a-coming though. Then they would stop and seemed wondering what kind of fighting is this, anyhow? At last they broke and started to beat it. A French observer reported he had never seen such accurate shooting as what we did.

Then the German batteries opened up and it was Hell sure enough. Shells busting everywhere.

That night Lt. Marshall, Pvt. Moore & myself crawled out to the German lines to find out if they were getting ready for a counter-attack. We just reached their lines & started to crawl snake fashion down into a small ravine when Marshall signalled to me & I crawled up close to him. My heart was going mighty fast—what we saw there was hundreds of Germans. It looked like they were going to attack & were just waiting for orders, so we crawled away from there to go back to our own lines & we encountered a German patrol who were scouting in our lines like we were in theirs. They never got back to their lines. We killed them all in hand to hand fighting. No attack came from the Germans that night.

Back of Lucy-le-Bocage. We were laying out in a wheat field. Runners come back from the 95th Company that the French were retreating. Major Sibley says, "Well, I can't help that. Let them go through. We have no orders to retreat."

He sent Marshall & I into the town of Lucy to see what the trouble was. A shell come along & hit a wall & knocked me into a Frenchman. I lit right on top of the frog and knocked him ten feet. It knocked Marshall down too. I got up & shook myself to see if I was all there and the lieut says, "You don't need to worry no more. You wrote home & told your mother the Germans did not make the shell with your address on it, didn't you?" I says, "Yes, but they are sure knocking next door."

Them fool Germans will hurt me yet. We got back from scouting this afternoon & I laid down in back of a tree and it seems like Fritz won't leave me rest. A shell bust close by & killed a mule and a piece of the shell tore a hole in my tree big enough to put my head in.

My feet are tired. I have not had my shoes off in four days. Also, no sleep. I have eat very little. Seemed though I was not hungry. I don't like artillery fire at all.

June 5th.   Major Sibley, Lt. Marshall & myself inspected our front line & he ordered all the companies to dig in. "Hold what you got," the Major says.

This is what we seen out there. Some of the boys was using dead marines for breast works. At another place there was a pile of them, arms and legs lying around. The Major ordered them buried. The boy he gave the order to says, "Major, they were buried once, sir, but the German's artillery blowed them out again."

Same night.   We were relieved & marched to the Paris-Metz road & camped the rest of the night in the woods.

At 4 P.M. June 6th we were ordered to leave everything but our emergency rations & we marched through open fields & were ordered to deploy in battle formation. There was 7 enemy observation balloons directing their artillery fire at us. Their range was good too.

Lt. Marshall called me over & showed me a map. "See this line here?

It's this little ravine, about 4 feet deep. Take any three men you want & go until you see Germans & find out where their machine-gun nests are and keep ahead of our line about 500 feet & send runners back so we'll know where they are." So I said a little prayer. It didn't look to me like there was any chance of coming back at all. My buddies from my old company said goodbye & wished me luck & I could tell they didn't ever expect to see me again neither.

I took Pvt Moore as the get-away man, Sleet & Pvt Howe to guard my flanks and to keep me in sight always for any signal. If I got bumped off, for Pvt Howe to take my place. We hunched along with our heads down. I spotted a bunch of Heinies around the bend of the ravine. I signalled back to Pvt Moore, he rushed back to headquarters, & then the attack started.

We stopped where we were until our men cleaned out that machine gun nest. I heard some shooting about 15 feet in back of a tree & I could not see this Heinie, so I crawled out of the ravine and walked on the side, stooping real low, & then I saw him in the bushes, so I took careful aim & fired & I got me another belt buckle.

I looked across the wheat field & there were our buddies still coming along through the machine-gun bullets. As fast as they would drop, another marine would take his place. Pvt. Howe didn't keep down and was hit.

I kept on crawling ahead & run into twenty more Germans. They were beating it for their own lines as hard as they could go & I helped them along with the old rifle. Lt. Marshall come up & said, "Form an outpost here and don't retreat, understand. We expect a counter-attack."

He sent up more men to reinforce us. The boys out in the wheat field— what was left of them—were digging in. The enemies' artillery were sending hundreds of shells into our lines. Lt. Marshall come back & stayed with us a while & said, "Guess we've got them going today all-right." He asked me how I felt and I said, "Nervous, and this waiting for a counter-attack is enough to drive a man crazy." I asked him, "Where the hell is our artillery? We sure could use those babies today."

The Germans counter-attacked in about an hour & I thought Hell had broke loose. They sent over high-explosive shells, gas shells, & their machine-guns were working overtime. Their infantry started advancing toward our line, but they never got there. My gun was good & hot from firing it so much & my ammunition was running low. Lt. Marshall sent back for hand grenades and rifle ammunition.

There were no more counter-attacks from the Germans the rest of the night, but their artillery sent over thousands of shells. Lt. Marshall stood guard while we laid down trying to get some rest.

Early the morning of June 7th he told us—"Stand by, they're going to counter-attack." We repulsed them again. After about two hours everything was quiet.

Lt. Marshall, Pvt. Trindad, Pvt. Moore & myself crawled across the open wheat field to the town of Bouresches. This town was taken by Lieut. Robertson of the 2nd Battalion with about twenty men, all that was left of his company. He took that town & he held it. The 97th Company went in & reinforced them.

When we got into the town we scouted around for German snipers. We were hiding any place for shelter. They were up on roofs, in trees, every point of vantage. We located a few and silenced them & while we was scouting around, we found a hog that the Germans had butchered, so being very hungry Lt. Marshall sent the other boys to find some cooking utensils & salt in order to have a meal. I was the chief chef & fried the whole hog before we'd had enough. The remains was put in our pockets for an emergency.

At dusk we started back for our outpost & ran across from the town through the wheat fields, zigzagging to this little ravine. The German snipers cracked down on us but they missed all their shots at us. We all felt better, because that was our first meal since May 31st—a whole week.

The other three companies of the 3rd Battalion, 6th Regiment, were having Hell in Belleau Woods. Our commander sent Lt. Marshall & myself into the woods to find out & report to him how the attack was progressing. The woods was trackless jungle and there was Germans in trees, behind woodpiles, in ravines, hid in piles of stone. We had to advance from tree to tree, looking all around to see where those shots were coming from. It was like playing Hide & Seek, only if you lost you were out for keeps.

We got back to hdqrs O. K. and reported there was Germans everywhere and the only way to get them out is blow the woods off the map with our artillery. We went back to our outposts to spend another night there. Lt. Marshall went on another scouting party.

About 1 A.M. the Germans opened an artillery barrage with hundreds of gas shells and I couldn't keep my gas mask on manoeuvering around in those bushes & the next thing I knew I woke up in a Field Hospital. I was gassed and hit in the head with a chunk of shrapnel.

My wounds were dressed and I was sent to Paris Base Hospital. There were hundreds of ambulances taking wounded back. The French people ran alongside our ambulance & gave us cookies and some were crying. They were tears of happiness as well as sadness, for the Germans were checked and their beloved Paris was saved.

In the Hospital I met a lot of my buddies and we fought the battle of Belleau Woods all over again. Among the casualties that was told were a number of my dearest friends. Pvt. Danley of Cleveland, Ohio, was one of them. While I laid there in bed & thought of how I ever come through alive, and all of the dead laying out there in the wheat fields—poor mothers, fathers & wives, they will hear the sad news your boy was killed in action, or your boy died of wounds or missing in action like Alarm Clock Bill from Chi, I forget his name, but a shell exploded under him & we found only his shoe.

Our emergency first aid station was in a little culvert under a road, four feet wide, eighteen feet long. That was where all the wounded were brought back & given first aid & they waited there for Ford ambulances that came there only at night, loaded up with wounded & drove without lights across fields to field hospital Bezu-le-Guery, about six miles in back of our lines. The wounded were transferred in G. M. C. ambulances to base hospitals & then hospital trains to the interior.

The dead out in the wheat fields near Belleau Wood laid where they had fallen. We had no chance to bury them. There were Frenchmen, Marines & Germans laying together. One place, a marine corporal & three Germans laying together in a heap, a story untold. At another place, a Marine in a prone position with his rifle to his shoulder, & finger on the trigger, just as he died. Another with his baynote [sic] still in a German and both dead. Such were the scenes they told at the hospital.

I was evacuated from the base hospital in Paris, put aboard hospital train to base hospital in Torys. Stayed there one week & was evacuated to Casual Camp St. Argonne. I called it St. Agony. It was worse than being up at the front.

I was equipped with rifle & heavy marching order & went back to the front. Arrived to battalion hdqrs 6th Marines on June 21st. They were in reserve then. Lt. Marshall come over & shook hands with me & wanted to know what happened & I told him. He said, "you are just in time, we go back in again tomorrow."

Corporal J. E. Rendinell was wounded during the counter-offensive on the Marne-Aisne front in July 1918. A shell exploded about 3 feet from him, and he picked up shrapnel in his right leg. On October 3rd, back in action, he was gassed at Champagne and spent seven weeks in the hospital.

The nurses asked him as he was lying in the ward, "When were you scared the most?"

He answered, "All the time."

The Corporal headed home February 1919 where he participated in a parade in Washington, D. C. He wrote, "We were given three citations, and the Croix de Guerre and the fourragere, the U. S. Marine Good Conduct Medal, Liberty Medal with 3 stars and a bar, sharp shooters medal, and the best of ALL, an Honorable Discharge."

Negro Combat Troops in the World War: The Story of the 371st Infantry

Captain Chester D. Heywood

ORIGINALLY PUBLISHED BY COMMONWEALTH PRESS, 1928

With the advent of the draft, the army found itself the recipient of black men for active service. Prejudice against the blacks ran high, and the new troops were looked upon as a mixed blessing. On the one hand, here was a reservoir of fighting men; on the other, integration in the armed forces was just about impossible. White men, generally, would not eat, sleep or train with blacks. While black troops had a valiant fighting record during the Civil War, little of it was written about or extolled publicly. Black servicemen were with Perry at Lake Erie, with Jackson at New Orleans; the 9th and 10th cavalry won glory at San Juan Hill.

In January 1863 when Lincoln's Emancipation Proclamation became effective, 50,000 black volunteers joined in the war before the year's end. By the time the Civil War was over, there were more than 180,000 black men in uniform. No measure of the war was more bitterly opposed than the project of arming the ex-slaves. It was denounced in the North, while in the South, the Confederate Congress threatened with death any white officer captured while in command of black troops.

With the birth and development of the Ku Klux Klan, black war veterans were sought out for floggings, lynchings, and victimized in shootings. Many of the ex-soldiers escaped to the North for safety. Educational facilities for blacks in the segregated South were almost non-existent, and the ghetto areas in the North were little better.

The black recruits in World War I were the fruits of the years of prejudice and segregation. The men were generally uneducated, many of them unable to read and write. Very few were eligible to attend Officers' Training camps, and it was a chore to find men with sufficient communication skills to serve as non-commissioned officers.

On 31 August 1917 there was organized at Camp Jackson, Columbia, South Carolina, in accordance with War Department General Order 109, The First Provisional Infantry Regiment (Colored) later designated as the 371st Infantry. The regiment was to be composed of blacks from the first draft and was to be commanded by white officers.

Colonel Perry L. Miles, a graduate of West Point, was placed in com-

*mand of this regiment on September 1, 1917 and Lieutenant Colonel Robert
M. Brambila, an officer of the regular army was assigned as second in
command. Ninety percent of the remaining officers, ironically or by design,
were from the states of North Carolina, South Carolina and Tennessee,
graduates of the first officers' training camps.*

*One of the first officers assigned to this new regiment was Captain Chester
D. Heywood. In a book published a few years after the war, he related some
of his experiences as a white officer among black troops.*

The arrival of the first draft of men was delayed by the War Department
until early October because of a shortage of labor in moving the 1917
cotton crop. On October 10 we received word that a large detachment was
on the way. Our regimental area had been ready for them for days. Each
company commander had his full complement of officers; the barracks
were in readiness even to cooks from the Divisional Cooks' and Bakers'
school.

The first intimation we had that the men had really arrived was the
sound of distant yelling, catcalling and laughter as our mob of embryo
warriors was led up through the divisional area and through the crowds of
convulsed white troops. No one who saw that outfit could keep from laughing. It was a sight never to be forgotten. There were big ones and little
ones; fat ones and skinny ones; black ones and tan ones; some in rags and
tatters; others in overalls and every sort of clothing imaginable. They came
with suit cases and sacks; with bundles and bandanna handkerchiefs full
of food, clothing and knick-knacks. Many were barefoot. Some came with
guitars or banjos hanging from their backs by strings or ropes. The halt,
the lame and the blind were there actually. Every colored derelict in certain
districts must have been picked up when the draft order was received. Our
section of the camp became as busy as a hive of bees and almost as
dangerous.

We had no non-commissioned officers from the regular army outfits
and none were ever assigned to our regiment. We had to train and make
N.C.O.'s from our own inexperienced men. The company commanders
and their lieutenants assumed all the duties of officers, and in addition, all
the duties of non-commissioned officers. They did the work of corporals,
sergeants, company clerks, mess and supply sergeants. Our work commenced at daybreak and lasted far into the night long after our tired men
were asleep. Hard work it was to be sure but it was interesting and many
humorous things occurred to lighten our burden. In the ragged hundreds
there were, of course, many clever, intelligent and educated men. These
were trained for non-coms and clerks as fast as possible.

The draft boards had advised the men that when they reached camp
they would be given brand new uniforms, consequently they left home,

even if they possessed good clothes, in things that they expected to throw away as soon as they arrived. It was many days before we got uniforms for them, and the setting-up exercises and the drills, humorous in themselves as they always are with recruits, were doubly so when almost every man was a living scarecrow. Large audiences from every section of the divisional area came to gaze upon us. The lack of a camp theater was not noticed in our recruit days for we furnished abundant entertainment, somewhat grudgingly I must admit, to the whole 81st Division.

The men were light-hearted and practically always in good spirits and were accustomed to taking orders and doing what they were told. Discipline was easily attained and necessarily strict, but just.

Clean clothes, well-cooked food in quantity, systematic exercises and drill, regular hours, plus strict but intelligent and helpful discipline, soon worked wonders. Lt. David M. Patten, as regimental athletic officer, organized various sports and teams that helped not only in a physical but in a recreational way as well. A regimental track meet was held in November, each company entering men in various events. B Company made the best company record. Smith of A Company made the best individual record. The officers soon forgot their disappointment at being assigned to the regiment and became tremendously enthusiastic about it and all its affairs. Many were the amusing incidents and many an officer saved himself from being convulsed with laughter in front of his men by bawling "Attention" and stepping quickly behind the rigid ranks.

"I remember distinctly," says one company commander, "the night that I put my newly arrived warriors into the shower baths. Very few of the men had ever heard of, much less seen, a shower and when stark-naked and clutching in their hands a cake of yellow laundry soap, a batch of twenty-five or thirty were pushed into the shower room and the water rushed down on them from the heads above, there was pandemonium. When they found that they were not hurt and that the water was warm, they yelled and danced with delight, and had to be ordered out to make room for the shivering and astonished squads waiting their turn outside.

"Nor will I forget the day that my company marched up to the regimental infirmary to have their teeth looked at by the dentists. A large room had been equipped with chairs, and as I remember it, there were two dentists, Lieutenants George N. Abbott and Aaron L. King, and their assistants, dressed in white coats and surrounded by glittering instruments on trays. I don't suppose that three men in my whole company had ever been in a dentist's hands in their lives. The company was lined up in single file, extending from the door through the hall, down the stairs, and out onto the parade ground.

"The two dentists had to look at the teeth of the whole regiment and they had evidently made up their minds that if they started to do any filling the job would not be completed until the end of the war, consequently no filling was done. The poor victims were led in two at a time, their eyes popping from their faces and beads of perspiration sticking out on their foreheads. Their mouths were pried open and the doctors, making a quick examination, commenced to yank out almost every tooth in which there appeared a cavity. Of course after the first yanks, the men began to scream bloody murder. Terror spread through the ranks in the halls and out onto the parade ground and a regular prayer meeting ensued. The poor victims waiting their turn shivered and shook, moaned and sobbed, calling on the Lord to save them from the agony that was coming.

"As long as I stayed in the room, the terror of the poor fellows kept me sober. The moment I went out into the halls to try to quell the tumult, laughter took hold of me so that I controlled myself with difficulty. I did not blame the poor devils for being terrified, for above the shrieks and groans could be heard a sound which was very similar to hail upon a tin roof—the extracted teeth being thrown into tin buckets at the side of the chairs. It was a terrible morning, and many a man was confined to quarters, having had from two to five teeth yanked out in almost as many seconds."

While administering the third "shot" of paratyphoid serum to a number of recruits at the regimental hospital, one of the medical officers noticed a rather dejected looking specimen in line and asked him, "Well, George, what do you think of the army now?" George sighed deeply and then replied, "Cap's, I done sot m'self to die, an' I don't think much about it any mo'."

By the time the elementary school of the soldier had been mastered, regular infantry equipment was issued and close order drill followed. Step by step came guard mounting, parades, reviews, signalling, route marching and the hundred and one things that a "dough-boy" has to know. The physically and mentally unfit were weeded out, and from the pick of those that remained came the various non-commissioned officers. The training of these men was no easy task, but eventually we developed excellent regimental, battalion, and company clerks, first sergeants, supply sergeants, line sergeants and corporals.

These new N.C.O.'s were hard workers and many of them quite impressed with their own importance. The drilling of their squads and platoons brought forth humorous commands and instructions. One of the sergeants forming his platoon barks: "Right Dress—Hey, you Niggahs, *slick* yo' eyes up and down dat line." Another, laboriously instructing his squad in the manoeuver, "By the right flank march," explains that the command is given as the right foot strikes the ground and illustrates it by placing his *left* foot forward. A nearby officer calls the instructor's attention to the fact that he has placed the wrong foot forward. The non-com wheels about, faces his squad and says in an earnest manner, "Niggahs, I's *doin'* it wrong, but I's *tellin'* you right!"

When it came to cooks, we had, I think, a shade on all the white regiments in the camp. Almost every one of our companies could boast a real peace-time chef.

Several times during our training, orders were received to send many hundreds of men to Newport News and other places to be used in labor battalions which were being readied for over-seas duty. Whenever these orders were received, each company commander picked out the dumbest men in his outfit and sent them along.

Our regiment, although an orphan at this stage of its existence, received the most considerate treatment at the hands of the camp commander, General Charles Bailey, and his staff. The First Provisional Regiment was offered the same facilities for training and the same interested supervision by the camp commander as regiments of his own 81st Division.

A story is told about another colored regiment that found it impossible to induce their men to sign up for Uncle Sam's war insurance. The colored boys agreed that the United States Government was reliable, but for one reason and another would have nothing to do with the insurance. Finally a colored non-com from another regiment heard of the situation and volunteered to sell the soldiers insurance.

"Listen, heah," he said in his speech to them, "if you' is insu'ed, Uncle Sam values yo' at ten thousand dollahs each. If'n yo' ain't insu'ed, Uncle Sam done stan' to lose nuthin' does de Germans get yo'. Now, Ah leaves it to yo'. Which bunch of men does Uncle Sam put in de front-line trenches where de killin' is de thickest—ten-thousand-dollah men, or de cheap colored boys?" The boys signed up—*pronto!*

During the (training) period there were constant efforts to get some of the 371st personnel away from the regiment, but Major General Bailey, who was commanding the camp, put both feet down on these attempts at grand larceny. Meanwhile the regiment was progressing remarkably. The recruits were being brought up to standard through industry which was deserving of all praise. The highly capable critics in the 81st Division admitted that 'Col. Miles's outfit was the smartest in camp.'

March 23 the Adjutant General of the Army wired (Maj. Gen. Bailey) in code to know when the 371st could move; this because its departure was earnestly desired. Colonel Miles agreed that the movement could take place within four days of orders. That gave another opportunity to send more wires as to shortages of equipment. Meanwhile Colonel Miles plunged at once into the job of packing.

Through the latter days of March many burning telegrams were sent to the Committee on Education and Special Service (the Adjutant General's department) for a sufficient clerical force, brigade and regimental. The Committee refused to do anything whereupon a sharp protest was sent which resulted in the Committee revoking its own decision. Then it suggested that a representative be sent to interview several presidents of colored colleges, widely scattered, to select and furnish needed clerks. All this when orders were expected at any moment to move, so the Committee was wired that it was at liberty to do the interviewing and selecting and when the selections were made to its satisfaction, to ship them to Camp Jackson if the regiment was still there, or if we had departed, then to France.

Within a few hours of that ultimatum, Colonel Miles made a hurry-up appearance; this because a War Department order (inexcusably assuming that he was in the Dept. Brigade) assigned him to the command of the 321st Infantry. What a ridiculous situation viewed from the standpoint of ordinary efficiency, when the records of the A.G.O. showed that Miles was Colonel of the 371st and under orders for overseas! Two hours later General Bailey had a telegram ordering the inspection and movement to Newport News of Headquarters 186 Brigade and the 371st Infantry; furthermore General Bailey (in order that there be no slip in the program) directed an inspection of the regiment and to report any inadequacies. This inspection started March 28 at 8:00 A.M. One humorous feature was the interestingly unsanitary showing made by the Sanitary Troops; for only a small percentage of the personnel showed up with either soap or toothbrushes.

An episode during the inspection (from the notes of a company commander):

The General (stopping in front of a terrified private, snatching the rifle from him, pulling the bolt and glaring into the chamber): "*That's* the way I like to see a piece kept."

Terrified private (in a burst of confidence): "Ys, suh, Gen'el, des year new toof brushes show do git in toe de cracks an' crannies."

"Toothbrushes are issued to clean teeth, not rifles," bawls the General, glaring at the Colonel, who glares at the platoon commander, who indicates by *his* glare that there is a certain private who will most probably die the death shortly.

The inspections were rigid for both officers and men. A missing identification tag or a shy tent pin brought forth the wrath of the inspectors and the threat that unless the final "look over" was perfect, we would be held up. Those were terrible days, checking and rechecking the men's belongings to be sure that *your* company would not be the one to hold up the entire regiment.

"Privit Willium Scriggs, sah, repots de loss ub two tent-pins, an' a toof brush."

"Do you want to be left behind when we start for France, Scriggs?"

"No, sah, Cap'n, I's done set ma mine on carvin' up some o'dem Bushes." [Our men always called the Boche "The Bushes."] "Ah recon ah kin fine dem missin' equipments somewheres, sah."

"Don't borrow them from anyone in *this* company, Scriggs."

"No, sah," replies Scriggs, with a smile and a knowing look that bodes ill for some luckless private or N.C.O. in an adjoining outfit.

The last articles are issued; the boxes painted, packed and stenciled. The mess sergeant is using up the last of the supplies in his kitchen. Men and officers, living near, are given twenty-four hours leave. Friends throughout the Division drop in to say goodbye and bemoan their own fate. On March 31 the following telegram was received at Divisional Headquarters:

CONFIDENTIAL
4 DNA 36 GVT NEWPORT NEWS VA 1130 AM MCH 31 1918.
COMMANDING GENERAL CAMP JACKSON COLUMBIA SC.
SEND 186th Brigade Headquarters and 371st Infantry now at your camp so as to arrive at this port between one AM and five AM April 5th, acknowledge receipt.

Hutcheson

On April 4, the bugles sound "Officers Call." The Colonel is trying not to look too well pleased as he reads the order that starts us off early next morning for the port of embarkation and France.

Before we go with the Regiment to Newport News, I want to say a word about the conduct of the 371st Infantry while in training. Camp Jackson was near Columbia, S. C., the heart of the so-called "fire-eating, Negro-hating South." There were at Camp Jackson approximately twenty-five thousand white soldiers of the 81st Division at the same time that the 371st Infantry was in training. White soldiers completely surrounded the area of the 371st and there was not the slightest friction between the two. No difficulties were experienced with the Southern authorities. Newspapers throughout South Carolina were unstinted in their praise of the conduct of the men and predicted an enviable record for them overseas.

The regiment debarked on April 23 and marched to the Pontenazean Barracks on the heights beyond the town. Here it remained to get rid of its sea legs and assemble its baggage until April 26 when it packed up and entrained.

By some oversight, the regimental commander had not been informed at the time of departure from Brest, or before, that the regiment was to serve with the French. His manner of getting this important information was unique. Our destination when we entrained was Givry en Argonne. We had not yet learned that the only thing we could be sure about the destination given in our orders was that it was certainly not the place directed therein. We later got onto the system. Shortly after starting we would get a new order directing us to the place to which they really meant us to go. It was figured, I suppose, that it would be very difficult for the Germans to keep up with the movement of French troops if the troops themselves didn't know where they were going until well on their way. As I say, we didn't know when we left Brest anything about this system, or that we had been turned over to the French, and we confidently expected to be met upon our arrival at the destination given in our orders by an American staff officer who would inform us as to billets, etc.

Something went wrong with the system that night. We were permitted to go all the way to Givry en Argonne. When we arrived we found no American officers, in fact no officers of any kind. The station master knew of no American troops in the vicinity and he, himself, was surprised to see us. Since we evidently were not expected there, the regimental commander had the train run back a few kilometers to a junction where he hoped to be able to get into telephone communcation with G.H.Q. at Chaumont.

When we arrived at this junction we found a French railway transportation officer who claimed that he knew where we were supposed to go— a short distance up the other branch of the railroad to a town called Vaubecourt. The Colonel, however, decided that he had better stop goose chasing and get himself and the regiment coordinated, so with the help of the interpreter we had aboard, he managed to get G. H. Q. on the wire. When the call went through, he told the adjutant at American Headquarters that a French officer at the station had given information that Vaubecourt was our destination. The adjutant seemed a little surprised that he had been appealed to and wanted to know why we didn't go to Vaubecourt.

"This is the first information I have had," said the Colonel, "that I am to obey any French Army officer I happen to find at a railway station or anywhere else." Then was imparted, for the first time, the very important and surprising information that we had been turned over to the French Command. That cleared up our present difficulties, and gave us many new things to think about as were quickly transported to Vaubecourt, which was to be our railhead and supply point for several weeks thereafter.

French staff officers were there to meet us, but stood aghast when they saw the length of our train and the amount of our baggage. The thousands of rounds of ammunition (Springfield) and the many other bulky, but as we had been made to understand, most essential articles of equipment that we had so laboriously acquired in order to be able to report ourselves ready for overseas service, gave those French officers anything but pleasurable thrills. They knew that it all had to be turned in and storage found for it some place.

While they worried about this, we crawled out of our cramped quarters in the "40 Hommes, 8 Chevaux" toy French freight cars. It was one o'clock in the morning and, of course, raining. We marched through the wet darkness about six kilometers to the town of Rembercourt aux Pots, where the 3rd Battalion and Regimental Headquarters found billets. The 1st and 2nd Battalions had gone the previous day to the small village of Marats-la-Grande, a few kilometers from Rembercourt.

These three towns were in the devastated district and had been partially demolished in the great German drive of 1914. They were the highwater mark of the enemy advance at that time. From the moment of our arrival the war became a reality. The ruined houses and the distant but ominous booming of the guns on the Verdun battle front gave a real meaning to our training now and brought the war home in a vivid way.

The regiment was to be fully armed and equipped as well as organized exactly as a French regiment of infantry and, furthermore, was to be rationed with the French. (We started using French rations on May 9.) This matter of rations was serious as it was likely to affect our physical condition and our morale. The French ration was quite different from ours. An exceedingly important feature of their meal was soup and the French soldier seemed to be able to make an appetizing soup from a minimum of vegetables and stocks. Our soldiers were not brought up on soups and they seemed a weak and poor substitute for the corn bread, meat stews and other substantial elements of the American ration to which they had been accustomed.

The wine was also a problem, for it was never a part of the American ration. Arrangements were made with the French to increase our sugar ration in lieu of wine.

We were considerably befuddled when we received the French order for the reorganization of the regiment. The one matter, beside clothing, that the French were not going to attend to for us was that of pay. We still had to depend on our Uncle Sam for this important item. Our men, and many of the officers, too, couldn't for a time make heads or tails out of the French money. Difficulties in the local shops, in regard to change, caused each company to have a "school of finance." The French money was laid out and explained in terms of American: "This is a franc and it's like our quarter," etc. The paper pieces—five, ten and twenty franc notes didn't look like real money to the boys and were dirty and torn like no American bill, even the worst of them. Then, too, the smallness of the French paper made it hard to realize that it represented real money.

The pay of our men, a dollar a day plus extra for overseas service, made a great showing when handed out in francs even though there were deductions for allotments and insurance. None of the Allied soldiers, with the possible exception of the Canadians, were paid as well as our men and the French were astounded at the display of wealth each pay day.

Of course our men had included in their equipment their dice ("bones," "galloping dominoes"). In most places where we billeted, until after the Armistice, there was not much to buy and pay day, consequently, saw some of the best "rollin' " you ever laid your eyes on. The first time the French saw our men sit down, roll the bones and pick up anywhere from twenty to five hundred francs at one cast of the dice, they nearly died. A day or so after pay-off most of the money in each company would be found in the possession of a few artists whose "bones" responded to special pleadings or on whom Lady Luck had smiled.

While training in this sector many of our officers were sent in small groups to the front lines for a week to live with the officers of French units, and to learn from the the details of actual life in the trenches and the methods used in this type of warfare. The first group of about twenty-five went up early in May. These officers saw more action than had been anticipated for their initial experience in the trenches. On the first night a German raid was made on the adjacent regimental sector and a considerable artillery concentration made on the subsector we were in. The next day we were spectators of an attack made, as we later learned, by two German regiments against Fort Douamont, east of the Meuse. The attack was accompanied by a great display of artillery fire from both sides. Many of us could plainly see the constant flashes of the French guns and the great clouds of smoke and dirt made by the rolling and protective barrages.

News soon reached us that the Germans were making a great attack toward the Marne and Paris, west of Rheims, and it was evident that the activities we had been observing in our vicinity were the noisy and attention-attracting proceedings of a demonstration to hold units and reserves on our front so that they could not reach the main show in time to be of help.

The German offensive toward Paris, which began May 9, was stopped only after it had crossed the Marne and made a great salient in the line between Rheims and Soissons.

On this trip to the front some of our officers went into the lines on the famous Hill 304 (Verdun sector). During instruction here, many of them went over to Dead Man's Hill and from the observatory there saw through the high-powered telescope their first Boche. They looked with interest and with awe at the heights of Montfaucon which was later stormed and captured by the 79th American division. It was from here that the Crown Prince in 1916 watched for days the unsuccessful attacks on Verdun that cost thousands of lives on both sides. From these heights of Montfaucon, the Germans had a view of the whole network of French trenches and rear areas on this front that was invaluable.

On May 25 we received the first order for men to leave for various schools and from this time on both men and officers were continually absent from their units.

Irvin S. Cobb saw our regiment in training and in his "The Glory of the Coming" he says:

"Word has come, no matter how, that Negro troops of ours were in the line. No authoritative announcement to that effect having been forthcoming, we were at the first hearing of the news skeptical. To be sure, the big movement overseas was at last definitely and audaciously under way; the current month's programme called for the landing on French soil of two hundred thousand Americans of fighting age and fighting dispositions, which contract, I might add, was carried out so thoroughly that not only the promised two hundred thousand but a good and heaping measure of nearly sixty thousand more on top of that arrived before the thirtieth. It is the Glory of the Coming all right, this great thing that has happened this summer over here, and I am glad that mine eyes have seen it. It is almost the finest thing that the eye of an American of this generation has yet seen or is likely to see before Germany herself is invaded.

"But even though the sealanes were streaky with the the wakes of our convoys and the disembarkation ports cluttered with our transports, we doubted that colored troops were as yet facing the enemy across the barbed wire boundaries that separate him from us. Possibly this was because we had grown accustomed to thinking of our Negroes as members of labour battalions working along the lines of communications—unloading ships and putting up warehouses and building depots and felling trees in the forest of France, which seem doomed to fall either through shelling or by the axes of the timbering crews of the allies.

" 'You must be wrong,' we said to him who brought us the report. 'You must have seen an unusually big lot of Negroes going up to work in the lumber camps in the woods at the North.'

" 'No such thing,' he said. 'I tell you that we've got black soldiers on the job—at least two regiments of them. There's a draft regiment from somewhere down South (author's note—the 371st) and another regiment from one of the Eastern States—one of the old National Guard outfits I think it is—about fifteen miles to the east of the first lot. Here, I can show you about where they are—if anybody's got a map handy.'

"Everybody had a map handy. A correspondent no more thinks of moving about without a gas mask and a white paper which is a pass. He wouldn't dare move without the mask; he couldn't move far without the pass, and next to these two the map is the most needful part of his travelling equipment.

"So that was how the quest started. As we came nearer to the somewhat indefinitely located spot for which we sought, the signs that we were on a true trail multiplied, in bits of evidence offered by supply train drivers who told us they lately had met Negro troopers on the march in considerable number. As a matter of fact, there were then four black regiments instead of two taking up sector positions in our plan of defence. However, that fact was to develop later through a statement put forth with the approval of the censor at General Headquarters.

"After some seven hours of reasonably swift travel in a high-powered car we had left behind the more peaceful districts back of the debatable areas, and were entering into the edges of a village (Rembercourt) that had been shot to bits in the great offensive of 1914, which afterward had been partially rebuilt and which lately had been abandoned again, after the great offensive of 1918 started.

"Right here from somewhere in the impending clutter of nondescript ruination we heard many voices singing all together. The song was a strange enough song for these surroundings. Once before in my life and only once have I heard it and that was five years ago on an island off the coast of Georgia. I don't think it ever had a name and the author of it had somehow got the Crucifixion and the Discovery of America confused in his mind.

"We halted the car behind the damaged wall of an abandoned garden, not wishing to come upon the unseen choristers until they had finished. Their voices rose with the true camp-meeting quaver, giving reverence to the lines:

> *In Fo'teen Hunnerd an' Ninety-one*
> *'Twuz den my Saviour's work begun.*

and next the chorus, long-drawn-out and mournful:

> *Oh, dey nailed my Saviour 'pon de cross,*
> *But he never spoke a mumblin' word.*

I was explaining to my companions, both of them Northern-born, that mumbling in the language of the tidewater darky means complaining and not what it means with us, but they bade me hush while we harkened to the next two verses, each of two lines, with the chorus repeated after the second line:

> *In Fo'teen Hunnerd an' Ninety-two*
> *My Lawd began his work to do!*
> *In Fo'teen Hunnerd and Ninety-three*
> *Dey nailed my Saviour on de gallows tree.*

And back to the first verse—there were only three verses, it seemed—and through to the third, over and over again.

"An invisible choir leader broke in with a different song and the others caught it up. But this one we all knew "My Soul Bears Witness to de Lawd" so we started the machine and rode around from back of the wall. The singers, twenty or more of them, were lying at ease on the earth alongside a house in the bright, baking sunshine of a still young but very ardent summer. On beyond them every where the place swarmed with their fellows in khaki, some doing nothing at all and some doing the things that an American soldier, be he black or white, is apt to do when off duty in billets. Almost without exception they were big men, with broad shoulders and necks like bullocks and their muscles bulged their sleeves almost to bursting. From the fact that nine out of ten were coal-black and from a certain intonation in their voices never found among up-country Negroes, a man familiar with the dialects and the types of the Far South might know them for natives of the rice fields and the palmetto barrens of the coast. Lower Georgia and South Carolina—that was where they had come from plainly enough, with perhaps a sprinkling among them of Florida Negroes. Our course, steered as it was by chance reckoning, had nevertheless been a true one.

"We halted a while to pay our respects to the commander of these strapping big black men—a West Pointer, still in his thirties and inordinately proud of the outfit that was under him. He had cause to be. I used to think that sitting down was the natural gait of the tidewater darky; but here, as any one who looked might see, were soldiers who bore themselves as smartly, who were as snappy at the salute and as sharp set at the drill as any of their lighter-skinned fellow Americans in service anywhere. Most of the officers were Southern born men, they having been purposely picked because of a belief that they would understand the Negro temperament. That the choosing of Southern officers had been a sane choosing was proved already, I think, by what we saw as well as by things we heard that day.

As we left the regimental headquarters, which was a half-shattered wine shop with breaches in the wall and less than half a roof to its top floor, the young major went along with us to our car to give our chauffeur better directions touching on a maze of crossroads along the last lap of the run.

"The Negro troopers we encountered now (369th Infantry, formerly 15th New York National Guard) here in the copses, sometimes singly or oftener still in squads and details, were dissimilar physically as well as in certain temperamental respects to their fellows of the draft regiment we had seen a little while before. They were apt to be mulattoes or to have light-brown complexions instead of clear black; they were sophisticated and town-wise in their bearing; their idioms differed from those others, and their accents, too; for almost without exception they were city dwellers and many of them had been born North, whereas the Negroes from Dixie were rural products drawn out of the heart of the Farther South. But for all of them might be said these things: they were soldiers who wore their uniforms with a smartened pride; who were jaunty and alert and prompt in their movements; and who expressed, as some did vocally in my hearing and all did by their attitude, a sincere and heartfelt inclination to get a whack at the foe with the shortest possible delay. I am of the opinion personally—and I make the assertion with all the better grace, I think, seeing that I am a Southerner with all of the Southerner's inherited and acquired prejudices touching on the race question—that as a result of what our black soldiers are going to do in this war, a word that has been uttered billions of times in our country, sometimes in derision, sometimes in hate, sometimes in all kindliness—but which I am sure never fell on black ears but it left behind a sting for the heart—is going to have a new meaning for all of us, South and North, too, and that hereafter n-i-g-g-e-r will merely be another way of spelling the word American.

"Coming away—and we came reluctantly—we skirted the edge of the billeting area where the regiment of Southern Negroes was quartered, and again we heard them singing. But this time they sang no plaintive meeting-house air. They sang a ringing triumphant, Glory-Glory-Hallelujah song.

For—so we learned—to them the word had come that they were about to move up and perhaps come to grips with the Bush-Germans. Yes, most assuredly n-i-g-g-e-r is going to have a different meaning when this war ends."

At the time that the regiment made its first relief and entered the trenches, a new German offensive was expected daily.

On the night of June 26, due to the strain of the expected attack and to the strangeness of their surroundings and inexperience in trench life, the men did some needless firing. This is the only time that nervous firing ever took place during the regiment's service. The French General and the French Colonel commanding the Infantry of the division inquired whether the men left the trenches during the firing. When they learned that the men, though alarmed, had no disposition other than to stand their ground, these commanders seemed at once to gain confidence in the American Negro soldier. These commanders also made inquiries about the way our men withstood the daily harassing artillery fire. They knew the effect on some of their own colored troops and until they had observed the conduct of our men, they had some misgivings.

Colonel Quillet decided to make a raid, using regular trained raiding parties from the 333rd Infantry of our division with attached officers from our regiment and the 372nd.

Captain Allen Thurman's story of the raid of August 5:

"The raid on the night of August 5 was originally planned for the middle of July and we began to train for it a few miles behind the lines, directly south of Vauquois. For some reason it was called off but later on we were ordered to a spot between Sivry le Perche and Esnes to resume training. I had two non-commissioned officers with me and there was also an officer from the 372 Infantry. There were about seventy men in all in this raid which included a French captain and two French lieutenants. The two lieutenants and myself made a preliminary reconnaissance of the sector on the night of July 24. After this we laid out miniature trenches of the sector we were to attack and rehearsed our act about two weeks.

"The attack was made at nine-five in the evening, just after dark. The area to be raided was known as The Triangle. There had been wonderful artillery preparation and we ran through the first two lines of enemy wire but found the third still intact. The barrage behind the German lines formed a perfect horseshoe and they were frantically sending up hundreds of flares. We were all kneeling in front of the third line of wire, the French lieutenant in charge was hunting for an entrance, when suddenly there were three terrific explosions in our midst which killed and wounded about thirty men. Littlejohn was killed and Kearns badly wounded. Finding that we could not get through we were ordered back to our own lines carrying as many wounded as possible.

"Everybody, including the officers, seemed satisfied that it was our own trench mortars which did all the damage although the Germans were firing at us with machine guns on our way back and one or two shells fell in our midst. The explanation the French gave us was that the heavy rains of August 5 made the trench mortars shoot short although I cannot understand why. The men were very bitter at the artillery men.

"One very significant thing happened about an hour before the raid, which may have had some bearing on it. While we were hiding in the trenches, waiting for the barrage to begin, a Boche plane, flying very low, came from behind the enemy lines, circled over us and then flew back. This was the only time that summer that I ever remember a plane flying over The Triangle. Just as we hopped off I could see the flash of a few German batteries.

I believe the shells which did all the damage were the ones which were supposed to cut the third line of wire. Whether they were firing short or we were ahead of schedule will always be a matter for argument but the fact remains that some of the wire was not cut which I think proves our point."

Lieutenant Joe Roddey's story of the Stokes mortars in the raid of August 5:

"Our trench mortar battery was organized at Camp Jackson where we did practically all of our training with wooden sticks. It was not until the last of our training that we got a chance to use the guns themselves which we fired once or twice with a small charge and dummy shells. Unable to get permanent guns and equipment, our battery was finally broken up and the various men, including myself, were sent back to their original units.

"While we were in the trenches at Hermont the regiment received four guns and I was called upon to reorganize the battery. Many of the men who had originally been in the battery were now scattered or were no longer in the regiment. We were able therefore to collect but half of the men who had made up the battery at Camp Jackson. These men we were training when we were called upon to go over to Vigneville to participate in a raid.

"Up to this time, none of our men had ever seen fired or fired the gun with the regular charge and the regular ammunition. Consequently the French lieutenant who had charge of the raid had his men fire the gun several times for us.

"In this raid (August 5) we spent one night carrying ammunition up to the outpost, and as the position which we were to fire from was on the reverse slope of the hill, we were able to put up the guns and prepare the ammunition during the following day. In this raid, because of our inexperience, only two of our guns were used and about four of our men scattered around with the other gun teams, one man to a team. The rest of the men were kept back under cover. The raid was pulled off at 9:05

just about twilight. Our signal to commence firing was the bursting of the first seventy-five shell in the territory to be raided. We were then to fire for nine minutes, a total of approximately nine hundred shells using ten guns, our target being the first line of German wire. As soon as the firing was over our men ran back to cover. The enemy artillery was quite prompt in its response and hit one gun position shortly after the men had left, upsetting the gun without doing it appreciable injury. In returning to cover we were halted several times on account of this shell fire. After things had quieted down, we went back to our positions and took out the guns. In this operation our objective was the first line of enemy barbed wire. The men making the raid reported that it was completely destroyed. We returned to Vigneville that night. The raid itself was a failure.

"This coup de main was a test of endurance for the Stokes unit. The place of the raid was about five to six kilometers from our quarters. The night before, until after midnight, we had spent carrying ammunition. We got two wagons, or really carts, and first carried the ammunition from the sector behind Le Mort-Homme (Dead-man's Hill) a mile or so to a little railroad track which used push cars. Next we moved it a mile or so on those and finally had to carry it another half mile by hand. Six shells, weighing about 75 pounds, was a man's load. We finally got our ammunition into a dugout and went back to Vigneville. Next day, bright and early, we went back to the raiding position and carried the ammunition from our dugout to our gun positions, placed the guns and prepared the ammunition for firing. We were able to do this unobserved as the day was rainy and cloudy. The trenches, however, were of red clay and filled with water rapidly so that they finally became as slippery as ice. A good portion of the distance from dugout to gun positions was up hill and by the time the men had made six or eight trips with their seventy-five pounds, they were as nearly exhausted as I ever saw them. We rested a while during the afternoon.

"That night as soon as we finished firing, we came back to a dugout to wait until after the raid was over. Naturally we were very much excited and crazy to know the results of the raid. First one of the French officers came in, flopped down on a bench and buried his head in his hands. He was the most despondent man I ever saw in my life. I tried firing some of my French at him and from the outburst that followed, gathered that everybody had been killed. Then we began collecting our guns and men as best we could, wandering hither and thither in the dark. The French lieutenant was assisting in bringing in the wounded so turned over his men to me.

"As soon as he had gone they began to yell 'Allez' while I was tearing my hair in desperation trying to find out if all of the guns and men were accounted for. I had one man missing and had to take a chance on the guns being there. Finally I calmed things down some by sending one contingent on ahead, while a few stayed to straighten things out. What mixed us up so was the fact that the French had used our guns so that no one seemed really responsible for them and I couldn't understand enough French to get any information. The missing man turned up eventually. He had been used to help bring in the wounded.

"That night going back to Vigneville our morale was of the wrong kind, if we had any. We were wet to the skin, hardly able to keep going and feeling as if our first attempt at the game have been a miserable failure. During our ten minute rest practically all of the men went to sleep.

"We were sent back to school for further instruction, where our course was interrupted to participate in the second raid."

A Poet of the Air:
Letters Written in the Aviation Service

Jack Wright

HARPER'S MAGAZINE, October 1918

As noted before, undoubtedly the most glamorous arm of the fighting armies was the Air Force, the knights of old all over again, donning armor and going out to do battle with lance and steed. Except in the Air Force, the modern steed was little more than a bicycle with motor and canvas while the lance was a machine gun.

The service was romanticized and there developed a chivalry observed by the flyers on both sides. Some would break off a fighting engagement if they suspected the opponent's guns were jammed, graves of fallen aviators were marked and decorated by their former foes, and captured aviators received exceptionally good treatment where foemen flyers could procure such treatment for them.

The Air Force was the dream of young men who had neither the bulk nor stamina to qualify for the Army or Navy. They believed they would be able to participate in the war in a clean and pleasant environment, sleep in a clean bed every night, and enjoy hot meals and drink when on the ground. There was no slogging through mud, living in trenches and under fire for weeks at a time. The Air Force represented the "ideal" way to fight a war.

The letters from a young cadet reveals the dreams and ambitions of a fighter pilot in 1917.

November 20, 1917

My darling Muzzie,

Well, your son is now a full-fledged aviator, diplomaed with the *brevet* of the French government and a member of the Aero Club of France. I don't know how far along I was in my tests when I last wrote you, but I think since then I've done a triangle first; I did it in three hours, which laid me up with fever and headache for three days. Then to-day, I did a voyage up to X, where there is an English Naval Aviation School.

It is a model camp and painted up to be decorative against the little groves that background it. Everything is clean and pretty and the whole looks like one of those little toy towns you see in windows.

They have a number of planes, well kept; students in their English naval uniforms, very cocky, and all the mechanics outfitted in the same uniforms; all of which is very different from the French camp, which is somewhat humorous by its mixture of attires and bonnets, and—peculiar for the French—barren grounds and barnlike barracks and hangars. The French only care that their machines run, which they usually do.

Back from X, where I got some English cigarettes, some English food at their officers' canteen, and a general taste of those wonderful English-gentleman manners, which seem bred into the lowest classes as well as those aristocratic thin boys who were student-aviators.

I took a little nap and some food, and was off to make up some time and landings of which I was short. This done, I walked into the "pilotage" very proudly and expected the clouds to part, the sun to rise, and the stars to dance.

Instead, the secretary exclaimed, "Another one!" And thus I was knighted with my pilot's license.

After signing some papers, I came back to get my suit pressed for Paris, which was the first actual joy and realization that I was at last an aviator.

How the first days of double-control work back in September seemed far away! Yet from the time I decided to join, in July, to now it has been about a third of a year. Never has a third of a year rushed past my bewildered eyes so rapidly. It passed like a comet, furious and glowing. It has been a wonderful period of youth, of adventure, of romance, that which is now the ideal I strive to attain. Thank God I am living up to my dreams. Thank God my dreams are not fancies, are not dreamt in vain, and perhaps the forgings of a real mind and the real prospect of a man.

Love,
Jack

I've gone through the school without breaking a thing—rather clever—eh, what?

December 18, 1917

Dear, Dear Nana,

As a true grandmother you're saying now and then, "Oh, I'd like to know just what he *is* doing!" And then you blame the censor, poor man, and afterward you blame the Kaiser and then the whole worldly system of things that so veil the exact and every movement of little Jack—how he washes his teeth or whether he does at all.

Well, I get up in the morning by moonlight. We never wash. After roll call I immediately race to get first in the breakfast line, and usually find fifty or so ahead of me. Before breakfast is over I must race back, climb up into my bunk, and turn into chambermaid. As the last blanket is folded I jump down from my bunk, into my flying clothes, and out to formation, with the moon still shining and the winter's night on full blast. Then I march to the field of my class, where we build a fire in a tent and sleep until smoked out; by that time our teacher and the planes will almost have arrived; that is, we'll only have another half-hour to wait.

The morning passes between stamping our feet in the snow and flying through it up in the air. The flying is wonderful when you don't have too much of it; so I'm enjoying it immensely just now. Everything becomes white—the snowy ground and roofs, the sky, the silver painted machine. Here and there tints of rosy clouds or veils of violet or amber gently spread their warming glow across the vast white world you fly through. It is much prettier than summer flying. Things are quieter and more serene, whiter and more saintly.

Flying appears, also, when everything is white, more in its natural aspect—that of everything being a sea through which you swim as serpentine as a fish, or a sky through which you sail and dive. No earth and wheeled vehicles seem to exist.

Well, then we march back again and equally again do we race for grub, wash our dishes, and go out for a class on motors or archeology or how to make chocolates. Then about the time you are telling Tee to stop clawing your dress while you serve tea, I am entering that famous rendezvous for all the camp, where, after work-hours, we gather (or push, rather) to the Red Cross counter to buy tea and sandwiches and spread all the last rumors of the camp, of how the Germans have nearly taken Paris, or the opposite.

If I have any extra time I use it most valuably in washing. If not, I don't wash; perfectly natural, perfectly simple. After dinner I either go to the Y.M.C.A. to hear that the band has fallen sick, or else I roll into bed as fast as I can arrange the blankets.

So you see your Jacky tumbles from here to here throughout the day, from formation to classes, and at last back to bed for a night of beloved rest and dreams of home—happy Christmas visions, and silent thanks for the little comforts, such as the sweater and mitts, that are sent from "back there."

Merry Christmas!
Jack

December 27, 1917

Darling Muzzie,

It is awful the way the days go by without my writing you, but my time is very filled with formations and waiting in line and all the rest, which, though it does not accomplish much, nevertheless takes the time away.

At noon I have no extra time and at night a few tired moments are all. Your little diary came the day before Christmas. I was on the point of buying just such a little note book.

Sylvia sent me three huge packages of cigarettes, chocolate, plum pudding, gloves, soap, socks, a cigarette case, preserves, and everything fine that shops could turn out.

As a climax, several letters blew in from you and one from Nana.

The next day, Christmas, Mrs. F.'s outfit came in cleverly wrapped in pictorial supplements of the Sunday papers. So far, lucky boy, I have received no useless presents, excepting that I don't need any more sweaters.

Christmas Eve I heard Mrs.—sing at the Y.M.C.A., and listened to taps afterward as soldiers wended their way back to the different barracks through the silent, snow-covered streets of the camp. Night covered all, most conventionally, and the Christmas Eve seemed but a myth. The only difference it held this first time away from home, this Christmas Eve at war, was that I could get up when I felt like it, instead of 5:30 the next morning.

Christmas morning, when the boys woke up, gave one a sight gladder than any Christmas morn yet. They hollered, as six-year-olds, from blanket to blanket, up and down through the bunks and over the trunks, "Merry Christmas!"

The next day I was up by moonlight again and off to fly. I was at last on those beautiful, dear, sweet, beloved coffins called the modern *chasse* machine. Delicate to handle and therefore dangerous, but powerful, fast, conquering, and therefore Paradise! Months had I watched, here and there and at Tours, experienced and glorious pilots rip up the air with them and in a second darting from one corner of space to another, doing impossible acrobatics and conquering the greatest forces of the world—those of the unknown infinite, so that as I sped through the air for the first time on them I was almost purring with the silent joy to know that at last I was doing what my idols had done—that I was piloting these little devils—these little beauties.

December 28, 1917

This morning we flew while it was snowing, and I certainly realized it. Bumpy! Oh, how bumpy! Whiffs that tickle your nerves till they're silly.

This afternoon we had a lecture, and most of the time off, so I'm sitting cuddled up in my upper berth, scribbling and reading and smoking and feeling like a comfortable, leisurely clubman, perfectly satisfied with life. I caught a chance to wash, so I feel better still. I expect your little *souvenirs de Noel* this evening; in fact, I've made a bet on receiving them.

My vanity is quite tickled to tell you that the government has considered me worth being a First Lieutenant, so—well, I am one. I feel like a Christmas tree, for I'm buying all sorts of cute gold cords and silver bars and things. On the side, though, it's rather nice to attain that position at nineteen.

Most devotedly, your 1st Lieut. A.S., S.O.R.C., A.E.F., U.S.R., U.S.A.

Jack

January 7, 1918

My Very Dear Muzzie,

I am still flying *tour de piste*, but soon hope to leave those miserable, monotonous classes of landing—going up and landing—for the spiral class. A good spiral is the hardest acrobatic feat, and much fun is promised to break up the long hours we stand around in the snow, waiting.

Every one that goes up for a spiral always entertains the crowd, so I'm looking forward to a good time. After that my course is—altitude, acrobatics (in general), group flying, reconnaissance and duel training. Then I'm shipped to the front. Oh! the blessed day! Every one is dying to get there.

There have been some accidents lately, each of which should have been fatal. One was, but the others escaped miraculously. Jack S. should have been killed yesterday, but he escaped with a broken arm and a broken shoulder—probably it will put him out of flying. Anyway, it puts him up for a couple of months, thereby spoiling many of our chummy plans.

It also makes quite a hole in my existence to see my daily comrade taken away for the rest of the war. He had my teddy bear suit on and it's hopelessly ripped up from the smash.

The camp life has a great deal of beauty about it. The barrack life is beautiful in that you are in immediate touch with the crude necessities of life—not the luxuries—barren food, long beds, a fire. It is beautifully rude and ugly—it is barbarous; it expresses strength and force; it is in true harmony with war.

The main thing now is to get to the front. As soon as I get there I will begin to live. I intend to have a little home there, charming friends, writing and drawing spasms, luxuries and some independence, with the added thrills of my daily adventures against the Huns. All my present is in that future, despite the idiocy of being the least bit in the future in this game. But here, a great deal of my present is made on planning the near future which I can permit myself, seeing that there is more reliability in futurity while yet in the stages of training.

I don't suppose that the war could possibly have affected the character of the people at home; it's too new and too far away. I suppose that the teas are just as frivolous and the dinner parties just as indifferent. I can see the gatherings in salons and studios surrounded by their luxury and intellect and chatting and discussing just as before, flirtation and art in the dim lights or the gay lights midst a rustling of gowns and a tinkling of cups and glasses. Everything is undoubtedly the same. You all seem to be passing through this world crisis, in which men agonize, hope, and die, without more than a political, a very scant tangency to it.

Over here the people are very changed. True that their gatherings are still chatty and gay and intellectual, but there is always the influence of the conflict at the gates of Paris, as though it were just behind the very curtains of the particular salon or studio. There is always keen comprehension and appreciation of the struggles of the days and nights and years, and always a ready heart of sympathy for the worshiped men who are on leave. You notice the difference if you watch closely; you notice it everywhere, even in the cold hearts of the café girls, even in the way people walk to and fro along the boulevards. There seems to be a spirit of friendship unknown to peace-times, and it draws you closer to the gray houses, their balconies and their windows; to the towers and curving bridges—to all the silent smiling soul of Paris, the city of war. There is where I hold a great deal of pity for you all at home. You are not finding the new spirit that the war has brought.

Beans are Sunday's charm here, and I must join the mess-line to wait some more; then I wait in line to wash dishes. Ye gods! how I'm sick of washing dishes! Then I come back to get ready to wait some more. Now you do a little waiting, too, until my next letter.

Lovingly,
Jack

January 15, 1918

Very Dear Muzzie,

Well, I expected to tell you I would be in "spirals" by now, but on my last landing of the *tour de piste* class, having a machine that bent to the left, it twined on me when the wheel touched and broke a piece or two. It is the first time I have ever broken anything, which is a nice record.

One's first forced landing is disagreeable to have when you're on a "15"—these modern machines—especially when, as the motor "poops" on you and dies, you look over-board on nothing but vineyards stretching a network of wires under you so to better catch your wheels on coming down and "flip" you.

However, I "pancaked" so as to touch all points at once and not roll ahead, thereby smashing down on top of the wires instead of swooping into them. As a result not a scratch was made to the machine and I was very happy.

Another friend fell yesterday. His face is all done up in bandages with a hole for his mouth. But he is cheery and glad to be alive.

As I look about me, I find the bunk opposite empty. He's laid up from a fall. The bunk across the way, the same: the bunk below, the boy was shot and badly laid up. The bunk next to me—the lad is laid up in the hospital, too, and "laid up" means for three months over here, for after your physical injuries you have to cure your nervous system by going to Nice or somewhere.

Much love to you,

Jack

January 16, 1918

My Very Dear Mother,

What awful news I have received! Ye gods! For reasons I cannot tell you, it appears that all of us advanced men in *chasse* work are to be doomed to drive those awkward, elephant uninteresting machines of *reconnaissance* and *artillerie reglage*. I, who counted so much upon speeding through the fire of combat on a small, fast duel machine, and setting out independently in the skies to make my reputation, am to be tied down to directing artillery fire and other such long, monotonous, negative, unfighting drudging. It will only be for this spring, but that means three months, and three months means a lot in this game—they are a lifetime with us—a lifetime in two ways.

Not counting the regret of giving up this duel-training (*chasse*) which held my heart so intimately, not counting the insipid training for the rest of the winter, or those craft as big as houses with front verandas and just about as capable of flying.

This sport is beginning to show itself up, too. It is, in short, a little world, somewhat aerial, and very fast turning, where that which takes years to be done in civilian life here takes a day, an hour. Your plans are broken, your friends disappear, and your intimate chums are scattered away from you as soon as you have gained their friendship.

The scenery is shifted constantly, rapidly, in the climax of the act—in its very beginning—just before its wondrous end.

To-day the wind is blowing sixty an hour and the clay mud is feet deep; so we're not exactly flying—just a lecture now and then, so you won't go entirely mad. But believe me, with all that I so sincerely and constantly regret in my exile, I would never, for any fortune, change places and go back again to what I left—to all the art and luxury and sympathy I left behind. Never, never! And there, in spite of all war's trickery, I'm just devilish enough to have a wee hope in the near future; in fact, I firmly intend to sound life to a very deep degree. That is a great deal, though without *chasse* work it is not enough. Perhaps, too, I'll come through to at last be able to take up *chasse* work when this summer it will be possible; then I'll have my chance, for I'm with the first American aviators in France against the Hun.

Now, dearest woman I know, do not take war so seriously. You are blessedly far away from it all, so don't bother to try and hypnotize yourself about it. Just enjoy, enjoy, enjoy—all the joys and laughter the world contains, for it will make me happy to catch the feeble echo of your laugh through the lines of your letters—your dear, sweet letters,

I am your servitor and son,

Jack

January 19, 1918

My Dearest Mommie,

I have just received my active orders. I can wear all the paraphernalia, silver bars, gold-and-black hat-cord, black braids, gold silk braids, collar decorations and also the gold aviation eagle on my heart. I can dress up to beat the Kaiser, and, more thanks, have somewhere to go.

Oh yes! I've had my first salute—a beauty, *just the way these privates ought to!!* I, who in the French army as *poilu* covered with dust on a banging truck, and in the American army was a blinking, gawking door-keeper, jumping up and down to attention for second lieutenants and being kicked from the first to the fifth flight by thousands of corporals, I am now ye honorable and much-respected, much-waited-upon First Lieutenant and pilot. I'll have to grow a beard, too, for I look like a baby.

One private guessed immediately that I had just put on my stripes, probably because I had been moving a garbage can with him half an hour previous, and as he saluted a broad grin spread across his tough cheeks— it was beautifully sincere and I couldn't help laughing.

All the boys, as I walk down the barracks, wish me good luck, stand at attention, and then jump on me and muss me all up. Confound these lower creatures! I must move immediately to the officers' barracks.

The next thing to do, now that I'm a gentleman again for the first time in many months, was to go and have tea. Imagine having tea, but such is the gentle and civilized custom of the officers; so off I went to the Biltmore—which is the Red Cross. Now the Red Cross is divided distinctly in two. In front of the counter a long line of soldiers and cadets wait to buy a tin cup of coffee and a sandwich, to the worn-out needle of a phonograph. Behind the counter, laughing as easy life permits, sit the favorite privileged few—the officers sipping chocolate, dipping into choice *confitures*, and being waited on with chinaware—that they do not wash afterward, either— at a few long white tables surrounded by a whirligig of white-and-blue nurses.

The tea was just exquisite—a couple of friends, newly commissioned, were with me. It was the first time we had been clean in two months, so we felt as in tuxedos and were immediately very affected in voice, awkward in gesture, and insipid in conversation—fluent chat, such as officers—the higher wits—*always* are supposed to be keeping up among their intellectual circles. Then, oh, wonderful sight of brilliant chandeliers and glistening tables of feasting, I walked over to the officers' mess, embarrassed and wondering why I wasn't banging my good old mess-kit in a line unending, such as I had always done for the last nine months. Decidedly I had been enthroned, blessed by God, sought by fortune, transported, for some vague but important merits, high into the celestial on the kind wings of smiling, suddenly visible angels from heaven—that is, Headquarters.

I ate on china; I ate a feast and I ate without the forecast of standing in another line out in the cold night to wash a greasy tin dish in cold water and freeze my hands all the way back home to the barracks.

More still, German prisoners ran around to get the platters and see that I was served. The sergeants of the mess addressed me, "Sir." The privates stood silently at attention, daring not to utter so much as the title "Sir" lest it disturb my tranquility of thought.

The next morning I was awakened by the rush of my friends to stand at roll call at 5:30 A.M. I grunted and rolled over to doze off another hour or two. Then I proceeded to dress, received the compliments of the morning from the sergeant who, the night before, had had me working on hands and knees all over the barracks floor, and when he asked me if I would leave everything straight in the bunk when I left for the officers' barracks, I merely remarked, "I'm not living here any more."

Then I brought my baggage over, after a luxurious breakfast, to the new barracks, where an orderly opened the door for me as I entered. At noon a chicken dinner with a fine dessert awaited me, and I sat opposite the next room, where I could watch with a broad grin the boys I had left standing in the winding, serpentine, sleepy line to receive their Sunday beans.

Just heard of a witty trick done recently by a friend. He was doing acrobatics when he went into a *vrille*. That's very bad near the ground if it happens accidentally; he came out but to go into another—the ground coming up like lightning—when he kept his calm enough to notice an *aileron* flapping, useless, and traced the break back to a missing bolt, whereupon he—marvelous brain, he must have divine control—undid his belt and stood up a little full in the dash of a death-spin, a sure, fatal fall, grabbed the disjointed piece and held it together; with one hand over his head while with the other he made his landing safely.

He is a hero whom not only the papers ignore, but most of the camp. He has the compliments of us aviators, and I can assure you that means something.

Great joy! To-morrow morning I enter spirals; that will be the beginning of more rapidly succeeding and more vital events of interest; that is, more dangerous slips and drops to be caught up in true, more businesslike, warlike flying.

Now good-by for the while.

Very lovingly,
Jack

January 22, 1918

Dearest Dear,

Just a word to tell you how my world is turning around. It is turning very rapidly, for I have just been doing spirals yesterday. That is to say, you're hung up in space some three thousand feet, when you cut down the motor and start. For a second everything is silent, as the silence of night when you're walking toward a precipice, as the silence just before the hand strikes down to plunge in the dagger. Just then I tried to think of my instructions—absolutely useless. I was thoroughly stage-frightened, but I was nearing the precipice, the dagger was quivering to plunge down, so I started. I pulled the plane over in a perpendicular and down; then back a little on the stick to make her spin lightly, and off she went, the clouds whirling by as in a cyclone—a war of the gods and the wind roaring at me like a continual fog-horn and pulling on me hard. Round like a top, down, down toward the earth, as in a falling merry-go-round, the plane led me like a bolt, through space.

I remember vaguely acknowledging that if the bus did smash, it was nevertheless, a great experience, and that was the height of the game. It was a great adventure, midst the wild, invisible forces of the clouds, high up from other humans. It seemed, so to speak, like when the movie shows angels sweeping by diagonally in the heavens, with the clouds whizzing around.

The spiral was increasing in rapidity on my left, rather behind me, for I was turned to the right, watching the needle on my tecometer, pushing with my feet, accordingly, and trying to convince my hands, in spite of them, to pull back farther and over, so as to make the plane spin tighter and on a perpendicular; however, my hands refused to go far. I just couldn't make them.

By then the wind was roaring so loudly and the plane whizzing me around so fast and downward that I started to wonder whether I was in a *vrille* or not. (Fatal if you don't come out of it.)

I looked over my left shoulder and saw the houses spinning around regularly, and decided all was well; by chance I glanced over my right shoulder at the clouds. O-o-o-oh! that empty feeling.

I looked back inside the machine again and recovered promptly and with another one thousand and one prayers to something, some one, somewhere. Looking over at the sky when you're spinning seems to create a cone with the fat end in the bottom of the sky. Anyway, you can wager no sailor, even of a submarine would take more than one look at it.

Enfin! I came out ages later from the circle I was supposed to reach without pulling on the motor again, so just had to. When I felt the machine grip earth again I felt as though I had just finished a heated debate in the

Senate, and won; had just finished a complicated trial for suicide, and won; had just finished a desperate suit for a star in the century, and won.

I immediately was sent up for my second, which is a good plan while you've still got the confidence left in you. My second, I felt, was better, so that when I came out of it it was as though I had held my breath under water a long time. I just burst loose and sang and shouted at the top of my voice in English, French, and Yiddish. On my third spiral, when coming out, I was evidently dangerously flat, for my propeller just about stopped, and then did, which cut off the chance of pulling on the motor again, which I needed to, being over a forest a half-mile from where I should be. (The wind had drifted me.) So I tried to crank the propeller—not that I got out and did it! I dove down a couple of hundred feet, and the force of the wind, just as a private chauffeur, cranked it up for me. I pulled on the gasoline; she winced, and the motor gave a whoop and a pull and up I skimmed over the trees.

I might add, too, that in between the spirals, yesterday, I saw the last twirl that was the farewell second in life of a boy in the class next to mine. I don't feel heartbroken for him so much as for the mother back home.

The letters abruptly end with these words of tragic coincidence. Two days later an official telegram brought the news of the young aviator's last flight.

Fighting the Flying Circus

Captain Edward V. Rickenbacker

FREDERICK A. STOKES, CO, 1919

Flyers who survived their arduous, rigorous training found their way to the front lines and fought the war in the air the best way they could. In the early days of the conflict, pilots were simply observers reporting on troop movements or locations of artillery; or they tossed bombs from their cockpits at enemy troops. If they were approached by enemy planes, the pilots would resort to their side arms, firing generally with little or no effect. Eventually a machine gun was placed on the top of the wing so that the bullets could clear the propeller, and the pilot wouldn't shoot himself down. Later, the machine gun was placed on the cowling when it was learned how to synchronize the firing of the guns with the rotating propeller. Larger models sported a cockpit forward of the propeller with a free swinging machine gun that could be aimed in many directions.

Some of the planes carried two men, some four; bombers on occasion carried more, but the real knight of the skies was the pilot in the single seater pursuit plane. He was the hunter, the stalker, the killer, living from day to day, from mission to mission. It took a special breed of man to engage in this new kind of warfare where his life or his death depended solely on his skills and his machine.

But this was to be a temporary phenomenon according to Orville Wright, one of the brothers who invented the airplane. In an interview with Collier's Weekly *magazine in 1917, he predicted, "The greatest use of the airplane eventually will be to prevent war. Some day there will be neither war nor rumors of war, and the reason may be flying machines. The airplane will prevent war by making it too expensive, too slow, too difficult, too long drawn out—in brief, by making the cost prohibitive."*

The warriors of the air captured the imagination of all peoples. When an aviator shot down five enemy planes he became an "Ace," making it an occasion for the press who descended upon the flyer for pictures and story. The young man was an instant celebrity, his likeness reproduced in newspapers and magazines around the world.

Only the British shielded their airmen from this type of publicity. It was handled in the same manner governing the publication of submarine sinkings. They argued that the naming of British, Canadian and Australian aces would direct the attacks of German aviators against the most useful men in the British forces.

The outstanding aces in the French forces who received much press were George Guynemer, a mechanic who became a fighter pilot and gained the reputation of "The Fighting Machine" (subsequently he was shot down in flames) and the ace of aces, renowned at the time, Lieutenant Rene Fronk. When the war ended, Lieutenant Fronk was credited with 75 official victories, and an additional 40 "unconfirmed" downed planes. His quickest work was shooting down three German planes in 20 seconds. On May 8, 1918 he brought down six airplanes firing only 56 shots!

The Germans, too, had their air heroes. Captain Boelke had developed a maneuver whereby he hid in the clouds, and then, diving down on an unsuspecting enemy, blew him out of the sky. His speed carried him past his opponent in a rush so that if he missed, he was too far away to be engaged in battle. He seldom re-attacked, and ran up a respectable score of kills. The grand air hero of the German people was Baron Manfred von Richthofen who flew a plane flamboyantly painted flaming red, and led a squadron of gaily colored planes known as "The Flying Circus." He started his war career at the age of 20, an officer in the Uhlans, but the cavalry was too dull for this young man. He had been a hunter of animals since childhood, and he missed the personal element in modern war; the opportunity of attacking a man and killing him, enjoying the risk of being hunted by another man.

Baron von Richthofen was credited with 80 downed planes! Ironically, he was shot down while pursuing a novice fighter pilot who was fleeing for his life. The Baron, intent upon his kill, wasn't paying attention to his rear as Captain Roy Brown, a 24-year-old Canadian, sick with war fatigue, and living on milk and brandy for several weeks, came down behind Richthofen, and brought the war career of the illustrious "Red Baron" to an end.

The death of Richthofen was mourned by all of Germany, and Chief of Staff Major General Erich Ludendorff, upon hearing the news said, "He (Richthofen) was worth as much to us as three divisions."

Three fighting pilots from the United States received broad coverage when they attained the status of "Ace." Quentin Roosevelt (the son of Theodore Roosevelt), Raoul Lufbery and Edward Rickenbacker were covered extensively by the news media making them international heroes. Roosevelt and Lufbery were killed in action, but Rickenbacker managed to get through the war without a scratch, and ran up a score of 26 confirmed victories.

Captain Edward Rickenbacker, commander of the 94th (Hat in the Ring) Squadron, started his military career as a private in the Infantry; a driver for General Pershing!

The Captain's memoirs, published in 1919, are a sensitive record of the insecurities, fears, and emotions of a fighter pilot that could very well apply to every aviator who participated in the war.

It will be noticed that my preparation for combat fighting in the air was a gradual one. As I look back upon it now, it seems that I had the rare good fortune to experience almost every variety of danger that can beset the war pilot before I ever fired a shot at an enemy from an aeroplane.

This good fortune is rare, it appears to me. Many a better man than myself has leaped into his stride and begun accumulating victories from his very first flight over the lines. It was a brilliant start for him and his successes brought him instant renown. But he had been living on the cream at the start and was unused to the skim-milk of aviation. One day the cream gave out and the first dose of skim-milk terminated his career.

So despite the weeks and weeks of disappointment that attended my early fighting career, I appreciated even then the enourmous benefit that I would reap later from these experiences. I can now most solemnly affirm that had I won my first victory during my first trips over the lines I believe I would never have survived a dozen combats. Every disappointment that came to me brought with it an enduring lesson that repaid me eventually tenfold. If any one of my antagonists had been through the same school of disappointments that had so annoyed me it is probable that he, instead of me, would now be telling his friends back home about his series of victories over the enemy.

April in France is much like April anywhere else. Rains and cloudy weather appear suddenly out of a very clear sky and flying becomes out of the question or very precarious at best. On the 29th of April, 1918, we rose at six o'clock and stuck our heads out of doors as usual for a hasty survey of a dismal sky. For the past three or four days it had rained steadily. No patrols had gone out from our aerodrome. If they had gone they would not have found any enemy aircraft about, for none had been sighted from the lines along our sector.

About noon the sun suddenly broke through and our hopes began to rise. I was slated for a patrol that afternoon and from three o'clock on I waited about the hangars watching the steadily clearing sky. Captain Hall and I were to stand on alert until six o'clock that night at the aerodrome. Precisely at five o'clock Captain Hall received a telephone call from the French headquarters at Beaumont stating that an enemy two-seater machine had just crossed our lines and was flying south over their heads.

Captain Hall and I had been walking about the field with our flying clothes on and our machines were standing side by side with their noses pointing into the wind. Within the minute we had jumped into our seats and our mechanics were twirling the propellers. Just then the telephone sergeant came running out to us and told Captain Hall to hold his flight until the Major was ready. He was to accompany us and would be on the field in two minutes.

While the sergeant was delivering the message I was scanning the northern heavens and there I suddenly picked up a tiny speck against the clouds above the Forêt de la Reine, which I was convinced must be the enemy plane we were after. The Major was not yet in sight. Our motors were smoothly turning over and everything was ready.

Pointing out the distant speck to Jimmy Hall, I begged him to give the word to go before we lost sight of our easy victim. If we waited for the Major we might be too late.

To my great joy Captain Hall acquiesced and immediately ordered the boys to pull away the blocks from our wheels. His motor roared as he opened up his throttle and in a twinkling both our machines were running rapidly over the surface of the field. Almost side by side we arose and climbing swiftly, soared away in a straight line after our distant Boche.

In five minutes we were above our observation balloon line which stretches along some two miles or so behind the front. I was on Jimmy's right wing and off to my right in the direction of Pont-à-Mousson I could still distinguish our unsuspecting quarry. Try as I might I could not induce the Captain to turn in that direction, though I dipped my wings, darted away from him, and tried in every way to attract his attention to the target which was so conspicuous to me. He stupidly continued on straight North.

I determined to sever relations with him and take on the Boche alone, since he evidently was generous enough to give me a clear field. Accordingly I swerved swiftly away from Captain Hall and within five minutes overhauled the enemy and adroitly maneuvered myself into an ideal position just under his sheltering tail. It was a large three-seater machine and a brace of guns poked their noses out to the rear over my head. With fingers closing on my triggers I prepared for a dash upwards and quickly pulled back my stick. Up I zoomed until my sights began to travel along the length of the fusilage overhead. Suddenly they rested on a curiously familiar looking device. It was the French circular cocard painted brightly under each wing! Up to this time I had not even thought of looking for its nationality, so certain had I been that this must be the Boche machine that had been sighted by the French headquarters.

Completely disgusted with myself, I viraged abruptly away from my latest blunder, finding some little satisfaction in witnessing the startled surprise of the three Frenchmen aboard the craft, who had not become aware of my proximity until they saw me flash past them. At any rate I had stalked them successfully and might have easily downed them if they had been Boches. But as it was, it would be a trifle difficult to face Jimmy Hall again and explain to him why I had left him alone to get myself five miles away under the tail of a perfectly harmless ally three-seater. I looked about to discover Jimmy's whereabout.

There he was cavorting about amidst a thick barrage of black shell-bursts across the German lines. He was half-way to St. Mihiel and a mile or two inside Hun territory. Evidently he was waiting for me to discover my mistake and then overtake him, for he was having a delightful time with the Archy gunner, doing loops, barrels, side-slips and spins immediately over their heads to show them his contempt for them, while he waited for his comrade. Finally he came out of the Archy area with a long graceful dive and swinging up alongside my machine he wiggled his wings as though he were laughing at me and then suddenly he set a course back towards Pont-à-Mousson. Whether or not he knew all along that a German craft was in that region I could not tell. But when he began to change his direction and curve up into the sun I followed close behind him knowing that there was a good reason for this maneuver. I looked earnestly about me in every direction.

Yes! There was a scout coming towards us from north of Pont-à-Mousson. It was about our altitude. I knew it was a Hun the moment I saw it, for it had the familiar lines of their new Pfalz. Moverover, my confidence in James Norman Hall was such that I knew he couldn't make a mistake. And he was still climbing into the sun, carefully keeping his position between its glare and the oncoming fighting plane. I clung as closely to Hall as I could. The Hun was steadily approaching us, unconscious of his danger, for we were full in the sun.

With the first downward dive of Jimmy's machine I was by his side. We had at least a thousand feet advantage over the enemy and we were two to one numerically. He might outdive our machines, for the Pfalz is a famous diver, while our faster climbing Nieuports had a droll little habit of shedding their fabric when plunged too furiously through the air. The Boche hadn't a chance to outfly us. His only salvation would be in a dive towards his own lines.

These thoughts passed through my mind in a flash and I instantly determined upon my tactics. While Hall went in for his attack I would keep my altitude and get a position the other side of the Pfalz, to cut off his retreat.

No sooner had I altered my line of flight than the German pilot saw me leave the sun's rays. Hall was already half-way to him when he stuck up his nose and began furiously climbing to the upper ceiling. I let him pass me and found myself on the other side just as Hall began firing. I doubt if the Boche had seen Hall's Nieuport at all.

Surprised by discovering this new antagonist, Hall, ahead of him, the Pfalz immediately abandoned all idea of a battle and banking around to the right started for home, just as I had expected him to do. In a trice I was on his tail. Down, down we sped with throttles both full open. Hall was coming on somewhere in my rear. The Boche had no heart for evolutions or maneuvers. He was running like a scared rabbit. I was gaining upon him every instant and I had my sights trained dead upon his seat before I fired my first shot.

At 150 yards I pressed my triggers. The tracer bullets cut a streak of living fire into the rear of the Pfalz tail. Raising the nose of my aeroplane slightly the fiery streak lifted itself like the stream of water pouring from a garden hose. Gradually it settled into the pilot's seat. The swerving of the Pfalz course indicated that its rudder no longer was held by a directing hand. At 2000 feet above the enemy's lines I pulled up my headlong dive and watched the enemy machine continuing on its course. Curving slightly to the left the Pfalz circled a little to the south and the next minute crashed onto the ground just at the edge of the woods a mile inside their own lines. I had brought down my first enemy aeroplane and had not been subjected to a single shot!

Hall was immediately beside me. He was evidently as pleased as I was over our success, for he danced his machine about in incredible maneuvers. And then I realized that old friend Archy was back on the job. We were not two miles away from the German anti-aircraft batteries and they put a furious bombardment of shrapnel all about us. I was quite ready to call it a day and go home, but Captain Hall deliberately returned to the barrage and entered it with me at his heels. Machine-guns and rifle fire from the trenches greeted us and I do not mind admitting that I got out quickly the way I came in without any unnecessary delay, but Hall continued to do stunts over their heads for ten minutes, surpassing all the acrobatics that the enraged Boches had ever seen even over their own peaceful aerodromes.

Jimmy exhausted his spirits at about the time the Huns had exhausted their available ammunition and we started blithely for home. Swooping down to our field side by side, we made a quick landing and taxied our victorious machines up to the hangars. Then jumping out we ran to each other, extending glad hands for our first exchange of congratulations. And then we noticed that the squadron pilots and mechanics were streaming across the aerodrome towards us from all directions. They had heard the news while we were still dodging shrapnel and were hastening out to welcome our return. The French had telephoned in a confirmation of my first victory, before I had had time to reach home. Not a single bullet hole had punctured any part of my machine.

There is a peculiar gratification in receiving congratulations from one's squadron for a victory in the air. It is worth more to a pilot than the applause of the whole outside world. It means that one has won the confidence of men who share the misgivings, the aspirations, the trials and the dangers of aeroplane fighting. And with each victory comes a renewal and re-cementing of ties that bind together these brothers-in-arms. No closer fraternity exists in the world than that of the air-fighters in this great war. And I have yet to find one single individual who has attained conspicuous success in bringing down enemy aeroplanes who can be said to be spoiled either by his successes or by the generous congratulations of his comrades. If he were capable of being spoiled he would not have had the character to have won continuous victories, for the smallest amount of vanity is fatal in aeroplane fighting. Self-distrust rather is the quality to which many a pilot owes his protracted existence.

It was with a very humble gratitude then that I received the war congratulations of Lufbery, whom I had always revered for his seventeen victories—of Doug Campbell and Alan Winslow who had brought down the first machines that were credited to the American Squadrons, and of many others of 94 Squadron who had seen far more service in the battle areas than had I. I was glad to be at last included in the proud roll of victors of this squadron. These pals of mine were to see old 94 lead all American Squadrons in the number of successes over the Huns.

The following day I was notified that General Gerard, the Commanding Officer of the Sixth French Army, had offered to decorate Captain Hall and myself in the name of the French Government for our victory of the day before. We were then operating in conjunction with this branch of the French Army. The Croix de Guerre with palm was to be accorded each of us, provided such an order met the approval of our own government. But at that time officers in the American Army could not accept decorations from a foreign Government, so the ceremony of presentation was denied us. Both Captain Hall and myself had been included, as such was the French rule where two pilots had participated in a victory.

The truth was that in the tense excitement of this first victory, I was quite blind to the fact that I was shooting deadly bullets at another aviator; and if I had been by myself, there is no doubt in my own mind but that I should have made a blunder again in some particular which would have reversed the situation. Captain Hall's presence, if not his actual bullets, had won the victory and had given me that wonderful feeling of self-confidence which made it possible for me subsequently to return to battle without him and handle similar situations successfully.

October (1918) was a month of glorious successes for 94 Squadron, having brought us thirty-nine victories with but five losses. For, besides Captain Coolidge and Lieutenant Nutt the Squadron had lost Lieutenant Saunders of Billings, Montana, shot down on the 22nd, when out after balloons with Cook and Jeffers. Cook on this occasion succeeded in setting fire to the balloon he was attacking, and Jeffers turning upon the Fokker which had just sunk Saunders, shot him down in flames sixty seconds later.

On the 29th, Lt. Garnsey of Grand Haven, Michigan, fell in our lines near Exermont, after having fought a brilliant combat against greatly superior numbers. Reed Chambers, after bringing down an enemy machine of the 22nd, which he attacked at the tail of a Fokker formation containing five aeroplanes, returned to the aerodrome in considerable pain from a sudden seizure of appendicitis and next day was sent to the hospital, where he had the appendix removed.

The Squadron had developed eight aces, including Lufbery, Campbell,

Coolidge, Meissner and Chambers, all of whom were now absent, and Cook, Taylor and myself, who were left to carry on to the end of the war. Meissner was absent only in the sense that he was now in command of the 147th Squadron and his victories were going to swell the score for his newly adopted squadron instead of our own.

Many others were "going strong" at the end of October and needed but the opportunity to fight their way up into the leading scores of the group. Rain and dud weather kept us on the ground much of the time and when we did get away for brief patrols we found the enemy machines were even more particular about flying in bad weather than we were. None put in an appearance and we were forced to return empty-handed so far as fighting laurels were concerned.

Our first Night Flying Squadron had been formed early in October, under command of Captain Seth Low of New York, and its hangars on our Group aerodrome. This was not a squadron of bomb-carrying aeroplanes, but one with which to attack bombing machines of the enemy and prevent their reaching their intended targets over our lines. The night-flying aeroplanes were the English Sopwith Camels, a light single-seater capable of extraordinary evolutions in the air and able to land upon the ground in the darkness at a very low speed. The British had inaugurated this special defense against the Hun bombers in their raids upon London. Later the same system was tried at the British front with such success that over a score of German bombers were brought down in a single month by one Squadron of Night Flying Camels.

On the next to the last day of October I won my 25th and 26th victories, which were the last that I was to see added to my score. Two others that I had previously brought down were never confirmed. After the deplorable death of Frank Luke, who had won eighteen victories in less than six weeks of active flying at the front, there were no other American air-fighters who were rivaling me in my number of victories. But ever since I had been Captain of the 94th Squadron the spur of rivalry had been entirely supplanted in me by the necessity of illustrating to the pilots under my orders that I would ask them to do nothing that I myself would not do. So covetously did I guard this understanding with myself that I took my machine out frequently after the day's patrol was finished and spent another hour or two over the lines. The obligations that must attend leadership were a constant thought to me. Greater confidence in my leadership was given me when I noticed that my pilots appreciated my activity and my reasons for it. Never did I permit any pilot in my squadron to exceed the number of hours flying over the lines that was credited to me in the flight sheets. At the close of the war only Reed Chambers' record approached my own in number of hours spent in the air.

I allude to this fact because I am convinced after my six weeks' experience as Squadron Commander that my obedience to this principle did much to account for the wholehearted and enthusiastic support the pilots of my Squadron gave me. And only by their loyalty and enthusiasm was their Squadron to lead all the others at the front in number of victories and number of hours over enemy's lines.

With Reed Chambers' forced absence at the hospital the leadership of our First Flight was put in charge of Lt. Kaye. On October 30th I had been out on two patrols in the forenoon, both of which had been without unusual incident or result. When Kaye left the field with his flight at three o'clock in the afternoon I decided to accompany him to observe his tactics as Flight Leader. This formation, composed of only four machines, two of which were piloted by new men, was to fly at only 2,000 feet elevation and was to patrol the enemy's lines between Grand Pré and Brieulles. I took my place considerably in their rear and perhaps 1,000 feet above them. In this position we reached Brieulles and made two round trips with them between our two towns without discovering any hostile aeroplanes.

As we turned west for the third trip, however, I noticed two lone Fokkers coming out of Germany at a low elevation. From their maneuvers I decided that they were stalking Lt. Kaye's flight and were only waiting until they had placed themselves in a favorable position before beginning their attack. I accordingly turned my own machine away into Germany to get behind them, still keeping my altitude and trusting that they would be too intent on the larger quarry to notice me.

I had hardly begun to turn back when I saw that they had set their machines in motion for their attack. Opening up myself I put down my nose and tried to overtake them, but they had too great a start. I saw that Kaye had not seen them and in spite of the odds in our favor I feared for the two new men, who were at the end of the formation and who must assuredly bear the first diving assault of the Fokkers. Fortunately, Kaye saw them coming before they had reached firing range and he immediately turned his formation south in the direction of home. "Cook is with Kaye and those two will be able to defend the two youngsters if the Fokkers really get to close quarters," I thought to myself. I could not hope to overtake them myself, anyway, if they continued back into France. So, after a little reflection I stayed where I was, witnessing a daring attempt of the Fokkers to break up Kaye's Formation which, nevertheless, was unsuccessful. Both Fokkers attacked the rear Spad, which was piloted by Lt. Evitt, one of our new men. Instead of trying to maneuver them off he continued to fly straight ahead, affording them every opportunity in the world of correcting their aim and getting their bullets home. Evitt discovered upon landing that one of his right struts was severed by their bullets!

After this one attack the Fokkers turned back. I was in the meantime flying deeper into Germany, keeping one eye upon the two enemy machines to discover in which direction they would cross the lines to reach their own side. They seemed in no hurry to get back, but continued westward, heading towards Grand Pré. Very well! This suited me perfectly. I would make a great detour, coming back out of Germany immediately over Grand Pré with the hope that if they saw me they might believe me one of their own until we got to close quarters.

But before I reached Grand Pré I noticed them coming towards me. I was then almost over the town of Emecourt and quite a little distance within their lines. They were very low, and not more than a thousand feet above the ground at most. I was quite twice this height. Like lambs to the slaughter they came unsuspectingly on not half a mile to the east of me. Letting them pass I immediately dipped over, swung around as I fell and opening up my motor piqued with all speed on the tail of the nearest Fokker. With less than twenty rounds, all of which poured full into the center of the fusilage, I ceased firing and watched the Fokker drop helplessly to earth. As it began to revolve slowly I noticed for the first time that again I had outwitted a member of the von Richthofen crowd. The dying Fokker wore an especially brilliant nose-piece of bright red!

As my first tracer bullets began to streak past the Fokker his companion put down his nose and dived for the ground. As he was well within his own territory I did not venture to follow him at this low altitude, but at once began climbing to avoid the coming storm of Archy and machine-gun fire. Little or none of this came my way, however, and I continued homeward, passing en route over the little village of St. George, which was then about two miles inside the enemy lines. And there directly under my right wing lay in its bed a German observation balloon just at the edge of the village. On a sudden impulse I kicked over my rudder, pointed my nose at the huge target and pulled the triggers. Both guns worked perfectly. I continued my sloping dive within a hundred feet of the sleeping Drachen, firing up and down its whole length by slightly shifting the course of my aeroplane. Not a human being was in sight! Evidently the Huns thought they were quite safe in this spot, since this balloon had not yet been run up and its location could not be known to our side. I zoomed up and climbed a few hundred feet for another attack if it should be necessary. But as I balanced my machine and looked behind me I saw the fire take effect. These flaming bullets sometimes require a long time to ignite the balloon fabric. Doubtless they travel too fast to ignite the pure gas, unmixed with air.

The towering flames soon lit up the sky with a vivid glare and keeping it behind me I speeded homeward, with many self-satisfied chuckles at my good fortune. But too much self-satisfaction always receives a jolt. I had not gone ten miles before I received the worst kind of scare.

It had become quite dark and I was very near to the ground. Still some distance inside the German lines, for I had kept east in the hope that another Hun balloon might be left for my last rounds of ammunition, I thought of looking at my watch to see how late it really was. I had fuel for only two hours and ten minutes. A vague sort of premonition warned me that I had been overlooking something of importance in the past few minutes. One glance at my watch and I realized exactly what had been weighing in the back of my mind. The time indicated that I had now been out exactly two hours and ten minutes.

A real terror seized me for a moment. I was not up far enough above earth to glide for any distance when my motor stopped. Even as I banked over and turned southward I wondered whether my motor would gasp and expire in the turning. I feared to climb and I feared to stay low. I gazed over the sides of my office and tried to make out the nature of the landing ground below. Throttling down to the slowest possible speed to save fuel I crept towards the lines. It was dark enough to see that suspicious Heinies below were shooting at me on the chance that I might be an enemy. Glad I was to see those flashes receding farther and farther to my rear. I had passed the lines somewhere west of Verdun and must chance any open field I came to when the engine gave its last cough. Why didn't it stop? I wondered. It was now five or six minutes overdue. In miserable anticipation of the lot Fate had in store for me I struggled on, noting with additional gloom that the searchlight that should long ago be pointing out the way to my aerodrome had not been lighted. I could not be more than ten miles from home. Why couldn't those men attend to their business when pilots were known to be out? I took out my Very pistol and fitted in a red light. That would notify them at home that I was trouble and in a hurry to land.

Just as I fired the second Very light I heard the motor begin its final sputtering. And then just as I felt cold chills running up my back the blessed landing lights flashed out and I saw I was almost over the field. Forgetting all my recent joy I made myself as wretched as possible the following few seconds in concluding that I could not by any possibility reach the smooth field. It seemed to work—the treatment. I had expatiated my sins of over-confidence and appeased the Goddess of Luck, for I cleared the road, landed with the wind and struck the ground with a quiet thud less than a hundred feet from the entrance to 94's hangar—right side up! But I walked over to mess with a chastened spirit.

The following morning was rainy and the afternoon it continued to pour. Just before dusk we received orders to have our whole force over the lines at daybreak to protect an infantry advance from Grand Pre to Buzancy. We all felt that we were to witness the last great attack of the war. And we were right.

A heavy fog of the genuine Meuse Valley variety prevented our planes leaving the ground until the middle of the forenoon. All the morning we heard the tremendous artillery duel at the north of us and very impatiently waited for a clearing of the weather. That dull morning was somewhat relieved by our receipt of newspapers stating that Turkey had surrendered unconditionally and that Austria was expected to follow suit the following day. Placing about 100 of these journals in my plane, I set out for the lines with our patrol at 9:30 o'clock.

Arrived over the front lines near the town of Lapelle, I flew at an altitude of only a hundred feet from the ground. And there I saw our doughboys after their victorious advance of the morning crouching in every available shell-hole and lying several deep in every depression while looking forward for a snipe shot at any enemy's head that came into view. Others were posted behind woods and buildings with bayonets fixed, waiting for the word to go forward. As I passed overhead I threw overboard handfuls of morning papers to them and was amused to see how eagerly the dough-boys ran out of their holes to pick them up. With utter disdain for the nearby Hun snipers they exposed themselves gladly for the opportunity of getting the latest news from an aeroplane. I knew the news they would get would repay them for the momentary risk they ran.

Dropping half my load there I flew on over the Mozelle valley where I distributed the remainder of the papers among the men in the front line trenches along that sector. Returning then to the region of Buzancy I first caught sight of a huge supply depot burning. A closer view disclosed the fact that it was German and German soldiers were still on the premises. They were destroying materials that they knew they would be unable to save. In other words they were contemplating a fast retreat.

A few dashes up and down the highways leading to the north quickly confirmed the impression. Every road was filled with lorries and retreating artillery. All were hurrying toward Longuyon and the German border.

All the way up the Meuse as far as Stenay I found the same mad rush for the rear. Every road was filled with retreating heinies. They were going while the "going was good" and their very gestures seemed to indicate that for them it was indeed "*finis de la guerre.*" I hurried home to make my report which I felt certain would be welcome to those in authority.

The following day I obtained permission to visit Paris on a three days' leave. For the first time since I had been in France I found the streets of Paris illuminated at night and gaiety unrestrained possessing the boulevards and cafés. With the Place de la Concord and the Champs Elysées crammed with captured German guns and German aeroplanes, with flags and bunting astream everywhere it looked here too that people thought it was the "*finis de la guerre.*" I am told that Paris did not go raving mad until that unfor-gettable night of the signing of the Armistice; but from the street scenes I saw there during those first days of November while the Huns were in full retreat from the soil of France that had so long been polluted by their feet it is difficult to imagine how any people could express greater happiness.

Personally I am glad that I was with my Squadron instead of Paris on the night the war ended. For great as were the sights there, none of them could have expressed to an aviator such a view of the sentiment and feeling of aviation over the termination of this game of killing as was exhibited at our own aerodrome on the night the official order "Cease Firing!" came to us.

Returning from Paris on November 5th I found it still raining. Almost no flying had been possible along this sector since my departure. In fact no patrol left our field until November 8th, the same day on which we caught by wireless the information that the Boche delegates had crossed the lines between Haudry and Cheme on the La Chapelle road to sign the armistice. Peace then was actually in sight.

For weeks there had been a feeling in the air that the end of the war was near. To the aviators who had been flying over the lines and who had with their own eyes seen the continuous withdrawals of the Germans to the rear there was no doubt but that the Huns had lost their immoderate love for fighting and were sneaking homewards as fast as their legs would carry them. Such a certainty of victory should have operated to produce a desire to live and let live among men who were desirous of "seeing the end of the war," that is, men who preferred to survive rather than run the risks of combat fighting now that the war was fairly over.

But it was at this very period of my leadership of the 94th Squadron that I found my pilots most infatuated with fighting. They importuned me for permission to go out at times when a single glance at the fog and rain showed the foolishness of such a request. Not content with the collapse of the enemy forces the pilots wanted to humiliate them further with flights deep within their country where they might strafe aeroplane hangars and retreating troops for the last time. It must be done at once, they feared, or it would be too late.

On the 9th of November Lt. Dewitt and Capt. Fauntleroy came to me after lunch and begged me to go to the door of my hut and look at the weather with them. I laughed at them but did as they requested. It was dark and windy outside, heavy low clouds driving across the sky, though for the moment no rain was falling. I took a good look around the heavens and came back to my room, the two officers following me. Here they cornered me and talked volubly for ten minutes, urging my permission to let them go over the lines and attack one last balloon, which they heard was still swinging back of the Meuse. They overcame every objection of mine with such eagerness that finally against my best judgement I acquiesced and permitted them to go. At this moment Major Kirby who had just joined 94 Squadron for a little experience in air fighting before taking command of a new group of Squadrons that was being formed, and who as yet had never flown over the lines stepped into the room and requested permission to join Dewitt and Fauntleroy in their expedition. Lt. Cook would go along with him, he said, and they would hunt in pairs. If they didn't take this opportunity the war might end overnight and he would never have had a whack at an enemy plane.

Full of misgivings at my own weakness I walked out on the field and watched the four pilots get away. I noted the time on my watch, noted that a heavy wind was blowing them away and would increase their difficulties in returning, blamed myself exceedingly that I had permitted them to influence me against my judgement. The next two hours were miserable ones for me.

The weather grew steadily worse, rain fell and the wind grew stronger. When darkness fell, shortly after four o'clock, I ordered all the lights turned on on the field and, taking my seat at the mouth of our hangar, I anxiously waited for a glimpse of the homecoming Spads. It was nearing the limit of their fuel supply and another ten minutes must either bring some word from them or I should know that by my orders four pilots had sacrificed themselves needlessly after hostilities had practically ceased. I believe that hour was the worst one I have ever endured.

Night fell and no aeroplanes appeared. The searchlights continued to throw their long fingers into the clouds, pointing the way home to any wandering scouts who might be lost in the storm. Foolish as it was to longer expect them I could not order the lights extinguished and they shone on all through the night.

The next day was Sunday and another Decorations Ceremony was scheduled to take place at our field at eleven o'clock. A number of pilots from other aerodromes were coming over to receive the Distinguished Service Cross from the hands of Gen. Ligget for bravery and heroic exploits over enemy's lines. Several of our own group, including myself, were to be among the recipients.

The band played, generals addressed us and all the men stood at attention in front of our line of fighting planes while the dignified ceremony was performed. Two more palms were presented to me to be attached to my decoration. The Army orders were read aloud praising me for shooting down enemy aeroplanes. How bitter such compliments were to me that morning nobody ever suspected. Not a word had come from any of my four pilots that I had sent over the lines the day before. No explanation but one was possible. All four had been forced to descend in enemy territory—crashed, killed or captured—it little mattered so far as my culpability was concerned.

In fact a message had come in the night before that a Spad had collided in air with a French two-seater near Beaumont late that afternoon. A hurried investigation by telephone disclosed the fact that no other Spads were missing but our own—thus filling me with woeful conjectures as to which one of my four pilots had thus been killed in our own lines.

At the conclusion of the presentation of decorations I walked back to the hangar and put on my coat, for it was a freezing day and we had been forced to stand for half an hour without movement in dress tunic and breeches. The field was so thick with fog that the photographers present could scarcely get light enough to snap the group of officers standing in line. No aeroplanes could possibly be out to-day or I should have flown over to Beaumont at daybreak to ascertain which of my pilots had been killed there.

I was invited to mess with 95 Squadron that noon and I fear I did not make a merry guest. The compliments I received for my newly received decorations fell on deaf ears. As soon as I decently could get away I made my adieus and walked back across the aerodrome. And about half-way across I saw an aeroplane standing in the center of the field. I looked at it idly wondering what idiot had tried to get away in such a fog. Suddenly I stopped dead in my tracks. The Spad had a Hat-in-the-Ring painted on its fusilage—and a large number "3" was painted just beyond it. Number "3" was Fauntleroy's machine!

I fairly ran the rest of the way to my hangar where I demanded of the mechanics what news they had heard about Capt. Fauntleroy. I was informed that he had just landed and had reported that Lt. Dewitt had crashed last night inside our lines but would be back during the course of the day. And to cap this joyful climax to a day's misery I was told five minutes later at Group Headquarters that Major Kirby had just telephoned in that he had shot down an enemy aeroplane across the Meuse this morning at ten o'clock, after which he had landed at an aerodrome near the front and would return to us when the fog lifted!

It was a wild afternoon we had at 94 mess upon receipt of this wonderful news. Cookie too was later heard from, he having experienced a rather more serious catastrophe the previous afternoon. He had attacked an observation balloon near Beaumont. The Hun defenses shot off one blade of his propeller and he had barely made his way back across the lines when he was compelled to land in the shell-holes which covered this area. He escaped on foot to the nearest American trench and late Sunday afternoon reached our mess.

Major Kirby's victory was quickly confirmed, later inquiries disclosing the wonderful fact that this first remarkable victory of his was in truth the last aeroplane shot down in the Great War! Our old 94 Squadron had won the first American victory over enemy aeroplanes when Alan Winslow and Douglas Campbell had dropped two biplane machines on the Toul aerodrome. 94 Squadron had been first to fly over the lines and had completed more hours flying at the front than any other American organization. It had won more victories than any other—and now, for the last word, it had the credit of bringing down the last enemy aeroplane of the war! One can imagine the celebration with which 94 Squadron would signalize the end of the war! What could Paris or any other community in the whole world offer in comparison?

And the celebration came even before we had lost the zest of our present gratitude and emotion. The story of Major Kirby's sensational victory can be told in a paragraph. He had become lost the night before and had landed on the first field he saw. Not realizing the importance of telephoning us of his safety, he took off early next morning to come home. This time he got lost in the fog which surrounded our district. When he again emerged into clear air he found he was over Etain, a small town just north of Verdun. And there flying almost alongside of his Spad was another aeroplane which a second informed him was an enemy Fokker! Both pilots were so surprised for a moment that they simply gazed at each other. The Fokker pilot recovered his senses first and began a dive towards earth. Major Kirby immediately piqued on his tail, followed him down to within fifty feet of the ground firing all the way. The Fokker crashed head on, and Kirby zoomed up just in time to avoid the same fate. With his usual modesty Major Kirby insisted he had scared the pilot to death. Thus ended the War in the Air on the American front.

While listening to these details that evening after mess, our spirits bubbling over with excitement and happiness, the telephone sounded and I stepped over and took it up, waving the room to silence. It was a message to bring my husky braves over across to the 95 Mess to celebrate the beginning of a new era. I demanded of the speaker, (it was Jack Mitchell, Captain of the 95th) what he was talking about.

"Peace has been declared! No more fighting! he shouted. *"C'est le finis de la Guerre."*

Without reply I dropped the phone and turned around and faced the pilots of 94 Squadron. Not a sound was heard, every eye was upon me but no one made a movement or drew a breath. It was one of those peculiar psychological moments when instinct tells every one that something big is impending.

In the midst of this uncanny silence a sudden BOOM-BOOM of our Arch battery outside was heard. And then pandemonium broke loose. Shouting like mad, tumbling over one another in their excitement the daring pilots of the Hat-in-the-Ring Squadron, sensing the truth, darted into trunks and kit bags, drew out revolvers, German Lugers that some of them had found or bought as souvenirs from French *poilus*, very pistols and shooting tools of all descriptions and burst out of doors. There the sky over our old aerodrome and indeed in every direction of the compass was aglow and shivering with bursts of fire. Searchlights were madly cavorting across the heavens, paling to dimness the thousands of colored lights that shot up from every conceivable direction. Shrill yells pierced the darkness around us, punctuated with the fierce rat-tat-tat-tat-tat of a score of machine-guns which now added their noise to the clamor. Roars of laughter and hysterical whoopings came to us from the men's quarters beside the hangars. Pistol shots were fired in salvos, filled and emptied again and again until the weapon became too hot to hold.

At the corner of our hangar I encountered a group of my pilots rolling out tanks of gasoline. Instead of attempting the impossible task of trying to stop them I helped them get it through the mud and struck the match myself and lighted it. A dancing ring of crazy lunatics joined hands and circled around the blazing pyre, similar howling and revolving circuses surrounding several other burning tanks of good United States gasoline that would never more carry fighting aeroplanes over enemy's lines. The stars were shining brightly overhead and the day's mist was gone. But at times even the stars were hidden by the thousands of rockets that darted up over our heads and exploded with their soft 'plonks, releasing varicolored lights which floated softly through this epochal night until they withered away and died. Star shells, parachute flares, and streams of Very lights continued to light our way through the aerodrome seemingly thronged with madmen. Everybody was laughing—drunk with the outgushing of their long pent-up emotions. *"I've lived through the war!"* I heard one whirling Dervish of a pilot shouting to himself as he pirouetted along in the center of a mud hole. Regardless of who heard the inmost secret of his soul, now that the war was over, he had retired off to one side to repeat this fact over and over to himself until he might make himself sure of its truth.

Another pilot, this one an ace of 27 Squadron, grasped me securely by the arm and shouted almost incredulously, *"We won't be shot at any more!"* Without waiting for a reply he hastened on to another friend and repeated this important bit of information as though he were doubtful of a complete understanding on this trivial point. What sort of a new world will this be without the excitement of danger in it? How queer it will be in future to fly over the dead line of the silent Meuse—that significant boundary line that was marked by Archie shells to warn the pilot of his entrance into danger.

How can one enjoy life without this highly spiced sauce of danger? What else is there left to living now that the zest and excitement of fighting aeroplanes is gone? Thoughts such as these held me entranced for the moment and were afterwards recalled to illustrate how tightly strung were the nerves of these boys of twenty who had for continuous months been living on the very peaks of mental excitement.

In the mess hall of Mitchell's Squadron we found gathered the entire officer personnel of the Group. Orderlies were running back and forth with cups brimming with a hastily concocted punch, with which to drink to the success and personal appearance of every pilot in aviation. Songs were bellowed forth accompanied by crashing sounds from the Boche piano— the proudest of 95's souvenirs, selected from an officer's mess of an abandoned German camp. Chairs and benches were pushed back to the walls and soon the whole roomful was dancing, struggling and whooping for joy, to the imminent peril of the rather temporary walls and floor. Some unfortunate pilot fell and in a trice everybody in the room was forming a pyramid on top of him. The appearance of the C. O. of the Group brought the living mass to its feet in a score of rousing cheers to the best C. O. in France. Major Hartney was hoisted upon the piano, while a hundred voices shouted, "SPEECH—SPEECH!" No sooner did he open his lips than a whirlwind of sound from outside made him pause and reduced the room to quiet. But only for an instant.

"It's the Jazz Band from old 147!" yelled the pilots and like a tumultuous waterfall they poured *en masse* through a doorway that was only wide enough for one at a time.

Whooping, shrieking and singing, the victors of some 400-odd combats with enemy airmen encircled the musicians from the enlisted men of 147 Squadron. The clinging clay mud of France lay ankle deep around them. Within a minute the dancing throng had with their hopping and skipping plowed it into an almost bottomless bog. Some one went down, dragging down with him the portly bass drummer. Upon this foundation human forms in the spotless uniforms of the American Air Service piled themselves until the entire Group lay prostrate in one huge pyramid of joyous aviators. It was later bitterly disputed as to who was and who was not at the very bottom of this historic monument erected that night under the starry skies of France to celebrate the extraordinary fact that we had lived through the war and were not to be shot at to-morrow.

It was the *"finis de la Guerre!"* It was the *finis d'aviation*. It was to us, perhaps unconsciously, the end of the intimate relationship that since the beginning of the war had cemented together brothers-in-arms into a closer fraternity than is known to any other friendship in the whole world. When again will that pyramid of entwined comrades—interlacing together in one mass boys from every State in our Union—when again will it be formed and bound together in mutual devotion?

Revolt in the Desert

T. E. Lawrence

"FIGHTING FOR TAFILEH"
JONATHAN CAPE, 1927

The war churned on and on at the Western front devouring men, munitions and whole cities. The world watched this violent action with a trance-like fascination, yet only a thousand miles away an arm of the same war was being fought, and was almost unnoticed by the citizens of the warring nations.

The war in Africa was brimming over. German agents planted there years ago had done their work well, and large groups of natives had been agitated to take up arms against the British and the French. In addition, Germany brought the Ottoman Empire into the war with the object of opening a road to the East and attacking the British Empire at what appeared to be her most vital and vulnerable points. The prime objects were to block the Suez Canal, to obtain access to the Persian Gulf and to gain a road through Persia to the frontiers of India.

German agents were at work among the tribes of Darfur, far to the south of Omdurman, and aroused the religious fanaticism of the Senoussi of the Eastern Sahara while The Ottoman Sultan was urged into attacking Egypt by the promise of obtaining it as a province of the Ottoman Empire.

The Sultan was building a railway from the frontier of Palestine and if they had been allowed to extend it and make an arrangement for storing water, they would be able to attack Egypt in force and this would place the Suez Canal in jeopardy. It was of the highest importance to the British to keep the canal open at all times as through it passed large numbers of men and tons of foodstuffs and material from India and Australia for both the British and French armies.

It was discovered the brackish water available for drinking in the pools and wells had no effect on Arabs or Ottomans but acted as a strong laxative on European men and their horses. Water for the army had to be piped in from Egypt for the troops. In addition to the water problem, the struggle against the sand was perpetual and arduous. It required great labor to keep the railway clear, and it was almost impossible to build roads that would support armored vehicles for no solid bottom to be used as a foundation under the shifting sand could be found.

The British, too, had agents out among the natives of Africa attempting to stimulate them into action against the Germans and Turks either for past grievances or for gold. Among the men working with militant Arab groups was Thomas Edward Lawrence, a British adventurer, soldier and scholar (an Oxford graduate). He had set out on a walking tour of Syria in 1910, later joining an archeological expedition in Mesopotamia and remained in the area until 1914. After the outbreak of war, Lawrence was attached to British Intelligence in Egypt and went into the Arab world to promote active support for the Allies.

In 1916, feeling the need for a closer relationship with the forces under Feisal al Husain, he helped them revolt against domination by Constantinople. Lawrence disrupted the Ottomans' communication by leading attacks against the Hejaz railroad. He urged the Arab forces under Feisal to cooperate with General Allenby and they moved northwards to attack trains and rail lines. In 1918, Lawrence entered Damascus with the Arab forces before General Allenby.

T. E. Lawrence, who earned the appellation Lawrence of Arabia, completed writing his war memoirs in 1919.

We waited in Guweira for news of the opening of our operation against Tafileh, the knot of villages commanding the south end of the Dead Sea. We planned to tackle it from west, south and east at once; the east opening the ball by attacking Jurf, its nearest station on the Hejaz line. Conduct of this attack had been trusted to Sherif Nasir, the Fortunate. With him went Nuri Said, Jaafar's chief of staff, commanding some regulars, a gun, and some machine guns. They were working from Jefer. After three days their post came in. As usual Nasir had directed his raid with skill and deliberation. Jurf, the objective, was a strong station of three stone buildings with outer-works and trenches. Behind the station was a low mound, trenched and walled, on which the Turks had set two machine-guns and a mountain-gun. Beyond the mound lay a high, sharp ridge, the last spur of the hills which divided Jefer from Bair.

The weakness of the defence lay in this ridge, for the Turks were too few to hold both it and the knoll or station, and its crest overlooked the railway. Nasir one night occupied the whole top of the hill without alarm, and then cut the line above and below the station. A few minutes later, when it was light enough to see, Nuri Said brought his mountain-gun to the edge of the ridge; and, with a third lucky shot, a direct hit, silenced the Turkish gun beneath his view.

Nasir grew greatly excited; the Beni Sakhr mounted their camels, swearing they would charge in forthwith. Nuri thought it madness while Turkish machine-guns were still in action from trenches; but his words had no effect upon the Bedu. In desperation he opened a rattling fire with all he had against the Turkish position, and the Beni Sakhr swept round the foot of the main ridge and up over the knoll in a flash. When they saw this camel-horde racing at them, the Turks flung away their rifles and fled into the station. Only two Arabs were fatally hurt.

Nuri ran down to the knoll. The Turkish gun was undamaged. He slewed it round and discharged it point blank into the ticket office. The Beni Sakhr mob yelled with joy to see the wood and stones flying, jumped again on their camels and loped into the station just as the enemy surrendered. Nearly two hundred Turks, including seven officers, survived as our prisoners.

After the looting, the engineers fired charges under the two engines, against the water-tower, in the pump, and between the points of the sidings. They burned the captured trucks and damaged a bridge; but perfunctorily, for, as usual after victory, every one was too loaded and too hot to care for altruistic labour.

Then the weather once more broke. For three successive days came falls of snow. Nasir's force with difficulty regained the tents at Jefer. This plateau about Maan lay between three and five thousand feet above sea level, open to all winds from north and east. They blew from Central Asia, or from Caucasus, terribly over the great desert to these low hills of Edom, against which their first fury broke. The surplus bitterness lipped the crest and made a winter, quite severe of its degree, below, in Judea and Sinai.

Outside Beersheba and Jerusalem the British found it cold; but our Arabs fled there to get warm. Unhappily the British supply staff realized too late that we were fighting in a little Alp. They would not give us tents for one-quarter of our troops, nor serge clothing, nor boots, nor blankets enough to issue two to each man of the mountain garrisons. Our soldiers, if they neither deserted nor died, existed in an aching misery which froze the hope out of them.

According to our plan the good news of Jurf was to send the Arabs of Petra, under Sherif Abd el Mayin, at once up their hills into the forest towards Shobek. It was an uncanny march in the hoar mist, that of these frozen footed peasants in their sheepskins, up and down sharp valleys and dangerous hillsides, out of whose snowdrifts the heavy trunks of junipers, grudging in leaves, jutted like castings in grey iron. The ice and frost broke down the animals, and many of the men; yet these hardy highlanders, used to being too cold throughout their winter, persisted in the advance.

The Turks heard of them as they struggled slowly nearer, and fled from the caves and shelters among the trees to the branch railhead, littering the roads of their panic with cast baggage and equipment.

However, the advantage lay with Nasir, who leaped in one day from Jefer, and after a whirlwind night appeared at dawn on the rocky brink of the ravine in which Tafileh hid, and summoned it to surrender on pain of bombardment: an idle threat, for Nuri Said with the guns had gone back to Guweira. There were only one hundred and eighty Turks in the village, but they had supporters in the Muhaisin, a clan of the peasantry; not for love so much as because Dhiab, the vulgar head-man of another faction, had declared for Feisal. So they shot up at Nasir a stream of ill-directed bullets.

The Howeitat spread out along the cliffs to return the peasants' fire. This manner of going displeased Auda, the old lion, who raged that a mercenary village folk should dare to resist their secular masters, the Abu Tayi. So he jerked his halter, cantered his mare down the path, and rode out plain to view beneath the easternmost houses of the village. There he reined in, and shook a hand at them, booming in his wonderful voice: 'Dogs, do you not know Auda?' When they realized it was that implacable son of war their hearts failed them, and an hour later Sherif Nasir in the town-house was sipping tea with his guest, the Turkish Governor, trying to console him for the sudden change of fortune.

At dark Mastur rode in. His Motalga looked blackly at their blood-enemies the Abu Tayi, lolling in the best houses. The two Sherifs divided up the place, to keep their unruly followers apart.

Feisal had delegated command of this push towards the Dead Sea to his young half-brother Zeid. It was Zeid's first office in the north, and he set out eager with hope. As adviser he had Jaafar Pasha, our general. His infantry, gunners and machine-gunners stuck, for lack of food, at Petra; but Zeid himself and Jaafar rode on to Tafileh.

Things were almost at a break. Auda affected a magnanimity very galling to the Motalga boys, Metaab and Annad, sons of Abtan, whom Auda's son had killed. They, lithe, definite, self-conscious figures, began to talk about revenge—tom-tits threatening a hawk. Auda declared he would whip them in the market-place if they were rude. This was very well, but their followers were two to every man of his, and we should have the village in a blaze. The young fellows, with Rahail, my ruffler, went flaunting in every street.

Zeid thanked and paid Auda, and sent him back to his desert. The enlightened heads of the Muhaisin had to go as forced guests to Feisal's tent. Dhiab, their enemy, was our friend: we remembered regretfully the adage that the best allies of a violently successful new regime were not its partisans, but its opponents. By Zeid's plenty of gold the economic situation improved. We appointed an officer-governor and organized our five villages for further attack.

Notwithstanding, these plans quickly went adrift. Before they had been agreed upon we were astonished by a sudden try of the Turks to dislodge us. We had never dreamed of this, for it seemed out of the question that they should hope to keep Tafileh, or want to keep it. Allenby was just in Jerusalem, and for the Turks the issue of the war might depend on their successful defence of the Jordan against him. Unless Jericho fell, or until it fell, Tafileh was an obscure village of no interest. Nor did we value it as a possession; our desire was to get past it towards the enemy. For men so critically placed as the Turks to waste one single casualty on its recapture appeared the rankest folly.

Hamid Fakhri Pasha, commanding the 48th Division and the Amman sector, thought otherwise, or had his orders. He collected about nine hundred infantry, made up of three battalions (in January 1918 a Turkish battalion was a poor thing) with a hundred cavalry, two mountain howitzers, and twenty-seven machine guns, and sent them by rail and road to Kerak. There he impressed all the local transport, drew a complete set of civil officials to staff his new administration in Tafileh, and marched southward to surprise us.

Surprise us he did. We first heard of him when his cavalry feelers fell on our pickets in Wadi Hesa, the gorge of great width and depth and difficulty which cut off Kerak from Tafileh, Moab from Edom. By dusk he had driven them back, and was upon us.

Jaafer Pasha had sketched a defence position on the south bank of the great ravine of Tafileh; proposing, if the Turks attacked, to give them the village, and defend the heights which overhung it, behind. This seemed to me doubly unsound. The slopes were dead, and their defence as difficult as their attack. They could be turned from the east; and by quitting the village we threw away the local people, whose votes and hands would be for the occupiers of their houses.

However, it was the ruling idea—all Zeid had—and so about midnight he gave the order, and servants and retainers loaded up their stuff. The men-at-arms proceeded to the southern crest, while the baggage train was sent off by the lower road to safety. This move created panic in the town. The peasants thought we were running away (I think we were) and rushed to save their goods and lives. It was freezing hard, and the ground was crusted with noisy ice. In the blustering dark the confusion and crying through the narrow streets were terrible.

Dhiab the Sheikh had told us harrowing tales of the disaffection of the townspeople, to increase the splendour of his own loyalty; but my impression was that they were stout fellows of great potential use. To prove it I sat out on my roof, or walked in the dark up and down the steep alleys, cloaked against recognition, with my guards unobrusively about me within call. So we heard what passed. The people were in a very passion of fear, nearly dangerous, abusing everybody and everything; but there was nothing pro-Turkish abroad. They were in horror of the Turks returning, ready to do all in their physical capacity to support against them a leader with fighting intention. This was satisfactory, for it chimed with my hankering to stand where we were and fight stiffly.

Finally, I met the young Jazi sheikhs Metaab and Annad, beautiful in silks and gleaming silver arms, and sent them to find their uncle, Hamd el

Arar. Him I asked to ride away north of the ravine, to tell the peasantry, who, by the noise, were still fighting the Turks, that we were on our way up to help them. Hamd, a melancholy, courtly, gallant cavalier, galloped off at once with twenty of his relations, all that he could gather in the distracted moment.

Their passage at speed through the streets added the last touch required to perfect the terror. The housewives bundled their goods pell-mell out of doors and windows, though no men were waiting to receive them. Children were trampled on, and yelled, while their mothers were yelling anyhow. The Motalga during their gallop fired shot after shot into the air to encourage themselves, and, as though to answer them, the flashes of the enemy rifles became visible, outlining the northern cliffs in that last blackness of sky before the dawn. I walked up the opposite heights to consult with Sherif Zeid.

Zeid sat gravely on a rock, sweeping the country with field-glasses for the enemy. As crises deepened, Zeid grew detached, nonchalant. I was in a furious rage. The Turks should never, by the rules of sane generalship, have ventured back to Tafileh at all. It was simple greed, a dog-in-the-manger attitude unworthy of a serious enemy, just the sort of hopeless thing a Turk would do. How could they expect a proper war when they gave us no chance to honour them? Our morale was continually being ruined by their follies, for neither could our men respect their courage, nor our officers respect their brains. Also, it was an icy morning, and I had been up all night and was Teutonic enough to decide that they should pay for my changed mind and plan.

First I suggested that Abdulla go forward with two Hotchkiss guns to test the strength and disposition of the enemy. Then we talked of what next; very usefully, for Zeid was a cool and gallant little fighter, with the temperament of a professional officer. We saw Abdulla climb the other bank. The shooting became intense for a time, and then faded into distance. His coming had stimulated the Motalga horsemen and the villagers, who fell on the Turkish cavalry and drove them over a first ridge, across a plain two miles wide, and over a ridge beyond it down the first step of the great Hesa depression.

Behind this lay the Turkish main body, just getting on the road again after a severe night which had stiffened them in their places. They came properly into action, and Abdulla was checked at once. We heard the distant rolling of machine-gun fire, growing up in huge bursts, laced by desultory shelling. Our ears told us what was happening as well as if we saw it, and the news was excellent. I wanted Zeid to come forward at once on that authority: but his caution stepped in and he insisted that we wait exact word from his advance guard, Abdulla.

This was not necessary, according to book, but they knew I was a sham soldier, and took license to hesitate over my advice when it came peremptorily. However, I held a hand worth two of that, and went off myself for the front to prejudge their decision. On the way I saw my bodyguard, turning over the goods exposed for removal in the streets, and finding much of interest to themselves. I told them to recover our camels and to bring their Hotchkiss automatic to the north bank of the gorge in a hurry.

The road dipped into a grove of fig-trees, knots of blue snaky boughs; bare, as they would be long after the rest of nature was grown green. Thence it turned eastward, to wind lengthily in the valley to the crest. I left it, climbing straight up the cliffs. An advantage of going barefoot was a new and incredible sureness upon rock when the soles had got hard by painful insistence, or were too chilled to feel jags and scrapes. The new way, while warming me, also shortened my time appreciably, and very soon, at the top, I found a level bit, and then a last ridge overlooking the plateau.

This last straight bank, with Byzantine foundations in it, seemed very proper for a reserve or ultimate line of defense for Tafileh. To be sure, we had no reserve as yet—no one had the least notion who or what we would have anywhere—but, if we did have anybody, here was their place: and at precise moment Zeid's personal Ageyl became visible, hiding coyly in a hollow. To make them move required words of a strength to unravel their plaited hair: but at last I had them sitting along the skyline of Reserve Ridge. They were about twenty, and for a distance looked beautiful, like 'points' of a considerable army. I gave them my signet as a token, with orders to collect there all newcomers, especially my fellows with their gun.

As I walked northward towards the fighting, Abdulla met me, on his way to Zeid with news. He had finished his ammunition, lost five men from shell-fire, and had one automatic gun destroyed. Two guns, he thought the Turks had. His idea was to get up Zeid with all his men and fight: so nothing remained for me to add to his message; and there was no subtlety in leaving alone my happy masters to cross and dot their own right decision.

He gave me leisure in which to study the coming battlefield. The tiny plain was about two miles across, bounded by low green ridges, and roughly triangular, with my reserve ridge as a base. Through it ran the road to Kerak, dipping in the Hesa valley. The Turks were fighting their way up this road. Abdulla's charge had taken the western or left-hand ridge, which was now our firing-line.

Shells were falling in the plain as I walked across it, with harsh stalks of wormwood stabbing into my wounded feet. The enemy fuzing was too long, so that the shells grazed the ridge and burst way behind. One fell near me, and I learned its calibre from the hot cap. As I went they began to shorten range, and by the time I got to the ridge it was being freely sprinkled with shrapnel. Obviously the Turks had got observation some-how, and looking round I saw them climbing along the eastern side beyond the gap of the Kerak road. They would soon outflank us at our end of the western ridge.

'Us' proved to be about sixty men, clustered behind the ridge in two bunches, one near the bottom, one by the top. The lower was made up of peasants, on foot, blown, miserable, and yet the only warm things I had seen that day. They said their ammunition was finished, and it was all over. I assured them it was just beginning and pointed to my populous reserve ridge, saying that all arms were there in support. I told them to hurry back, and refill their belts and hold on to it for good. Meanwhile we would cover their retreat by sticking here for the few minutes yet possible.

They ran off, cheered, and I walked about among the upper group quoting how one should not quit firing from one position till ready to fire from the next. In command was young Metaab, stripped to his skimp riding-drawers for hard work, with his black love-curls awry, his face stained and haggard. He was beating his hands together and crying hoarsely with baffled vexation, for he had meant to do so well in this, his first fight for us.

My presence at the last moment, when the Turks were breaking through, was bitter; and he got angrier when I said that I only wanted to study the landscape. He thought it flippancy, and screamed something about a Christian going into battle unarmed. I retorted with a quip from Clausewitz, about a rearguard effecting its purpose more by being than by doing: but he was past laughter, and perhaps with justice, for the little flinty bank behind which we sheltered was crackling with fire. The Turks, knowing we were there, had turned twenty machine-guns upon it. It was four feet high and fifty feet long, of bare flinty ribs, off which the bullets slapped deafeningly: while the air above so hummed or whistled with ricochets and chips that it felt like death to look over. Clearly we must leave very soon, and as I had no horse I went off first, with Metaab's promise that he would wait where he was, if he dared, for another ten minutes.

The run warmed me. I counted my paces, to help in ranging the Turks when they ousted us; since there was only that one position for them, and it was poorly protected against the south. In losing this Motalga ridge we would probably win the battle. The horsemen held on for almost their ten minutes, and then galloped off without hurt. Metaab lent me his stirrup to hurry me along, till we found ourselves breathless among the Ageyl. It was just noon, and we had leisure and quiet in which to think.

Our new ridge was about forty feet up, and a nice shape for defence. We had eighty men on it, and more were constantly arriving. My guards were in place with their gun; Lutfi, an engine destroyer, rushed up hotly with his two, and after him came another hundred Ageyl. The thing was becoming a picnic, and by saying 'excellent' and looking overjoyed, we puzzled the men, and made them consider the position dispassionately. The automatics were put on the skyline, with orders to fire occasional shots, short, to disturb the Turks a little, but not too much, after the expedient of Massena in delaying enemy deployment. Otherwise a lull fell; I lay down in a sheltered place which caught a little sun, and no wind, and slept a blessed hour, while the Turks occupied the old ridge, extending over it like a school of geese, and about as wisely. Our men left them alone, being contented with a free exhibition of themselves.

In the middle of the afternoon Zeid arrived, with Mastur, Rasim and Abdulla. They brought our main body, comprising twenty mounted infantry on mules, thirty Motalga horsemen, two hundred villagers, five automatic rifles, four machine-guns and the Egyptian Army mountain-gun which had fought about Medina, Petra and Jurf. This was magnificent, and I woke up to welcome them.

The Turks saw us crowding, and opened with shrapnel and machine-gun fire: but they had not the range and fumbled it. We reminded one another that movement was the law of strategy, and started moving. Rasim became a cavalry officer, and mounted with all our eighty riders of animals to make a circuit about the eastern ridge and envelop the enemy's left wing, since the books advised attack not upon a line, but upon a point, and by going far enough along any finite wing it would be found eventually reduced to a point of one single man. Rasim liked this, my conception of his target.

He promised grinningly to bring us that last man: but Hamd el Arar took the occasion more fittingly. Before riding off he devoted himself to the death for the Arab cause, drew his sword ceremoniously, and made to it, by name, a heroic speech. Rasim took five automatic guns with him; which was good.

We in the centre paraded about, so that their departure might be unseen of the enemy, who were bringing up an apparently endless procession of machine-guns and dressing them by the left at intervals along the ridge, as though in a museum. It was lunatic tactics. The ridge was flint, without cover for a lizard. We had seen how, when a bullet struck the ground, it and the ground spattered up in a shower of deadly chips. Also we knew the range, and elevated our Vickers' guns carefully, blessing their long, old-fashioned sights; our mountain-gun was propped into place ready to let go a sudden burst of shrapnel over the enemy when Rasim was at grips.

As we waited, a reinforcement was announced of one hundred men from Aima. They had fallen out with Zeid over war-wages the day previous, but had grandly decided to sink old scores in the crisis. Their arrival convinced us to abandon Marshal Foch and to attack from, at any rate, three sides at once. So we sent the Aima men, with three automatic guns, to out flank the right, or western wing. Then we opened against the Turks from our central position, and bothered their exposed lines with hits and ricochets.

The enemy felt the day no longer favourable. It was passing, and sunset often gave victory to defenders yet in place. Old General Hamid Fakhri collected his Staff and Headquarters, and told each man to take a rifle. 'I have been forty years a soldier, but never saw rebels fight like these. Enter the ranks' . . . but he was too late. Rasim pushed forward an attack of his five automatic guns, each with its two-man crew. They went in rapidly, unseen till they were in position, and crumpled the Turkish left.

The Aima men who knew every blade of grass on these, their own village pastures, crept, unharmed, within three hundred yards of the Turkish machine-guns. The enemy, held by our frontal threat, first knew of the Aima men when they, by a sudden burst of fire, wiped out the gun-teams and flung the right wing into disorder. We saw it, and cried advance to the camel men and levies about us.

Mohamed el Ghasib, comptroller of Zeid's household, led them on his camel, in shining wind-billowed robes, with the crimson banner of the Ageyl over his head. All who had remained in the centre with us, our servants, gunners and machine-gunners, rushed after him in a wide, vivid line.

The day had been too long for me, and I was now only shaking with desire to see the end: but Zeid beside me clapped his hands with joy at the beautiful order of our plan unrolling in the frosty redness of the setting sun. On the one hand Rasim's cavalry were sweeping a broken left wing into the pit beyond the ridge: on the other the men of Aima were bloodily cutting down fugitives. The enemy centre was pouring back in disorder through the gap, with our men after them on foot, on horse, on camel. The Armenians, crouching behind us all day anxiously, now drew their knives and howled to one another in Turkish as they leaped forward.

I thought of the depths between here and Kerak, the ravine of Hesa, with its broken, precipitous paths, the undergrowth, the narrows and defiles of the way. It was going to be a massacre and I should have been crying-sorry for the enemy; but after the angers and exertions of the battle my mind was too tired to care to go down into that awful place and spend the night saving them. By my decision to fight, I had killed twenty or thirty of our six hundred men, and the wounded would be perhaps three times as many. It was one-sixth of our force gone on a verbal triumph, for the destruction of this thousand poor Turks would not affect the issue of the war.

In the end we had taken their two mountain howitzers (Skoda guns, very useful to us), twenty-seven machine-guns, two hundred horses and mules, two hundred and fifty prisoners. Men said only fifty got back, exhausted fugitives, to the railway. The Arabs on their track rose against them and shot them ignobly as they ran. Our own men gave up the pursuit quickly, for they were tired and sore and hungry, and it was pitifully cold.

As we turned back it began to snow; and only very late, and by a last effort did we get our hurt men in. The Turkish wounded lay out, and were dead next day.

With the Tanks

Harold A. Littledale

THE ATLANTIC MONTHLY, December 1918

Many new weapons were invented and developed in an attempt to break the stalemate of trench warfare. The Germans were intrigued with flame throwers and poison gas. The British found interest in an armored cabin that was propelled by caterpillar tractors invented in America. While the Belgians had armored cars (automobiles with iron plating and a mounted machine gun), the Italians had built an iron-plated automobile with a small cannon poking out of a revolving turret. But both of these mobile machines were open on top and depended upon uncluttered roads for freedom of movement.

As stated the caterpillar tractor pulled a fully enclosed armored cabin over uneven terrain scarred by the big guns. These lumbering monsters were used for the first time in battle in September 1916. While they enabled the British to take Flers, Corcelette and other German positions, the new weapon was not fully understood, was used incorrectly, and to some, seemed a failure.

It wasn't until November 1917 that tanks achieved a major success in an attack near Cambrai. In the final months of the war they proved a valuable and efficient weapon in the hands of the Allies.

That they were particularly effective was proved by the ease with which the tanks of all varieties tore through the barbed wire entanglements and pierced the Hindenburg and Krienhild lines supposed by the Germans to be impregnable.

Heavy anti-tank rifles that carried a charge calculated to pierce armor were designed and produced by the Germans and issued to the soldiers in the front line trenches at the rate of three to a company, but they proved to be ineffective. The tanks spread death and terror to the entrenched enemy. In effect, they had developed into mobile artillery and were used as such by the Allied army. The tank had become one of the instrumental factors that helped bring final victory to the Allies.

We were not always with the Tanks. We came from the infantry, from the cavalry, from the artillery, from the Machine-Gun Corps, the Motor Machine guns, the Flying Corps, the Army Service Corps, and even from the navy. We came at first in the varied uniforms of our various regiments, and a motley crowd we were—the British infantry man in his turned-over trousers, the Scotsman in his kilt, the artillery boys in riding breeches and jaunty bandoliers, and he of the senior service in regulation navy blue. Some of us came with the mud of the trenches on our boots and the stains of war on our clothing; others, who had not been overseas, were more presentable in clean khaki.

We were not always known as the Tanks. At first, a great deal of secrecy was thrown about us, and we were called the Heavy Branch, Machine-Gun Corps, wearing the crossed-machine-gun insignia of that service. Later, in the summer of 1917, after we had cut our teeth and done a little biting on our own account, we became the Tank Corps, and the insignia was changed to a tank surrounded by laurel leaves, surmounted by a crown. By that time we had grown, and four original companies had become many battalions, the first handful of tanks had been multiplied and were legion, and we had established a depot in France in addition to depots in England, schools for gunnery and for driving, great workshops and stores behind the line, and advanced workshops and stores near the line. Also, we had taken part in many battles, and done a little toward winning some of them, perhaps, learning how most effectively to use our new engine of war, and improving upon it so much that, when the enemy used tanks against us, we were able to outdistance and outmanoeuvre his machines to his very great astonishment and dismay.

The spirit of adventure called most of us to the Tanks. This was not because we were any braver than our comrades-in-arms, but because our natures demanded a change. And so the call for volunteers found us ready, and when the word of acceptance came, our hearts beat quickly and our hopes rose high; for we were tired of the monotony of the trenches and the monotony of the guns. And yet, when we came together, we wondered why many of us were there; for while some of us were selected because we were machine-gunners, and others because we were motor-drivers, there were many of us to whom the machine-gun and the motor were incomprehensible things. But in the end we did not find this lack of knowledge any handicap; for the army authorities, who were wiser than we, knew that to men of average intelligence and education these things were easy to learn; and to our very great amazement, we found that a week was all that was necessary thoroughly to master any machine-gun and to qualify with it at the range, and that was necessary to grasp the principle of the internal-combustion engine and the mechanism of the tank.

All that, however, was only the preliminary training and there followed weeks and often months of instruction and of drill until we became letter-perfect. In those later weeks, of course, some of us fell by the wayside and were returned to the infantry or the cavalry or the guns.

There were times when the spirit of adventure within us received a severe jolt. That was when we had to haul about cases of petrol, drums of oil, and tins of grease; for with every move—and we were constantly moving—it was necessary to form a 'dump' of such things as were necessary for the beast to move and have its being; and our minds will always turn back to nights of rain, and to roads of mud along which we struggled bitterly, bearing upon our shoulders or our backs great loads, the petrol leaking from its tins against our heads and so into our eyes, the thick oil escaping from its drums and trickling down our backs. All this was sheer navvying and not at all what we expected, but it was most necessary.

Later, when we converted obsolete tanks into supply-tanks, much of this work was done by them and it became so organized that supply-tanks brought petrol, oil and grease up to us in action, or established dumps at certain designated points to which we turned back during the course of the battle, so that we could refill, return, and carry on. Thus the beast of prey did not altogether lose its usefulness with old age, but became a beast of burden and, as such, took no small part in making the fighting tank an efficient and formidable weapon.

Not all tanks were to survive for this service, however, for many went into action never to return; others sank from view in the Flanders mud, and our men dug down to them and converted them into bomb-proofs; and six of the first ever to be used lie along the Arras-Albert highroad, some on their sides, some on their backs, others still head-on toward the enemy's line, all of them broken and black with rust; for time and battle have shown them little mercy and left them merely unattractive hulks on the high tide of the German trenches.

Our first impression of the tank was one of disappointment. So much had been printed, after their first appearance in battle, of their freakish appearance and their great size, that we expected something far more strange in design, more monstrous, more dragon-like, and twice as big. However, when we came to go into action with them and to see some of them lurch clumsily when they were struck by armor-piercing shells, we inclined to the belief that they were quite large enough, and we even came to cherish a secret feeling that it would be much nicer and more comfortable and safer and healthier all round, if the tank could be made smaller and less conspicuous. Later it was made smaller; but the small tank was for special work and the large tank remained as large as ever, although certain internal improvements made it easier to handle and thereby increasingly difficult to hit. How increasingly difficult to hit they became may be appreciated when it is known that the first time the improved tanks were used in battle, not one of them was lost. That action took place during the merciful shelter of the darkness of a morning in the early summer of 1918; and while sixty tanks were used, the German official statement gave the number as eight hundred!

We were disappointed, too, to find that the tank could not do all that we had heard it could do. We had quite expected to climb to the house-tops, or, failing that, to go right through houses, to uproot great trees, and to waddle through wide rivers. The newspapers had depicted the tanks doing all those things; but we were to learn that roofs have a habit of giving way under the weight of 35 tons, which is the weight of a large tank, and that it was easier to go round houses than to go straight through them; and we were to learn that large trees, deeply rooted, successfully resist great force, and that the rivers of France are so muddy in the bed, that to cross them, as indeed once we had to in action, it was necessary to lay down a causeway of barrels filled with cement.

But, in spite of these early disappointments, there was much about the tank that satisfied the spirit of adventure, and there is not one of us who will ever forget his first ride—the crawling in at the sides, the discovery that the height did not permit a man of medium stature to stand erect, the sudden starting of the engine, the roar of it all when the throttle opened, the jolt forward, and the sliding through the mud that followed, until at last we came to the 'jump' which had been prepared. Then came the downward motion, which suddenly threw us off our feet and caused us to stretch trusting hands toward the nearest object—usually, at first, a hot pipe through which the water from the cylinder jackets flowed to the condenser. So, down and down and down, the throttle almost closed, the engine just 'ticking over,' until at last the bottom was reached, and as the power was turned full on, the tank raised herself to the incline, like a ship rising on a wave, and we were all jolted the other way, only to clutch again frantically for things which were hot and burned, until at last, with a swing over the top, we regained level ground. And in that moment we discovered that the trenches and the mud and the rain and the shells and the daily curse of bully beef had not killed everything within, for there came to us a thrill of happiness in that we were to sail over stranger seas than man had ever crossed, and set out on a great adventure. And some of us were to do great deeds, and others were to do simple things; some of us were to win great glory, and others of us were to crumple up against the engine or the guns, never again to stir; but all of us were to learn that it is not life that matters, but the courage which one brings to life.

Each one of us who transferred in France came to the reinforcement and training depot with a secret hope that he might be sent to Blighty for instruction. (Blighty is the soldiers' name for England. It is a corruption of the Indian word for home.) But in the first five minutes at the depot, that hope disappeared, and we knew that we should not see Blighty except in the ordinary routine of leave and wounds. As leave is granted only about every fifteen months, and even wounds are frequently difficult to get, the prospect of going home was soon dispelled.

In those days the depot was only in its infancy. It consisted of a score of tents for the men, and half a dozen small Armstrong huts for the officers.

But each week it grew, and after we left and went to various battalions, it was moved elsewhere, and huts such as are used in the British camps were erected.

On our arrival at the depot we were classified in two lots—drivers and gunners—the sheep and the goats, as it turned out to be later, for the better pay fell to the drivers and the dirtier work to the gunners. We were all given the rank of gunner, however. This was a relief. In the infantry we had been privates, but the term private soldier had ever been a source of mystery to us, for we had never discovered anything private in our lives to warrant the title. Even our private letters were not sealed, and had to be censored before they could be dispatched. Also, we were not permitted to have any private property; for a soldier belongs, body, soul, and belongings, to the army, at least theoretically, for of course we did have private property. This consisted mostly of the photographs of our wives, our children, and our sweethearts. The rest was what we bought in the way of soap and polish; for the one piece of soap and the single tin of blacking which the army issues to each recruit upon joining can scarcely be expected to last through a campaign, be the soldier ever so economical in washing his body or in cleaning his boots!

Just what was the mode of procedure in selecting some men to be drivers and other men to be gunners, we never knew. Perhaps it was gauged by the size of one's boots or the color of one's eyes. At any rate, quite frequently a skilled motor-mechanic would be sent to the gunners' company, while an expert machine-gunner, who knew nothing about internal-combustion engines, would find himself among the drivers. In the long run, however, it did not matter much, for each driver had to qualify as a gunner, and each gunner was given an elementary tank course and taught how to drive.

The reasons for so complete a training were obvious. In case a tank was knocked out or developed serious engine-trouble, the entire crew could carry on in the trenches or the field with the guns; whereas, if all the drivers were killed, any gunner could bring the tank back. But to the average Tommy this dual instruction boded ill, for the soldier believes that the less you know, the better off you are. For instance, if you are a machine-gunner, a bomber, and a signaller, you will probably come in for more 'shows' than if you are simply a rifleman; wherefore a little knowledge is considered a dangerous thing. But later each one of us thanked his lucky stars that he was gunner and driver too; for there came a time when we did have to carry on in the trenches or the field with the guns, and there came a time, too, when the drivers all 'went West,' and the gunners had to bring back the tanks.

With the rank of gunner we drew slightly higher pay. In the infantry our rate of pay had been one shilling a day, half of which we turned over toward the support of our dependents, the government supplementing the allowance. As the Tanks were classified as artillery, and the daily rate of pay in the artillery was one shilling and twopence halfpenny, we drew this additional twopence halfpenny. Later, when the Tank Corps was established and pay in the army generally increased, we drew as much as two shillings and eightpence a day as first drivers, plus war-pay of a penny a day extra for each year we had been in the army; and the government relieved us of compulsorily contributing to the support of our dependents and itself undertook their entire support, which however, we were permitted to increase by voluntary contributions from our pay.

The depot was in a back area. The site was ideal, a valley with woods on either side, making it difficult to observe from the air. Not infrequently hostile aircraft sailed overhead as if in search of us; but they failed to find us, for we were never subjected to aerial attack.

The camp was in a large field. The field itself was used as a parade and sports ground. Along either side were two rows of tents in which the men were housed. At one end was the mess-hall and at the other end the officers' quarters. The entire camp was surrounded by a hedge and poplar trees so that little could be seen from the road which bordered the eastern side. Along the western side ran a double-track, wide-gauge railway, and a spur of this led into Central Workshops, less than a quarter of a mile away. In a sense, Central Workshops was a tank hospital, for it was there that tanks which had been damaged in action went for overhauling and repair, and there at any time one could see tanks with great wounds in their sides, and, searching among the heap of cartridges on the floor, find some button or shred of clothing which told only too clearly what had happened. Later we were to see much of Central Works, for it was here, too, that all new tanks arriving from England were first tested before being turned over to the men who were to take them into battle; and it was upon flat cars moved into this siding that we were to drive our tanks, and so move to within striking distance of the fighting line.

It was to a tent on the side-lines that the new arrival was sent. If he was lucky, he found himself in one occupied mostly by cooks. The luck manifested itself after 'Lights Out,' when tins of sardines and jam and pieces of bread and cheese would mysteriously appear and be passed around; for while the army ration is sufficient, manna from the soldiers' heaven, which is the cookhouse, is always welcome. And almost nightly this manna rained upon this tent, and from the beginning the new arrival got a portion, for soldiers always share.

For the most part the men at the depot were recruits from England sent out to reinforce battalions which had suffered losses in action. A few battalion men were there, though, and these could be distinguished by the colors on their shoulder-straps. In those days the battalions were designated by the letters of the alphabet: A Battalion, B Battalion, C Battalion, and so on, and the colors of A Battalion were red, of B Battalion yellow, of

C Battalion green, of D Battalion blue. Later, the lettering system was discontinued—why, we never knew—and A Battalion became the First Battalion, B the Second, C the Third, and so on.

At that time those of us who had only had instruction on tanks in England, and those of us who had never seen a tank, looked with awe upon these battalion men; for most of them had seen action in the tanks, and many of them had been wounded, gone to hospital, and subsequently been dispatched to the depot for return to their respective units. And because so much mystery was attached to the tanks, we came to think that their risks had been greater than any we ourselves had run, and we often tried to get them to talk of it all; but found them strangely silent. Later, we were to learn how ridiculous this sense of awe had been, for we in turn were to suffer from much the same sort of thing and were to hear people murmur hoarsely to each other, 'He's with the Tanks,' as if we were the pick of the army, undergoing greater hardships than anyone else.

The officers at the depot were there under circumstances similar to our own. Some of them were battalion officers who had been wounded; others were reinforcements sent from England, and others were officers who had transferred in France from as many different units as ourselves.

Usually the routine of the day included physical training, squad-drill, gas-drill machine-gun instruction, preliminary tank instruction, and fatigues. Fatigues were doing any odd job around the camp, from peeling potatoes for the cooks to unloading quartermasters' stores. And, the day finally ended, there were still pickets and guards to be done in turn. The fire picket was a more or less informed affair which we did not mind; but guard had to be mounted in full marching order, and so searching was the inspection that a spot of grease on your pack might cause you to lose three days' pay and be confined to camp as well. Guard-mounting in steel hats some thirty miles behind the line seemed to us only a ceremonial instituted purposely to aggravate the soldier, and we groused a great deal about it until we heard the reason, which may or may not be the true one. It was said that, in the first few weeks after the depot was started, and when there was one tank there, guard was mounted in the usual manner, the men wearing the soft field-service cap. A sentry was posted at the tank, and that night, when the corporal of the guard marched the relief to that point, he fell over the prostate body of the sentry. He picked him up and carried him to the guard-house and later had him removed to a hospital, for he had been struck over the head with some blunt weapon. Why or how he had been struck, he never knew, nor how long he had been unconscious; but the affair was put down to espionage and resulted in an order to wear our shrapnel helmets when on guard. Color was lent to the theory of espionage by a later incident; for through papers found on a man arrested in England the intelligence officers traced a German spy, and caught him on that spur of the railway track leading to Central Workshops.

It was while marching to the baths that many of us saw our first tank. For two days rain had been falling and the parade-ground was camouflaged by two inches of water and four inches of mud. Of the two the water was probably thicker than the mud; so, because we could not do squad-drill, we were warned for the baths. These were shower-baths, two kilometres distant, but they were more like an anaemic fire-sprinkler system than anything else. They were housed in a dilapidated old barn, the roof of which leaked more water than came through the sprinklers.

With towels over our left shoulders we were lined up and marched off, grousing a good deal, for it was still raining and the road was in a wretched condition. We had just passed Central Workshops when the tank appeared, moving along the road slowly, making less noise than we expected, for we were to learn that most of the noise is internal and little except the exhaust can be heard from without.

We marched to the side of the road to let Behemoth pass, and in that moment forgot the mud and the rain, and laughed as it slid past, much as the infantry are said to have laughed on that summer morning which marked the beginning of the Battle of the Somme. But our merriment lasted only a moment, for a sharp order brought us to a realization that we were marching to attention; so we set our faces and trudged on.

It has been printed that the tanks were called 'Willies.' We ourselves never used the name. At first they were known as landships, and H. M. I. S. Campania comes to mind. In those days all the tanks were named. There were Explorer and Explosive, for instance; and when the Germans came to use tanks we found that they had named theirs, too; for one of the first German tank-commanders called the tank Elfreda, probably after his sweetheart. But Elfreda turned out to be fickle and quickly deserted to our side, and we made much of her, for she was the first of her type to be captured. With us, however, names quickly fell into disfavor, and in the end were discontinued, and tanks fell to the military routine of carrying regimental numbers.

In those early days a tank always to be relied upon to create more than usual interest was one presented to the British army by a councilor of the Malay States. In front of the tank, on either side, was painted a large staring eye, such as may be seen on the bows of Chinese junks; and the idea probably was the same, for the Chinese say, if a ship has not got eyes, how in the world can it possibly see to go?

To-day tanks are largely of four types: the male tank, the female tank, the gun-carrier (or supply) tank, and the 'whippet.' The male and female tanks are of the heavy type, and are identical in size. They differ only in armament, for the male tank carries two large cannons and five machine-guns, whereas the female variety is armed with seven machine-guns, reversing the poet's assertion that the female of the species is deadlier than the male.

While male and female work together and probably would have entered the Ark side by side had they existed in those days, they are used for entirely different work. Generally speaking, the male tank is used first to pass over barbed wire and flatten it, so that infantry may walk through, and then goes on to the more important work of destroying 'pill-boxes'—machine-gun emplacements—so called because of their appearance. It is for this work that the cannons are used and armor-piercing shells are fired, and not infrequently what remains of the emplacement is sat upon by the tank itself. That, however, is a dangerous undertaking, for the tank might be hoist with its own petard and ditched in its own destruction.

The female tank, moving in the wake of the male, passes over the wire in the same spot, effectively flattening it, and acts as 'mopper-up' of the infantry, with the exception of those who come into direct observation of the male; for while the male is pounding the 'pill-boxes' with her guns, the female is going across the enemy's trenches and moving along the tops of them, firing her machine-guns at the infantry there.

In shape male and female, as they are to-day, are identical with that first tank used at the Battle of the Somme. One attachment that was immediately discarded, however, was the trailer of wheels. These great wheels were used to assist in steering the tank, and were so devised that, when it went into a shell-hole or a trench, they could be lifted clear by internal mechanism. They were found to be of little value, however, and were discarded without delay. That was the first improvement, and later, when certain other internal changes were made, the tank manoeuvred so much better and went so much faster that, when those which had been captured from us were patched up and used against us, we found that we were able to run circles around them and defeat them at each encounter.

Of all our tanks the least successful was the gun-carrier. This was of greater length than the fighting tank; and was designed to carry a piece of ordinance of large calibre into advanced positions, newly captured; and the arrangement was such that the gun could either be fired from the tank or be dismounted and put on wheels. For some reason, however, this plan did not work out as well as was expected, and many of the gun-carrier tanks were used to bring up supplies, and as such did highly efficient work, more than making up for their early failure.

Of all our tanks the 'whippet' was the big surprise. This was a small tank, built for the purpose of pursuit on ground which could not be traversed by an armored car. The surprise came when the whippet, built much along the lines of the gun-carrier, succeeded in traversing ground which invariably ditched the bigger supply-tank.

With the failure of the gun-carrier, we of the heavy fighting tanks came to the belief that to have the tracks—or caterpillar tread—pass completely round the hull was an essential to success; for in the gun-carriers this was not done and they found difficulty in getting out of holes. But when the whippet, whose tracks, like those of the gun-carrier, did not pass completely round the hull, proved a success, we came to change our views and to lay the blame to incorrect balance.

While whippets were first used in the early part of 1918, it was not until the second defeat of the German army on the Marne and the Somme that this type came to be generally known. The enemy's forced retreat to the old Hindenburg line was an ideal condition for the whippet, and these little tanks, which have a greater speed than their bigger brothers and sisters, were able to harass the foe and to break up the rear-guard machine-gun fighting which he attempted to put up. This they did so effectively that, in the late summer of that year, civilians seemed to talk in terms of whippets, not realizing that the preliminary work of the male and female tanks in flattening down wire, breaking 'pill-boxes,' and causing the enemy to give up his lines of defense, was needed before the whippet's effectiveness could be complete.

These, then, were the tanks which our men took into action. In the beginning none of us knew anything about tanks. We had learned the engine and the mechanism, and had driven them over holes and trenches; but battle conditions are found to be entirely different. And because this engine of war was new, our high command had to learn tank tactics; and not before all of us had made many mistakes, did we learn how tanks should be handled and where they should be used. Those mistakes cost us dear, both in men and in tanks, and there was a time when, although we ourselves knew the tank to be a valuable instrument, we quite understood that the confidence of the public had been shaken by our failures.

How near the Tank Corps came to being abandoned, few persons know. Its fate was decided by one single engagement, and only a minor operation at that.

At one point on our line there was a German position of seven machine-gun emplacements or 'pill-boxes,' which was forever causing trouble. It was planned to take that position, and the commander there was ordered to draw up a plan of attack and an estimate of casualties; for in the British army no attack is made without an estimate of casualties, and if they are out of proportion to the zenith of success, the attack is never made. In this instance the number was placed between 400 and 500. This figure the high command thought too high, and the Tanks were asked if they could capture the position. Officers of our corps looked over the ground and examined aeroplane maps. Then they announced that they could take the position, and that, as the infantry would be used only to consolidate the ground won, the casualties would not be nearly so high as the first estimate. And so the attack was made, and the position was taken. The casualties were only seventeen and the Tank Corps was saved.

We called them 'busses,' and the name stuck. 'Landship' was too long and too clumsy to last. Even 'tank' did not stand the test of time, except officially in the army forms and the army correspondence. Always it was busses.

To each bus a crew was assigned. The duties of the crew were to keep the mechanism and the guns in working order, and to take the tank into battle. With the large busses the crew consisted of one commissioned officer, one non-commissioned officer, and six men. In the case of the gun-carrier, when those busses were relegated to supply-work, only drivers were carried, as there were no guns. With the whippets the crew was not so numerous as with the male and female tanks, because the whippet was smaller, and there were fewer guns to be operated.

The general shape of the heavy British fighting tank is well known. The elevation is roughly that of a rhombus, with the two acute angles rounded off. The plan resembles somewhat the letter H, with a heavy cross-bar for the body, the sides of the letter representing the tracks.

For the most part the tanks are made of armor-plating. In some places the armor is thicker than in others, but at the thickest it is not more than three eighths of an inch. This may seem ridiculously inadequate, but the armor is hardened by a process used for ships of the British navy. It is bullet-proof and bomb-proof, and shrapnel more often than not does no harm. Armor-piercing shells, however, are effective when direct hits are made. The Germans even use an armor-piercing shell weighing only one pound, and seem to think it quite satisfactory. These shells are fired from specially designed anti-tank guns, which are kept in the front lines or in concealed places just behind the line.

Even the tracks are made of armor-plate. These tracks in the heavy fighting-tanks run completely round the body, and are made of individual plates, so that they can be 'broken,' opened up, anywhere, to permit the mechanism underneath them to be examined. This mechanism, in a general way, consists of rollers, chains, and sprocket-wheels and differs little from that of the average American tractor, but is greatly improved. The rollers need constant lubrication, and after every trip men are assigned to greasing up. This is a job which all of us hate cordially, because it consists of forcing grease into these rollers from outside, with a grease-gun, and one not only gets very dirty but, as there are fifty-four rollers to each tank and most of these are within two inches of the ground, the job is back-breaking and often necessitates sitting down in the mud. Usually greasing up outside falls to the gunners, for the drivers have other work inside, not always so arduous but equally important, and needing their greater knowledge of the engine and controls.

Projecting from either side of the male tank are two large sponsons. These are not quite one-third the entire length of the bus and are placed amidships. They are emplacements for the guns, and give the heavy cannon a wide traverse. The sponsons are removable and can be pushed in flush with the side. Were this not so, tanks could not be taken on trains because of their great width with the sponsons in position, and every move by train involves the arduous job of pushing in sponsons when entraining and pushing them out after detraining.

In the female tank the sponsons are comparatively small. The large one is not needed in this case, as the female has only machine-guns; but even the small sponson of the female is made to shut in. The supply-tanks and the whippets do not have sponsons.

Entrance, in the case of the male tank, is effected by means of doors at the back of each of the sponsons. In the case of the female these doors are underneath the sponson and open into the side. There is also a door at the rear of the heavy fighting tank, and a fourth place of entrance or exit elsewhere. All these doors are provided with locks, which are proof even against the Hun; there have been times when he has come around and tried to open them, to be greeted with revolver-fire; for each member of the tank crew carries a revolver for personal protection and close-quarters work.

The engine is installed along the centre-line of the tank and slightly forward of the middle. At first, a powerful engine designed for heavy tractor-work was used; but this was found to be scarcely strong enough, and another engine was specially designed and contributed no small part of the success of the improved tank.

It is in the front of the tank that the driver sits; for there are the throttle and the controls and the brakes and the gauges which register the oil- and petrol-pressure. Beside him usually is the non-commissioned officer, who operates the forward machine-gun; and by no means the least among the driver's annoyances are the empty cartridge-cases which are ejected from this gun and which usually find the driver's left ear or eye as a target.

The tank officer usually sits in the conning tower amidships. Observation from the driver's seat is restricted on either side because of the tracks, but from the conning tower the lookout has an unrestricted view in all directions. Thus he can watch for 'targets,' and, being in the middle of the tank, is well situated to command it. He is so close to most of the gunners that he can communicate with them either by shouting or by making signs, but so terrific is the noise of the engine that it would be utterly impossible for the non-commissioned officer and the driver to hear him, so speaking-tubes run from the conning tower to the driver's cab.

In action in a tank, heat is one of the great hardships, for it is so exhausting that the men frequently have to buck themselves up with restoratives, carried in the tank's medicine bag.

Usually, in the ordinary course of travel, or going up, men walk outside the tank, or ride on the top, the driver alone being inside; but in action all have to be inside, and the tank is shut up so that in broad daylight it is quite dark within. Observation for the driver and gunners is made possible by lookout ports, in which eight tiny holes are drilled. Strangely enough, observation is not so difficult as might be imagined. It is above these holes that the only padding in the tank is placed; for, contrary to the general impression, tanks are not padded inside, nor are men strapped into seats. The gunners for the most part stand; the two men forward are seated, and when the driver is about to take a severe drop or incline, he shouts back through the speaking-tube and the men hang on, bracing themselves against the engine or the guns. The padding over the lookout holes consists of a head-rest against which one presses the forehead in order to bring the eyes as close to the holes as possible. These lookout holes superseded periscopic prisms, which proved unsatisfactory. The prisms were made of glass about two inches thick; but bullets striking the glass, while not breaking it, starred it so that observation became difficult if not quite impossible. To meet this, a steel reflector was tried out, but did not answer the purpose; and so the holes were resorted to, and while observation involves an unnatural straining of the neck, it is effective.

While bullets do not penetrate the armor, but only ruffle it up a bit at the point where they are deflected, a great deal of bullet 'splash' does come in. This is more annoying than serious, and after an action one could pick out any number of these tiny splinters from one's face. So, as a means of protection against 'splash,' face-armor was invented. This looks much like a bandit's mask, with a steel-mesh chain hanging from it. The mask itself is of thin steel, with slits for the eyes, the whole padded for the face and adjustable to it.

The greatest danger, however, whether in or out of action, is that of fire. Smoking inside a tank is forbidden. Usually smoking is not permitted within twenty yards of one. This is because of the great amount of petrol, or gasoline, carried, and because of the fumes. Thus an armor-piercing shell entering the tank not only explodes in a confined area, but usually sets the machine on fire. When that happens, men have to escape as best they can, tumbling out of the doors, usually to be greeted by the enemy's machine-gun fire. Often, however, so much damage was done by the shell itself, that only those nearest the doors ever escaped. The rest perished in the flames, and those who have ever had to go back to a tank and see their comrades burned almost beyond recognition will bear testimony that death by fire was feared more than anything else.

Such, then, is the tank. It came at a time when intense artillery barrages made the ground in front and behind the lines almost impossible to traverse. Thus the infantry was hampered in movement, and often reached the enemy's barbed wire only to find that, while its form had been destroyed, it lay there as tangled and as dangerous as ever. Furthermore these barrages were enormously expensive, and one British barrage lasting three days cost more than $63,000,000.

Perhaps the most serious fault of the barrage, however, was the notice of attack which it gave the enemy. While an attack might be on a limited front and the barrage on an extended front, it was like sending a visiting card. So the Germans watched and prayed. Often they prayed for the attack to begin; for after two or three days and nights of intense artillery and trench-mortar fire one longs to have it over and done with.

The tank virtually abolished this method of attack. Artillery barrages were kept up even after the tanks were perfected, but frequently the element of surprise was attained by the use of tanks without a preliminary fire. And so, in the dark of the early morning, the tanks go over, male and female, ahead of all others, and they cross the enemy's wire and flatten that, and then press on against his 'pill-boxes,' leaving the infantry with their bombs to settle affairs in the dugouts. Often the artillery assists the tanks, once the battle has begun, and particularly when dawn breaks and visibility exists. Then they put up a smoke-barrage, and the tanks carry on with the assistance of these screens, smashing down defenses, mopping up personnel, and creating terror in the hearts of the enemy.

PART VII

WITNESSES TO WAR

At the war's beginning not one of the fighting countries cared for war correspondents. The reporter's dispatches often gave information the generals considered vital dealing with the location of forces, their strength and their armaments. Newspaper reporters and magazine writers had a difficult time getting the news back to their readers. And when the belligerent nation's propaganda mills began to grind out stories of their own, correspondents were steered and monitored, and "information" began to flow to the printed page.

Correspondents covered all types of events during the war years. Some of them became observers by choice, travelling deliberately into ravaged areas to convey information from the fighting lines to news-starved countries. Publications from books to magazines and newspapers sought to fill the communication gap. They offered stories (sometimes sensational) of citizens and soldiers embroiled in the war.

One such correspondent was ex-Senator Albert Jeremiah Beveridge, a staunch supporter of Theodore Roosevelt's policies. He had lost his Senate seat in 1911 and his bid for governor of Indiana in 1912. The ex-Senator turned to the writing of history and traveled extensively in Europe noting conditions and the reactions of the citizens in various countries. As noted earlier in this work, he assessed public opinion in England. He moved on to other countries, possibly at their request, for at this time popular support in the United States was divided between the Central Powers and the Allies. Senator Beveridge reported on the activities of the German and French armies, seeing them in "their best Sunday suits."

It might also be noted that in Senator Beveridge's reporting the conversation with a French soldier, a prisoner of war, the Senator quoted him as saying "They treat us like white men, sir," which may be more Indiana than France.

Training New German Armies

All over Germany fresh troops are in training. This has been going on for many months. Every possible detail of every possible experience at the front is gone over and over and over, time and time and time again. You may see every phase of a real battle, except of course the actual wounding and killing, in the country adjoining any one of the innumerable training camps scattered throughout the Empire: artillery action, trench fighting, advances in the open, cavalry work, scouting, management of supplies, both food and ammunition—in short every conceivable thing that occurs in active service. Excepting only casualties, one could take photographs on these practise fields, and in these training camps, or one could write descriptions, and both photograph and description would faithfully portray scenes at and near the battle line, so exactly are conditions at the front reproduced.

The thoroughness of this training of the common soldier cannot be put too strongly or too often. When finally the recruit is allowed to go to the scene of the action, he already is a seasoned soldier, except for the experience of hearing and feeling hostile lead and steel. Most of these men have had much physical and disciplinary education. Therefore in these camps at present, the theory itself is being carefully modified by actual experience in the present war. It is reasonably safe to say that the German soldier of 1915 will be a more efficient man than was his comrade who rallied to the colors last August. As to military training, it should be noticed that scholars like the great theologian Harnack, or the Socialist leader Suedekum, think it is so good a thing for developing health, strength, and efficiency, that the German people are more than repaid for this investment. "Aside from the military phase—if no army were needed and no war possible—I should earnestly favor our system of military training, physically, mentally, and morally, as a vital part of our educational system," said Professor Harnack. If such a thing were possible, the instruction and drill of those preparing to be officers is far more careful and complete than the exacting and exhaustive military schooling given the common soldier. And these future officers are spared no hardship. They are toughened and seasoned quite as much as the men whom they soon are to command. You study with keen interest company after company of these young men who are striving for commissions. You are struck by the high intelligence of their faces; character and education is written on every feature. Their bearing is manful and soldierly. Germany's worst enemy could not fail to be impressed by the appearance of these men, even though he looked at them through the glasses of hatred.

Of the hundreds studied in one immense training camp in January, 1915, none looked younger than twenty or older than thirty. From their appearance and conduct they seemed to be prime soldier stock.

The training differs from that of peace times only in its continuity. It is intensive training upon soil well prepared. These things are stated only because they are facts, precisely as one might describe any fact, such as a tree, bridge, railway train, house, field, hill.

No one but the military authorities knows the number of men now in training. Certainly it is very great. And waiting eagerly for their turn are hundreds upon hundreds of thousands. To the casual and unskilled observer, ignorant of military things, there seems to be no end of men in Germany.

These may or may not be fit war material—you do not know, personally.

But as to numbers, they at least seem to be myriads. By careful questioning in every quarter, and in different parts of Germany, during several weeks, and piecing together, weighing and testing information thus garnered, the conclusion seems justified that Germany expects to keep 5,000,000 men actively in the field, year in and year out, no matter how long the war lasts, and more than 5,000,000 cannot be used to advantage. By 5,000,000 is meant soldiers and officers as well trained as those called to the colors last August. All this, too, in the regular, ordinary course of events, without straining her human resources.

Care of Germany's Wounded

But what of the wounded and disabled? Of these, by semi-official estimate up to January 15, there were 543,000, of whom 322,000 were only slightly wounded, and at that time nearly ready to go to the front again; and 221,000 more seriously wounded, of whom 35 per cent would soon be ready for duty once more. A more generous computation gave 650,000 wounded, of whom 60 per cent, or 390,000 men, could return to the front within a short time.

The care of these injured ones is infinitesimal in scientific detail and very tender on its human side. The best hospital trains are marvels of comfort, convenience, efficiency. In each regulation hospital train there are twenty cars; in each car, there are beds for ten patients. Each bed is suspended on powerful springs fixed at the ends so as to absorb the shock. Above each bed are two looped straps which the wounded one may rest his weary arms and hands. In a case at the side is a glass, water, and toothbrush; in short, no mechanical convenience has been neglected. Then, of course, there are operating cars, surgeons' cars. Above all, on these hospital trains there are women nurses, carefully chosen not only for their knowledge, nerve and skill, but also for their gift of human sympathy.

These maimed men are promptly cared for before reaching hospital trains, in the field hospital, very near the scene of the casualty, and next in a division base hospital within sound of the firing line. Go into one of these latter establishments of succor. Here a soldier is recovering, and is very happy, almost joyful. His only thought, he tells you, is to get back to the fighting. There another is too badly hurt to talk or even think.

Yonder, a man lies dying, and he expires in your presence; but it does not astonish, for you have seen the same thing in the Philippines, down to the smallest detail of sunken cheek, stertorous breathing, rattling throat, and final silence. Also you have seen the same thing but more sordidly, and without the least tinge of romance or glory, in New York hospitals.

But what is this? The general commanding that corps comes in. He does not stride. He walks softly. He goes to the bedside of a common soldier, sore wounded, on whose breast he pins, by a black and white ribbon, the Iron Cross with words of praise for gallantry. Three times this happens; once the prostrate figure answers with articulate words of thanks. The other two are too sick to speak; but appreciation shines from their eyes.

Finally comes the transfer of the wounded to the great permanent hospitals located at central points in every large German city. Witness the unloading of the maimed from the newly arrived hospital train.

It is early morning. A chill rain is falling. Two- or three-score men with red cross bands on their coat sleeves carry the disabled soldiers on stretchers to waiting vehicles which haul them to hospital buildings—there are red cross ambulances, luxurious limousines, great furniture vans with reclining places for the wounded, much like the beds on the trains. A few women, who have relatives in those cars, stand patiently about.

A well-dressed, gray-haired man is looking for his son, whom he soon finds, desperately hurt, and walks by the stretcher's side to the limousine. There are no tears. Each person, man or woman, holds back all emotion with firm hand. Having settled down to the business of war, they are doing it in steady fashion, facing the ugly as well as the stirring with equal patience and fortitude.

Of dozens of convalescing, wounded soldiers talked to, all but one expressed their eagerness to get back to the front. There was no false enthusiasm about them, no pretense. You could not doubt their earnestness and sincerity. The expression of the face, tone of voice, above all the look from the eye, left no room for doubt. One soldier who had been shot in the leg at the Battle of Tannenberg said he was quite comfortable where he was. He would not be able to walk very well anyhow, he thought, and did not seem to regret it. But he was the one exception. Of the total number of wounded in every way, at least 60 per cent go to the front again. Cautious and conservative estimates place the percentage even higher, more indeed than 70 per cent. The anxiety of the men to return to the firing line equals their desire to get well. Indeed this state of mind has something to do with the quickness of their recovery. Great numbers of German soldiers have been wounded, treated, and have gone back to service three separate times.

Professor Dr. O. Kiliani, of New York, one of the principal surgeons with the German forces operating near Lille, France, has personally observed many cases of this kind. The uncomplaining fortitude of the wounded, their astonishing vitality and power of resistance, their ardor and determination to get into the fighting as soon as possible, Professor Kiliani thinks the most notable physical and psychological facts coming under the observation of the scientist.

Dr. Charles Haddon Sanders, of Washington, D. C., head of the American Red Cross hospital at Gleiwitz, Germany, on the Russian frontier, testifies to the same thing. "Every man of them," said Dr. Sanders, "is anxious to get back to the front and the fighting. Not one of them wants to go home. Their spirit and confidence is beyond belief. I want to say this for these wounded German soldiers whom we have operated upon and treated: no patients could be more appreciative of what is done for them. I have been impressed by their cleanliness of mind and manner."

Germany's Prisoners

Germany has within her borders at the present moment not far from 700,000 prisoners of war. At the end of December, the exact number was 586,000 of whom 310,000 were Russians, 220,000 French, 40,000 Belgian, and 16,000 British. These specific figures are those of the railway department which is the only mathematically accurate authority. British are included Sikhs, Gurkhas, and others from India; among the French, Arabs, Moors, and others from Africa.

On January 15 a semi-official but fairly reliable estimate placed the total number of prisoners at 633,000. While this latter figure is not from the railway records it is believed to be reasonably dependable. At the date of this writing, February 10, 1915, it is known that many thousands of additional prisoners have been taken. Thus an approximation of 700,000 would seem to be not unfair. These numbers include no civilians, but only soldiers who had been actually engaged in hostilities.

This same semi-official but sufficiently authoritative estimate placed the total number of German missing and prisoners at 154,000. It is possible, of course, that all of these may be prisoners.

Thus Germany has on her hands, in unwounded, able-bodied, captured enemies, about one per cent of her total population of men, women and children. To feed these prisoners means the providing of enough food to supply the whole German nation for about three days out of a year. Yet it is firmly expected in Germany that the number of prisoners taken by the German forces will be very greatly increased during the present year, and Germany is preparing, now, for that contingency.

These soldiers of the Allies held in Germany are concentrated in prison camps scattered all over the Empire. Let us, then, go carefully through two of these camps, which are typical of all. Yet all these places are not alike; for, although the same general orders govern all, and the same quantity and quality of food is supplied everywhere, the character, ability and inclination of the camp commander has much to do with the camp management.

"We have no complaint to make, sir, considering that we are prisoners of war," was the answer of a French common soldier when questioned about their treatment; "and," added he, of his own accord, "they treat us like white men, sir." This particular prisoner spoke English perfectly, having worked in London for three or four years.

As I was permitted to talk freely with the prisoners, more than a score were questioned and conversed with, Russians and French, as well as English. This was done through an interpreter, whom I have known personally for many years, brought with me for such work from my own home town in America where he was born, and who has no German associations or connections whatever. No German interpreted anything here reported; nor did anyone object or interfere in the slightest with my conversing with the prisoners.

In this camp were more than 12,000 men, the great majority of them being French, the next largest number being Russians. There are perhaps 300 or 400 Sikhs, Gurkhas, and Turcos, and only thirty Englishmen.

Very lonely, these last appear among so many thousands of their fellow prisoners, whose language they do not speak or understand and with whom, it would seem, they associate but little. Perhaps this is the reason for the sour frame of mind in which this tiny group of men was found, which was in striking contrast with the comparative contentment of the French, Russians, Sikhs, and Gurkhas.

"Do you get enough to eat?"

"Only a bare existence, sir."

"But can you not buy what you want at the camp canteen? Do you not get money from home?"

"No, sir. I wrote to my brother in the States for money the end of last November, and I have had no answer yet—" It was then the nineteenth of January!

Such are fair samples of the comments of several of these thirty English prisoners.

On the contrary:

"How are you getting along?" was asked of a Russian.

"All right," he answered. "We have nothing to complain of."

"Do you get enough to eat?"

"Yes, plenty," came the contented reply.

"I'll wager," broke in the German camp commander, "that he is getting more to eat than he ever had before in his life!"

This exact exchange of question and answer was in substance the same as that which occurred with all Russian prisoners talked to. Without exception, each of them grinned with bovine good humor.

"Considering that you are a prisoner, I take it that you are satisfied, from what you have said," was the concluding remark to a hearty, pleasant-faced Frenchmen, after many questions and answers about food, treatment and occupation.

"Yes, considering, as you say, that we are prisoners."

"But of course you don't like prison life," was the visitor's banal and silly remark.

"Of course not," he smiled. He was too polite to laugh outright. "But we get along very well. Considering that we are prisoners, much better than we had expected."

And here is another scrap of conversation, with another French prisoner in this camp:

"How do you get along with the German officers and guards?"

"Why, very well indeed," he answered.

"Do you mean that the relations between you Frenchmen and the Germans are good?" was the surprised query.

"Why, yes," he answered, "that is our personal relations. But," he added quickly, "of course that has nothing to do with our patriotic feeling. That is stronger than ever, if possible."

Since the subject of food was mentioned in every conversation, the question was asked of the German commander:

"What do you give them to eat?"

"In the morning, bread and coffee; at midday, bread and a thick soup made of potatoes with some other vegetable in which five times a week, meat is included; at evening, bread and a thinner soup. The water, of course, is filtered." It was the lack of meat of which the English chiefly complained.

The prisoners' barracks are large, well built, wooden affairs, much better than those occupied by the interned Belgian soldiers in Holland. Sometimes there are three or four tiers of bunks, one above another, supported by heavy, upright timbers. These are not close or crowded. The mattress is made of a rough substance, like gunnysack, filled with straw. There are plenty of blankets; several stoves were observed. It was a cold snowy day, but the interior of every barrack visited was comfortably warm.

The prisoners appeared to be well-nourished and healthy. In two camps and among many hundreds of prisoners personally inspected, only one was found who looked in poor health and said he felt badly—a small-statured Russian. The commanders of both camps said that little or no sickness had as yet developed.

In the barracks occupied by the prisoners from India, there is an unusual feature: every Hindu cooks and in every way prepares his own food, for he will not eat anything touched by Christian hands. Many of them were observed at this private and religio-culinary occupation. The Gurkha sergeant in charge of this barrack spoke English very well. He and his companions were treated very well, he said, much better than they expected.

Would he like to get back to India? He would, more than anything.

Why had he come to the war?

"Orders, sir."

He good-naturedly interpreted for a group of tall, grave-faced Sikhs, statues of dignity and gravity.

Why had they come to fight?

"The service" was the answer; and the Gurkha sergeant tried to make their meaning clear by such expressions as "their duty," "their profession," "their business." As to wanting to go home, one gathered that they were quite indifferent, that it was all the same to them and that they took things as they happened.

In the barracks where the Turcos lived came the one disagreeable, even shocking, surprise of the day. It is impossible to imagine more villainous-looking creatures. Nearly all of them are small men, and most of them have viciousness stamped on every feature. Their evil eyes follow you expressionless, unblinking, like those of a serpent. Some of these men undoubtedly are criminals—the forehead, jaw, mouth, back head, and above all the merciless, soulless eyes spell depravity. The Sikhs and Gurkhas from India, some of whom have fine and even noble features, are infinitely superior to this scum of Northern Africa; for such at least most of these particular Turcos must be. There are some faces among them that are not bad; but, most of them justify the harshest description.

They were clad in an amazing array of garments—here one, an Arab, a blue mark on his forehead, wearing the bornous of the desert; there another, of a different ethnology, clad in a totally unfamiliar uniform of dark blue, with brass buttons; still another with the braided jacket and baggy trousers of the zouave—and so on throughout as outré a collection of costumes as the imagination of a Lewis Carroll could picture.

Another prisoners' camp was exactly like the first you had seen in the food and occupations of the captured. But it had no landscape gardening, no sculptor, no chorus; perhaps because there were comparatively few French, or because of the lack of initiative, invention, and sympathy of the German camp commander. Doubtless it was both. In this camp, the nationalities of the prisoners were almost reversed; a large number of the English, very many Russians, comparatively few French, and no blacks. Here the English were more cheerful and less complaining than their thirty desolate brothers in the first camp visited; but here, also, the hostility between the English and Germans was even more pronounced.

"The English are very difficult," the genial commander of the first camp visted had remarked, and:

"We can't get along with the English. They won't work. They object to everything." was the comment of the somewhat rheumatic German commander of the second prison camp visited.

On their part, the dislike of the English prisoners for the Germans was still more pointed and acid. While most of them frankly said that they thought themselves very well off as to food and quarters in view of the fact that they were prisoners of war, still when one was asked:

"Would you rather be here or in the trenches?" the answer came with a snap:

"In the trenches, sir. I'd like to get a crack at them, sir!"

And another, this time a tailor, one of the fewer than a dozen Englishmen actually seen at voluntary work, answering the same question, said sharply: "In the trenches with my comrades, sir. Anything is better than this."

In general, the hostility of the English prisoners to their German captors was plainly apparent, and indeed, unconcealed. One could not help admiring the openness and boldness of it. Conversely, the dislike of the German officers and guards for their stubborn wards was no less manifest. You could not but like the frankness displayed by both. The only difference in their mutual dislike seemed to be that the Germans gave reasons, such as: "The English won't work." Or: "The English are quarrelsome." Or: "The English fight the French with their fists." Or: "The English are always complaining."

On the other hand, with the English antipathy for the Germans, it was a case of:

"I do not like you, Dr. Fell!
The reason why I cannot tell
But this one thing I know full well:
I do not like you, Dr. Fell!"

Yet it seems that both Germans and English respect one another highly as first-class fighting men. For example: take the comment of a German officer at Lille, France, noted for his gallantry, which was agreed to by his fellow officers:

"The English whom we have met are good soldiers. The officers are fine."

Reciprocally: "Oh, yes, the Germans fight well enough; like devils, sir." was the comment of an English prisoner who had just expressed his dislike for the Germans and his earnest wish to "get at them" again.

"Do you get enough to eat?" you ask a bearded English sailor.

"I suppose so; but not as much as we should like, sir." He said he got money from home and could buy what he liked in the canteen. "But," said he; "we can't get jam, sir."

"Jam!" you exclaim, in ill-mannered surprise. "Yes, sir. Jam, sir, and chocolate and such other, the dainties, sir."

The camp post office is the liveliest place of all. Always these stations of intelligence seem to be crowded. Also, they are disbursement centers. In one camp 33,000 marks had been paid to French prisoners by the end of the year 1914. This money was sent from France by the friends or relatives of the captured relatives of the captured prisoners. It is not given out in bulk or cash by the German officials. Ten marks a week is the maximum allowed to a private soldier, so that he will not spend it recklessly. At the canteen are sold only food and clothing; the sale of intoxicants are forbidden.

Of many thousands of prisoners personally inspected, all but one appeared to be in robust health. You were surprised at their rosy cheeks, well-nourished condition and general fitness. As far as is possible, those who will not work voluntarily, making articles which are sold and paid for, are compelled to do labor of some kind. Hundreds are compelled to draw and push wagons laden with camp provisions. Other hundreds keep clean the streets of German cities and the approaching roads. Nuremburg is an example of this. But with every possible employment, only a fraction of Germany's 700,000 prisoners can be given useful occupations during the winter.

When Spring and Summer come, however, there will be another story. It is planned, at least in parts of Germany, in certain portions of Bavaria, for example, to employ the prisoners in tilling the soil, sowing the seed, and gathering the harvest. For this work, the French are willing and the Russians more than eager. No woman, child, or old man need work in the fields of Germany during the present year, unless they insist upon doing so, for there are enough prisoners anxious to perform the labor in preference to the confinement of the camps.

Kings, Queens and Pawns

Mary Roberts Rinehart

"NIGHT IN THE TRENCHES"
GEORGE H. DORAN CO., 1915

The antagonism toward correspondents in the early days of the war was to discourage many newsmen and magazine writers to feed on the tragedy sweeping Europe. That didn't deter Mary Roberts Rinehart, a young married woman, registered nurse, member of the American Red Cross, and up to the date of the war, the writer of three mystery books and one novel, from applying for a tour of the front lines.

She listed her occupation as 'writer,' but one of her main concerns for the trip was the distribution of medical supplies contributed by the United States. Mrs. Rinehart was interested in the type of supplies, the need for them, and the conditions under which they were administered. Rumors in America were that the medical situation in Europe was chaotic.

She also wished to get the full picture of the war so that she could show it for the horror that it is; a picture that might give pause to ". . . that certain percentage of the American people that is always so eager to force a conservative government into conflict with other nations."

America was sending large amounts of money and vast quantities of supplies to the Belgians on both sides of the line. What was being done in Belgium was well known, but those hospital supplies and other things shipped to northern France were swallowed up in great silence.

"Let me see conditions as they really are," Mary Roberts Rinehart said. "It's no use telling me about them. Then I can tell the American people what they have already done in the war zone, and what they may be asked to do."

There was much debate at the Anglo-Belgium Committee for correspondents were allowed in to the battle zones in limited numbers and for no more than 24 hours—after which they were shipped across the channel or to some innocuous destination in the South.

Rinehart stayed for a short time in the Hôtel des Arcades in Dunkirk. Around the corner, the police had closed a house for a month as punishment because a room had been rented to a news correspondent. He had been sentenced to five years imprisonment, but had been released after five weeks.

Rinehart emphasized that she was a writer, not a correspondent, and received her card permitting her to visit hospitals and the front lines.

Because of the inundation directly in front, (the trenches) are rather shallow, and at this point were built against the railroad embankment with earth, boards, and here and there a steel rail from the track. Some of them were covered, too, but not with bombproof material. The tops were merely shelters from the rain and biting wind.

The men lay or sat in them—it was impossible to stand. Some of them were like tiny houses into which the men crawled from the rear, and by placing a board, which served as a door, managed to keep out at least a part of the bitter wind.

In the first trench I was presented to a bearded major. He was lying flat and apologised for not being able to rise. There was a machine gun beside him. He told me with some pride that it was an American gun, and that it never jammed. When a machine gun jams the man in charge of it dies and his comrades die, and things happen with great rapidity. On the other side of him was a cat, curled up and sound asleep. There was a telephone instrument there. It was necessary to step over the wire that was stretched along the ground.

All night long he lies there with his gun, watching for the first movement in the trenches across. For here, at the House of the Barrier, has taken place some of the most furious fighting of this part of the line.

In the next division of the trench were three men. They were cleaning and oiling their rifles around a candle.

The surprise of all of these men at seeing a woman was almost absurd. Word went down the trenches that a woman was visiting. Heads popped out and cautious comments were made. It was concluded that I was visiting royalty, but the excitement died when it was discovered that I was not the Queen. Now and then, when a trench looked clean and dry, I was invited in. It was necessary to get down and crawl in on hands and knees.

Here was a man warming his hands over a tiny fire kindled in a tin pail. He had bored holes in the bottom of the pail for air, and was shielding the glow carefully with his overcoat.

Many people have written about the trenches—the mud, the odours, the inhumanity of compelling men to live under such foul conditions. Nothing that they have said can be too strong. Under the best conditions the life is ghastly, horrible, impossible.

That night, when from a semi-shielded position I could look across to the German line, the contrast between the condition of the men in the trenches and the beauty of the scenery was appalling. In each direction, as far as one could see, lay a gleaming lagoon of water. The moon made a silver path across it, and here and there on its borders were broken and twisted winter trees.

"It is beautiful," said Captain F——, beside me, in a low voice. "But it is full of the dead. They are taken out whenever it is possible; but it is not often possible."

"And when there is an attack the attacking side must go through the water?"

"Not always, but in many places."

"What will happen if it freezes over?"

He explained that it was salt water, and would not freeze easily. And the cold of that part of the country is not the cold of America in the same latitude. It is not a cold of low temperature; it is a damp, penetrating cold that goes through garments of every weight and seems to chill the very blood in a man's body.

"How deep is the water?" I asked.

"It varies—from two to eight feet. Here it is shallow."

"I should think they would come over."

"The water is full of barbed wire," he said grimly. "And some, a great many, have tried—and failed."

As of the trenches, many have written of the stenches of this war. But the odour of that beautiful lagoon was horrible. I do not care to emphasize it. It is one of the things best forgotten. But any lingering belief I may have had in the grandeur and glory of war died that night beside that silver lake—died of an odour and will never live again.

And now came a discussion.

The road crossing the railroad embankment turned sharply to the left and proceeded in front of the trenches. There was no shelter on that side of the embankment. The inundation bordered the road, and just beyond the inundation were the German trenches.

There were no trees, no shrubbery, no houses; just a flat road, paved with Belgian blocks, that gleamed in the moonlight.

At last the decision was made. We would go along the road, provided I realised from the first that it was dangerous. One or two could walk there with a good chance for safety, but no more. The little group had been augmented. It must break up; two might walk together, and then two a safe distance behind. Four would certanly be fired on.

I wanted to go. It was not a matter of courage. I had simply, parrot-fashion, mimicked the attitude of mind of the officers. One after another I had seen men go into danger with a shrug of the shoulders.

"If it comes, it comes!" they said, and went on. So I, too, had become a fatalist. If I was to be shot it would happen, if I had to buy a rifle and try to clean it myself to fulfil my destiny.

So they let me go. I went farther than they expected, as it turned out. There was a great deal of indignation and relief when it was over. But that was later on.

A very tall Belgian officer took me in charge. It was necessary to work through a barbed-wire barricade, twisting and turning through its mazes. The moonlight helped. It was at once a comfort and an anxiety, for it seemed to me that my khaki-coloured suit gleamed in it. The Belgian officers in their dark blue were less conspicuous. I thought they had an unfair advantage of me, and that it was idiotic of the British to wear and advocate anything so abusurd as khaki. My cape ballooned like a sail in the wind. I felt at least double my ordinary size, and that even a sniper with a squint could hardly miss me. And, by way of comfort, I had one last instruction before I started:

"If a *fusée* goes up, stand perfectly still. If you move they will fire."

The entire safety of the excursion depended on a sort of tacit agreement that, in part at least, obtains as to sentries.

This is a new warfare, one of artillery, supported by infantry in trenches. And it has been necessary to make new laws for it. One of the most curious is a sort of *modus vivendi* by which each side protects its own sentries by leaving the enemy's sentries unmolested so long as there is no active fighting. They are always in plain view before the trenches. In case of a charge they are the first to be shot, of course. But long nights and days have gone by along certain parts of the front where the hostile trenches are close together, and the sentries, keeping their monotonous lookout, have been undisturbed.

No doubt by this time the situation has changed to a certain extent; there has been more active fighting, larger bodies of men are involved. The spring floods south of the inundation will have dried up. No Man's Land will have ceased to be a swamp and the deadlock may be broken.

But on that February night I put my faith in this agreement, and it held.

The tall Belgian officer asked me if I was frightened. I said I was not. This was not exactly the truth; but it was no time for the truth.

"They are not shooting," I said. "It looks perfectly safe."

He shrugged his shoulders, and glanced toward the German trenches.

"They have been sleeping during the rain," he said briefly. "But when one of them wakes up, look out!"

After that there was little conversation, and what there was was in whispers.

As we proceeded the stench from the beautiful moonlit water grew overpowering. The officer told me the reason.

A little farther along a path of fascines had been built out over the inundation to an outpost halfway to the German trenches. The building of this narrow roadway had cost many lives.

Half a mile along the road we were sharply challenged by a sentry. When he had received the password he stood back and let us pass. Alone in that bleak and exposed position in front of the trenches, always in full view as he paced back and forward, carbine on shoulder, with not even a tree trunk or a hedge for shelter, the first to go at the whim of some German sniper or at any indication of an attack, he was a pathetic, almost a tragic figure. He looked very young too. I stopped and asked him in a whisper how old he was.

He said he was nineteen!

He may have been. I know something about boys, and I think he was seventeen at the most. There are plenty of boys of that age doing just what that lad was doing.

Afterward I learned that it was no part of the original plan to take a woman over the fascine path to the outpost; that Captain F—— ground his teeth in impotent rage when he saw where I was being taken. But it was not possible to call or even to come up to us. So, blithely and unconsciously the tall Belgian officer and I turned to the right, and I was innocently on my way to the German trenches.

After a little I realised that this was rather more war than I had expected. The fascines were slippery; the path only four or five feet wide. On each side was the water, hideous with many secrets.

I stopped, a third of the way out, and looked back. It looked about as dangerous in one direction as another. So we went on. Once I slipped and fell. And now, looming out of the moonlight, I could see the outpost which was the object of our visit.

I have always been grateful to that Belgian lieutenant for his mistake. Just how grateful I might have been had anything untoward happened, I cannot say. But the excursion was worth all the risk, and more.

On a bit of high ground stands what was once the tiny hamlet of Oudstuyvenskerke—the ruins of two small white houses and the tower of the destroyed church—hardly a tower any more, for only three sides of it are standing and they are riddled with great shell holes.

Six hundred feet beyond this tower were the German trenches. The little island was hardly a hundred feet in its greatest dimension.

I wish I could make those people who think that war is good for a country see that Belgian outpost as I saw it that night under the moonlight. Perhaps we were under suspicion; I do not know. Suddenly the *fusées*, which had ceased for a time, began again, and with their white light added to that of the moon the desolate picture of that tiny island was a picture of the war. There was nothing lacking. There was the beauty of the moonlit waters, there was the tragedy of the destroyed homes and the church, and there was the horror of unburied bodies.

There was heroism, too, of the kind that will make Belgium live in history. For in the top of that church tower for months a Capuchin monk has held his position alone and unrelieved. He has a telephone, and he gains access to his position in the tower by means of a rope ladder which he draws up after him.

Furious fighting has taken place again and again round the base of the tower. The German shells assail it constantly. But when I left Belgium the Capuchin monk, who has become a soldier, was still on duty; still telephoning the ranges of the gun; still notifying headquarters of German preparations for a charge.

Some day the church tower will fall and he will go with it, or it will be captured; one or the other is inevitable. Perhaps it has already happened; for not long ago I saw in the newspapers that furious fighting was taking place at this very spot.

He came down and I talked to him—a little man, regarding his situation as quite ordinary, and looking quaintly unpriestlike in his uniform of a Belgian officer with its tasselled cap. Some day a great story will be written of these priests of Belgium who have left their churches to fight.

We spoke in whispers. There was after all very little to say. It would have embarrassed him horribly had any one told him that he was a heroic figure. And the ordinary small talk is not currency in such a situation.

We shook hands and I think I wished him luck. Then he went back again to the long hours and days of waiting.

I passed under his telephone wires. Some day he will telephone that a charge is coming. He will give all the particulars calmly, concisely. Then the message will break off abruptly. He will have sent his last warning. For that is the way these men at the advance posts die.

As we started again I was no longer frightened. Something of his courage had communicated itself to me, his courage and his philosophy; perhaps his faith.

The priest had become a soldier; but he was still a priest in his heart. For he had buried the German dead in one great grave before the church, and over them had put the cross of his belief.

It was rather absurd on the way back over the path of death to be escorted by a cat. It led the way over the fascines, treading daintily and cautiously. Perhaps one of the destroyed houses at the outpost had been its home, and with a cat's fondness for places it remained there, though everything it knew had gone; though battle and sudden death had usurped the place of its peaceful fireside, though that very fireside had become a heap of stone and plaster, open to winds and rain.

Again and again in destroyed towns I have seen these forlorn cats stalking about, trying vainly to adjust themselves to new conditions, cold and hungry and homeless.

We were challenged repeatedly on the way back. Coming from the direction we did we were open to suspicion. It was necessary each time to halt some forty feet from the sentry, who stood with his rifle pointed at us. Then the officer advanced with the word.

Back again, then, along the road, past the youthful sentry, past other sentries, winding through the barbed wire barricade, and at last, quite whole, to the House of the Barrier again. We had walked three miles in front of the Belgian advanced trenches, in full view of the Germans. There had been no protecting hedge or bank or tree between us and that ominous line two hundred yards across. And nothing whatever had happened.

Captain F—— was indignant. The officers in the House of the Barrier held up their hands. For men such a risk was legitimate, necessary. In a woman it was foolhardy. Nevertheless, now that it was safely over, they were keenly interested and rather amused. But I have learned that the gallant captain and the officer with him had arranged, in case shooting began, to jump into the water, and by splashing about draw the fire in their direction!

We went back to the automobile, a long walk over the shell-eaten roads in the teeth of a biting wind. But a glow of exultation kept me warm. I had been to the front. I had been far beyond the front, indeed, and I had seen such a picture of war and its desolation there in the the centre of No Man's Land as perhaps no one not connected with an army had seen before; such a picture as would live in my mind forever.

I visited other advance trenches that night as we followed the Belgian lines slowly northward toward Nieuport.

Save the varying conditions of discomfort, they were all similar. Always they were behind the railroad embankment. Always they were dirty and cold. Frequently they were full of mud and water. To reach them one waded through swamps and pools. Just beyond them there was always the moonlit stretch of water, now narrow, now wide.

I was to see other trenches later on, French and English. But only along the inundation was there that curious combination of beauty and hideousness, of rippling water with the moonlight across it in a silver path, and in that water things that had been men.

In one place a cow and a pig were standing on ground a little bit raised. They had been there for weeks between the two armies. Neither side would shoot them, in the hope of some time obtaining them for food.

They looked peaceful, rather absurd.

Now so near that one felt like whispering, and now a quarter of a mile away, were the German trenches. We moved under their *fusées*, passing destroyed towns where shell holes have become vast graves.

One such town was most impressive. It had been a very beautiful town, rather larger than the others. At the foot of the main street ran the railroad embankment and the line of trenches. There was not a house left.

It had been, but a day or two before, the scene of a street fight, when the Germans, swarming across the inundation, had captured the trenches at the railroad and got into the town itself.

At the intersection of two streets, in a shell hole, twenty bodies had been thrown for burial. But that was not novel or new. Shell-hole graves and destroyed houses were nothing. The thing I shall never forget is the cemetery round the great church.

Continental cemeteries are always crowded. They are old, and graves almost touch one another. The crosses which mark them stand like rows of men in close formation.

This cemetery had been shelled. There was not a cross in place; they lay flung about in every grotesque position. The quiet God's Acre had become a hell. Graves were uncovered, the dust of centuries exposed. In one the cross had been lifted up by an explosion and had settled back again upside down, so that the Christ was inverted.

It was curious to stand in that chaos of destruction, that ribald havoc, that desecration of all we think of as sacred, and see, stretched from one broken tombstone to another, the telephone wires that connect the trenches at the foot of the street with headquarters and with the "château."

Ninety-six German soldiers had been buried in one shell hole in that cemetery. Close beside it there was another, a great gaping wound in the earth, half full of water from the evening's rain.

An officer beside me looked down into it.

"See," he said, "they dig their own graves!"

It was almost morning. The automobile left the pathetic ruin of the town and turned back toward the "château." There was no talking; a sort of heaviness of spirit lay on us all. The officers were seeing again the destruction of the their country through my shocked eyes. We were tired and cold, and I was heartsick.

A long drive through the dawn, and then the "château."

The officers were still up, waiting. They had prepared, against our arrival, sandwiches and hot drinks.

The American typewriters in the next room clicked and rattled. At the telephone board messages were coming in from the very places we had just left—from the instrument at the major's elbow as he lay in his trench beside the House of the Barrier; from the priest who had left his cell and become a soldier; from that desecrated and ruined graveyard with its gaping shell holes that waited, open-mouthed, for—what?

When we had eaten, Captain F—— rose and made a little speech. It was simply done, in the words of a soldier and a patriot speaking out of a full heart.

"You have seen to-night a part of what is happening to our country," he said. "You have seen that the Belgian Army still exists; that it is still fighting and will continue to fight. The men in those trenches fought at Liege, at Louvain, at Antwerp, at the Yser. They will fight as long as there is a drop of Belgian blood to shed.

"Beyond the enemy's trenches lies our country, devastated; our national life destroyed; our people under the iron heel of Germany. But Belgium lives. Tell America, tell the world, that destroyed, injured as she is, Belgium lives and will rise again, greater than before!"

PART VIII
ESPIONAGE

Since gathering information on troop movements and munitions was vital, aerial reconnaisance, observation balloons and spies were employed by both sides. Secret agents were used to disrupt factories and shipping, blow up munition plants, explore restricted areas or attend parties where women could seduce officers of the army and navy to get them to talk. Coded messages were used to alert commanders in the field. It could be an exciting life, but the penalty when caught was often the firing squad.

Fighting Germany's Spies:
The First Glimpse of the Ship Bombs

French Strother
Managing Editor

THE WORLD'S WORK, April 1918

The spies from the Central Powers had a dual objective in the United States. They sought to ferret out information that could be of interest to the military and to destroy where possible public and military installations to disrupt the war effort. They were adept at creating and spreading rumors to frighten and confuse the general populace. One story rumored that President Wilson's secretary, Joseph Tumulty, had been imprisoned and shot as a German spy. Tumulty had to make a public appearance and announce that he was alive and well. Another story claimed that horses to be shipped to France had been poisoned with a slow-acting bacteria, bandages rolled by the Red Cross for the wounded soldiers had been infected, and would kill those on the road to recovery. There was a rumor that Mexicans were on the border, just waiting for the word to invade the United States. There were whispers that enemy agents were on the Atlantic coast, slinking along the beaches and flashing secret messages to enemy submarines.

On July 24, 1915 Dr. Heinrich Albert had his briefcase snatched by a United States Secret Service agent and it revealed that Albert had received $28 million from the German government to finance a variety of disruptive acts. He had agents place a time bomb on a commercial steamer bound for France; some of his paid provocateurs created "accidents" on railroads and munitions plants. Others of Albert's agents produced pro-German motion pictures, and in an effort to project the Central Powers view of the news, he purchased a New York daily newspaper, The Mail.

So Americans would not be confused by the facts, in December of 1915 the German government sent to the United States for general publication in newspapers across the country the following statement:

> *The German government has naturally never knowingly accepted the support of any person, group of persons, society or organization seeking to promote the cause of Germany in the United States by illegal acts, by counsel of violence, by contravention of law, or by any means whatever that could offend the American people in the pride of their own authority.*

Patient President Wilson waited until April 1917, when he urged the declaration of war on Germany to take into consideration the statement issued in 1915. He said in part:

> *One of the things that has served to convince us that the Prussian autocracy was not and could never be our friend is that from the very outset of the present war it has filled our unsuspecting communities and even our offices of government with spies and set criminal intrigues everywhere afoot against our national unity of counsel, our peace within and without, our industries and our commerce. Indeed it is now evident that its spies were here even before the war began; and it is unhappily not a matter of conjecture, but a fact proved in our courts of justice, that the intrigues which have more than once come perilously near to disturbing the place and dislocating the industries of the country have been carried on at the instigation, with the support, and even under the personal direction of official agents of the Imperial Government accredited to the government of the United States.*

The United States Constitution's first amendment was bent out of shape with the arrest of 6,000 people, and 1,500 were convicted of offenses that consisted of criticizing the Red Cross or the Y.M.C.A.

The film, "The Spirit of '76" showed British soldiers killing American children during the American Revolution. This earned, for the producer of the film, a three-year prison sentence!

Mrs. Rose Stokes landed in prison facing a ten-year term after she wrote a letter to a newspaper that read, "I am for the people, and the government is for the profiteers!" (Her conviction was later set aside.)

German agents continued to bore from within. They persuaded people who bore English names to take leading places in organizations which concealed their origin and real purpose. The American Embargo Conference arose out of the ashes of Labor's Peace Council, and its president was American, though the funds were not. Others tampered with were journalists who lent themselves to German propaganda and served as couriers between the Teutonic embassies in Washington and government offices in Berlin and Vienna. A check of $5,000 paid to Marcus Braun, editor of "Fair Play," by Count von Bernstorff was revealed. There is a record of $3,000 paid through the German Embassy to finance the lecture tour of Miss Ray Beveridge, an American artist, who was also supplied with German war pictures.

In view of these revelations, headlined in newspapers and featured in magazine articles, the government embarked on witch hunts that curtailed civil liberties to an extent that would not have been dreamed possible before the war. Yet despite the frantic efforts by all the police agencies, only a handful of those convicted were actually spies. As one federal judge declared a year after the war's end, "In my best judgement more than 90 percent of the reported pro-German plots never existed." A second opinion was voiced by John Lord O'Brian, an official in the Department of Justice, ". . . no other one cause contributed so much to the oppression of innocent men as the war time hysteria of what was supposedly an all-pervasive system of German espionage."

ROBERT FAY AND THE SHIP BOMBS
A Plot That Proved To Have Been Made in Germany and Financed by the German Government—The Infernal Machine Which Fay Invented, and the Story of the Weak Link That Broke to His Undoing—One of the Most Atrocious of the German Schemes—Von Papen's Hand Again

Robert Fay landed in New York on April 23, 1915. He landed in jail just six months and one day later—on October 24th. In those six months he slowly perfected one of the most infernal devices that ever emerged from the mind of man. He painfully had it manufactured piece by piece. With true German thoroughness he covered his trail at every point—excepting one. And five days after he had aroused suspicion at that point, he and his entire group of fellow conspirators were in jail. The agents of American justice who put him there had unravelled his whole ingenious scheme and had evidence enough to have sent him to the penitentiary for life if laws since passed had then been in effect.

Only the mind that conceived the sinking of the *Lusitania* could have improved upon the devilish device which Robert Fay invented and had ready for use when he was arrested. It was a box containing forty pounds of trinitrotoluol, to be fastened to the rudder post of a vessel, and so geared to the rudder itself that its oscillations would slowly release the catch of a spring, which would then drive home the firing pin and cause an explosion that would instantly tear off the whole stern of the ship, sinking it in midocean in a few minutes. Experts in mechanics and experts in explosives and experts in shipbuilding all tested the machine, and all agreed that it was perfect for the work which Fay had planned that it should do.

Fay had three of these machines completed, he had others in course of construction, he had bought and tested the explosive to go into them, he had cruised New York Harbor in a motor boat and proved by experience that he could attach them undetected where he wished, and he had the names and sailing dates of the vessels that he meant to sink without a trace. Only one little link that broke—and the quick and thorough work of American justice—robbed him of another Iron Cross besides the one he wore. That link—but that comes later in the story.

Fay and his device came straight from the heart of the German Army, with the approval and the money of his Government behind him. He, like Werner Horn, came originally from Cologne; but they were very different men. Where Horn was almost childishly simple, Fay's mind was subtle and quick to an extraordinary degree. Where Horn had been humane to the point of risking his life to save others, Fay had spent months in a cold-blooded solution of a complex problem in destruction that he knew certainly involved a horrible death for dozens, and more likely hundreds, of helpless human beings. Horn refused to swear to a lie even where the lie was a matter of no great moment. Fay told at his trial a story so ingenious that it would have done credit to a novelist and would have been wholly convincing if other evidence had not disproved the substance of it. The truth of the case runs like this:

Fay was in Germany when the war broke out and was sent to the Vosges Mountains in the early days of the conflict. Soon men were needed in the Champagne sector, and Fay was transferred to that front. Here he saw some of the bitterest fighting of the war, and here he led a detachment of Germans in a surprise attack on a trench full of Frenchmen in superior force. His success in this dangerous business won him an Iron Cross of the second class. During these days the superiority of the Allied artillery over the German caused the Germans great distress, and they became very bitter when they realized from a study of the shells that exploded around them how much of this superiority was due to the material that came from the United States for use by the French and British guns. Fay's ingenious mind formed a scheme to stop this supply, and he put his plan before his superior officers. The result was that, in a few weeks, he left the army and left Germany, armed with passports and $3,500 in American money, bound for the United States on the steamer *Rotterdam*. He reached New York on April 23, 1915.

One of Fay's qualifications for the task he had set for himself was his familiarity with the English language and with the United States. He had come to America in 1902, spending a few months on a farm in Manitoba and then going on to Chicago, where he had worked for several years for the J. I. Case Machinery Company, makers of agricultural implements. During these years, Fay was taking an extended correspondence school course in electrical and steam engineering so that altogether he had a good technical background for the events of 1915. In 1906, he went back to Germany.

What he may have lacked in technical equipment, Fay made up by the first connection he made when he reached New York in 1915. The first man he looked up was Walter Scholz, his brother-in-law, who had been in this country for four years and who was a civil engineer who had worked here chiefly as a draftsmen—part of the time for the Lackawanna Railroad—and who had studied mechanical engineering on the side. When Fay arrived, Scholz had been out of a job in his own profession and was working on a rich man's estate in Connecticut. Fay, armed with plenty of money and his big idea, got Scholz to go into the scheme with him, and the two were soon living together in a boarding house at 28 Fourth Street, Weehawken, across the river from uptown New York.

To conceal the true nature of their operations they hired a small building on Main Street and put a sign over the door announcing themselves in business as "The Riverside Garage." They added verisimilitude in this scheme by buying a second-hand car in bad condition and dismantling it, scattering the parts around the room so that it would look as if they were engaged in making repairs. Every once in a while they would shift these parts about so as to alter the appearance of the place. However, they did not accept any business—whenever a man took the sign at its face value and came in asking to have work done. Fay or Scholz would take him to a nearby saloon and buy him a few drinks and pass him along by referring him to some other garage.

The most of their time they spent about the real business in hand. They took care to have the windows of their room in the boarding house heavily curtained to keep out prying eyes, and here under a student lamp, they spent hours over mechanical drawings which were afterward produced in evidence at the trial of their case. The mechanism that Fay had conceived was carefully perfected on paper, and then they confronted the task of getting the machinery assembled. Some of the parts were standard—that is, they could be bought at any big hardware store. Others, however, were peculiar to the device and had to be made to order from the drawings. They had the tanks made by a sheet metal worker named Ignatz Schiering, at 344 West 42nd Street, New York. Scholz went to him with a drawing, telling him that it was for a gasolene tank for a motor boat. Scholz made several trips to the shop to supervise some of the details of the construction and once to order more tanks of a new size and shape.

At the same time Scholz went to Bernard McMillan, doing business under the name of McMillan & Werner, 81 Centre Street, New York, to have him make a special kind of wheels and gears for the internal mechanism of the bomb, from sketches which Scholz supplied. At odd times between June 10th and October 20th McMillan was working on these things and delivered the last of them to Scholz just a few days before he was arrested.

In the meanwhile Fay was taking care of the other necessary elements of his scheme. Besides the mechanism of the bomb, he had to become familiar with the shipping in the port of New York, and he had to get the explosive with which to charge the bomb. For the former purpose he and Scholz bought a motor boat—a 28-footer—and in this they cruised about New York Harbor at odd times, studying the docks at which ships were being loaded with supplies for the Allies and calculating the best means and time for placing the bombs on the rudder posts of these ships. Fay finally determined by experience that between two and three o'clock in the morning was the best time. The watchmen on board the ships were at that hour most likely to be asleep or the night dark enough so that he could work in safety. He made some actual experiments in fastening the empty tanks to the rudder posts, and found that it was perfectly feasible to do so. His scheme was to fasten them just above the water line on a ship while it was light, so that when it was loaded they were submerged and all possibility of detection was removed.

The getting of explosives was, however, the most difficult part of Fay's undertaking. This was true not only because he was here most likely to arouse suspicion, but also because of his relative lack of knowledge of the thing he was dealing with. He did know enough, however, to begin his search for explosives in the least suspicious field, and it was only as he became ambitious to produce a more powerful effect that he came to grief.

The material he decided to use at first was chlorate of potash. This substance in itself is so harmless that it is an ingredient of tooth powders, and is used commonly in other ways. When, however, it is mixed with any substance high in carbons, such as sugar, sulphur, charcoal, or kerosene, it becomes an explosive of considerable power. Fay set about to get some of the chlorate.

But it is now time to get acquainted with Fay's fellow conspirators, and to follow them through the drama of human relationships that led to Fay's undoing. All these men were Germans—some of them German-Americans—and each in his own way was doing the work of the Kaiser in this country. Herbert Kienzle was a dealer in clocks with a store on Park Place, in New York. He had learned the business in his father's clock factory deep in the Black Forest in Germany and had come to this country years ago to go into the same business, getting his start by acting as agent for his father's factory over here. After the war broke out he had become obsessed with the wild tales which German propaganda had spread in this country about dum dum bullets being shipped back for use against the soldiers of the Fatherland. He had brooded on the subject, had written very feelingly about it to the folks at home, and had prepared for distribution in the United States a pamphlet denouncing this traffic. Fay had heard of Kienzle before leaving Germany, and soon after he had got to New York he got in touch with him as a man with a fellow feeling for the kind of work he was undertaking to do.

One of the first things in Fay's carefully worked out plan was to locate a place to which he could quietly retire when his work of destruction should be done—a place where he felt he could be safe from suspicion. After a talk with Kienzle he decided that Lusk's Sanatorium at Butler, N. J., would serve the purpose. This sanitorium was run by Germans and Kienzle was well known there. Acting on a prearranged plan with Kienzle, Fay went to Butler and was met at the station by a man named Bronkhorst, who was in charge of the grounds at the sanatorium. They identified each other by prearranged signals and Fay made various arrangements, some which are of importance later in the story.

Another friend of Kienzle's was Max Breitung, a young German employed by his uncle, E. N. Breitung, who was in the shipping business in New York. Young Breitung was consequently in a position to know at first hand about the movements of ships out of New York Harbor. Breitung supplied Fay with information he needed regarding which ships Fay should elect to destroy. But first Breitung made himself useful in another way.

Fay asked Kienzle how he could get some chlorate of potash, and Kienzle asked his young friend Breitung if he could help him out. Breitung said he could, and went at once to another German who was operating in New York ostensibly as a broker in copper under the name of Carl L. Oppegaard.

It is just as well to get better acquainted with Oppegaard because he was a vital link in Fay's undoing. His real name was Paul Siebs and for the purpose of this story he might as well be known by that name. Siebs had also been in this country in earlier days and during his residence in Chicago, from 1910 to 1913, he had gotten acquainted with young Breitung. He, too, had gone back to Germany before the war, but soon after it began he had come back to the United States under his false name, ostensibly as an agent of an electrical concern in Gothenburg, Sweden, for the purpose of buying copper. He frankly admitted later that this copper was intended for re-export to Germany to be used in the manufacture of munitions of war. He did not have much success in his enterprise and he was finally forced to make a living from hand to mouth by small business transactions of almost any kind. He could not afford a separate office, so he rented desk room in the office of the Whitehall Trading Company, a small subsidiary of the Raymond-Hadley Corporation. His desk was in the same room with the manager of the company, Carl L. Wettig.

When Breitung asked Siebs to buy him some chlorate of potash Siebs was delighted at the opportunity to make some money and immediately undertook the commission. He had been instructed to get a small amount, perhaps 200 pounds. He needed money so badly, however, that he was very glad to find that the smallest kegs of the chlorate of potash were 112 pounds each, and he ordered three kegs. He paid for them with money supplied by Breitung and took a delivery slip for it. Ultimately this delivery slip was presented by Scholz who appeared one day with a truck and driver and took the chemical away.

Fay and Scholz made some experiments with the chlorate of potash and Fay decided it was not strong enough to serve his purpose. He then determined to try dynamite. Again he wished to avoid suspicion and this time, after consultation with Kienzle, he recalled Bronkhorst down at the Lusk Sanatorium in New Jersey. Bronkhorst, in his work as superintendent of the grounds at the sanatorium, was occasionally engaged in laying water mains in the rocky soil there, and for this purpose kept dynamite on hand. Fay got a quantity of dynamite from him. Later, however, he decided that he wanted a still more powerful explosive.

Again he applied to Kienzle, and this time Kienzle got in touch with Siebs direct. By prearrangement, Kienzle and Siebs met Fay underneath the Manhattan end of the Brooklyn Bridge, and there Seibs was introduced to Fay. They walked around City Hall Park together discussing the subject; and Fay, not knowing the name of what he was after tried to make Seibs understand what explosive he wanted by describing its properties. Siebs finally realized that what Fay had in mind was trinitrotoluol, one of the three highest explosives known. Siebs finally undertook to get some of it for him, but pointed out to him the obvious difficulties of buying it in as small quantities as he wanted. It was easy enough to buy chlorate of potash because that was in common commercial use for many purposes. It was also easy to buy dynamite because that also is used in all kinds of quantities and for many purposes. But trinitrotoluol is too powerful for any but military use, and it is consequently handled only in large lots and practically invariably is made to the order of some government. However, Siebs had an idea and proceeded to act on it.

He went back to the Whitehall Trading Company, where he had desk room, and saw his fellow occupant, Carl Wettig. Wettig had been engaged in a small way in a brokerage business in war supplies, and had even taken a few small turns in the handling of explosives. Siebs had overheard him discussing with a customer the market price of trinitrotoluol some weeks before, and on this account thought possibly Wetting might help him out. When he put the proposition up to Wettig the latter agreed to do what he could to fill the order.

In the meanwhile, Fay had sent another friend of Breitung's to Bridge-port to see if he could get trinitrotoluol in that great city of munitions. There he called upon another German who was running an employment agency—finding jobs for Austro-Hungarians who were working in the munitions plants, so that he could take them out of the plants and divert their labor from the making of war supplies for use against the Teutons. The only result of this visit was that Breitung's friend brought back some loaded rifle cartridges which ultimately were used in the bombs as caps to fire the charge. But otherwise his trip was of no use to Fay.

Carl Wettig was the weak link in Fay's chain of fortune. He did indeed secure the high explosive that Fay wanted, and was in other ways obliging. But he got the explosive from a source that would have given Fay heart failure if he had known of it, and he was obliging for reasons that Fay lived to regret. Siebs made his inquiry of Wetting on the 19th of October. The small quantity of explosives that he asked for aroused Wettig's suspicions and as soon as he promised to get it he went to the French Chamber of Commerce near by and told them what he suspected and asked to be put in touch with responsible police authorities under whose direction he wished to act in supplying the trinitrotoluol.

From that moment Fay, Siebs, and Kienzle were "waked up in the morning and put to bed at night" by detectives from the police department of New York City and operatives of the Secret Service of the United States. By arrangement with them Wettig obtained a keg containing 25 pounds of trinitrotoluol, and in the absence of Fay and Scholz from their boarding house in Weehawken, he delivered it personally to their room and left it on their dresser. He told Siebs he had delivered it and Siebs promptly set about collecting his commission from Fay.

Siebs had some difficulty in doing this, because Fay and Scholz being unfamiliar with the use of the explosive were unable to explode a sample of it and decided that it was no good. They had come home in the evening and found the keg on their dresser and had opened it. Inside they found the explosive in the form of loose white flakes. To keep it more safely, they poured it out into several small cloth bags. They then took a sample of it and tried by every means they could think of to explode it. They even laid some of it on an anvil and broke two or three hammers pounding on it, but could get no result. They then told Siebs that the stuff he had delivered was useless. Siebs reported their complaint to Wettig and Wettig volunteered to show them how it should be handled. Accordingly, he joined them the following day at their room in Weehawken and went with them out into the woods behind Fort Lee, taking along a small sample of the powder in a paper bag. In the woods the men picked up the top of a small tin can, built a fire in the stump of a tree, and melted some of the flake "T.N.T." in it. Before it cooled, Wettig embedded in it a mercury cap. When cooled after being melted, T.N.T. forms a solid mass resembling resin in appearance, and is more powerful because more compact.

However, before the experiment could be concluded, one of the swarm of detectives who had followed them into the woods stepped on a dry twig, and when the men started at its crackling, the detectives concluded they had better make their arrests before the men might get away; and so all were taken into custody. A quick search of their boarding house, the garage, a storage warehouse in which Fay had stored some trunks, and the boathouse where the boat was stored resulted in rounding up the entire paraphernalia that had been used in working out the whole plot. All the people connected with every phase of it were soon arrested.

Out of the stories these men told upon examination emerged not only the hideous perfection of the bomb itself, but the direct hand that the German Government and its agents in this country had in the scheme of putting it to its fiendish purpose. First of all appeared Fay's admission that he had left Germany with money and a passport supplied by a man in the German Secret Service. Later, on the witness stand, when Fay had had time enough carefully to think out the most plausible story, he attempted to get away from this admission by claiming to have deserted from the German Army. He said that he had been financed in his exit from the German Empire by a group of business men who had put up a lot of money to back an automobile invention of his, which he had worked on before the war began. These men, so he claimed, were afraid they would lose all their money if he should happen to be killed before the invention was perfected. This tale, ingenious though it was, was too fantastic to be swallowed when taken in connection with all the things found in Fay's possession when he was arrested. Beyond all doubt his scheme to destroy ships was studied and approved by his military superiors in Germany before he left, and that scheme alone was his errand to this country.

Far less ingenious and equally damning was his attempt to explain away his relations with Von Papen. The sinister figure of the military attaché of the German Embassy at Washington leers from the background of all the German plots; and this case was no exception. It was known that Fay had had dealings with Von Papen in New York and on the witness stand he felt called upon to explain them in a way that would clear the diplomatic service of implication in his evil doings. He declared that he had taken his invention to Von Papen and that Von Papen had resolutely refused to have anything to do with it. This would have been well enough if Fay's explanation had stopped here.

But Fay's evil genius prompted him to make his explanation more convincing by elaboration of the story, so he gave Von Papen's reason for refusal. These were not at all that the device was calculated to do murder upon hundreds of helpless men, nor at all that to have any part in the business was to play the unneutral villain under the cloak of diplomatic privilege. Not at all. At the first interview, seeing only a rough sketch and hearing only Fay's description of preliminary experiments, Von Papen's sole objection was:

"Well, you might obtain an explosion once and the next ten apparatuses might fail."

To continue Fay's explanation:

"He casually asked me what the cost of it would be and I told him in my estimation the cost would not be more than $20 apiece. [$20 apiece for the destruction of thirty lives and a million-dollar ship and cargo!] As a matter of fact in Germany I will be able to get these things made for half that price. 'If it is not more than that,' Von Papen said, 'you might go ahead, but I cannot promise you anything whatever.' "

Fay then went back to his experiments and when he felt that he had practically perfected his device he called upon Von Papen for the second time. This time Von Papen's reply was:

"Well, this thing has been placed before our experts and also we have gone into the political condition of the whole suggestion. Now in the first place our experts say this apparatus is not at all seaworthy; but as regards political conditions I am sorry to say we cannot consider it and, therefore, we cannot consider the whole situation."

In other words, with no thought of the moral turpitude of the scheme, with no thought of the abuse of diplomatic freedom, but only with thoughts of the practicability of this device and of the effect upon political conditions of its use, Von Papen had put the question before technical men and before Von Bernstorff and their decision had been adverse solely on those considerations—first, that it would not work, and second, that it would arouse hostility in the United States. At no stage, according to Fay's best face upon the matter, was any thought given to its character as a hideous crime.

The device itself was studied independently by two sets of military experts of the United States Government with these results:

First, that it was mechanically perfect, second, that it was practical under the conditions of adjustment to a ship's rudder which Fay had devised; and third, that the charge of trinitrotoluol for which the container was designed was nearly half the quantity which is used on our own floating mines and which is calculated upon explosion twenty feet from a battleship to put it out of action, and upon explosion in direct contact, absolutely to destroy and sink the heaviest superdreadnaught. In other words, beyond all question the bomb would have shattered the entire stern of any ship to which it was attached, and would have caused it to sink in a few minutes.

A brief description of the contrivance reveals the mechanical ingenuity and practical efficiency of Fay's bomb. A rod attached to the rudder, at every swing the rudder gave, turned up, by one notch, the first of the beveled wheels within the bomb. After a certain number of revolutions of that wheel, it in turn gave one revolution to the next; and so on through the series. The last wheel was connected with the threaded cap around the upper end of the square bolt, and made this cap slowly unscrew, until at length the bolt dropped clear of it and yielded to the waiting pressure of the strong steel spring above. This pressure drove it downward and brought the sharp points at its lower end down on the caps of the two rifle cartridges fixed below it—like the blow of a rifle's hammer. The detonation from the explosion of these cartridges would set off a small charge of the more sluggish but stronger dynamite, and that in turn would explode the still more sluggish but tremendously more powerful trinitrotoluol.

The whole operation, once the spring was free, would take place in a flash; and instantly its deadly work would be accomplished.

Picture the scene that Fay had in his mind as he toiled his six laborious months upon this dark invention. He saw himself, in imagination, fixing his infernal box upon the rudder post of a ship loading at a dock in New York Harbor. As the cargo weighed the ship down, the box would disappear beneath the water. At length the ship starts on its voyage, and, as the rudder swings her into the stream, the first beat in the slow, sure knell of death for ship and crew is clicked out by its very turning. Out upon the sea the shift of wind and blow of wave require a constant correction with the rudder to hold the true course forward. At every swing the helmsman unconsciously taps out another of the lurking beats of death. Somewhere in midocean, perhaps at black midnight, in the driving storm, the patient mechanism hid below has turned the last of its calculated revolutions. The neck piece from the bolt slips loose, the spring device drives downward, there is a flash, a deafening explosion, and five minutes later a few mangled bodies and a chaos of floating wreckage are all that is left above the water's surface.

This is the hideous dream Fay dreamed in the methodical 180 days of his planning and experimenting in New York. This is the dream to realize which he was able to enlist the cooperation of half a dozen other Germans. This is the dream his superiors in Germany viewed with favor, and financed.

| **German Codes and Ciphers** |
| French Strother |
| Managing Editor |

THE WORLD'S WORK, June 1918

"Fighting Germany's Spies" was spread over five issues in The World's
Work, *with two pieces on the subject in each issue. The enemy was painted
as clever and ruthless, the forces in the United States, brave and bright.
People that would in peace time be labeled busybodies and gossips were
now considered alert and properly suspicious Americans. While the series
on espionage undoubtedly helped sell more copies of the magazine, it also
fanned the flames of hysteria and paranoia. German-Americans suffered the
most. There were millions with Teutonic-sounding names in the United
States, and they were the victims of the spy witch hunts. Employers were
requested to check the national origin of their workers and to guarantee their
patriotism. As a result of this policy, many Americans with German names
were fired from their jobs. In some work areas men with foreign accents
were forced to crawl on their hands and knees across a room and kiss the
American flag. Those that were accused of making seditious statements were
publicly flogged, and a mob in southern Illinois succeeded in lynching a
German-American.*

*Spies and spying brought the war alive to people on the homefront, and
now all could participate in the fight against the Hun. Even though the case
histories presented in the magazines were a few years old, the nearness of
the war to all civilians solidified opinion and strengthened the determination
of each individual to back the "boys" at the front and help with the war.*

The Bolo Pasha Messages—How the Hindus, Recently Convicted in
San Francisco, Communicated with One Another—The Cohalan and
Devoy Messages Concerning the Roger Casement Revolution in Ireland—Enciphered Code Used to Direct German Cruiser Operations in
the West Indies

Secrecy is, of course, the most important consideration in the German
plots in this country. When Bernstorff wished to arrange with Berlin to
give Bolo Pasha 10 million francs to betray his country, he naturally did
not write out his messages in plain English for every wireless station on

both sides of the Atlantic to read them as they went through the air. He did, to be sure, write the messages in English, and they looked plain enough—and innocent enough—but they meant something very different from what they seemed to mean. And when it got down to the actual transfer of the money, another German agent in New York signed the messages, which likewise were not what they seemed.

These messages were in *code*.

Now *code* should not be confused with *cipher*. When some Hindus in New York, subsidized by Berlin, wished to write their plans to some other Hindus in San Francisco, concerning their common purpose of fomenting revolution against British rule in India, they wrote out messages that consisted entirely of groups of Arabic numerals.

Those messages were in *cipher*.

To any one but an expert, many code messages look simple and harmless, and cipher messages usually look unintelligible and suspicious. Yet, oddly enough, the cipher messages are by far the easier to make out. Indeed, unless you have a copy of the code, code messages can almost never be translated, whereas a straight cipher message can almost invariably be unraveled by an expert, if you give him enough time and material. Hence, by people who know the subject (and nobody has mastered it so thoroughly as the Germans) codes are used for *secrecy*, and ciphers are used simply as an added precaution and to *delay* the unraveling of a message if, by any chance, the enemy has gotten possession of a copy of the code.

German plot messages, therefore, are usually written out first in plain German, then coded, and the code then put into cipher. Such messages are called *enciphered code*.

For an enemy to get them to make sense, he had first to decipher them, and then decode them. Any expert can decipher them—in time. Decoding them is a very different matter.

Before taking up some of the German code and cipher messages that have been translated with dramatic results, it will be well to discuss codes and ciphers in general.

A *code* is an arrangement by which two people agree, when exchanging messages, always to substitute certain words or symbols for the real words of the message. Thus, they might agree on these substitutions:

$$
\begin{aligned}
\text{a} &= \text{the} \\
\text{French ship} &= \text{market} \\
\text{sailed from New York} &= \text{price} \\
\text{sailed from Boston} &= \text{quotation} \\
\text{to-day} &= \text{is} \\
\text{for Marseilles} &= \text{any even number} \\
\text{for Bordeaux} &= \text{any number with a fraction}
\end{aligned}
$$

With such a code, a German spy in New York could cable a seemingly harmless message to a friend in Holland, such as:

"The market price is 110."

That would mean, of course:

"A French ship sailed from New York to-day for Marseilles."

Whereas a very slight change in wording:

"The market quotation is 110½" would mean

"A French ship sailed from Boston to-day for Bordeaux."

Messages of that sort could be exchanged daily between a broker in Wall Street and a broker in Amsterdam, and by the addition of a few more words, could be infinitely varied and would look like perfectly legitimate commercial correspondence. In fact, most international business before the war (the Government now requires that all messages appear in plain English) was carried on by coded cables which turned long messages into short groups of words that of themselves made gibberish. Several code books, for business use, were on the market, containing hundreds of pages of these arbitrary substitutions, which were useful, not for secrecy, but for economy. A dozen words could be made to say what normally would require five hundred words.

Ciphers, however, have almost always been resorted to when secrecy was desired. This sounds like a contradiction. But people who are not experts use them because they think they are more secret, since they look so. And experts use them when they are concerned only with *temporary* secrecy. They use them, then, because cipher messages can be written and translated (by one's correspondent) without any equipment like a code book, and much more rapidly than code. Thus, if a general in the field wishes to send a message ordering a colonel to advance in two hours, he sends it in cipher, because it would take the enemy more than two hours to decipher the message even if he intercepted it immediately, and because after the two hours have elapsed the information in the message would be of no value to him.

A *cipher* is the substitution of some symbol for a letter of the alphabet. The substituted symbol may be another letter—as writing *e* when you mean *a*. Or it may be a figure—as using 42 when you mean *m*. Or it may be an arbitrary sign—as * to mean *c*. In cipher, then, every word is spelled out, but the word *Washington* might be spelled x = ± ½?!§:°B if you had agreed that

$$
\begin{array}{ll}
w = x & n = ! \\
a = = & g = § \\
s = ± & t = : \\
h = ½ & o = ° \\
i = ? & n = B
\end{array}
$$

That is called *substitution* cipher, because some other letter or symbol is arbitrarily substituted for every letter.

But another kind is called a *transposition* cipher, because in this the letters of the alphabet are simply transposed by agreement—the simplest

Fig. A

G	A	R	D	E
N	I J			

Fig. B

G	A	R	D	E
N	I J	B	C	F
H	K	L	M	O
P	Q	S	T	U
V	W	X	Y	Z

and most obvious example being to reverse the alphabet, so that *z* stands for *a*, and *y* for *b*, etc. Such a transposition cipher would read:

Alphabet of plain text:

a   b   c   d   e   f   g   h   i   j   k   l   m
n   o   p   q   r   s   t   u   v   w   x   y   z

Alphabet of cipher:

z   y   x   w   v   u   t   s   r   q   p   o   n
m   l   k   j   i   h   g   f   e   d   c   b   a

and *Washington* would be spelled *dzhsrmtglm*.

Perhaps the cleverest transposition cipher ever devised—it is so good that the British Army uses it in the field and nevertheless has published text books about it—is the very simple "Playfair" cipher. First a square is drawn, divided into fifths each way. This arrangement gives twenty-five spaces, to contain the letters of the alphabet—*I* and *J* being put in one square because there would never be any plain sentence in which it would not be quite obvious which one of them is needed to complete a word of which the other letters are known.

Next a "key word" is chosen—and herein lies the cleverness and the simplicity of this cipher, because every time the key word is changed, the whole pattern of the alphabet is changed. Suppose the key word is *gardenia*. It is now spelled out in the squares [See fig. A.]

The second A is left out, as there must not, of course, be duplicates on the keyboard. Now the rest of the alphabet is written into the squares in their regular sequence. [See fig. B.]

The message is written out in plain text; for example:
DESTROY BRIDGE AT ONCE
(Only capital letters are commonly used in cipher work.) This message is now divided into groups of two letters, in the same order, so that it reads:
DE ST RO YB RI DG EA TO NC EX
(The X is added to complete the group and is called a *null*.) These groups of twos are now ciphered from the keyboard into other groups of twos, by the following method:

Where two joined letters of the original message appear in the same *horizontal* row on the keyboard, the next letter to the right is substituted for each. Thus, the first two letters of our message are DE. They occur in the same horizontal row on our keyboard. Consequently, for D we write E, and for E we go "on around the world" to the right, or back to the other end of the row, and write G for E. This gives us DE enciphered as EG.

Where two joined letters of the original message appear in the same *vertical* row on the keyboard, the next letter below is substituted for each.

Where two joined letters of the original message appear neither in the same horizontal nor the same vertical row on the keyboard, we imagine a rectangle with the two letters at the opposite corners, and in each case substitute the letter found on the keyboard at the other corner of the same horizontal row. This sounds complicated, but in reality is very simple. For example, take the third two-letter group of our message—RO. The rectangle in this case is

```
R   D   E
B   C   F
L   M   O
```

and for R we substitute E, and for O we substitute L.

Substituting our whole message by this system, it reads:

Original	DE	ST	RO	YB	RI	DG	EA	TO	NC	EX
Cipher	EG	TU	EL	XC	AB	EA	GR	UM	IF	RZ

As telegraph operators are accustomed to send these gibberish messages in groups of five letters (so that they can check errors, knowing that when only four appear in a group, for example, something has been left out) these enciphered groups of two are now combined into groups of fives, so that the finished cipher reads:

EGTUE LXCAB EAGRU MIFRZ

The foregoing sounds extremely complicated, but the truth is that anybody, after half an hour's practice, can put a message into this kind of cipher ("Playfair" cipher) almost as fast as he can print the straight English of it in capital letters. And unless the person who reads it knows the key word which determined the pattern on his keyboard, he would have to be an expert to decipher it, and even he could do it only after a good deal of work.

Another ingenious cipher is called the "Chess Board." First, a sheet of paper is ruled into squares exactly like a chess board—that is, a square divided into eighths each way. This arrangement gives, of course, sixty-four small squares. Then, by agreement between the people who intend to use this cipher, sixteen of these squares are agreed upon and are cut

Fig. C

Fig. D

A		U					
	T		H				
		O		R			
I		Z			E		
			P				
A							Y
	M	E					
	N						T

Fig. E

A	⊃	U	⌐				
⋁	⌐	T		H			⊣
	⌐		O	–	R	Z	
I		Z	Z		–	E	⊡
			P			Σ	
A				⌐			Y
	M	E		O			
⋊	N	O					T

Fig. F

S	A	⊃	U	⌐	⋊	⋊	⋁
⋁	⌐	T	O	H	O	ⅎ	⊣
⋊	⌐	Z	O	–	R	Z	⅁
I	Σ	Z	Z	⅁	–	E	⅁
–	⅁	⅁	P	⅁	O	Σ	O
A	⅁	⋏	⊢	⊓	⌐	⋏	Y
⊥	M	E	⅁	O	O	Σ	Z
⋊	N	O	⊢	I	⅁	S	T

Fig. G

S	A	D	U	L	R	R	Y
A	L	T	O	H	O	F	T
R	L	N	O	I	R	N	E
I	M	Z	N	P	I	E	E
I	P	E	P	G	O	M	C
A	P	Y	T	U	L	A	Y
H	M	E	B	O	O	M	N
R	N	O	T	T	E	S	T

out of the sheet with a knife. Suppose for example, this pattern is chosen [See fig. C.] and the squares showing in white are cut out.

Next, another sheet of paper is ruled into a chess board, of exactly the same size as the first. The perforated sheet is now laid on top of the second sheet, so that the squares on the one exactly cover the squares on the other. Now, with a pen or pencil, the plain text of the secret message is printed on the under sheet by writing through the perforations of the upper sheet, only one letter being written in each square. This, of course, permits the writing of sixteen letters of the message.

Suppose the complete message is to be:

"Authorize payment ten million dollars to buy copper for shipment to Germany." Then the lower sheet, after we have written through the perforations will look like this. [See fig. D.]

The perforated sheet is now turned to the right through one-fourth of a complete revolution, so that the top of it is at the right side of the lower sheet and so that the two chess boards again "match up." This operation exposes, through the perforations, a new set of sixteen open squares on the lower sheet. The writing of the message is continued, and the lower sheet now looks like this. [See fig. E.]

Again the perforated sheet is turned to the right, and sixteen more letters are written. Once more, and the whole sixty-four squares are utilized, looking like this. [See fig. F.]

These letters are now put upright, like this. [See fig. G.]

These letters are now read from left to right and from the first line down, like ordinary reading matter. They are then grouped into fives for telegraphic transmission, and an X added at the end to make an even five-group there. Thus the message, as transmitted, reads:

SADUL RRYAL TOHOF TRLNO IRNEI MZNPI EEIPE PGOMC
APYTU LAYHM EBOOM NRNOT TESTX

When this message is received, it can, of course, be quickly deciphered by printing it out on a chess board and placing over it a sheet perforated according to the prearranged pattern.

This survey of codes and ciphers does not more than scratch the surface of the subject, nor more than suggest the almost infinite variations that are possible—in ciphers especially. It simply gives a groundwork for an understanding of the German secret messages now to be described.

Among the most interesting of these secret messages is the series of wireless telegrams by means of which the German money was paid to Bolo Pasha for the purchase of the Paris *Journal*—one of the principal episodes in the treasonable intrigue for which Bolo was recently executed by a French firing squad. These messages were in English, and meant exactly what they said, except for the proper names and the figures, which were *code*. To decode them, it was necessary only to make the following substitutions:

William Foxley = Foreign office
Charles Gledhill = Count Bernstorff
Fred Hooven = Guaranty Trust Company (New York)
$500 = $500,000

and to all other figures add three ciphers to arrive at the real amount. For example, one of these messages read: "Paid Charles Gledhill five hundred dollars through Fred Hooven." This meant: "Paid Count Bernstorff five hundred *thousand* dollars through Guaranty Trust Company."

The story of these messages is briefly this: Marie Paul Bolo started life as a barber, became an adventurer and, in the service of the Khedive of Egypt, received the title of Pasha for a financial service which he rendered him. Returning to France as Bolo Pasha, he married two wealthy women and lived in grand style on their money. He became an intimate of Charles Humbert, another adventurer, who achieved political power by question-able methods and became a member of the French Senate. In the mean-time, the Khedive had been deposed by the British on account of his pro-Turkish (and hence pro-German) activities after the Great War began. Abbas Hilmi joined the colony of ex-rulers in Switzerland, and there be-came a part of the German system of intrigue. He received money from the Germans and, after he had deducted his "squeeze" (which sometimes amounted to half the total), he paid over the rest to Bolo, to be used by Bolo, Humbert, and ex-Premier Caillaux in an effort to restore Caillaux to power and then to further the propaganda for an early and hence in-conclusive peace.

Either this method of supplying the French traitors with funds became too dangerous, or the Germans preferred to keep their gold and wished to use their credit in the United States to get American gold for this purpose. In any event, Bolo Pasha appeared in New York early in March, 1916. Strangely enough, the French subject bore letters of introduction to several Germans. The most important was addressed to Adolf Pavenstedt, who was senior partner in G. Amsinch & Company and for many years chief paymaster of the German spy system in this country (the United States). Through Pavenstedt, Bolo met Hugo Schmidt, a director of the Deutsche Bank of Berlin, a Government institution, who had been sent to this country soon after the war broke out to provide complete cooperation between the older representatives of the Deutsche Bank here and the management in Berlin.

Through Pavenstedt as messenger, Bolo also got in touch with Bernstorff, and arranged the final details of the plan by which Bolo was to receive 10 million francs from the German Government. He was to use this money to buy the Paris *Journal*, which would then be edited by Senator Humbert, who agreed to change its editorial policy to favor an immediate peace. As the *Journal* is one of the most powerful dailies in France, with a circulation among more than a million and a half readers, the sinister possibilities of this scheme are readily seen.

Bernstorff committed the financial details to Hugo Schmidt. He, in turn, wirelessed Berlin for suitable credits in American banking houses. These were arranged with the Guaranty Trust Company and the National Park Bank—for many years American correspondents of the Deutsche Bank. These credits were then credited to G. Amsinck & Company, of which Pavenstedt had long been senior partner. He, in turn, placed them, with the New York branch of the Royal Bank of Canada, to the account of Bolo Pasha. As the exchange rate at the time ran in favor of American dollars and against French francs, the 10 million francs (normally equal to about 2 million dollars) which Bolo got, required only $1,683,500 of American money—which is just the sum of the amounts named in the wireless messages.

The *Journal* was actually bought by Bolo and Humbert, but before they could do much damage with it, they were arrested, and Bolo has already been executed.

The Hindus in this country, who were plotting with the Germans the revolution that should destroy the British rule in India, used two systems for their secret messages: The first was this *substitution cipher:*

	1	2	3	4	5	6	7
1	A	B	C	D	E	F	G
2	H	I	J	K	L	M	N
3	0	P	Q	R	S	T	U
4	V	W	X	Y	Z		

The message, "Leave San Francisco" would be written in cipher as follows:

25 15 11 41 15 35 11 27 16 34 11 27 13 22 35 13 31

by giving each letter of the message the number to the left of it combined with the number above it.

The other system used by the Hindus was a *book code*. They agreed upon a small English dictionary of a certain edition, and wrote from it messages that were also groups of numbers after this fashion: 625-2-11 27-1-36 45-2-20 and so on. The first figure in each group was the number of the page on which the word would be found, the second figure gave the column, and the third figure was the number of the word in the column counting from the top of the page.

The case of the *Odenwald* reveals an example of German *enciphered code*. The *Odenwald* was a German steamer, requisitioned on March 17, 1915, by the German Government for service as a naval auxiliary. Our Government detected the *Odenwald* engaging to go to sea periodically with supplies to be delivered to the German cruiser *Prinz Eitel Friedrich*, whereupon our officers interned her at Ponce, Porto Rico, which had been her headquarters. In the process of unearthing her illegal activities, our Government intercepted nearly one hundred secret wireless messages and cablegrams.

The *Odenwald* was one of several German vessels that happened to be in the West Indies when the war broke out. They were all set at the task of supplying, at sea, the German commerce raiders and squadrons of cruisers, like Von Spee's. They acted under the local orders of Captain Schlimbach, of the *Praesident*, which was anchored in the harbor at Ponce. Schlimbach kept in touch with his superiors in the United States through Körber & Company, a German banking house in Ponce. The head of this concern was a typical example of the German business agent charged by his government with the task of carrying German commerce to every part of the world and of becoming not merely an emissary of trade, but also a permanent agent of the German Government in any work, military or otherwise, that it should have to do. After the universal custom of these men, he made his outlying post his permanent home. He married a Porto Rican woman, and became, to all appearances, an integral part of the life of Ponce. When his son was in his early teens, he sent him to Germany to finish his education under the *kultural* aegis of the Fatherland, and then to New York for a few years of experience in American commercial methods in a commission house in Wall Street. Several members of the staff of the *World's Work* (including the writer of this article) very well remember little blond "Willie" Körber, when he boarded the same house with them at 128 East Sixteenth Street, in New York, in 1903 and 1904. His English was still broken, but he was learning rapidly, and every evening, after his day's work was done, he climbed to his little room at the fourth floor, front, and delved into his books of English. They were chiefly books of travel and books on business methods, but he had, besides, an excellent knowledge of standard English literature. He, too, was doubtless preparing to do his part in the worldwide spread of *Deutschtum*.

The method by which Körber kept Captain Schlimbach in touch was this: Karl Boy-Ed, the German naval attaché at Washington, had moved to an office in New York. Here he worked out his orders for the German ships, basing them upon his own instructions from Berlin. These orders were cabled to a German firm in Havana—Scheidt-Heilbut & Company— and signed with the name of Schwarz. The company in Havana then cabled the messages on to Körber, in Ponce, and Körber passed them on to Schlimbach. To cover up the military character of the ships' operations, open messages were sent to Körber, from time to time, by the agency of the Hamburg-American Line at St. Thomas, which was then a possession of Denmark (now part of the United States and re-named as the Virgin Islands).

The *Odenwald*, the *Praesident*, the *Gladstone*, and the *Farn*, at one time or another, were under German orders to coal and otherwise supply the *Kronprinz Wilhelm*, the *Eitel Friedrich*, the *Karlsruhe*, and the *Dresden* in South Atlantic waters, besides reporting information concerning the movements of French and British cruisers patrolling this region. The intercepted messages, when unraveled, not only put a stop to the German naval operations, but disclosed the chain of German agents in the West Indies whom we needed to beware of for the protection of our own interests in the war, and after. Körber's position, for example, became quite clear, despite his long-time surface enthusiasm for American control of Porto Rico, and he is now interned, and will be carefully watched the rest of his life.

But perhaps the most dramatic of all the intercepted messages (except the Luxburg and Zimmerman notes, of which the story cannot yet be told) were those which revealed the part played by well known Irish-American leaders in the ill-fated Casement revolution in Ireland.* The story of the

---

* Justice Cohalan, of the Supreme Court of New York, sent a coded message that went from Von Papen's office to Bernstroff, advising the Germans upon the best means to make Sir Roger Casement's revolution in Ireland a success. The message: "No. 335—16 *very secret* New York, April 17, 1916. Judge Cohalan requests the transmission of the following remarks: 'The Revolution in Ireland can only be successful if supported from Germany. Otherwise, England will be able to suppress it, even though it be only after hard struggles. Therefore, help is necessary. This should consist primarily of aerial attacks in England and a diversion of the fleet simultaneously with Irish revolution. Then, if possible, a landing of troops, arms and ammunition in Ireland, and possibly some officers from Zepplins. This would enable the Irish ports to be closed against England and the establishment of stations for submarines on the Irish coast, and the cutting off of the supply of food for England. The success of the revolution may therefore decide the war." He asks that a telegram to this effect be sent to Berlin. 5132 8167 0230 *To His Excellency Count von Bernstorff, Imperial Ambassador, Washington, D.C.*

Casement expedition.is too familiar to need to be retold. And comment upon the political morals of Justice Cohalan and John Devoy becomes superfluous in the light of these messages. American citizens (one of them signally honored with public office in New York), both held their Irish blood superior, in their duty of loyalty, to the United States, using their citizenship as a cloak under which to strike at Great Britain, which has been for a quarter century the chief bulwark of this country against Germany's plan to conquer us and to impose upon our country the most hateful tyranny in the history of the world.

PART IX

THE BIRTH OF MODERN COMMUNISM

Communism and other utopian forms of governments had been tried many times before in small countries and movements and always failed, but toward the end of the war, an uprising in Russia left that country with a communist government based on the philosophies of Marx and Lenin. Initially the new administration was applauded as a better alternative to the Czar's government, but in time, their oppressive policies led many people throughout the world to consider the USSR a potential enemy who must be watched and contained.

The New Russia

Charles Johnston

THE AMERICAN REVIEW OF REVIEWS, May 1915

World War I created the condition for a centuries-old dream of many people to become a reality. An entire country was under Communist philosophy and control.

Real property and the means of production shared by all members in a community was not a new idea promulgated by a handful of Russian revolutionaries. Communism as a theory of government and social reform may be said, in a limited sense, to have begun with the Greek vision of the Golden Age, particularly with Plato, who in the Republic *outlined a society with communal holding of property, but also with a hierarchic social system including slavery; this has by some been called "aristocratic communism."*

The idea of common property was strong in some religious groups such as the Jewish Essenes (approximately 2nd century, B.C.) and certain early Christian communities. These religious opponents of private property held that property holding was evil and that God had created the world for the use of all humankind. These ideas were particularly strong among the Bogomils, the Cathari, and the Albigenses. Paradoxically, feudalism, which had as its base private ownership of land, had on the lower level of the Manorial system common cultivation of the fields and communal use of the village commons.

The Aztec Indians in Mexico practiced ejido *when the land was expropriated from private holdings and redistributed to small farmers. The intent of the* ejido *system was to remedy the social injustice of the past and to increase Mexican production of subsistence foods. The land was owned by the government and the* ejido *was financed by a special national bank that supplied the capital for such things as seeding and reclamation. Communal ownership was in decline before the Spanish arrived.*

The term communism is defined to include such types of community living as that of the Jesuit Reductions in Paraguay and on occasion is even intended to mean the communal life instituted in Monasticism.

It was partly on the basis of common rights that the rebellious peasants in 14th century England and the insurgents of the great Peasants' War in 16th century Germany advocated common ownership of land and the means of production.

The mixture of religious enthusiasm and economic reform was shown in 17th century England by the Levellers and more particularly by the sect of the Diggers. They sought to put their theories into practice on expropriated land, a significant action to protest against the inclosures of land.

Capitalism, reinforced by the Industrial Revolution which began in the 18th century, brought about the conditions that gave rise to modern communism. The living conditions of the workers in the new industrial factories were by the beginning of the 19th century so appalling that even highly conservative humanitarians saw the necessity of some relief.

In Germany, Immanuel Kant attacked the institution of private property. In France, Francois (Grocchus) Babeuf's fight for the abolition of private property led him to the guillotine, and in England the cause was pursued by the poet, Percy Shelley.

In the 19th century the idealists were not content with literary expression. They organized small cults and launched communist settlements including some in the United States. One group in Red River, Texas (1848) lasted less than a year. Another group settled in Nauvoo, Illinois (1849) and they lasted until 1856 when dissension disposed of their president and leader, Étienne Cabet. Some of the branch communities survived until 1898.

A revival of Babeuvism by revolutionary secret societies in France and Italy was intent on overthrowing the established governments and establishing a new and propertyless world. It was among them that the words communism and socialism took root. The terms were used loosely and interchangeably, although there was a tendency to call those who stressed a strong state as the owner of all means of production socialists, and those who stressed the abolition of all private property (except immediate personal goods) communists.

It was 1848 when the Communist Manifesto *of Karl Marx and Frederich Engels appeared. With it the radical movement took a completely new turn and very soon Marxist theories and programs dominated left-wing thought.*

Although the party (founded in 1847) for which the manifesto was written was called the Communist League, the whole movement which went forward with the founding of the First International and of Social Democratic parties in the various countries of the Western world was generally called socialism.

The modern form of Communism began its development with the split in 1903 within the Russian Social Democratic Party (founded in 1898). The more radical wing, the Bolsheviks, were led by Lenin and advocated immediate and violent revolution instead of gradual and constitutional means of bringing about the downfall of capitalism and the establishment of an international socialist state across the world. The triumph of the Bolsheviks within the Russian party, and even more, their triumph in the Russian Revolution of 1917, gave them the leadership in socialist action.

Some of the birth pangs of the Russian Revolution, the first Communist nation in the world is recorded by eyewitness reports detailing the confusion and the hardships of the people in those early days of 1917 when anarchy

*ruled the population contained in more than eight million square miles of
the earth's surface.*

*Feature writer Charles Johnston filed the following report in 1915, paint-
ing a glowing report of Russia as a nation. He was enthusiastic about the
Czar, Russian agriculture and industry and the Russian peasant. He depre-
cated the Jewish minority and all those who did not recognize the greatness
of the "new" Russia. What was supposed to be a news report, in the light
of history, is nothing more than a sly piece of propaganda, and as one reads
the article carefully, one can recognize that the seeds of revolution are being
sown.*

The Birth of Modern Communism

"With the war and without vodka, Russia is more prosperous than with
vodka and without the war." This, the greatest single sentence ever uttered
for prohibition, comes, not from a professional Prohibitionist, but from
M. Kharitonoff, Controller of the Treasury, speaking before the Budget
Committee of the Russian Parliament on January 25. The Controller added
that, owing to the extraordinary increase in the national savings due to
prohibition, the enormous outlay occasioned by the war had caused no
widespread hardship in Russia. As a proof of this, M. Kharitonoff cited
the figures. The national savings, as shown in bank deposits between December 1913 (seven months before the war) and December, 1914 (after
five months of war), had been increased by 147 per cent. What a contrast,
this, with the country's condition just ten years ago! For it is exactly ten
years since the fall of Port Arthur, and the great battle of Mukden, which
broke the power of Russia in Manchuria, was fought and lost in March,
1905.

In these ten years Russia has gained:

1. Civil and religious liberty
2. A Parliament, of two houses, rapidly becoming fitted to the national
   genius
3. A new principle of citizenship, affecting a hundred million Russian
   peasants
4. A new ideal in education
5. A new cultivated area of 50,000,000 acres
6. An increase in national revenue of $500,000,000
7. A new epoch of agricultural and industrial prosperity
8. An added population of 40,000,000

It is doubtful whether, since the world began, any nation has ever made
an equal ten-year's gain.

The Russian Parliament was added to a strong sovereignty, not substituted for a sovereignty weak or already abolished. The result is, both

elements of the national organism, the sovereignty and the Parliament, continue to operate together, producing an admirably stable union. The one gives continuity and poise. The other gives free respiration to the national life. So Russia has a government not exactly like that of any other nation; in some things, like that of England; in some more like that of the United States; in both, well fitted to her own needs.

As in England, the governing power in Russia is made up of three elements: the sovereign; the upper house; the lower house. The upper house consists of just under 200 members, and is somewhat like the upper house designed, but not yet formed by the English Liberals; one-half appointed by the crown (for the king's creation of peers is, a fact, appointment to the upper house); one-half representing different powers and classes in the state. To show how thorough, thoughtful, and fair the Russian system is, it is worth while describing exactly in what way the elected half of Russia's upper house is made up. It is as follows:

Six are elected by the Clergy.
Eighteen by the hereditary Nobility.
Six by the Academy of Sciences and the Universities.
Six by the Chamber of Commerce.
Six by the Industrial Councils.
Thirty-four by the gubernias with local self-government (states).
Sixteen by the gubernias without local self-government (territories).
Six by Poland.

or 98 in all, as against 98 appointed by the crown—a total of 196. The lower house (Duma) elected in a way presently to be considered, numbers just under 450; about the size of the House of Commons, or our own House of Representatives.

We think of the Duma as the Russian Parliament. It is, in reality, the lower house of a bicameral Parliament; the upper house, which was developed from the Council of the Empire being, as we have seen, in part elective. The Duma owes its existence to the Czar's famous proclamation of October 17, 1905.

The First Duma met on April 27, 1906. It was largely made up of wild-eyed theorists and revolutionaries, who "made laws for an imaginary world," but had no grasp at all on the world as it now is. It was dissolved as hopelessly impracticable, on July 9, thus closing a tempestuous existence of seventy-four days. The Second Duma was like unto it. Meeting on February 20, 1907, it was dissolved on June 3, with just over a hundred days to its credit.

Then the sovereign saw that he had opened the doors too wide. He made changes in the electoral system, applying the principle of the electoral college which, nominally, elects our Presidents. These changes had the effect of throwing preponderant power into the hands of the landed gentry;

the class which made the ablest parliaments the world has ever seen, the English Parliaments of the nineteenth century. On this basis the Third Duma was chosen, and met on November 1, 1907. It served the full five years of its legal existence, and was succeeded by the Fourth, the present Duma, which met November, 1912. In this Fourth Duma, there are nine parties, somewhat as in France, ranging from the Monarchists on the right, to the Socialists on the left. But one may say that practically two-thirds of the members are Moderates, while one-third are Radicals of various shades.

Curiously enough, it was only after the election of the Third (the effective) Duma, that the Russian Revolution really got under way. But even while the revolution raged, the Duma, acting with the Czar's Ministers and the upper house, was doing very effective work.

In his early days, Parnell asked Davitt whether there was any chance for an agrarian agitation in Ireland; whether the Irish peasants would follow his lead in a struggle for the land. "Yes!" answered Davitt; "they will follow you to the gates of hell!" There was something of the same fervor in the attitude of the Russian peasants toward the land; and, just as, in Ireland, the practical settlement of the agrarian question by the various Land Purchase Acts knocked the bottom out of the revolutionary movements there, and turned the Irish peasants into staunch Conservatives, so the settlement of the land question in Russia, in a somewhat similar way, has taken all the steam out of "the Russian Revolution," and is turning the Russian peasant into a sober, practical citizen of a wholly new and very desirable type.

To make a man, an independent peasant proprietor, of the Irish serf, it was necessary to buy out his landlord. In Russia, it was not the landlord, but the village-community, that had to be bought out. It is true that, in 1861, Alexander II, planned a scheme by which the former serfs might purchase land from the landlords, paying for it in installments to the state; exactly along the lines followed by Gladstone in 1881, and by Wyndham in 1903. But the vast majority of the peasants were left in thraldom to their ancient socialistic village-communities; for, as Sir Henry Maine so convincingly showed, the real place of Socialism is the past, not the future. Socialistic experiments are throw-backs to ancient history.

There were in Russia, at the time of the Japanese war, some seventy million peasants, gathered in village-communities, with a huge, straggling settlement of log houses as the center of each. Of villages with not more than 100 inhabitants, there were more than half a million. The land about these villages, owned in common, was distributed every seven years, being cut up into little parcels, so as to give some land of each kind and quality to each household. So it might often happen that the holding of a peasant's family consisted of a hundred strips of land, some of them no larger than ten square feet, and as much as twenty miles from his home. He wore out soul and shoes walking from one little "cemetery-plot" to another; and, at the end, if he had made improvements, drainage, clearings, or fertilizing, he saw them all "redistributed"—practically confiscated—at the end of seven years. The results were poverty, thriftlessness, apathy.

Why are the peasants of France the happiest, the richest, the most effective in the world? Because each one of them knows that he owns his farm down to the center of the earth; and that every stroke of work he puts into it, every ounce of fertilizer, will come back to him, and to his wife and children. On such terms, any man will work and save; and the reaction on his character, in thrift, energy, providence, self-respect, will be of incalculable value.

It was to bring about a like happy result in Russia, that the policy of Land Purchase, chiefly associated with the name of the late Premier Stolypin, was directed, and "Stolypin's farmers," as the new Russian peasant-proprietors are called, are already counted by the million. Within a few years they will number a hundred million; a new race, strengthened, invigorated, rendered responsible and self-reliant; busy, through intensive cultivation, enriching themselves and their nation.

The practical difficulties in the way of this great transformation were enormous; but the most serious have already been overcome. It required an army of land-surveyors merely to take stock of the lands to be converted and this army had to be created and trained. This was successfully and rapidly done. Then the village-communities had to be brought round to the new view, since their lands could only be distributed with their consent and goodwill. Then, for every village which did thus consent, it became necessary to lay out parcels of land from thirty to forty acres for each family, in such a way that all would feel that they were fairly treated. Then of each such plot two maps had to be made, one of which was kept by the owner, while the other was filed at the Ministry of Agriculture. And, last but not least, the new farmer had to transfer his house to the center of his farm. This was comparatively simple, seeing that a log house can be taken to pieces and put together again, almost like a house of children's building-blocks.

Already some 10,000,000 acres a year are being redistributed in this way—turned from communal to individual ownership; and as the peasants see the great practical benefits the change will go on still more rapidly.

Meanwhile, the older land-purchase, not from the village-communities, but from the landlords, had been making good headway. To aid this process, the Peasants' Land Bank had been established, in 1882, and up to the time of the Japanese war, some 20,000,000 acres had been bought in this way. In November, 1906, a law was promulgated permitting all peasants who had begun the purchase of their holdings at the time of the emancipation to become freeholders of their allotments, all redemption payments still due being remitted. This splendid concession applied to about 280,000,000 acres.

So that in these two ways a new race of peasant proprietors is being built up in European Russia, while in the wheat belt of Siberia free grants of forty acres each are being distributed by the government. There is enough land of the highest quality in Siberia to settle ten million Russian families.

The old-time Russian peasants grouped in village-communities ruled by their own customary law—practically, little self-contained republics— were nevertheless blended in a common unity—largely by the fervor and sincerity of their religion. "The people of the land," said an English writer two years ago, "have made it a vast sanctuary, perfumed with prayer, and filled with the memories of their faith."

Through this great religious nation, a new spirit is now stirring, a spirit of energy, of vigor, of hope. It is expressing itself, among other ways, in a new movement of education, applying primarily to the children of the vast peasant class, which now numbers a hundred million. And with admirable good sense they are laying stress on the things practically useful to the new nation of peasant-proprietors. Thus very many villages possess their school fields and gardens, in which the children learn to plant and cultivate the fruits and vegetables and grains of their district. In addition to this, there are a thousand schools that teach beekeeping. Three hundred give instruction in the culture of the silkworm. In nearly a thousand, trades and industries are taught, and hundreds more specialize in manual training. During the last ten years there has been much activity in the establishment of new educational institutions all over Russia, notably technical and commercial schools, under the new Ministry of Commerce. It is curious that the ministry and the Duma are pulling somewhat in opposite directions, in one part of the field of education, the ministry favoring the classical side of the schools, while the Duma rather favors the scientific side. It is worth noting, too, that Russia has long held an advanced position in the education of girls. In university education, the drift at present is toward physics, chemistry, and the natural sciences generally.

The long white winters have had a peculiar influence on the industrial life of Russia, developing not so much "cottage industries" as "village industries," in which many hundreds of men and women take part in a common enterprise. The whole village, which may number thousands, is generally devoted to some special occupation, one village producing felt shoes, another flax thread, another wooden spoons, a fourth iron nails or chains, and so on. So certain gubernias (states) have grown famous for certain commodities. Moscow produces wicker-work, baskets, and furniture; Kostroma carves wooden bowls and silver ware; Yaroslav and Tula produce samovars and sauce pans; Vladimir makes ikons; Nijni Novgorod makes a specialty of knives and scissors; Tver produces saddlery and harness. Thus we have, among the peasantry themselves and as a part of their indigenous life, the beginnings of an enormously productive industrial system, side by side with their agriculture.

Out of these village industries, which seem to be absolutely peculiar to Russia, at least among European nations, large factories are springing up in the villages, doing the same things better, more systematically, more commodiously, and employing as many as ten or twelve thousand hands. Among the more rapidly growing industries are cotton-spinning, the making of linen, from the rude peasant fabric to the most beautiful damask, the spinning of silk, and the manufacture of beet-sugar. In Petrograd, Moscow, and Warsaw, there has been a great development of tanning, and the dependent industries of shoe and glove making; while new and well-built factories are turning out paper, flour, tobacco, and hemp ropes.

The list of these industries suggests—what is one of the strongest points of the situation—that, in every one of these lines, Russia has her own practically inexhaustible supplies of raw material. She is as self-contained and as self-supporting as it is possible for a nation to be. Of raw materials, there are two great classes; those which grow in the ground, and those which are dug out of the ground. In both, Russia is marvelously supplied. In lumber, she possesses the largest forests on earth, stretching from the Baltic to the Pacific Ocean. Her cereals are one of the world's great supplies. She has long been a great flax country. Her expansion into Turkestan has made her a great cotton country. In the north, she grows millions of tons of rye and oats. In the south, fine grapes, tea, oranges, and tobacco flourish. There is, in fact, practically nothing that grows that Russia does not produce.

As for metals and minerals, only two facts need be quoted. At one end of the scale, Russia is running France neck and neck for fourth place among the iron-producing nations of the world. At the other end, she supplies, from the Ural mines, almost the entire platinum output of the world. Her railroads are increasing enormously in mileage, there being few engineering difficulties on her vast, flat plains. In 1860, Russia had 1,000 miles of railroads; in 1885, 16,000 miles; in 1905, 40,000 miles; and the increase since has been equally rapid.

Russia numbers, to-day, 180,000,000—the greatest white nation the world has ever seen. On her western frontier, there are settled some 5,000,000 Jews, chiefly inherited from Poland, which offered them an asylum when the nations of Western Europe were persecuting them. Towards these Jews Russia's policy had been negative. It has practically amounted to bidding them remain where they were, when the Western districts were annexed. That is the real history of "the Jewish Pole." It is a question of political inertia and economic precaution, not of religious persecution.

On this last point, let me quote an authority as impartial as the *Encyclopaedia Brittanica*: "In his relations with Moslems, Buddhists, and even fetishists the Russian peasant looks rather to conduct than to creed, the latter being in his view simply a matter of nationality. . . . The numerous outbreaks against the Jews are directed, not against their creed, but against them as keen business men and extortionate money-lenders. Any idea of proselytism is quite foreign to the ordinary Russian mind," as indeed is sufficiently shown by the continuous satisfactory relations between Russia and her millions of Mohammedan and Buddhist subjects.

Nevertheless, the Jews of Russia's western frontier have felt pressure, and have bitterly resented it, filling the ranks of the revolutionary societies at home, and fiercely attacking Russia when they go abroad. So it has come about that we in America are prone to see the vast nation of 180,000,000 through the hostile eyes of 5,000,000 aliens,—or, indeed, far less than 5,000,000; for many Jews are well-disposed to Russia, both at home and among those who have emigrated. In just the same way, we have been prone to see England through the eyes of the Irish Fenigans, who came here after the abortive outbreak of 1867. In both cases, a narrow, bitter, and essentially unjust view resulted.

But, just as the Irish-American irreconcilables of the Clan-na-Gael have long ceased to represent even their own fellow countrymen, so the anti-Russian opinion here is becoming unrepresentative and out of date. And this from two causes. The Czar's proclamation of religious liberty was followed, in 1907, by a relaxation of the rules which kept the former Polish Jews within the Pale; and, as occasion has permitted, there have been other ameliorations of the position of the Russian Jews. Notable so, since the opening of the great war, in which new opportunities to serve with distinction in the army have been given to Jews, of which they have splendidly taken advantage; showing that they possess high qualities of military valor, and that they are fired with the same love of their fatherland that flames in the hearts of all Russian soldiers.

So that, in Russia, the question of that little minority of Jews is settling itself. Much can be done in this country to add and soften that settlement: first, by American Jews; next, by the American Government. Let the Jews here recognize that the wrongs are not all on the Russian side—that seldom happens in this vale of tears—and, admitting the difficulty of Russia's task, and her sincere effort to fulfil it, let them drop the bad habit of ceaselessly girding at Russia, whether she be right or wrong. And let our Administration remember that we have our own problems of citizenship here. Since the Civil War, which was to confer equal rights on the negro, we have deprived millions of negroes of certain political rights; and, to the citizens of the land of Confucius, the oldest civilized nation in the world, the nation which has been, for centuries, the most literate, we have denied any rights of citizenship at all. There may be a necessity for this. That is not the question. But, while laboring under this necessity—if so it be—at home, let me not be priggish and Pharisaical about the difficulties of others.

Russia has gained, in the last ten years, a population of forty million. In the next ten years she will gain still more, having then a population of 225,000,000 or more. The bulk of this vast population are of one blood, sane and unspoiled, with high ideals, saturated with humane and religious principle. They are, as we saw, just entering on a new era of free yet stable government, of new development in agriculture, in education, in industry, and still more, in manhood and citizenship. To such a nation the heritage of the future belongs; and the splendid moral and physical qualities of the Russian millions are a magnificent promise to the human race. Writing in the *Vorwaerts* at the end of March, Professor Vogt, a well-known German authority on Russian affairs, said: "It will take a long time, great energy and patience, and many victories to gain headway against this new Russia. Russia's offensive powers have hardly been touched. Her staying powers are enormous. Her army has done magnificent work, while the Russian financial and economic position has seldom been better."

The German publicist may not be a willing witness to the greatness of Russia, formidable to her enemy, full of promise to her friends; but we may be assured that his testimony is true.

The Reawakening of Russia

Staff

THE AMERICAN REVIEW OF REVIEWS, May 1915

Also in the May 1915 issue of the American Review of Reviews there appeared a short article pieced together from various sources that reflect upon Russian conditions, and the possibility of internal problems.

Although the Russian Government is no doubt receiving hearty support from the people in prosecuting the war, yet there is a struggle going on within the Empire in which the two sides that present a united front to the foreign enemy stand arrayed against each other in a fight for power and mastery. Between the bureaucracy and the popular will there is less harmony to-day than at any time since the suppression of the revolution. More and more strongly the people are asserting themselves in emphatic demands for greater liberties.

The last session of the Dumas voted additional three milliards of rubles for the war, but before doing so the deputies wanted to know what the government was going to give the people in return. The government at first declared that it would do nothing at all, that it would follow the same policy in the future as in the past. Then the significant thing happened, which shows that the spirit of rebellion against despotism is again active in Russia. The people's representatives raised such a storm of protest that to placate them the government was compelled to modify its uncompromising attitude and to yield to the extent of at least making some vague promises. In the Petrograd *Nashe Slovo* the following account is given of the deliberations that took place in the short Duma session:

> The questions of the terms of peace and of internal reforms were discussed. The government declared that it does not wish to deprive Germany of any of its territory. It wants nothing but Galicia and the Dardanelles. The Constitutional Democratic deputies insisted mainly upon the Dardanelles.
>
> In the second sitting, when it came to the question of reforms, Maklakov, the minister of the interior, declared that the government would make no concessions. It would pursue the same course as heretofore. His statement produced a scene of the greatest disorder in the house. The deputies jumped from their seats, and the president was

obliged to declare a recess. When the Duma reassembled, Goremykin made a statement somewhat softening the harsh impression created by Maklakov's blunt refusal to consider the demands of the deputies for a freer Russia generally, for better treatment of Finland, and for guaranteeing equal rights to the Jews and stopping Jewish persecutions.

The insistence of the Duma upon an extension of the people's rights is not the only sign of the reawakening of Russia. All over the Empire the people are combining in efforts to force concessions from the government. They seem to be perfectly aware of their advantage in the present crisis and are determined to make use of it for the liberalization and modernization of Russia. A Russian soldier, in a letter printed in the New York *Forward* writes:

> All the nationalities throughout the Czar's dominions are keenly alert for their chance to obtain freedom. The Poles have displayed great skill in seizing the advantage offered by the extraordinary situation of the war. For the present they actually possess a state of their own in Warsaw, from which they control the whole of Poland.

Russian society is also on its guard. Two powerful organizations have been founded, the Territorial Assembly League and the League of the Cities. Their power and activity are daily increasing, and the Russian Government knows it has to reckon with them. The Russian press and the Russian intelligent classes have raised their heads. The alliance with the English and the French, who are fighting for freedom, has put the stamp of liberty upon Russia and ennobled the crude, uncultured pan-Slavism.

It is strange but true. The activity of the Black Hundreds has ceased. They are as if congealed. Here and there they are still stirring, Maklakov and Scheglavitev raise their voices occasionally. The Jew is driven hither and thither. But generally speaking, they have fallen into a lethargy. A new life is developing in Russia. The old tolerates the new without protest. There are two Russias.

All are awakening to a new life, all are organizing, all are demanding a place in the sun.

Nevertheless, the Russian people realize that the government will not yield an iota of its power without a fierce struggle. It is generally understood that it is ready to back up its policy as expressed by Maklakov in the Duma with all the forces at its command.

Commenting on Maklakov's declaration, the *Novy Mir*, a Russian daily published in New York, writes:

> This means that the Russian Government will continue to rule as it has hitherto with the nagaika and the knout, disregarding the people's representative and the demands of the various Russian organizations and societies. As until now, the government will continue to kill every manifestation of popular self-activity. It will continue to favor the pa-

rochial schools and keep the secular schools under the strict and constant surveillance of its officials. As hitherto, it will imprison or send to Siberia all those who dare to express dissatisfaction with the government. It will continue to persecute the Poles and the Armenians and to stir up the dark, ignorant masses against the Jews. it will continue its policy of fanning the flame of race hatred by pitting one nation of the Empire against the other.

Nevertheless, there are ample signs of a gradual Russian reawakening, if we turn our gaze from above to the people themselves. The very war which seemed to strengthen czarism compelled the Czar's government to tolerate certain organizations and societies, both in the cities and villages, which it prohibited before. And the people are taking advantage of this freedom. Not only the propertied classes, but the peasants also are organizing. And though their organization will temporarily serve the victory of czarism, there can be no doubt, if we consider recent events in Russian history, that they are bound sooner or later to be used for overthrowing a government system which is antagonistic to the most elementry needs of the country in the economic and cultural development.

Russia in the Throes of Re-birth

Isaac Don Levine

THE AMERICAN REVIEW OF REVIEWS, June 1917

The causes of the Russian Revolution were many. When Russia entered the World War, the fabric of government was already devoid of vitality and force. If a victory might conceivably contribute to restore the obedience of the people to the Czar, it was inevitable that defeat and corruption would lead to the collapse of the entire system.

From Peter the Great to microscopic (and last) Nicholas, Russian autocracy, directing a huge army, had acquired province after province. Yet the Pole, the Lett, the Lithuanian, the Armenian, the innumerable people of Asia, retained a consciousness of a racial independence which persisted under Russian rule.

Not only were the people from the Arctic to the Caspian, from the Dniester to the Pacific unassimilated, but the Russian family itself was divided. The vast country was held together by the forces of bureaucracy and the army.

The small but influential element inhabiting the cities was not affected by the issues of the World War, but as far as many of their leaders were concerned it was capitalism, not Germanism, that was the enemy.

The autocracy and the army had accepted the challenge and made war upon Germany, but this very fact discredited the war in the eyes of Russian Socialism. Other elements in the population had suffered iniquities, oppression and abuse of the bureaucracy and only felt hatred and hostility toward the Czar.

The revolution, it is said, began with the assassination of a single man, Gregory Novikh, known as Rasputin. A Siberian peasant by birth, immoral and physically filthy, with no formal education, he was a drunkard and a libertine, posing as a sort of saint and miracle worker. He tramped about barefoot, and in a country where men wore their hair short, his unwashed hair reached his shoulders.

Rasputin (the Russian word for ne'er-do-well) left his district of Tobolsk for Moscow where he started a new cult mingling seances with debauchery. He was introduced to the Empress and soon exercised an extraordinary influence upon the Czarina, and through her, the Czar. Many of the credulous public believed Rasputin to be the evil spirit of the Imperial circle.

After his assasination, the Duma was postponed for a month, censorship grew tighter, the numbers of the secret police increased, and an attempt to abort the growing sentiment for revolution was made and failed. Hunger was a serious problem. It was almost impossible to obtain bread; crowds gathered in the streets, often breaking into bakeries. The police had orders to disperse the crowds—anyone who refused to return to work would be sent to the trenches. The crowds were enormous and disorderly. More than two hundred rioters were killed the first day.

Isaac Don Levine gives the American people a more detailed report on the birth of Communism in war-torn Russia.

To understand the seemingly puzzling events in the new Russia since the revolution last March, it is necessary to bear in mind one cardinal fact which was disclosed only recently. And this is that the Russian Revolution was not the work of the Duma, and the upper classes, but wholly of the labor masses.

This was not made clear by the Petrograd correspondents at the time of the upheaval. On the other hand, they tried to convey the idea that the Duma was the ring-leader of the revolt. This impression became so deeply rooted that the minds of the world were utterly confused by the developments of April and May.

Here are the revised facts about the revolt: Demonstrations occurred in Petrograd the first week in March. The government of Protopopoff, minister of the Interior, provoked the masses to further excesses in order to spread unrest and create a basis for a separate peace. When the demonstrations first occurred the workers said: "This is not a Zabastovka, but a Protopovka," which meant: "This is not a strike, but a trap of Protopopoff." However the continued provocations of the police drove more and more workers into the ranks of the strikers.

On March 10, when the strike assumed the proportions of a general movement, the leaders of the various secret Socialist and revolutionary organizations met in conference with several labor chiefs, to have control of the strike. A temporary Council of Labor Deputies, such as had directed the revolution of 1905, was formed. This council placed itself in charge of the spreading revolutionary tide, of course, without knowing whither this tide would carry it. In 1905 the Council had been swept into jail and Siberia. The Council of 1917 was ready for the same fate.

While this was going on, the Duma was in session. Fiery speeches were being made. The government was denounced from every quarter. But the Duma remained *inactive*. The Duma was rather sure that any attempt at revolution would be crushed by the police. As Paul Milyukoff [leader of the liberal Constitutional Democratic Party] said, when informed of the first revolutionary outbreaks: "The revolution will be crushed in a quarter of an hour." The Duma watched, with fear for Russia and the Allies in its heart, the expanding wave of rebellion.

The only revolutionary act of the Duma was its refusal to be dissolved after the Imperial decree calling for its dissolution was issued. When the revolution was at its height—a vast throng of rebel soldiers and workers marched to the Duma to find out where it stood. After that, the Duma formed on its own initiative a Committee of Safety. But all the time there was a labor council in charge of the revolution though the world was informed only of the Duma's Committee.

The Duma and Council then conferred and decided upon a Provisional Government. The Council's stand was not to participate in any government till the Constituent Assembly met. Meanwhile, the Dumas pulled all the time to "the right." The Council and the masses wanted the abolition of the monarchy, but the Duma decided to make Russia a Constitutional Monarchy. When Milyukoff announced to the waiting multitudes that Czar Nicholas would be deposed, there were cheers; but when he added that the Czarevitch would be retained and Grand Duke Michael made regent— there were cries: "Again the Romanoffs! Down with the Monarchy!"

The masses, therefore, found themselves early dissatisfied with the Duma. Through their Council they urged the ending of the monarchy altogether, and succeeded.

The labor class awoke to find that after it had originated and brought to a successful conclusion one of the most remarkable revolutions in history, the power was really taken out of its hands by the Duma—a body, but not radical enough to satisfy the revolutionists. The latter grew suspicious of the Provisional Government. The Council of Labor Deputies, combined with those of the soldiery, issued appeals to the masses to be on guard lest "the conquests of the revolution" be wrested from their hands. Intoxicated by the sudden rush of freedom, the Socialists composing the Council imagined that the millennium was at hand; that a revolution in Germany was imminent; that universal peace was, therefore, a matter of days; and that a new social order for humanity was about to be inaugurated.

The Council's function was to preserve the "conquests of the revolution" till the Constituent Assembly, elected on the basis of direct, equal and universal suffrage should meet. It was a laudable function. The Council's insistence on the abolition of the monarchy will be remembered in history as a great and glorious achievement. But still the "conquest of the revolution" is a rather uncertain term, which cannot be defined with exactitude. This resulted in many complications, mainly springing from foreign rather than internal policies.

The internal policies certainly presented a remarkable record. Independently or under pressure of the Council, the Provisional Government began the reconstruction of Russia as soon as the old regime fell. A political amnesty freed more than a hundred thousand prisoners and exiles in Siberia. Finland regained her autonomy; the Jews were fully emancipated; the Poles were promised independence; Armenia's restoration was pledged; while the Lithuanians and Ukrainians were promised autonomy. The Czar's and Grand Duke's estates were confiscated. Many radical labor laws were enacted, including an eight-hour working day. The police were superseded by militia. The peasants were promised the land. Naturally, all the promises relating to fundamental legislation will be carried out only by the Constituent Assembly. The army was reorganized on a more democratic basis. In a word—all essential reforms were promulgated promptly and through the proper channels.

But differences soon developed between the Council and the Provisional Government on matters relating to foreign policy. First, the Council was convinced that a revolution could be engendered in Germany through the Allies' restatement of their war aims in accordance with President Wilson's declaration last January in his famous Senate speech that all peoples should have the right to settle their own fortunes and destinies. The French Socialists, it will be recalled, made a similar demand on their government soon after President Wilson's address. The Russian Socialists in the Council believed that once the Allies came out with such a statement, renouncing annexations and indemnities, that German proletariat would rise, overthrow the Hohenzollerns, and bring about the end of the world slaughter.

Certainly there was nothing dangerous about their proposed experiment. But a couple of episodes occurred which lent to their demands a complexion that seemed disturbing to the world. First there was the case of Nikolai Lenin, the noted Socialist leader, who returned to Russia from Switzerland via Germany, and who is an extreme radical. Lenin's view is that the war is an imperialistic affair; that the proletariat of the world will suffer as much from British capitalism as from Prussianism; and that consequently its interest demand peace, peace at any price, so that it can devote itself to a European social revolution. Lenin's point of view was not understood by the Petrograd foreign correspondents, and they proceeded to paint him as a German agent, which irritated even his opponents.

A word or two may be said at this juncture of the Russian attitude toward the British after the revolution. The British showed little rejoicing at the fall of Czarism, regarding the revolution only from the point of view of its effect on the war. The British press also shed crocodile tears over the fate of Czar Nicholas, whom the Russian democracy considered a despot. Some of the leading London papers described the revolutionists as anarchists and outlaws. This British stupidity could have but one effect on the Russian radical masses. The latter felt irritated against Britain, for her treatment of Ireland, and for her former agreement with Czarism for aggressive purposes, as in the case of Persia. This created a fertile soil for Lenin's peace propaganda.

Misinformed correspondents and German agents spread the legend that the new Russia was ready to conclude a separate peace. But this was at no time true. There never was any danger of such an occurrence. Lenin and his followers were from the very beginning in the minority. The President of the Council of Labor and Soldiers' Deputies, Tcheidze, declared soon after Lenin's arrival in Petrograd that he would be absorbed by the new Russia. It was a remarkable prediction, and came true within a few weeks. Lenin lost followers by the thousand. The Russian masses, like the British and French masses, desired universal peace on certain radical conditions, but no separate peace under any circumstances.

One cannot emphasize too much the statement contained in the preceding sentence. It explains in a nutshell the real stand of the Council and its activities. Thus the first Milyukoff incident occurred on account of the Council's attitude toward peace. Paul Milyukoff, Foreign Minister in the Provisional Government, had always favored Russia's acquisition of the Dardanelles and Constantinople. In April he made a statement to that effect to a newspaper correspondent. This caused violent opposition since the masses and its Council wanted no annexations. The rest of the Cabinet hastened to announce that Milyukoff spoke for himself, and not for the Government, thus averting a crisis.

But the wedge was already driven between the Council and the Cabinet. The former felt that Milyukoff stood in the way of a German revolution, and did not express the will of the majority of the people, which undoubtedly was true. The Council, therefore, assumed a more watchful attitude than ever toward the Provisional Government. At the same time it began to exercise authority of its own, thus creating a duality of power. A national congress of all the Councils of Workmen's and Soldiers' Deputies, held in Petrograd in the middle of April, adopted among others, the following resolution:

> The Congress calls upon the revolutionary democracy of Russia, rallying around the Council, to be ready to vigorously suppress any attempt by the Government to elude the control of democracy or to renounce the carrying out of its pledges.

Two weeks later the Council found in an act of Milyukoff an "attempt by the Government to elude the control of democracy." The Foreign Minister, in transmitting to the Allies the Government's earlier repudiation of all annexations and indemnities, said: "The Provisional Government . . . will maintain a strict regard for its engagements with the Allies of Russia." This caused a storm. What those engagements were was unknown, but that they provided for Russia's acquisition of the Dardanelles was divulged last year by Premier Trepoff. The Council demanded an explanation of the Provisional Government. The revolutionary masses, incited by extremists and German agents, were turbulent. For a day or two Petrograd was the scene of some very dramatic events. There were cries of "Down with

Milyukoff! Down with the Provisional Government!" Another revolution was in the air.

Fortunately, the Council had full control of the situation. Its orders were obeyed by the populace. Paul Milyukoff himself courageously came out to defend his stand. He found many supporters in the crowds. It became clear to the Council that on its decision the fate of Russian freedom hinged; that civil war was inevitable in case it voted lack of confidence in the Provisional Government; and the radical council voted, by a small majority, it is true, its support of the Government.

At the same time, early in May, a serious condition developed in the Russian army as a result of the Socialist peace agitation. The soldiers, carried away by beautiful dreams, began to fraternize with the Germans. Discipline was rapidly declining. The authorities were powerless. Only the Council of Deputies had influence over most of the soldiers. And the Council was obviously not in full harmony with the Provisional Government. It even adopted a resolution calling for an international Socialist Conference for the purpose of forcing the Allies to restate their war aims and of bringing about universal peace. The rank and file of the army interpreted this as complete license to act without restraint. This afforded the Germans an opportunity to withdraw large forces from the eastern front to the western during last month.

The demoralization increased so rapidly that General Korniloff, the man who arrested the Czarina, resigned from the post of Petrograd commandant, protesting that the Council was interfering with his duties. The popular hero, General Brusiloff, and General Gurko had requested to be relieved of their offices, warning against the disintegration threatening the army.

The Provisional Government had invited the Council to participate in the Cabinet and end the duality of authority, but the Socialist Council by a majority of one rejected the proposal. The situation grew desperate. The Council had the power and influence, but refused responsibility. The Government had all the responsibility but lacked power. War Minister Gutchkoff resigned in protest. The Socialist Minister of Justice Kerensky made a passionate appeal to the people, declaring he wished he had died two months before, when the revolution was still a beautiful dream, rather than witness the reality of Russian freedom. He addressed better words to the democracy, asking if free Russians are serfs in need of a master's whip or citizens realizing their responsibility. The masses and the Council then awoke.

A coalition cabinet was now decided upon by the council by a large majority. Paul Milyukoff resigned as Foreign Minister to give way to M. I. Terestchenko, who held the post of Minister of Finance. Prince George E. Lvoff remained Premier and Minister of the Interior. Minister of Justice Kerensky became Minister of War. Several new Ministries were created for the Socialists. Victor Tchernoff, a leader in the Social-Revolutionary party, became Minister of Agriculture, while A. Shingaroff, who had held that post, was slated for the Ministry of Finance. Skobeloff, Vice-President of the Council of Workmen's and Soldiers' Deputies, entered the Cabinet. Altogether about six or seven Socialists became members of the Government in a total of thirteen or fourteen.

The transfer of the patriotic and socialistic Minister of Justice, A. F. Kerensky, to the post of War Minister was a fortunate stroke. The masses and the army idolize Kerensky. A visit of his to the front will do a great deal toward the restoration of the military organization and its fighting spirit. His knowledge of military affairs is, to be sure, very negligible. But his passionate love for the people may prove more of a motive power in the present circumstances than actual business experience. One of the first effects of Kerensky's assuming the office of War Minister was the return of Generals Brusiloff and Gurko to their posts. Michael I. Terestchenko, the successor of Milyukoff in the Foreign Office, is only thirty-two years old, but possesses enormous energy. He is one of the wealthiest men in Russia, his estates being worth about 60,000,000 rubles. His father was one of the leading sugar manufacturers in Europe, and perhaps the most generous philanthropist in all Russia.

During the present war, Terestchenko has been Vice-President of the War Industries Mobilization Committee, of which the resigned War Minister Guchoff was president. This committee was one of the leading social factors in the rehabilitation of the army after the military disasters of 1915. The new Foreign Minister was also a member of the Southwestern Zemstvo Union with the headquarters in Kieff. Terestchenko's political creed is not very different from that of his distinguished predecessor in the Foreign Office, Paul Milyukoff.

The new Coalition Cabinet means one power and one authority in Russia. It means the end of uncertainty. While disagreements between the opposing factions are yet likely to occur, there is certainly no reason to despair of Russia. The Russian radicals have proved that they are not insane fanatics. They can rise to the demands of the hour. The new Russia to-day holds out nothing but bright promises. She stands for very definite things, and if they can only be understood, it will become clear that to think of Russia in terms of anarchy is nothing short of a crime. Considering the vast changes wrought in her organism, Russia is behaving very well indeed. And those who know her feel that she will yet lead the world to true democracy, humanity, justice, and a higher civilization.

What Next in Russia?

Roger Lewis

THE WORLD'S WORK, April 1918

The revolution was a year old when Roger Lewis, an Associated Press correspondent in Petrograd, wrote of his experience for the American public. He gave a new perspective to the fledgling government's attempt at rule, and painted a vivid picture of a people involved in a war and revolution.

Whenever I feel tempted to hazard a prediction about Russia, my mind runs back to a certain dismal winter afternoon in Petrograd early in March, 1917. Guy Beringer, correspondent for Reuter's News Agency in Russia, and I were playing English billiards in a clubhouse on the Morskaya. Beringer suddenly laid down his cue and remarked with utter irrelevancy but great feeling: "I tell you that nothing is going to happen in this forsaken country. I can't see a particle of use in being miserable in Petrograd. It's a good time for me to go to the Crimea for a holiday."

The door opened and a uniformed attendant entered, betraying more emotion than it is commonly supposed possible for Slavic features or club servant to express.

"It's begun," he announced incoherently. "The Cossacks are charging the crowds in the streets . . . Revolution. . . ."

Reuter's correspondent was by no means the only person guilty of a mistaken judgment in this matter. The fine art of prophecy has won distinction for very few people in this war. Certainly no one has received any credit on this account in Russia. When the London *Times* reached Petrograd with glowing accounts of the brilliant Russian maneuver which was to envelop Lodz in the early part of the war, the city rested more firmly than ever in the hands of the Germans. Instead of trains bearing an entire corps of German prisoners into Russia, which the *Times* correspondent had vividly put before his readers, the trains were going in the other direction and carrying tens of thousands of Russian prisoners into Germany. When the American newspapers containing an optimistic statement concerning the unconquerable spirit of the Russian armies and the prospect of a general advance made their belated appearance in Russia, these armies, totally demoralized, were in headlong flight into the interior of the country. And to quote just one more instance out of a hundred, shortly after Washington received from Ambassador Francis in Petrograd, who was exceptionally well informed, the reassuring information that Russia was at last emerging from her difficulties, the country had plunged into an abyss of madness far exceeding anything which had gone before.

This introduction need deceive no one. The following prediction carries with it no guarantees. I wish only to lay before the reader my own sources of information and to see whether all signs do not point unmistakably in one direction. It may simplify matters to set down three main alternatives which, I believe, cover the possibilities, and to decide which of these is the most plausible.

The first is a gradual disintegration of Russia into independent states, later perhaps to become loosely federalized. The second is a perpetuation of a regime of ultra-radicalism, performing its political antics before a partly sympathetic but somewhat nettled audience. The third is a sudden or a gradual reversion to a relatively conservative government—an ebb-tide of extreme radicalism, dragging the Bolsheviki and their political platform back into the depths from which they were cast up by the temper of revolution.

As this is being written, the renewal of German military operations on the Eastern Front introduces a fresh possibility—the possibility of a German subjugation of western Russia and a careful German surveillance and control over Russia's internal problems. But whether the German armies continue their advance into Russia or the German Government concludes a definite peace treaty with the Bolshevist Government it is impossible to regard the situation thus created as permanent or even stable. If Germany makes peace with the Bolsheviki she has not made a lasting peace with Russia, and if her armies take Petrograd and Moscow, she has not conquered the Russian people. The will of the Russian people to settle their own destiny has gathered too strong an impetus to be permanently checked.

The first alternative has already matured beyond the stage of hypothesis. With the Ukranians recognized as a de facto government and with the Bolshevist Government's declaration that Russia is a republic of *soviets*, a federation of Russian states may be regarded as a distinct possibility. This, however, is not properly an answer to the question of Russia's future. If Russia splits up into smaller units along natural lines of cleavage, and becomes a republic of independent states, the same problem which confronts the empire will still perplex the republic. The class struggle, the decision whether Russia is to be ruled by the extremists, the moderate socialists, or one of the various conservative or bourgeois factions—which will, of course, involve the important question of Russia's future attitude toward us, our allies, and the Germans—must be fought to a finish by Russia united or divided. There is a certain national bond in this very conflict, common to all parts of the country, which is likely to postpone the possibility of disintegration. While the country is sharply broken up into national groups of radicals and conservatives, it will be difficult for a cross-current impelling a division into states to gather much headway. And, as I have said, if it does, its only effect will be to localize the social problem—to divide the national class struggle into an infinite series of local class struggles.

I shall, therefore, devote this article to a discussion of the alternatives which I have mentioned—the possibility of a reversion, violent or peaceful, sudden or gradual, to relative conservatism. Is Bolshevism to remain forever triumphant, forcing by tyrannic methods far exceeding those of the despised autocracy, its minority will upon the majority, or are there already signs of a reaction which will sweep Bolshevism off the political map?

In this connection let me attempt an explanation of that dreadful bogy of the Russian extremists—"counter-revolution." The prospect of such a movement is, in the words of the radical factions, "imperiling the safety of the democracy." It is easier to understand this fear of counter-revolution if one realizes that the Russian character is a victim of the constant illusion that some satanic influence is clouding the political horizon and threatening the liberty of the people.

There is and can be no counter-revolutionary organization in Russia, for the simple reason that the people will not allow it. There may be innumerable repetitions of the Kornilov uprising of last autumn. As long as Kornilov and Kaledine escape prison and death, they may conduct as many Cossack rebellions as they like, but until public opinion—that is to say, the opinion of the masses—veers around in their direction there is no possibility of a successful counter-revolution of violence. The impulse toward a counter-revolution can not come from a few discredited generals and a very much overrated band of cossacks. It must come from the people.

One must realize even here by this time that the masses are in absolute control of Russia. The autocracy of the mob is much more complete than the autocracy of the former Emperor and there is much less chance of conducting counter-revolutionary propaganda at present than there was of conducting revolutionary propaganda in the days of the imperial government. The newly acquired freedom of speech and of the press is a pure fiction. There is freedom of speech for any one who wishes to express socialistic or anarchistic beliefs, but there is no free speech or press for any one else. There is, in fact, a much stricter censorship at present than ever existed under the old regime.

If there are any doubts about this, it is easy to convince oneself by a simple experiment. Get up in a public square and express a few "bourgeois" ideas. Say, for instance, that the feelings of employers should be considered or that the best way to save Russia is by electing a coalition cabinet which will consult with the Entente Allies before making peace—and see how far you get with it. If you are a person judged sufficiently important to have real influence over the people, you will go to jail. Express the same sentiment in a Petrograd newspaper and both the newspaper and you will be effectively suppressed.

The moment a bourgeois leader begins to show any signs of spirit, the numerous factions of the proletariat cease squabbling among themselves and unite solidly against him. They have the power of completely muzzling any member of the bourgoise. The consequence is that most of the counter-revolutionary material is in retirement or hiding, burying itself in the obscurity of the Crimea or the Caucasus, slipping quietly out of the country, helpless and frightened, looking only for a place of refuge from the mad, topsy-turvy country which the fatherland has become.

After the Revolution an Irish friend of mine with a highly developed sense of humor, was traveling from England to Norway on a North Sea boat which was sunk by a German submarine. Among the wretched survivors who crowded into one of the lifeboats were several Russians. One of them who knew that the Irishman had spent most of his life in Russia and in whom the Russian love of political discussion triumphed even over the miseries of shipwreck, asked him to what Russian party he belonged.

"I belong," said the Irishman to his shivering shipmate, "to the party of the 'frightened intelligentsia.' "

The phrase has become classic in Russia as a description of the helpless and intimidated non-socialist classes. To expect vigorous action from them is like expecting a manacled prisoner in the dock to perform sleight-of-hand tricks. There is not a bourgeois leader who is not under suspicion, who is not living in a period of stern probation expecting imprisonment or death.

If this counter-revolution about which there has been so much fearful surmise, is really to take place—and it is my belief that it is as certain as anything can be in a country of infinite surprises, where logic leads one to false conclusions and the laws of cause and effect seem temporarily suspended—then it is not to be expected from the powerless aristocracy or bourgeoise; it must come from the proletariat which now shudders at the very idea. But before going further with assertions which may seem extravagant and unwarrantable, let us examine the evidence. I will try, with illustrations of what I saw and heard in Russia, to show how this counter-revolution of the people is coming about.

The counter-revolution of which I speak had already begun when I left Russia, but it did not consist in conspiracies of plots against the people or their representatives. It is a slow but steadily gaining disillusionment in the hearts of the Russian masses with the result of the Revolution, in which so many high hopes were placed. To use the words of M. Shingareff, first revolutionary minister of agriculture and later minister of finance, recently murdered by the red-guard of the Bolsheviki, it is not so much a "movement at it is a mood."

The mood of the soldiers and workmen has drooped from the high exaltation of the early days of the Revolution to a brooding scepticism. After all, what has the Revolution done for them? Where are the mighty things which the release from past oppression promised? Where even, indeed, are the things more lowly but more vital to the comforts and welfare of the people? They were hungry and now they are starving. They wanted land and all they have received they have been compelled to steal or take by force. Formerly, they were oppressed by corrupt representatives of the imperial authority under German influence; and now they are bossed by dishonest representatives of the proletariat who have played even more directly into the hands of Germany.

The arguments of the Bolshevik leaders appealed at the outset to the workmen and soldiers, chiefly because they stood stubbornly for immediate peace, which is what all Russia, except the bourgeois classes, has ardently desired since the Russian Revolution. But these arguments were based on the conception of two democratic states making peace according to the principle of no annexations and no indemnities. Not even the wildest of the radicals dreamed of a peace on the terms which Germany is now dictating. The leaders who have driven Russian Democracy into this trap will have difficulty retaining their hold over the outraged masses. It is not unreasonable to suppose that the definite acceptance of Germany's humiliating peace terms and the continued advance of German forces into the heart of Russia will both foment a counter-revolutionary spirit in the people against the Bolshevist Government which has brought the degradation upon Russian Democracy.

The immediate cause of the revolution last March was a vast swelling volume of political discontent, ignited and exploded by the spark, which, so far as I know, usually sets off revolutions—physical suffering and hunger. This cause of revolution has changed in no way in Russia except to become more acute. The food situation in Petrograd and Moscow and in a great part of western Russia has become steadily worse since the Revolution, until it is now desperate. Starving people lose sympathy rapidly with idealistic experiments which fail to supply their primitive wants. Hunger has a way of eclipsing abstractions and drawing a clear line between the foreground of physical necessity and the background of political privilege. The starving man is much less interested in his right to vote than he is in something to eat.

Since the food problem is contributing in such a definite way to the counter-revolutionary spirit, I may, without digressing, briefly sketch the conditions in the cities and in the country. The poorer classes in Petrograd are now living on less than half a pound a day of a soggy, almost inedible substance, euphemistically known as black bread. There is no milk; there are no eggs; there is no white flour. There is too little tea and coffee and sugar, and the prices for what little meat there is are prohibitive. In the factory districts, on the Viborg side of the Neva, there is not even any milk for babies. The infant mortality, I have been told by physicians, has risen to alarming figures.

The forever-vaunted German efficiency and power of organization will be put to the supreme test when it attempts to bring order out of the Russian chaos and to disentangle the economic resources of the country from the total wreck which Russia has become. For months Russia would certainly be more of a liability than an asset to Germany.

Petrograd has become, since the Revolution, a dismal, starving city with endless queues of desperate people filling its wide, desolate streets. Wherever there are provision stores, these lines form before midnight and stand until the bleak dawn, like long gaunt arms of hunger, stretching out for food in a foodless city. They are mostly wretched-looking women, with chalky faces, almost smothered in dark shawls, and supporting wicker baskets and other receptacles for food. Sometimes these queues stretch for a quarter of a mile, making a somber, ragged human fringe for the somber streets. Now and then someone collapses and is borne away to a hospital and often later to a morgue. When the stores open the line moves slowly up, but before the latter end has reached the shop, everything has been sold.

I do not like to dwell upon these conditions. I have lived too long among them to see anything picturesque or colorful in this spectacle of hungry people. Moreover, everyone is too meagerly fed in Petrograd at present to be able to regard the misery of the masses as a detached phenomenon for which he can display a proper sympathy. I lived in Petrograd at the Military Hotel (formerly the Astoria) which had unusual privileges in the matter of Government requisitions of food. One was supposed to fare better there than elsewhere. But the best I could do for breakfast was a square chunk of black half-cooked dough, sometimes with a small pat of rancid butter; and a cup of tea or chicory-coffee without milk, sometimes with a little sugar. A hundred dollars could not have procured an egg or a piece of white bread. You occasionally met some fortunate person who had mysteriously acquired a few pounds of white flour or a half dozen cans of condensed milk which he would offer you at an exhorbitant price. But if you were keeping house, there were equal difficulties. For example, wood which used to cost seven rubles a Russian cord, now costs more than seventy.

The food question as a topic of conversation has completely preempted the place formerly taken in polite social chatter by the opera, politics, or the war. In the manner in which an art collector used to exhibit to his friends some recently acquired masterpiece, a man now says instead, with the same pride of the collector, "I picked up something to-day which I think would interest you. It is a comparatively fresh and undoubtedly genuine Siberian ham."

Take this company of society women who are having lemonless, milkless tea in the five-o'clock room of the Military Hotel. They are not discussing music or clothes. They are debating the food question. And this prosperous-looking business man whose somewhat drooping and pendulous features are wrapped in a temporary grin of complacence. He has not signed a contract involving millions. I know because I asked him how he dared to smile in Russia. He said someone has just sent him a leg of lamb from the country. There is another man in the tea room whose mental state demands explanation. He is a long-haired intellectual with a flowing tie and an expression of antagonism toward everybody, eyeing the orchestra for the moment with particular suspicion. He is not considering the ethics of the social question. He is wondering how the devil he is going to get a square meal!

A few days before I left Petrograd I met on the Nevsky a business friend whom, it was easy to see, some tragedy had overtaken.

"I've just been robbed." he complained, "of two poods (about seventy-two pounds) of good white flour."

"How did it happen?" I asked.

"It was in the tonneau of my automobile in the garage," he said, "and someone stole the automobile!"

The usual explanation of the food shortage in Petrograd and Moscow is the lack of proper railroad organization and transportation facilities. It is true that the economic condition of the country has suffered greatly from railroad mismanagement, but there is a deeper reason. I can explain best by letting Ivan Petrovitch, a Russian peasant temporarily in Petrograd, tell the story. Imagine then, Ivan speaking as he spoke to me a little while ago in Petrograd.

"I live in Samara on the Volga, and until the war began I was very poor and miserable. Tomara Andrevna (his wife) and the two boys and I hardly managed to live. We had a small piece of land which might have been enough to support us if we worked well. But we didn't. We became drunk with vodka very often and sometimes the farm was idle for weeks at a time. Our *dacha* (cottage) was badly kept and we had little to eat. Nearly all the produce of the farm we had to sell to pay for clothes and other expenses. All we ate was black bread. We sent everything else to the city.

"Then the war began and my two boys had to fight. And there was no more vodka to drink. I found I was able to do all the farm work which three of us had done before. But every month the Government sent us money to make up for the service of our sons at home. And I saved all the money we used to spend on drinking. It was many rubles a month. We became rich. I had more than five hundred rubles in a savings bank.

"Then I found out there was nothing we could do with the money. We had all the food we wanted except sugar, and we couldn't buy sugar no matter how much money we had. And we couldn't buy plows or any other machinery for the farm. There wasn't any oil to be bought either. So all we were doing was selling our food and getting money which we couldn't spend. I talked about it with my wife and the other farmers, and we decided we would not sell our grain any more. We would keep it and we would eat more. We began to eat things we had never thought of eating in the old days. We ate eggs—all the eggs we wanted. We drank milk and we began to cook white bread. We had never eaten these things before and we hadn't missed them. But we got used to them and liked them very much. It was better to eat them than to get money for them, for you cannot eat money. There was lots of grain left over, of course. We stored this until we could either get very high prices or something in exchange for it that we needed.

"Besides, we don't like the way our *tovarishi* (comrades) in the cities and in the army are acting. I do not understand politics, but I do not think that everyone should stop working and fighting to talk. We are working in the country and if the soldiers and the men in the factories do not work, we do not see why we should send them our food."

It is impossible for me to improve upon this statement of Ivan Petrovitch. One might write a five-thousand-word thesis on the economic condition in Russia without getting to the heart of the matter as he has in a few words. M. Shingareff gave me exactly the same information in different language.

"We have," he said, "the unique situation of a country whose peasants are prosperous, well-fed, and living like princes, while the people in the cities are starving. Let me give you a few figures. The peasantry of this country has received since the beginning of the war four billion rubles in allowances made to families whose male members are fighting. They have saved two billion rubles on account of prohibition. They are not merely comparatively, but actually, wealthy. There is no reason in the world why they should want to sell their grain. If you wish to know the primary reason why the cities are without food, it is because the peasants are eating and storing it. They feel a natural resentment against the deserters, from the army and the men in the factories, and really believe, I think, that the best way of punishing them is not to send them food."

I asked M. Shingareff if he foresaw a counter-revolution.

"It seems inevitable," he said. "It will be precipatated by the starvation of the people in the cities. February and March will be our hardest months. Snowstorms as usual will tie up transportation, and the little food which we are now receiving from the country will be held up. It seems to me exceedingly doubtful if Petrograd will survive this winter, at least not without the help of many American locomotives and cars.

"Meantime, the discontent and indignation of the people is growing daily. It is producing a distinct counter-revolutionary movement. The masses which thought the old government was responsible for the food shortage are slowly coming to the conclusion that their own socialist government is making a far worse muddle of things. But the counter-revolution will not be a question of reasoning or political wisdom; it will be physical—a pure matter of food storage and hunger. When people are starving they revolt against their government."

One must banish, then, the conventional idea of a counter-revolution by the Russian aristocrats and conservatives and accept the notion of a disenchanted people rebelling against their own leaders. The power of the genuine reactionaries is gone beyond recall. I traveled across Finland into Sweden in the same compartment with a man typical of the class from which one has been led to expect counter-revolution. He was a captain in one of the old guard regiments. Every now and then he relapsed into fits of melancholy reminiscence and spoke tenderly of the glories, the pomp, and splendor of the old empire—of the days when he used to attend wonderful balls in the Winter Palace and was permitted to kiss the hand of his empress. But he always finished bitterly with the statement that he was no longer a Russian. "Not until my country has a government and a flag of her own, shall I again own or set foot in Russia." he said repeatedly.

There is pathos in the plight of these fugitives from the country which they once loved and honored, but there is little chance of a counter-revolution led by them.

The political pendulum has swung to its leftmost limit. It has run all the way from Lvoff and Miliukov to Lenin and Trotsky. It is inconceivable that it will rest with the latter much longer than it tarried with the former.

There is nothing unique in the political evolution which has happened in Russia. It is natural for an oppressed people to hail revolution as a millennium. The cause of their suffering and unhappiness was an iniquitous and unjust government. Remove the government and you automatically abolish injustice and tyranny. This, I mean to say, is the way it appears to the masses. The new government must either immediately fulfill all the exalted expectation of a new government by the people or it is doomed to failure. It is, of course, doomed. The people decide they have not chosen the men who really represent them. For have not the people a supreme, unfaltering, if somewhat vague and undemonstrated wisdom which will make errors and injustice impossible? This, at least, is the Russian socialist's hypothesis.

So they delve into another political stratum and elect new leaders. Again the experiment fails. They have not chosen the real champions of the people. They dig lower still. And so Russian democracy tries all experiments and their failure begets the mood of disenchantment and discontent which I have described. The proletariat is beginning to feel and to express its doubts. Perhaps the supposed wisdom of the people is a myth. Perhaps, at least until they are trained and educated, it would be better for them to depend for leadership upon the hated but most competent bourgoise.

This is the doubt which is assailing the disillusioned people of Russia. In this way, sobering public opinion, evolving slowly out of the turmoil, is about to push back the political pendulum. The question is, which experiment has been least costly, least dangerous, promising the nearest approximation to the revolutionary ideal. To this point the pendulum will race back and perhaps stick. Perhaps it will stop again with Kerensky or it may go back as far as Miliukov or some other representative of the cadet party. But it can not fail to go back. This will be the counter-revolution.

Traveling Through Siberian Chaos

Richard Orland Atkinson

HARPER'S MAGAZINE, November 1918

Aleksandr Feodorovich Kerensky was a representative of the moderate labor party in the fourth Dumas. He became, after the February Revolution of 1917, minister of justice then war minister in the government of Prince Lvov. He succeeded Lvov (July 1917) as provisional premier. His moderation and vacillation enabled the Bolsheviks under the leadership of Lenin to overthrow his government, causing him to flee the country to Paris.

Vladimir Ilyich Lenin, founder of Bolshevism and Soviet Russia, was born V. I. Ulyanov. Although various reference works list him as Nikolai Lenin, he never used Nikolai as a first name.

Lenin was residing in Switzerland during World War I since he had left Russia in 1907. He had managed to split the Russian Social Democratic party at a meeting held in London in 1903 into the Mensheviks, and the Bolsheviks, whom he headed. Lenin was the chief exponent of Bolshevik thought in the struggle for supremecy among the Marxists.

The German government aided Lenin in his attempt to leave Switzerland and return to Russia. They allowed him to cross Germany to Sweden in a sealed railway car. The Germans hoped to disrupt the Russian war effort with this ploy. And history proved them correct.

An abortive Bolshevik uprising (July 1917) against the Kerensky government forced Lenin to flee to Finland. Bolshevism represented a minority in the first all-Russian Soviet Congress, but soon gained the decisive power due to weakness and disorganization of the government. In November 1917 the Bolsheviks overthrew Kerensky and set about establishing a dictatorship of the proletariat by the organization of the Council of People's Commissars. Lenin became chairman of the council and virtual dictator. Trotsky, Stalin and Rykov were the other chief members. Their first acts were a decree proposing an armistice among the warring nations and another decree abolishing private ownership of the land, nationalization of industries, begun under Kerensky, was speeded up. Opposition was ruthlessly suppressed after the victory of the Bolsheviks (who became the Russian Communist party). Lenin accepted the humiliating treaty of Brest-Litovsk (1918) but fighting continued with the civil war in Russia and against western neighbors until 1920.

For the western Allies, for the men and women who were giving their best in life and treasure, the Russian defection became immediately, and remained, an act of treason, not easily forgiven nor at all understood.

Russian military power collapsed in July, and the Germans moved their troops from the Eastern front to Flanders and to Cambrai in sufficient numbers to defeat the British and precipitated the Italian disaster at Caporetto which almost put Italy out of the war.

The Russian Revolution on the political side divided the citizenry in the Allied countries, set in motion domestic protests and rebellion against Allied policy, and destroyed a German movement toward peace. And so the immediate result of the Russian Revolution was to weaken democracy in Allied countries, crush it in the Central Powers, check Allied military power on the French front, and break it on the Italian front.

Russia's overwhelming desire was peace without delay. The Allies' supreme concern was to pursue the war to victory. The Allies appealed to Russia to continue its battle; Russia appealed to the Allies to lay down its arms.

In July 1917 and in the succeeding months up to the treaty of Brest-Litovsk, Allied hopes touched the dead low-water mark of their dreams, prospects and courage. Every prediction of victory was based upon the participation of Russia. Again and again the Western citizenry had been solaced for failure on their own front by promises of the arrival of the Russian steam roller in Berlin and Vienna. Such promises could be made no longer. Even the American hope lost its appeal in the light of the Russian letdown.

American correspondents snaking their way through Russia managed to file stories keeping the American people informed of the chaotic revolution in progress and its effect upon the people as they saw it. Here again, we get an interesting blend of personal opinion and fact.

I was walking down the main street of Vladivostok one morning when I noticed a large crowd collected on the sidewalk just ahead of me. Soldiers and sailors came running from every direction. A few civilians, happening along, stopped at the outskirts of the mob, to see what it was all about. But the soldiers and sailors held first place.

A young Chinese had snatched a purse from a lady as he passed her. He had been caught in the act and handed over to some soldiers. They were asking the boy all kinds of questions without waiting for any answer. They were abusing him with filthy phrases. They were beating him over the head and kicking him with their heavy boots, until I thought they would surely kill him.

Finally, the woman who had been robbed appealed to them to spare the victim and take him away for trial. But nobody seemed to know where to take him. I wondered where the police could be, to allow such disgraceful scenes on the main thoroughfare. I asked a man who was standing a little apart.

"Police?" he replied, amazed at my ignorance. "There aren't any police now, except those brutes you saw abusing that poor devil. They don't even know where the lock-up is. Yet we citizens of 'Free Siberia' have only them to depend upon for the protection of our persons and our property. It is the soldiers and sailors that say what shall be done here in the East. And this is a sample. They claim to be policing this city efficiently. Bah!"

While he was talking, a half-dozen ringleaders were arguing in a loud voice as to the proper procedure in such a case. Finally, two soldiers sauntered up, claiming to be of higher civic authority, and, with the noisy throng following, they dragged the prisoner off up a side-street.

Vladivostok was a city of soldiers and sailors. They were everywhere— on the streets, in the parks, in the trams. Red flags floated on all sides, and the soldiers had painted a little, bright-red daub over the old "eye of the Czar" on the fronts of their caps. They straggled along, looking for amusement; they had no drill; they refused to guard the harbor fortifications; there was nothing to do but draw their wages and spend them. The civilian got out of their way when he saw them coming, for they would brook no interference from any man.

I spoke of the Chinese incident that evening at dinner. I was fortunate in being the guest of a prominent English importer, and his charming Russian wife, who had been educated in California.

"Oh, you're evidently just beginning to find Vladivostok out," commented my hostess. "It's still better than Petrograd and Moscow, I understand, but it's getting bad enough. Most of the soldiers you see are deserters from the army, or men called for service and never transferred. They all gravitate toward Vladivostok. They live in hovels up on the hills, packed like sardines, and existing under the worst possible moral and sanitary conditions.

"Agitators arrived shortly after the revolution, and stirred up the men in uniform to violent mischief. Vladivostok used to boast a pleasant social life, on account of its being the port of the Pacific fleet. We have a good many English and American families, and we all enjoyed life together. We welcomed the revolution because we thought it would help those who were downtrodden. It is amusing to think that *we* have taken their places, and now we are living from day to day in danger of losing everything we possess, even our lives.

"The sailors ordered the admiral of the fleet to hand over his mansion to them. You know the large, brownstone place overlooking the water, with its beautiful gardens. That is where most of the balls used to be given. The admiral left the building, but managed to take with him most of his furniture. He said the house might belong to the state, but the tables and chairs were his. The men seized his paintings, and you ought to see them now. They say they are cut and slashed, and fit well into the present general scheme of things there. The place is a club-room for the new owners."

I had visited the mansion that day, in company with an English sailor of the Russian fleet. All was as Mrs. B—— had described it, except that she could not picture with words the dilapidated condition of the walls and ceilings. Stains, cuts and broken frescoes gave an appearance of hideous ruin. The occupants were spending their time in ignorant idleness, wantonly destroying property, or flirting with some frowsy girl from the streets.

"Several times," continued Mrs. B——, "news has come from that house that there is going to be an organized 'confiscation' of the valuables from the homes of the *bourgeoisie* in the town. Finally, after some minor robberies and personal attacks, the men of the foreign colony persuaded their consuls to enter formal demand for protection against the proposed outrages. The Kerensky *Commissaire* was frightened, and did something to quiet things down for a while. If I could, I'd leave for America tomorrow; and I think you'd be wiser to travel in that direction, instead of toward the Urals!"

"What interests me most at present," interrupted Mr. B——, "is how this labor question is going to be settled. It's becoming a serious problem with us business men. For instance, the Canadian Pacific Railway used to pay its employees on the wharves, for loading and unloading its vessels, eighty copecks a day. Well, after the change in affairs wages naturally rose—with everything else. Eventually, the employees asked four rubles for the first hour, five for the second and so on, for an eight-hour day. That amounted to sixty rubles for the day, or seventy-five times the rate paid a year ago. The men ask some of us one hundred rubles a day, and it's useless to try to argue with them. I can't imagine where to think the money's coming from.

"Commodities are higher because of the abnormal cost in the unloading of imports. Then the family men come around and say: "We've got to have another raise. Prices have gone up again!" And so it goes on indefinitely. In spite of all we can do, the men strike and refuse to work—say they're tired of working. Then the Mongolians or Manchurians get their jobs. Discontent seizes them in time, and they quit. After that, the women leave the farms in the surrounding country and hurry into the city after the 'big pay.' The result is a scarcity of food-supplies and a poorer quality of city labor. And I understand this sort of thing is being repeated in all the commercial centers of Siberia.

During the days that followed I saw much to confirm my friends' statements of the chaotic conditions in the port city. A large building, much the style of the Sailors' Club, bore a placard announcing that here the Committee of Soldiers and Sailors met to settle all municipal questions and disputes. I attended one afternoon session, but found little of interest in the talkative proceedings. Another fine old residence, formerly used as an officers' club, was now doing active service as a club for soldiers. Officers might go there as guests, if they so desired. The rooms were stripped of everything in the way of furniture, and it was difficult to see where the "club" part came in. But the soldiers could not allow the sailors to get ahead of them.

The freight-yards of the Trans-Siberian were choked with goods awaiting shipment. Transportation was steadily falling off, owing, I was told, to three reasons: the old Minister of Communications had neglected the lines, following an "economic" policy; many cars had been captured by the Germans, and few new ones were being built; and the new administration had adopted a *laissez faire* attitude toward the roads.

Indeed, all along the water-front I noted acres of provisions of every kind, from America, Japan, and the South, covered with sail-cloth, and left there. Shortage of cars, of labor, of system all conspired to promote general stagnation. We had a car-load of materials from America, for use in our work in the army; we at least saw it safely on its way for Petrograd. It arrived there five months later, after tracers had trailed it all over Siberia. It reached its destination only to be hurried out of the city again to keep it from German hands. Yet the cities of Russia were depending almost entirely now upon the Pacific terminal and the Siberian road for their clothing, shoes, and food.

In these mountains of supplies in Vladivostok were millions of dollars' worth of American barbed wire and ammunition, *en route* to do battle for Russia and the Allies. It is still there!

The local stores were appreciating the tremendous trading opportunities, but even their stock was getting low, while the goods they needed were rotting in front of their doors. When I remarked on the high price of any article, the merchants always answered with: "Wait until you reach Petrograd. You can't buy this there at all, or, if you can, you'll pay five times what we're charging you." And in most cases I found, later on, that they were right.

We left for Petrograd one Thursday evening, on the Siberian Weekly Express. The station is one of the finest in the East, but inside was a dirty, swarming mass of soldiers, provocators, and thieves, filling every nook and corner of restaurant, waiting-room, and platforms. The majority were trying to arrange last-minute passage, or were there merely for the sake of loafing and making trouble. A Russian officer told me that we were more fortunate than the members of the Root Commission whose train was despatched in secret from a point outside the station for fear of a demonstration against the "American *bourgeoisie*."

At Harbin, twenty-four hours from Vladivostok, there was a lively hustling by the porters, trainmen, and many passengers, to load up with great quantities of Japanese loaf-sugar and all manner of non-spoilable foods. This, I learned, was the regular practice—people making the long trip for the sole purpose of smuggling across the Manchurian border thousands of rubles' worth of necessities for the hunger-stricken cities of Russia.

Among the passengers was Major D——, a Scotchman, born and bred in Russia. He always read the Siberian papers as we received them along the way, and often related tales of the plains he knew so well.

The major pointed out one station where several men had recently been killed by order of workmen who had come from the cities and found that too little had been changed from the old routine. Faded, torn red flags floated from every station. The old station-masters, however, have never been removed. They still dress in their bulky black coats, and go about their business, leaving politics to those who have more time. The Bolsheviki have recognized, as did Kerensky officials, that there was one institution it was unwise to interfere with too much; and so the trains have been left free to go along under their own momentum as long as they will.

We found most of the German prisoners quartered in the east; the Russians had taken no chance of their walking home. They were all securely interned and strictly watched. At Krasniarsk, a Danish prison-worker told us that he was looking after six thousand soldiers and four thousand officers. He remarked that they were receiving the same food rations as the poor classes in Petrograd, and they didn't have to stand in line all night to get it.

"But the men go mad without work," he added, "so I secured for many the privilege of helping on the streets. The Russian soldiers are really jealous, but they won't do the work themselves."

As we traveled on through the ever-fertile regions of waving meadows or through tracts of hardy woods, the weather became steadily colder, and in some parts fierce snow-storms were sweeping the country. We had left Vladivostok bathed in the maple tints of sunny autumn, and four days later the Rumanian military guards on our train were struggling to keep from freezing as we crept through the network of tunnels around Lake Baikal into Irkutsk.

But as the cold increased, so did the multitudes of soldiers waiting at the stations through which we passed. Sometimes we would see ten trains a day coming from the war, their box-cars loaded with human freight. "*Bourgeois* trains!" they would call us; and their animosity became so violent that before long we had to draw our shades carefully each evening, for fear our candles would serve as beacons for the stones hurled at our windows.

There were thousands of soldiers seeking to travel in the other direction as well. One evening, the major was explaining the difficulties of self-government among a people so intellectually dark and morbidly erratic, and he laid stress on the fact that the millions of freed soldiers and sailors constituted the great menace at present. "They are being led like sheep by a few idealists and clever traitors. I fear it is going to end in a terrible upheaval," he concluded, as we pulled into the station at Taiga.

As usual, we got off to walk around. A much-bewhiskered old fellow was telling the soldiers from his perch on top of our car why they had a better right to ride in that express train than we had. He convinced them, and there was a wild scramble for places. One soldier caught my coat-tail as I disappeared through the door and I left a piece of it with him. Usually the train guards kept the doors safely locked at the stations, but this time they were taken unawares, and only a few cars remained free from visitors. Strangely enough, the soldiers hesitated to break in the doors, although this little diffidence conveniently disappeared during the winter.

Those soldiers who got into the cars were generally content to travel in the aisles and block up the passageways. One confided to me that he had outstayed his leave from the line by more than a month, and was compelled to ride on the express to get back in time "to escape punishment." I discovered an under-officer hanging on the outside step, one bitter cold night, and I finally persuaded the attendant to let him come inside. He stammered his thanks and fell on the floor, exhausted and half frozen. He had hoped to be taken in; and had hung on for two hours, with his bare hands, trusting to reach another station before he should have to let go and drop under the wheels.

He related how the engine-driver on one of the trains now ahead of us had been thrown into his own fire-box because he had taken his post-train out of a station ahead of a troop-train. At several stations we had been delayed while two or three trains went on ahead. Not that the men were hurrying to get anywhere, but they loved to jeer playfully at the belated express. The station-agents good-naturedly let them have their own way— and thus lived to see another sun rise. We were ten days going from Vladivostok to Petrograd.

Peace had been signed and spring had arrived when I crossed the Urals again and stopped at the mining city of Cheliabinsk. Situated at the upper end of a broad, bleak street are the great sheds formerly used to quarter prisoners before they were distributed over Siberia. Now the buildings fly the red flag, and in front of the massive gates, in the center of the square, are the graves of the Bolsheviki who fell in the winter capture of the city from Kerensky defenders.

In a leading store we talked with two young Jewish proprietors. They had returned in 1917, from New York, where they had lived for several years. Both were ardent followers of Trotzky, they boasted, and both expressed a fond hope that Germany would win the war.

"And she will, too!" exclaimed one. "She'll win in spite of you in America. What right had America to mix herself up in this affair, anyway? It was none of her business. Trotzky will show New York a few new wrinkles before *he's* through."

We assured him that we were quite agreed that Trotzky had shown America, or any other decent nation, sufficient "new wrinkles," without attempting to add any more; and my California friend finally asked with exasperation: "If you love Germany so much, and favor her cause in this fight for world ideals, why don't you go and do your part to help her?"

"Oh," was the calm reply, "she doesn't need us, or we would."

Afterward it occurred to us that they no doubt *were* doing considerable to help Germany right there in Siberia.

We attended a picture show in the town, and there sat scores of German and Austrian prisoners with women friends, just as in the restaurant where we had eaten some hours before. In reply to my inquiries, the usher whispered that many of the prisoners had married Russian women and were preparing to settle down in Siberia after their formal release. Later we discovered a cafe run by the prisoners and equipped with an excellent Hungarian orchestra. And we were not surprised to find that the city was efficiently "guarded" by fifteen hundred prisoners, acting under the Bolsheviki.

In every city much the same thing was true; Germans, Austrians, and Bolsheviki mingled in friendly council, and the erstwhile prisoners now dominated the streets and public places. Most of them knew that America was in the war, but professed ignorance of any reason why she had entered. Others whom we met did not know that we were their enemies. They presented a striking contrast to the Red Guard, in the neat appearance of their clothes and the clean, healthy glow of their faces. There were some complaints that they did not get enough to eat, but I saw no evidence of hunger among any of them in Siberia.

The crowds of Russian soldiers which had been so prominent about the stations had for the most part disappeared. Since the peasants had no other clothing, they were still wearing their faded and buttonless uniforms around the farms; and they will doubtless continue to wear them so long as the shreds will hang together. Thousands were safely within the Bolsheviki fold, and were quarreling for the privilege of drawing fine wages to act as Red Guards.

By this time very few trains were crossing Siberia. Civil war and its attendant evils had hastened the ruin of traffic. There was no longer any coal mined, and the engines burned wood, which had been cut by the women and piled for miles along the track. The engines were fast falling to pieces through misuse and neglect, and our journey was punctuated every few hours while we changed engines or awaited orders. Several times our engines were taken away from us by a stray *tovarisch* train that did not want to go any farther with the old one it had.

Every station-master had become a law unto himself and had full control over all trains that came into his district. On more than one occasion I heard a loud uproar against the "chief," who had uncoupled through freight cars and hitched on local ones in their place, to accommodate special friends.

The lack of transportation had almost destroyed the business of the famous co-operative societies in Siberia. There are practically no roads through the country, so they did what little business they could with the trains passing through the villages. It was amusing to see the cheerful line-up of men and women at every little yellow station, offering for sale poultry, milk, eggs, butter, bread, apples, and all kinds of special Russian dishes.

At Omsk, where the Austrians were loafing about the station in full force, we encountered a very indignant representative of the International Harvester Company. His plant had been seized the night before, and his partner arrested. The consul got off the train and went with him to get the matter straightened up. Earlier that day we were all enjoying ourselves by entertaining the youngsters with a bit of American fun—and a baseball. A miscellaneous crowd quickly collected, but the Red Guard dispersed them with the angry accusation that we were American *bourgeois* making fun of them. One Russian gentleman, who had been enjoying the impromptu sports, turned away with an exclamation of annoyance.

"Wouldn't you think even our poor foolish peasants would know better than to be influenced by such rot? And yet they feel themselves highly capable of setting up and pulling down governments! This incident reminds me of what was done in the next village, where I live. Our peasant girls, you know, are now allowed to go to school. Well, the villagers took over a large manor-house down there, and decided to use it for a school for both boys and girls. A committee was appointed to get it ready, and went to visit it.

"What do you think they did? They reported that the house had so many doors that it was impossible to use it; the children would get lost in it. So they recommended that it be torn down or burned. And the peasants actually burned it. They haven't got their new school yet!

"They made the same mess of our mines down here. They insisted on taking them over completely, although they don't know the first rudiments of business. The owners lost patience and flooded the mines so that they can't be operated for five years or more. They preferred to ruin their own industries rather than leave them to slow destruction in the hands of irresponsible children."

It was at Krasniarsk that we barely missed a good joke on our Red Guard friends. They had received a telegram to prepare to receive sixty *barani*, which were to arrive on the train that day. Now, *barani* means "sheep;" so the Red Guards made ready wagons and an abundance of hay and feed for the welcome animals. Instead of sheep, however, there stepped off the train sixty aristocratic nobles, heavily guarded. They were being sent into exile from the northwest province of Russia. The telegraph operator had made the mistake of reporting *barani* instead of *baroni*. But it made good fun for the crowd at the station.

The best inside into true conditions was given me by Izenkin, whom I had known as a soldier at the front, a few months before. I chanced to run across him near Tomsk. I knew him to be a shrewd, prosperous peasant, and I took time to get his views.

"Now, Izenkin," I said, after greetings were over, "you're a good Bolshevik, or Communist—pardon me!—so tell me about the reforms you're putting through here in Siberia."

He comically winked at me with both eyes.

"Oh *Gospodin Atkinson*, you know very well why I pretend to be Bolshevik—because it isn't safe to be anything else. Most of us here in Siberia are descended from political exiles, and we've always tried to keep up our education a little and be worthy of our ancestors' fight for liberty. And now it seems as if everything had gone to pieces.

"My people tell me that even when Kerensky was in power a lot of low toughs from the Petrograd factories, to say nothing of Siberian convicts, were receiving pay from somebody to go through all our villages, trying to stir up the vilest kind of trouble. Deserting soldiers were coming home, so they repeated to our home folk the lies we all used to hear from Germany and the Bolsheviki, all about America and Japan stealing eastern Siberia, and about the 'deliverers, Lenin and Trotzky,' who were going to keep us from becoming slaves to foreigners.

"Our people didn't believe these stories, nor did they like the way the provocators were acting; so they decided that they'd set up a republic of their own with the capital near here, at Omsk or Tomsk.

"You know the rest," he continued, bitterly. "Trotzky while he was talking internationalism and the rights of free peoples, sent cannon and guns and ammunition, and a blood-red gang of cutthroats—and what could unarmed Siberia do? Every city fought to the last, but it had to end sometime. Thousands of our soldiers turned traitor and joined the invaders, getting good money for it. Of course the criminal elements were happy. Some of the women believed the stories of the deserters and thought it was a great battle for their freedom. But most of them are just waiting, like the men, for a chance to throw off the despicable rule of these tyrants!"

"But," I objected, "you always vote Bolshevik at those elections for your town-meeting soviets."

"Yes, of course we do, but why? It's an open, hand-raising vote. Those who have thought the thing through and know how the present government is running our country, daren't vote against the Bolsheviki, because the Red Guards stand armed at the elections, a gang ready to start a riot to kill at a moment's notice. It's only a very few who are brave enough to face an issue like that more than once. Most of us prefer to sit around and wait until something happens from outside to break up this combination. It's bound to come, sooner or later, if the prisoners don't make Siberia a German colony before that time." And he laughed and sighed alternately at the confused predicament of his native land.

I recalled to mind the scurrying around corners to avoid machine-guns which were being turned loose down principal streets in cities I had visited, and lying down on the floor of cars while bullets whistled blithely through the windows; and I thought I could quite understand the lack of conscientious objectors at a Siberian open-air election.

When we reached Irkutsk we began to feel we were indeed in "Little Germany." It was a marvel to us that our refugee trains were allowed to pass. I spoke of conditions to an American there.

"I don't understand, myself, why they don't get after us all," he said, "unless they think it's better policy to lie low a little longer. There are fifteen thousand German prisoners between Irkutsk and Tchita, and they've got access to Bolshevik arms. They have declared themselves Bolsheviki, and have been taken into partnership.

"We had a nice little fuss here in January," he went on, "at the time the Red Guards captured the city. Some of the finest buildings were shelled and three thousand citizens lost their lives, after a terrible siege in the public museum. Several Englishmen and Americans were killed. Living has been so abominable ever since that most of our foreign population has moved down to Harbin.

"I had a funny experience with the gang coming from Moscow. My passport was stolen, so I made a new one, myself. I knew it would be all right if I could find a seal for it. At last I thought of using a tomato-can that was kicking around the floor in the car. I cut a large seal out of the red tomato picture, and pasted it on. It worked. These Siberian 'police' didn't examine it any further."

The news-stands were selling only Bolshevik papers, and those contained mostly German news, including despatches about the popular topic of the great American revolution sweeping the Western Hemisphere. In one issue the Siberians were warned to prepare for the new double battle-front, to be situated on the boundary between Europe and Asia, and facing Germany on the one side and the Japanese-American menace on the other.

But the oddest papers discovered were two many-colored posters for sale in a station, illustrating the difference in the land under the Czar and under Messrs. Trotzky and Lenin. They are entitled "God Sleeps" (under the Czar), and "God Wakes" (under the Bolsheviki). The pictures illustrated the new blessings now enjoyed in family, business, and social relations. The idea was particularly startling, considering the atheistic attitude taken by the present government in Russia.

Our train rattled along over the winding roadbed, as far as Tchita, and then threatened to stop. We could not pass through Manchuria because Seminoff's Cossacks were waging war against the Bolsheviki in that territory. Finally we were off again, on the newly finished road which runs up north of the Manchurian border to Harbarovsk, and then drops south to Vladivostok. It was the roughest railroad I have ever been on, and I was not surprised to hear that a train ahead of us had been wrecked and many of the Austrian-German-Bolshevik soldiers, going to outflank the Cossacks, had been killed.

The little colonies clustering about the stations were very small, but remarkably well kept. New school buildings showed real fruits of the March revolution, and the men, women and children gave the best impression for cleverness and energy that we had received in all Siberia. But the Red Guards were here also in all their absurd pomp and power. Once we caught them assisting in the unloading of vodka in barrels marked "Fish." Again, an insolent youngster in workman's clothes, and armed with a gun, revolver, and sword, ordered my friend and me into the car to have "our papers examined." He intended to show *Americanitz* that he must be obeyed in that locality. We knew the "paper" story was a bluff, and we decided to have his photograph as a souvenir. I stood in front on the car steps to hold his attention, while my friend used his camera to good advantage.

Across the long bridge that spans the River Amur, we swerved around into the city of Harbarovsk. This modern town was throbbing with life. At that time its population was swelled by refugees on their way to the coast. One "French-British Mission" train, that left Moscow two weeks ahead of us, had just arrived that morning. And we had been nearly a month on the road. At the station was gathered a most cosmopolitan assemblage: Englishmen with their monocles and canes, Frenchmen, Russians, Americans, Japanese with babies on their backs, Chinese with red faces, and glossy pigtails, Mongolians, fierce-looking Tartars with black pointed beards, and the usual motley rabble of Red Guards, Germans and Austrians.

It was Sunday, and the thieves' market and horse-market were doing a rushing business up on the hills skirting the town. When we visited the horse-market, a scabby, old, dirty-white horse, attached to a low-wheeled nondescript vehicle was the prime object of loud voiced discussion. "Fifty rubles" appeared to be playing an important role in the proceedings.

We walked up the wide street along the ridge leading to the cathedral on the bluff that overlooked the bend of the broad river. The Swedish Red Cross was conspicuous as occupying the ground floor of one of the massive new business blocks. Across the valley, on another ridge, were situated the spacious detention camps of the German and Austrian prisoners.

The next afternoon we attended the exodus of German prisoners toward Irkutsk. There were privates and officers, with uniforms denoting every rank; men from the army, the navy, and the air fleet. Their clothes were practically new, rich and gay; there were fur coats, high hats, and spiked helmets. They were a clean, strapping-looking company; some extremely boyish, others imposing, distinguished officers.

There was an endless stream of Germans crossing the tracks to the box-cars waiting on the siding. They were carrying small trunks, chairs, mattresses, cellos, mandolins, carved canes, kettles, pails, teapots, wash-pans, bags, and baskets. They were hurrying to and fro and saluting; there was much giving of orders. Young Red Guards were very much in control. Their bayonets were set, and they were enjoying the excitement immensely. I tried to imagine the thoughts of the German superior officers as these smirking, cigarette-mouthed boys prodded them now and again with their bayonets, to keep them within certain bounds. But I could only judge by the terrible looks of disdain with which they favored their guardian angels.

One young fellow insisted that I was a prisoner, and tried to keep me herded toward the train, with his *"Nilsa! Nilsa!"* ("no! no!") whenever I attempted to get back "across the lines."

"Hi, there!" I laughingly protested, "I tell you I'm no German; I'm *Americanitz!"* Finally persuaded, he was highly amused at the mistake, and voiced his intention to go to America soon himself.

We dogged the heels of the departing troops, and took snapshots of the outfit as best we could. Some soldiers were good-natured and "posed," but the officers considered it an outrageous insult, and urged their men to keep out of focus of the cameras. I had bribed the Red Guards to allow us to photograph the prisoners by the simple expedient of expressing a keen desire for their pictures, also, as a remembrance of the occasion. The whole force gladly left the Germans to themselves and followed me some distance down the tracks, where my friend was waiting to "snap" them.

One German told me he had lived in North Dakota, but did not like America because it was so "greedy for gold"! Few of them were willing to talk, but at last I discovered a short, jolly-looking fellow with a heavy red beard. In answer to my questions, he told me his story in English.

"There are about sixteen thousand prisoners in this neighborhood, besides a considerable number of Austrians and Hungarians. We were all captured in 1914 and moved out here in November of that year. The first winter we suffered terribly, without winter clothing or overcoats. The Russians gave us but little food. Then came the Swedish Red Cross and helped us to get clothes and supplies from our home government. And an American Y.M.C.A. man helped us to get books and other comforts. Several of us studied English from the Berlitz books he brought for us, and that is how I learned to speak English. Most of the Germans studied Russian by order of their officers; I guess a lot of them are to stay in the country for colonization. When America went into the war we lost our helper, and lost our touch with your people. I am a Hungarian wood-cutter. Some day I hope to go to America; I have only the warmest feeling for your country and its people."

"But why are you leaving here now?" I asked. "And why don't the Red Guards seem more friendly to you? All through Siberia they're arm and arm with the Germans."

"I'm not going away—yet," he answered. "I'm only down here to see one of my German friends off. There is not the best of feeling between the German prisoners and the rest of us, as a general rule. They don't trust our loyalty altogether, and we're left behind until later. Word came from Irkutsk that the German prisoners were to leave for that city at once, to escape the Japanese and Americans, who are reported to be advancing from Vladivostok to cut off the railroad at Tchita. Irkutsk is the center for all German prisoners, anyway. An officer told me a few minutes ago that he thought you men must be an American scouting party.

"As for the Bolsheviki, they have kept us pretty well cooped up around here, but I think that's merely the idea of the local Red Guard. There was no trouble in securing these trains for the men to-day."

"Have you become a Bolshevik?" I pertinently inquired.

"I am still a soldier, and therefore must not discuss politics," he replied, with a shy smile. He saluted and went to join a comrade Austrian.

As their trains steamed out for Irkutsk, we called good-bys to the enemy refugees, but their words of answering farewell were not of a nature that is generally permitted to appear in print.

The American flag never looked so beautiful to us when our cars skirted the shore and came into full view of the battleship *Brooklyn*, in the bay at Vladivostok. Alongside was the British *Suffolk*, and near by were the Japanese and Chinese war-ships.

I had read so many conflicting stories concerning the "allied outrages" in this port, that I immediately sought out Colonel S——, to learn the truth of the landings.

"There isn't much to tell," he explained. "The Bolsheviki ran things about as badly here as everywhere else. Things were even far worse than they were before. There are a good many German firms in eastern Siberia, and it looked as though the Reds were likely to help the Germans—actively or passively—to spirit away a lot of the valuable supplies lying around here. We were becoming rather restless. Then something happened which cleared up the situation.

"One morning, about ten o'clock, some Japanese merchants were murdered in their store. It was merely an incident in the crime that was being committed throughout the city. But the Japanese landed five hundred marines that night and announced that hereafter they would see to it that the lives and property of their people were protected. The marines spend their time quietly doing sentry duty in front of the Japanese Consulate and in Japanese quarters of the city.

"The British landed fifty marines to guard their consulate. The Americans have so far kept their marines around the ship, fearing that the other course smacks somewhat of intervention."

Many changes could be seen in the city. The streets were alive with people, the population having almost doubled in a few months. All nationalities were clamoring for passage to Japan, on their way to America or "anywhere out of Russia." Yet there was an atmosphere of order abroad that had not been there before. True, the Red Guards were parading the streets and making much the same mess of things as their predecessors had made with the Chinese pickpocket. But for the foreigner there was a new and definite sense of security emanating from those four vessels at anchor in the harbor.

Crossing a corner one day, my attention was drawn to the splendid appearance of the blue-jacketed Japs, with their white puttees, as they came along the street toward me. Approaching from the other way was a body of British sailors, in perfect marching order. Just as they met, a mob of about fifteen Red Guards, surly and rough, shuffled down the cross-street, out of step and with rifles sadly awry. The British and Japanese kept on their way with true military dignity. But the Red Guards halted, while they jeered and made faces at their old allies. A minute more and they had all passed by.

I was coming down Main Street one night, when I heard shooting close ahead of me. Reminded of daily events in Petrograd, I stopped to await developments. But the appearance of two or three Japanese marines, on the run, quieted the disturbance, and I heard nothing more.

Shortly afterward Japanese soldiers were shot at by a man who jumped into a waiting carriage and drove off with his accomplice. The Japanese flew after them like lightning, and did not give up the chase until they had captured the pair of bandits. But it was impossible to establish law and order in the surrounding country, under the limited program of the Allies, and the chaplain of the *Suffolk* lost his life outside the city while I was there.

When it came time for me to leave Vladivostok I learned that my passport must be deposited in the Bolshevik offices three days before being viséd. Wishing to leave the next morning, I urged the Chinese clerk to hurry it through for me that day. "No can do!" he insisted, and I had to be satisfied with that.

I went over to the noted old Lone Dog Restaurant for lunch and thought of various ways and means of possible approach. Finally I went back to the office and hunted up a woman clerk whom I had noticed going in and out of the *Commissaire's* room with an air of unquestioned influence. When I found her I slipped a few rubles into her hand and carelessly remarked:

"Oh, by the way, do you suppose I can get the *Commissaire* to fix up my papers to-day? I've simply *got* to leave to-morrow."

She looked cautiously at the bill (to see that it was not bad "Kerensky money," perhaps), and sweetly replied that she certainly thought it could be managed. She led me into the *Commissaire's* presence and asked him please to attend to my case at once. He did, and I left on schedule time. I had already secured my Japanese visé in ten minutes, paying for the same just ninety-nine copecks.

I found Harbin, "the toughest city in the world," plainly endeavoring, in the present disorder, to prove worthy of its name. But however gay and dissolute it may be, it can be forgiven all, for there are now no Bolsheviki there!

Seminoff's officer-troops made a fine appearance on parade, with their short Japanese rifles, but they were pitifully few in numbers. Little could be expected of them, without much outside assistance, in their war against chaos in Siberia.

American engineers were also there, preparing to push on toward Irkutsk with their constructive operations, when the time was opportune to do their best work. And in all Siberian Asia there were just two emblems of hope and belief that the near future might hold some beautiful promise for the storm-tossed nation—those khaki suits on American engineers, and those mingled flags of sister Allies on the ships in the harbor of Vladivostok. Without them both it would take Siberia many decades to regain her balance and claim her rightful place among the fruitful regions of the world.

PART X
RELIGION AND THE WAR

Polite society in peacetime manages to suppress virtually all overt religious prejudice. Only the low-bred, the poor and the mentally unbalanced give in to the zeal for their church, and desecrate religious objects of others or deliberately hurt people of a different persuasion. But during war, when the fight is for *God* and country, different religions are not to be tolerated. The evil and suffering perpetrated by the prejudiced in God's name must make the devil shout for joy.

The German Catholic Viewpoint

Heinrich Schrörs

THE AMERICAN REVIEW OF REVIEWS, February 1915

An interesting note injected by the German Catholic Church was that the war was a religious conflict, and the enemy lay within the Russian borders. The church felt a strong kinship with France, and early in 1915 announced that it would find it difficult to accept a war that would reduce France to a second rate power. However, German Catholic youths continued to serve in the armed forces, carrying the war and its desolation deep into the heart of France.

The fear, though, was strong that lying within the heartlands of Russia was a foe devoted to doing away with Latin Christianity.

The Catholics in Germany, it has been said, may be regarded as forming a state within a state. There is a very distinct line of cleavage in the Fatherland between Catholics and other citizens, not only in the religious sphere, but in politics and to some extent in economics as well. Politically, the adherents of the Roman Church are represented by the Centrum, numerically one of the strongest parties in the Reichstag. In the economic field they have always striven to hold the mass of Catholic working-men within the fold and to guard against their desertions to the Socialist camp by maintaining special Catholic labor unions.

Bismarck was naturally displeased with their spearatistic tendencies and taunted them with not being strong enough nationalists. They cared more for the international idea of their religion than for the German idea of their fatherland, he complained. Yet by the remarkable unity they display in the present war Bismarck has been proved as wrong concerning the German Catholics as Wilhelm was wrong when he called the Socialists "fellows without a fatherland." Heinrich Schrörs, a Catholic theologian, professor at the University of Bonn, undertakes to show in the *Internationale Monatsschrift* the consistency between international Catholicism and fervent patriotism, and to explain the general attitude of the German Catholics in the present war:

It is true [Schrörs admits] that Catholicism in Italy, and still more so in France, and perhaps to a certain degree in North America, is more markedly national in character than it is with us in Germany, not only in the application of the Catholic religion to home affairs and church institutions, but also in the general formulation of Catholic ideas and in the conception of the principles and functions of our Church.

If in these matters we are not so nationalistic as in other countries, if we adhere more firmly to what constitutes the essence of our faith, maintaining the purity of its supernational character, then we lay ourselves the less open to the suspicion of being willing to make sacrifices upon the altar of chauvinism. The conviction and devotion with which we uphold the Kaiser and are determined to fight for the defense and honor of our Empire is therefore added proof that this war is not a war of cupidity and conquest, but a war into which we have been forced against our will. Were it not so, it would be irreconcilable with the fundamental principles of Catholicism.

The writer then goes on to show that from the Catholic point of view German militarism was justified only by the menace of militarism in other countries, and that on one occasion, when the demands of the government for an increase of the military burdens did not seem sufficiently warranted by necessity, the Catholic party offered such strong resistance as to lead to the dissolution of the Reichstag. Selfish militarism is antagonistic to the Christian religion, the cardinal principle of which is love and righteousness. Catholic theologians from the time of the Fathers on through the scholiasts of the middle ages down to the present have consistently and steadfastly condemned war and preparations for war. They have condemned unjust wars not only by nations, but have declared it sinful for the individual to fight in such wars.

It is one of the most painful necessities in the present situation [Schrörs continues] that we have to draw the sword against nations such as France, with whom we are united by the highest cultural interests and for whose science we have the deepest regard. This is true especially of German Catholic theology, which, more than any other science, shares its broad foundations with the same science in other countries, particularly France. In fact, in a certain sense, our theology is identical with French theology. This is natural in view of the essential unity of Catholicism, which goes much deeper than the unity of Protestant theology. Between the Protestanism of Germany and the Protestantism of England, for example, there are no such close ties.

In brief, between the Catholic theologians in Germany and those on the other side of the Vosges the relations are so close and intimate that to speak of national hostility between them is absurd. We should greatly deplore the humiliation of France or the impairing of its position as a civilized nation. If in the present war we could detect any such object on the part of the German Government, even as a secret tendency, we should be the first to oppose it.

It was Russia that was the immediate cause of the war, and to the

Catholic world that is of extreme significance. Pan-Slavism is bound up with the Orthodox Christianity of the East. The Russian cross on the Hagia Sophia of Constantinople is to become the symbol under which the Balkan nations are to join the Empire of the Czar, and under which the Greek-Russian Church is to dominate the whole world. The deep enmity of that church toward Latin Christianity, which has existed since their separation in the ninth century, has never been overcome. It still furnishes the fuel for the fire that welds the church communites of the East.

In the minds of the Russian people and of the Orthodox believers of the Balkan peninsula the present war is also a religious war. It is therefore difficult to understand how the French clergy can be enthusiastic over their alliance with the Muscovite Empire. Even the non-Catholic French have good reason to fear Russian victory. Their interests in the Orient are strongly protected by the Catholic missions and by the age-long protectorate over them. If the Greek-Russian influence becomes predominant there, three missions will be wiped out of existence.

The Jewish Flight from Palestine to Egypt

Martha L. Root

THE AMERICAN REVIEW OF REVIEWS, June 1915

The frenzy of World War I unleashed many undercurrents of racial, religious and national prejudice. What had been subtle and sly indignities exploded into vicious hatred. Property was confiscated, people were forced from homes and many were herded into sub-standard prisons; others were tortured and killed. Rape and pillage was committed in the name of nationalism and God.

Some of these horror stories crept into national publications, but generally they were buried amongst a selection of articles on all phases of the war, and fiction of the period. Concerned citizens could read about the atrocities inflicted upon non-combatants; however publications were careful about being too graphic so as not to offend the sensibility of the readers.

Always there were reasons and excuses offered for behavior bordering upon the barbaric, but the end was always the same: dislocation, poverty and death.

The first day of my arrival in Alexandria, Egypt, March 13, 1915, I came at once into the midst of "expelled Palestine." Six thousand refugees from the towns of Palestine were in Alexandria. I inquired of Mr. Arthur Darrels, the American Consul, how to find out about these poor outcasts, and he courteously gave me a note to Mrs. H. M. Broadbent, an Englishwoman in Cabbari. He sent a tall Arab to put me on a tram, and our way led through poverty-stricken and filthy sections of "old Alexandria" to an enormously big, round stone structure overlooking the Mediterranean Sea, and bearing the name "Quarantine Lazaret, Gabbari."

Thronging the entrance were hundreds of Jewish people attired in all manner of ill-fitting clothing. Mrs. Broadbent, clad in immaculate white linen, stood in the inner court smiling and speaking cheerfully to the refugees who were trying to tell her all their woes at once.

I discovered that Mrs. Broadbent was connected with the government quarantine department, and that the building, which might well have been a Khedive's residence, had been opened to the refugees, together with its pleasant gardens, lying close to the sea. The "Lazaret" had in fact once been the palace of Said Pasha. An immense bathtub cut from a piece of solid marble stood by the gardens and three little girls were dancing on a table where probably he used to dine al fresco. The gardens extended out in a perfect circle, and around the circle was a stone enclosure, where soldiers were housed, and a moat where horses had been kept. Every particle of space from moat to palace was utilized by the unfortunate Jewish refugees. Sometimes twenty-six families occupied one spacious room, or two families would share a horse stall. They had come to Alexandria from Jerusalem, Jaffa, Haifa, and the provinces of Palestine. All had been provided with clothing, beds, and cooking utensils. Cotton merchants had generously given the poorer quality of their staple and from this the refugees had fashioned mattresses. Bamboo had also been given them, and with it the men from Palestine had made low cots. Those who did not have the bamboo cots were furnished with straw matting.

"We give them tea and bread for breakfast," said Mrs. Broadbent. "At noon they have a thick nourishing soup with bread, and at night bread and tea. Each individual receives a loaf of bread a day and four lumps of sugar." On Sundays they are given olives and jam instead of hot soup, and each Friday they are given a meat dinner. Large as this immense quarantine station was, its population constituted only a small proportion of the total number of Jews now living in improvised refugee towns in Alexandria. About 4,500 of these Jewish refugees were brought over from Palestine by the American battleship, *Tennessee*, which made five trips, arriving in Alexandria, December 28, January 15, January 19, January 30, and February 16.

Mrs. Broadbent sent for some of the bright refugee children to tell me about the *Tennessee*. "Captain Decker is a living angel," they began. "He carried the babies in his arms and the sailors did, too. He gave his room to mothers with young babies, and he turned his bathrooms over to be used by mothers with young babies. He gave us soup, milk, and little cakes. We had a big entertainment, and there was a nice baby boy born on the *Tennessee*. The sailors on the *North Carolina* warship from your country said they were jealous that they were not the ones to bring us over."

A business man from Jaffa gave me the key to the whole Jewish situation. He said, "The Turks, who did not until recently hate the Jews, do so now because they fear their latent power as a nation. The Germans forsee the menace of the Jews in a commercial way. Many of these Jews are from France, Russia, and England, and they refuse to become Ottomans. They have migrated to Jerusalem for two main purposes—to establish the center of Jewish life in Palestine and to assert Jewish national individuality in the dispersed communities. They wish to bring the land without a people to the people without a land."

It is a national movement of an essentially spiritual kind. To become Ottomanized would kill these Jews nationally and spiritually. They aim to obtain the support of the European monarchs for Jewish colonization on an autonomous basis. The Jewish population in Palestine is 120,000, among a total of 600,000. There is no desire among them to form a separate province of the Ottoman Empire.

All of their stories were heartrending. Many of them had been shoved aboard ships having only the clothing they wore, and some had even been taken from their homes in their night clothes. Many were barefooted and without hats. Some of them did not have a moment to gather together any luggage or to even get their families together.

I asked one refugee how this happened. He replied: "Beha-El-Dine, secretary of the Generalissimo, announced at noon one day that all Jews who had not accepted Ottoman citizenship must quit the country on an Italian steamer leaving at four o'clock that afternoon. The police seized all of us Jews, who happened to be on the streets. Women were taken, too. They were not allowed to go home to get the barest necessities to protect them from the winter's cold. We were hurried to the port. The boatmen were there with poignards in their hands, and threatened to kill us if we did not hand over to them our money and our jewels. Women were disrobed and jewels torn from them. They were beaten so cruelly that their cries resounded on the shore.

Religious services are held in all the refugee quarters. There were old men with marvelously strong, spiritual faces and young men, students who were preparing to become rabbis. The "halos" of absolute faith even in this grim vicissitude were their "rich garments." Instinctively it came to me that this was not the first time they had been exiled. Many of the refugees were Russian and Galician Jews who were so persecuted that they had to leave their own country. Now, after they had built homes and become prosperous in an adopted land, this new calamity had overtaken them.

In the hospital fitted up in Gabbari, I saw thirty-five refugee mothers who had been cared for this week during childbirth by a distinguished refugee from Jerusalem, Dr. Abouchedid. He had been at the head of a hospital, and director of its ten dispensaries. He told me that he had been arrested as a spy and came near being shot. His wife, who is sharing his exile with him, invited me into their two small bare rooms in the quarantine.

Dr. Abouchedid explained the critical situation in Jerusalem: "All business is dead. All shops of the Jews, both of Allied and of Ottoman descent, were robbed by the authorities. They even took the silk cloaks, women's gloves, and perfumes, saying that these were needed by the soldiers. Waterproof overcoats and leggings were taken off from Jews in the streets. The wealthiest persons in Palestine have been actually turned into beggars.

A Jewish writer, also a refugee, said: "The economic situation of Palestine is terrible. The large orange crop of Jaffa is ruined because there is no petroleum to run the motive power for irrigation. Germans and Turks lay hands on everything. They seize such small plunder as a quarter of a pound of tea, and bakings of two loaves of bread. Candles or matches cannot be bought now at any price."

A tailor from Jaffa told me that all the tailors of his town who failed to produce a certain number of uniforms for the Turkish and German troops were savagely beaten on the soles of their feet.

Mention should be made of the noble work done by the Australian soldiers in caring for these enforced emigrants. They took their horses and wagons and brought over four thousand of these poor people to the places of inspection, and later helped them to the barracks where they were to be housed. All the Palestinians were given a physical examination and vaccinated before they were assigned to quarters. Mr. W. C. Hornblower, an athletic Englishman, is the Egyptian Government delegate to the two Alexandria Refugee committees. The influx is so great that the government is directing the relief.

At present besides Gabbari, the telegraph building, a baggage house, and a station for soldiers for His Highness, the deposed Khedive and "Wardian," a beautiful building which was recently erected as a private railway station for the Khedive, are overflowing with the Jewish influx. Mafrusa, a cattle quarantine, is the home of hundreds of others. In the yards at Mafrusa, I saw 600 young Jews drilling. Each day they ask to join the British troops to go out and fight for Palestine. Three hundred young men are housed in a moving picture theater. The benches had been converted into beds. A bakery has been fitted up where the refugees make their bread in several instances. Laundries are improvised; hundreds of women do washing; some of the men work in factories which have been fitted up for them. Sewing is provided and many refugees make a few pennies each day. The Jews are not encouraged to go to Alexandria to find employment, as Alexandria has a big problem in providing for its own poor.

The consuls of various countries have assumed responsibility for their nationals and the Egyptian Government will probably be reimbursed for the present expense. The Jews wish to return to Palestine as soon as the fate of war permits.

The Massacred Armenians

Filippo Meda
Italian Minister of Finance

THE AMERICAN REVIEW OF REVIEWS, December 1917

According to tradition, the Kingdom of Armenia was founded in the region of Lake Van by Haik, a descendant of Noah, and was ruled for centuries by Haik's successors. The Assyrians frequently invaded, but never fully subdued the Armenians. For years the country was a battleground for Assyrians, Medes, Persians and Romans. Christianity was introduced early, making Armenia the oldest Christian state. Persecution of Christianity created innumerable martyrs and kindled nationalism among the Armenians.

The Ottoman Turks held all Armenia by the 16th century. Under Ottoman rule the Armenians, though often persecuted and always discriminated against because of their religion, nevertheless acquired a vital economic role. Constantinople and all other large cities of the Ottoman Empire had colonies of Armenian merchants and financiers.

The worst period in Armenian history was between 1894 and 1915 when Abdu-l-Hamid II accused the Armenians of aiding the Russian invaders and offered them clemency if they converted to Mohammedism. The wave of attrition that swept the land offers little if any evidence that conversion saved a single life.

The sad fate that has befallen the Armenians of the Turkish Empire is the theme of a paper in *Nuova Antalogia* (Rome) by the Italian Minister of Finance, Senor Filippo Meda. He considers that one of the chief anxieties aroused by the Russian revolution concerns the future of the surviving Armenians in Asia Minor, which had seemed to be reasonably assured by the Russian victories.

He recalls the ringing proclamation of Nicholas II to the Armenians, in which the Czar tells them that after four centuries of oppression "the hour of liberty has at last sounded for you," and assures them that the Russian people will never, never forget its debt to illustrious Armenians, such as Laraseff and Loris Nelikoff, who fought side by side with their Slavonic brothers for the freedom of Armenia.

These fervent protestations were accompanied by an abandonment of the attempts to russify the Armenians in Russian territory by violent means, and by the institution of a more sympathetic policy toward them.

It is true that many of the more intelligent Armenians, especially those living in the centres of European civilization, were disposed to be somewhat sceptical as to the Russian promises, in view of previous experiences, after the Russo-Persian war of 1828, and the Russo-Turkish war of 1877. Nevertheless, the repeated declarations of the Allied powers as to their determination to satisfy the aspirations for liberty on the part of all oppressed peoples, seemed to justify the belief that the hour of Armenia's freedom had at last arrived.

Now, however, that revolutionary Russia boldly proclaims a policy of "no annexations and no indemnities," Senor Meda asks what is to be the fate of Armenia, into whose hands will she fall? The history of the past two years shows that unless the world is willing to see the Armenian race disappear entirely, it must be freed, once and for all, from Turkish dominations.

The frightful sufferings to which this unhappy race has been subjected are briefly but convincingly presented by Senor Meda, who draws his data from the "Blue Book" of July 1, 1916, prepared by Viscount Bryce. The latter took every possible precaution to exclude from the recital any statements unworthy of acceptance.

In almost every case, the course pursued by the Turks was to summon the male Armenian of a given district to present themselves without delay before the authorities. All who did not obey the summons were driven to the rendezvous by the Turkish gendarmes. On their appearance they were immediately arrested and cast into prison for a day or two, then they were bound one to the other, and driven out of the inhabited regions into the open country.

They were told that their destination was Mossoul or Bagdad, but as soon as the wretched exiles, snatched from their families without even taking a last leave of them, had reached a distant point where nothing could be seen of them from the road, they were all massacred. This was done at the order of the Minister of the Interior, Talaat Bey, in agreement with the Minister of War, Enver Pasha, who had charged himself with the task of exterminating that part of the Armenian population under his jurisdiction.

After the departure and the massacre of the able-bodied male population came the turn of the women, the children, the old men and the infirm. Notices were put up in every village that they must prepare to leave in a few days. The women were nominally accorded the privilege of escaping exile, if they became Mohammedan converts. But the mere profession of a change of religion did not suffice, they must ratify it by espousing a Mussulman.

For the children the illusory promise was made that they could enter

Turkish orphan-asylums, where they would be educated in the faith of Mohammed. However, in the greater part of the cities and in almost all the villages there were no such asylums in existence.

The miserable women were forced to march out into the open country. Under these conditions death by thirst, hunger, sunstroke, or infectious diseases soon reduced their numbers, and when they reached the mountainous district the old and infirm were massacred by Kurds.

The few exiles who finally reached Aleppo in a state of absolute destitution were assigned to the most unhealthy places, among enemies whose language they did not understand. It had been estimated that as many as 600,000 of the total population of 2,100,000 Turkish Armenians were in this way deliberately done to death by their Turkish persecutors.

CONCLUSION
THE ARMISTICE

The world, weary from the long war, saw the hostilities finally come to an end in November 1918. Both sides retreated to heal their wounds and the victors demanded treaties that they believed would make a better world and end the possibility of ever having to go to war again. But the terms for peace were harsh, and while the fighting came to a halt, the seeds for World War II were planted in the peace which followed.

Combed Out

F. A. Voigt

DIAL PRESS, 1929

On November 11, 1918, at 5 A.M., one hour before the expiration of the offer, the terms were accepted and the Armistice signed. At 10:59 A.M. the shells were still falling, bullets still striking, all the noise of destruction which had continued for 1,563 days, more than fifty-two months, was still audible on many fronts. But at eleven o'clock, exactly, there was silence—so abrupt, so complete as to be oppressive. The longest nightmare in human experience up to that time had ended.

The might of Germany was smashed by the forces under Marshal Ferdinand Foch in frontal attacks divided roughly into three great sectors. The first of these attacks was delivered by the French and Americans in the southern sector which included Verdun and the Argonne. The second thrust was delivered by British, French and Americans in the Cambrai sector. The third was delivered by British, Belgium, French and Americans in the Belgian sector on the north of the great battle line. The attack was opened in force September 18, 1918, and by the end of October peace rumors spread, and the smell of war's end was in the air. The death, the killing, the empty stomachs, the vermin-infested uniforms, the mud-caked bodies, the stench of rotting flesh, all this that had become a way of life, day to day living, the hour to hour existence—waiting to kill or be killed, was giving way to the feeling that permeated every being. All of it very soon would be part of the nightmarish past.

F. A. Voigt, a private in the British Army, was conscripted in 1916 and served at the fighting front in Flanders in various branches of the service from artillery to labor companies. His last days of the war were spent with the Royal Army Medical Corps.

His impressions of the final hours of the conflict in the front lines are a small part of his diary and letters later reproduced in book form.

I was fully awake long before reveille, sleepy and unrefreshed, and when reveille came we received orders to move within two hours.

Four of us and one N.C.O. were left behind to load a lorry. And then we, too, packed up and set out to follow the unit.

Thinking to take a short cut across country, we ascended the hill-slope, jumping and clambering across shell-holes and striding through long grass and weeds. Now and again we would chance upon some narrow winding track that soon lost itself again amid the tangled growth.

Low clouds burdened the sky and a fine rain began to fall. The top of the hill was hidden in grey mist.

We passed a heap of broken concrete blocks from which the twisted ends of iron rods projected. A little farther on a concrete shelter stood intact except for deep vertical fissures. I peered into the narrow entrance that sloped steeply down. I slipped in the soft mud, but by stretching out my arms and clasping the outer wall I just saved myself from falling flat on to a rotting corpse that lay half-immersed in greenish-black water. I drew slowly back, sick with horror.

The devastation increased with every mile and the shell-holes came closer and closer together. Dead horses, shattered guns, wagons, and limbers lay overturned in the ditches. At one spot on the roadside the legs and buttocks of a man, all brown and shrivelled, slanted upwards from a deep, wide rut, many heavy wheels having passed across the small of his back.

Gradually the houses, trees and bushes disappeared entirely. We reached the site of a village that before the war had sheltered several thousands of people. Nothing remained except small bits of brick mingling with the bare soil, piled up and scooped and churned and tossed by shell-fire.

Here, too, there were many dead. A little way off the road lay an Englishman who could not have fallen more than a few days before. His hands were clenched, his mouth wide open, his eyes fixed and staring. Near him was a tall German. He lay at full length with arms outstretched and legs crossed. His left hand, immersed in a pool, was white and puffy. His right hand was half closed and only slightly wrinkled. His side had been ripped open and fragments of entrail projected from the rent. The water beneath and around him was stained with blood. His pockets were turned inside out and papers and postcards lay scattered around in the usual manner. His cloak had been thrown across his face.

Other bodies had lain unburied for several months; others for several years, and of these only the mud-stained bones were left.

We marched in silence through this dismal land of ruin and desolation. At length, in the distance, we saw a solitary fragment of a brick wall standing in a wide hollow, a sign that we were nearing a habitable region once again.

We passed by riddled German sign-boards, and came to a litter of wreckage that had once been a village, and then we left the main road and entered a little wood, or rather an assembly of scarred tree-trunks leaning at all angles. It was crossed by a zigzag trench and all the refuse of battle lay scattered about.

An Australian soldier lay on a low mound. His head had dropped off and rolled backwards down the slope. The lower jaw had parted from the skull. His hands had been devoured by rats and two little heaps of clean bones were all that remained of them. The body was fully clothed and the legs encased in boots and puttees. One thigh-bone projected through a rent in the trousers and the rats had gnawed white grooves along it. A mouldy pocket-book lay by his side and several postcards and a soiled photograph of a woman and a child.

An attempt had been made to bury some of the dead, and several lay beneath heaps of loose earth with their boots projecting. But the rats had reached them all, and black, circular tunnels led down into the fetid depths of the rotting bodies. The stench that filled the air was so intolerable that we hastened to get out of this dreadful place.

As we walked on, the scattered houses drew closer and closer together until they formed continuous rows. A civilian passed by, pushing a wheelbarrow that clattered over the cobbles. Then there followed a woman with a bundle on her back.

We turned a corner and entered another street in which the houses had not been rifled. Several were occupied by civilians.

Before us, in an open field, lay our camp. Scribbled in chalk on a piece of board nailed across a broken window were the words:

"Der Friede wird stundlich erwartet"—Peace is expected every hour.

Ever since we had received news of the German peace offers and President Wilson's replies, rumours had multiplied enormously—the Kaiser had been assassinated, the German Fleet had surrendered, German troops were deserting in masses, German submarines were floating on the surface and flying white flags, a German Republic had been proclaimed with Liebknecht as President.

One evening after a day of unusually hard labour, we were laying exhausted in our tent. Suddenly the flap was thrown open, a man pushed his head in and shouted excitedly:

"I say, you chaps, the Armistice has been signed—it's official!"

"Who says so? Did you see it in print?"

"No, I just heard it from a despatch-rider. He got it from his C.O.— it's official."

"Don't believe it. We've heard that tale too often."

"All right, then, don't!" the man shouted angrily, and walked off.

No sooner had he gone when our Corporal said:

"It wouldn't surprise me if he were right. In any case, even if the Germans haven't signed yet, they'll have to do so soon. Bulgaria, Turkey, and Austria have collapsed. The Germans have decreasing resources and no reserves. The Allies have increasing resources and unlimited reserves. The longer the war goes on, the more desperate is Germany's position. She must accept our terms, she can't help herself."

"I do not think they will sign," I replied. "I think we can expect at least another year of war. I know Germany is in a bad way, but our terms mean unconditional surrender. The Germans will not be silly enough to imagine that, once they are disarmed and helpless, we shall stick to the Fourteen points or be bound by any promises of any kind. No, the Germans will fight on, they will shorten their front, and they will at least keep the Allies off German territory for an indefinite period until they can secure better terms."

"You overrate the strength of the Germans. I think the German army is becoming completely demoralized. I also think that the blockade has done its work amongst the civilian population. We shall have an armistice within the next few days. Perhaps rumour is correct for once and the war is already over. We haven't heard any guns for a long time—the front is extraordinarily quiet."

"Yes, but we would have heard officially—news like that would never be kept from us."

"That's true enough—I expect the thing is being discussed and a decision will be reached before long."

We all agreed that as soon as the fighting ceased, we would be informed. The news of the Armistice would be telegraphed to every unit and it would reach us within a few minutes from the actual signature. And then, what would we do then? How would our feelings find an outlet? It was impossible to say. Shouting, singing, dancing, would they give us relief? Speculation was useless, painfully useless. And yet what else could we think about?

It was Sunday, the 10th of November. We had no work to do and wandered restlessly round the town. An official communique was posted up outside the Mairie, but it contained nothing new. There was a crowd of soldiers round a Belgian boy who was selling English papers. We bought the last copies, but they were of the previous Thursday and did not add to our knowledge. The suspense was becoming unbearable. My conviction that the Germans would reject the terms of the Allies was shaken—not by any further evidence, but by the general atmosphere of excitement and hopeful expectation which communicated itself to me. I kept on repeating to myself, "They will not sign, they will not sign," and intellectually I believed my own words. And yet I was continually imagining the war already over and what I merely thought seemed unessential and irrelevant. The stress of wild hopes and mental agitation became almost a physical pain.

Darkness came on and we retired to our tents. I gradually became aware of a faint noise, so faint that I hardly knew whether it was real or not. As soon as I listened intently I could hear nothing. Then one of us said: "What's that funny noise?" There it was again, a low, hollow sound like that of a distant sea. It grew louder and then ceased. Then it became audible once more and grew louder and still louder. Suddenly we realized what it was—it was the sound of cheering. It came nearer and nearer, gathering speed. It flooded the whole town with a great rush, paused a moment, and then burst over our camp.

Everybody went mad. The men rushed out of the tents and shouted: "It's over—it's over—it's over!" I could hear one shrill voice screaming wildly: "No more bombs—no more shells—no more misery." The deafening clamor from innumerable throats was topped by the piercing blasts of whistles and the howling of cat calls. A huge bonfire was lit in the camp and sheets of flame shot skyward. The brilliant stars of signal-rockets rose and fell in tall parabolae and lit up all the neighbourhood. The Sergeant-Major blew his whistle with the intention of restoring order. He was answered by a hullabaloo of derisive hoots and yells. He gave up the attempt and instead he headed a procession that marched into the town, banging empty tins and whirling french-rattles. An anti-aircraft battery opened fire with blank charges. Aeroplanes flew overhead with all lights on.

Many of us went back into our tents and sang with all the power of our lungs.

So the war was over! The fact was too big to grasp all at once, but nevertheless I felt an extraordinarily serene satisfaction. Then someone said: "The people who've lost their sons and husbands—now's the time they'll feel it." The truth of his remark struck me with a sudden violence. My serenity was broken and looked into the blackness beneath it. I knew what I was going to see, but, nevertheless, I looked, in spite of myself, and saw innumerable rotting dead that lay unburied in all postures on the bare, shell-tossed earth. A horror of death such as I had never known before came upon me—a crushing, annihilating horror that seemed to impart a fiendish character to the shouting and singing in the camp, as though millions of demonic spirits were howling and dancing with devilish glee over the accomplishment of the greatest iniquity every known. At the same time I felt ashamed of not joining in the general jubilation, and bitterly disappointed that my own thoughts should obsess me at this supreme hour. But I knew that the war had lasted too long and that the world's misery had been too great ever to be shaken off, I also knew that all the dead had died in vain. In order to escape from my intolerable meditations I sat up and began to talk to my neighbour:

"I suppose it'll be read out officially tomorrow morning?"

"Sure—and we'll get a day off at least."

We continued to talk of commonplace things. It was several hours after midnight and the uproar was dying down a little. I felt sleepy and something like contentment was beginning to steal over me once again.

Reveille did not sound until nine o'clock on the Monday morning. The whistle blew for parade. There would, of course, be an official announcement that the Armistice had been signed, and perhaps a letter of thanks to the "splendid troops who had won the war" (which would bore us extremely) and a holiday (which would be welcomed with loud cheers).

We paraded. The Sergeant-Major addressed us:

"I'm sorry, boys, but nothing official's come through. You must go to work as usual. It's a damned shame, I know, but I can't help it. I expect the message'll come during the day and you're sure to get to-morrow off."

There was a murmur in the ranks, but bewilderment deprived us of the power of taking concerted action. A sudden fear seized me—could last night's celebration have been the result of a false alarm?

We marched off. But no one did a stroke of work the whole day. All discipline had gone. The N.C.O.'s had no vestige of authority left. Men from other units whom we met knew no more than we did. They said the Armistice had been signed, but there had been no official announcement.

We got back to the camp in the afternoon. No official news.

In the evening the celebrations were renewed. I was troubled by an intense anxiety which began to spread to the others. Still, there would certainly be an announcement the following morning.

We paraded on Tuesday. No announcement of any kind. We marched off to work as usual, but again no work was done. Suddenly I caught sight of a soldier walking along the road a long way off with a newspaper in his hand. I ran after him and caught him up.

"Any news?" I asked.

He gave me the paper. It was dated Monday, the 11th November— only a day old. The headline ran: "No Armistice yet."

So Sunday's demonstration had been a sham and a fraud!

I rejoined the others. They, too, had heard that no Armistice had been signed by Sunday midnight from a despatch-rider, who had, however, added that signature was expected every minute.

We were back in camp. Many new rumours were circulating—the Germans had rejected the terms, the Italians had renewed the offensive. In the evening some of us thought they could hear distinct gunfire. We listened carefully, but our mental tension destroyed our power of hearing very faint sounds.

Wednesday morning, and still no definite news. The suspense was becoming unbearable. No work was done. I questioned men from five other units, but none of them were any better informed than we were.

The expectation of peace had made us forget our bitterness towards the army, but it began to show itself again:

"They don't want us to know!"

"They're damned sorry it's all over!"

"There's too many of 'em wi' soft jobs what wants the war to go on for ever!"

"What are you grumbling about? What has the Armistice got to do with us? The Armistice concerns the Staff, not us. It's not our business— we're only common soldiers."

When we got back to camp a boy was selling papers at the entrance.

I bought a *Times*. It was Tuesday's. The Armistice had been signed on the Monday morning!

I went to my tent and sat down and thought it over. The terms were ominous. There was no doubt about it this time—the war had come to an end. I thought of home and of freedom. It almost seemed as though army-life had been a dream. I was still in the army, but a few months more or less would make no difference, for my thoughts would be all in the future.

In the evening the celebrations were resumed. They lacked the spontaneity of those that were held on the Sunday night. Nevertheless, the rejoicing was genuine, for our suspense had been followed by an immense relief.

As I lay in my tent amid the shouting and singing I again felt that bitter thoughts were gathering, but I was distracted by a man sitting two places from me, who said:

"It's a bloody shame we can't get any wine or spirits and get bloody well drunk to-night."

A man lying near him, who had kept very quiet all the evening suddenly sat up erect, glaring with fury, and shouted:

"That's all you think about, getting drunk—you dirty little blackguard! You don't deserve to have peace, you don't! Bloody lot of fools—all shouting and singing and wanting to get drunk! They ought to have more respect for the dead! The war's over, and we're bloody lucky to get out of it unharmed, but it's nothing to shout about when there's hundreds of thousands of our mates dead or maimed for life."

"Don't talk bloody sentimental rot—call yourself a soldier? You ought to be a bloody parson!"

"I don't call myself a soldier—it's a bloody insult to be called a soldier. I'm not a bloody patriot either—I reckon patriotism's a bloody curse. I kept out of the army as long as I could, but they combed me out (that's their polite way of putting it!), and shoved me into khaki, but they never made a soldier of me! I've never been any use to them! I only worked when they forced me to. I've been more expense and trouble to them than I'm worth. I haven't helped to win this wicked war, and I'm proud of it too! Sentimental rot be damned—if everyone had been my way of thinking there wouldn't have been a war, no, not in any country. The war's won, I know, and I'm sorry for it. But Fritz has come off best, not us. He's lost the war, but he's found his bloody soul! I'll tell the civvies something about war when I get home—I'll tell 'em we rob the dead, I'll tell 'em. . . ."

"For God's sake chuck it. . . ."

"All right, I'll chuck it—I know it's no bloody good talking to fellows like you. Go and get drunk, then, do as you bloody well please. That's all you're fit for. . . ."

He flung himself back into bed, wrapped himself up in his blanket and did not say another word.

The Armistice Negotiations

On January 8, 1918 President Woodrow Wilson, in an address before both houses of Congress, delivered an intensely idealistic message with certain very practical aims. It was intended to reach the liberal leaders of the Central Powers as a persuasive appeal for peace, and in that effort it was successful. It was also intended to serve notice to the Allies that the United States would not be a party to a selfish peace. There was also the hope that the 14 points President Wilson offered would provide a framework for peace discussions.

The President's plan follows.

1. Open covenants of peace, openly arrived at, after which there should be no private international understandings of any kind, but diplomacy shall proceed always frankly and in the public view.

2. Absolute freedom of navigation upon the seas, outside territorial waters, alike in peace and in war, except as the seas may be closed in whole or in part by international action for the enforcement of international covenants.

3. The removal, so far as possible, of all economic barriers and the establishment of an equality of trade conditions among all the nations consenting to the peace and associating themselves for its maintenance.

4. Adequate guaranties given and taken that national armaments will be reduced to the lowest points consistent with domestic safety.

5. A free, open-minded, and absolutely impartial adjustment of all colonial claims, based upon a strict observance of the principle that in determining all such questions of sovereignty the interests of the populations concerned must have equal weight with the equitable claims of the government whose title is to be determined.

6. The evacuation of all Russian territory and such a settlement of all questions affecting Russia as will secure the best and freest co-operation of the other nations of the world in obtaining for her an unhampered and unembarrassed opportunity for the independent determination of her own political development and national policy and assure her of a sincere welcome into the society of free nations under institutions of her own choosing, and more than a welcome, assistance also of every kind that she may need and may herself desire.

The treatment accorded Russia by her sister nations in the months to come will be the acid test of their good will, of their comprehension of her needs as distinguished from their own interests, and of their intelligent and unselfish sympathy.

7. Belgium, the whole world will agree, must be evacuated and restored, without any attempt to limit the sovereignty which she enjoys in common with all other free nations. No other single act will serve as this will serve to restore confidence among the nations in the laws which they have themselves set and determined for the government of their relations with one another. Without this healing act the whole structure and validity of international law is forever impaired.

8. All French territory should be freed and the invaded portions restored, and the wrong done to France by Prussia in 1871 in the matter of Alsace-Lorraine, which has unsettled the peace of the world for nearly fifty years, should be righted, in order that peace may once more be made secure in the interest of all.

9. A readjustment of the frontiers of Italy should be effected along clearly recognizable lines of nationality.

10. The peoples of Austria-Hungary, whose place among the nations we wish to see safeguarded and assured, should be accorded the freest opportunity of autonomous development.

11. Rumania, Serbia, and Montenegro should be evacuated; occupied territories restored; Serbia accorded free and secure access to the sea; and the relations of the several Balkan States to one another determined by friendly counsel along historically established lines of allegiance and nationality; and international guaranties of the political and economic independence and territorial integrity of the several Balkan States should be entered into.

12. The Turkish portions of the present Ottoman Empire should be assured a secure sovereignty, but the other nationalities which are now under Turkish rule should be assured an undoubted security of life and an absolute unmolested opportunity of autonomous development, and the Dardanelles should be permanently opened as a free passage to the ships and commerce of all nations, under international guaranties.

13. An independent Polish state should be erected which should include the territories inhabited by indisputably Polish populations, which should be assured a free and secure access to the sea, and whose political and economic independence and territorial integrity should be guaranteed by international covenant.

14. A general association of nations must be formed under specific covenants for the purpose of affording mutual guaranties of political independence and territorial integrity to great and small states alike.

The 14 points gave President Wilson immediately the position of moral leadership of the Allies. The peace proposal was studied in all countries and

*found special interest with the Central Powers because of the reverses be-
ginning to be felt on the battlefields by the German Army. By October 5th
the German Government sent its first peace feeler when General Haig's forces
had broken the Hindenburg Line between St. Quentin and Le Catelet and
General Pershing's forces were exerting enormous pressure between the
Meuse and the Argonne.*

This prompted the first German note to President Wilson:

> The German Government requests the President of the United
> States to take in hand the restoration of peace, acquaint all the bellig-
> erent states of this request, and invite them to send plenipotentiaries
> for the purpose of opening peace negotiations.
>
> It accepts the programme set forth by the President of the United
> States in his message to Congress on January 8th and in his later pron-
> ouncements, especially in his speech of September 28th, as a basis for
> peace negotiations.
>
> With a view to avoiding further bloodshed, the German Government
> requests the immediate conclusion of an armistice on land and sea.

*(The reference to the speech of September 28 referred to the President's
remark during the opening of the campaign for the Fourth Liberty Loan in
New York City where he said, "Militarism must go, root and branch.")*

*The President and his advisers were not interested in peace negotiations,
but unconditional surrender.*

*General Erich Ludendorff, Chief of Staff of Field Marshal Hindenburg,
was unhappy with the demand for "unconditional surrender," and advised
the Kaiser, "we must fight on."*

*By October 25th the Reichstag was shaken. The General who could not
win the battle, who had lost the victory, who had confessed that the fighting
line might be broken at any moment had advocated to continue the war.*

*Suddenly, completely, the homefront collapsed and Ludendorff recog-
nized that "Germany is lost!" He offered his resignation to the Kaiser, then
fled to Sweden.*

*On October 31st the Inter-Allied War council met at Versailles: Cle-
menceau, Lloyd George, Marshal Foch, and Colonel Edward House for
President Wilson.*

*By November 3rd a rumor of Navy mutinies came from Kiel. It was the
same day that Austria surrendered unconditionally. At Versailles the Inter-
Allied Conference had decided on the terms Germany could have by asking
Marshal Foch for them. Germany had informed President Wilson that it
had stopped air raids and was grieved that Allied planes were still spreading
panic in the Rhine Valley.*

*On November 5th German Headquarters asked for and received per-
mission to pass through Allied lines to get Marshal Foch's peace terms. The
German ambassadors were escorted through the ruins of St. Quentin and*

embarked on a special train to the Forest of Compiègne near the village of Rethondes where Marshal Foch awaited them in a railroad car. It was November 9th when the Germans walked into the cold railroad car while at home the revolution flared up and the Kaiser abdicated, leaving for Holland. The Crown Prince followed by another route. The next few days saw an influx of German royalty into Switzerland.

The chilling atmosphere, created by the memories of four years of atrocities, was understood by the German ambassadors. They were handed the terms of the Armistice, and were told that they must accept or reject the terms within 72 hours.

The actual text that was signed:

1. Military Clauses on Western Front

One. Cessation of operations by land and in the air six hours after the signature of the armistice.

Two. Immediate evacuation of invaded countries: Belgium, France, Alsace-Lorraine, Luxemburg, so ordered as to be completed within fourteen days from the signature of the armistice. German troops which have not left the above-mentioned territories within the period fixed will become prisoners of war. Occupation by the Allied and United States forces jointly will keep pace with evacuation in these areas. All movements of evacuation and occupation will be regulated in accordance with a note annexed to the stated terms.

Three. Repatriation, beginning at once, to be completed within fifteen days, of all the inhabitants of the countries above enumerated (including hostages, persons under trial, or convicted).

Four. Surrender in good condition by the German armies of the following war material: Five thousand guns (2,500 heavy and 2,500 field), 25,000 machine guns, 3,000 *minenwerfer*, 1,700 airplanes (fighters, bombers—firstly, all of the D 7's and the night bombing machines). The above to be delivered *in situ* to the Allied and United States troops in accordance with the detailed conditions laid down in the note (annexture No. 1) drawn up at the moment of the signing of the armistice.

Five. Evacuation by the German armies of the countries on the left bank of the Rhine. The countries on the left bank of the Rhine shall be administered by the local troops of occupation. The occupation of these territories will be carried out by Allied and United States garrisons holding the principal crossings of the Rhine (Mayence, Coblentz, Cologne), together with the bridgeheads at these points of a thirty kilometer radius on the right bank and by garrisons similarly holding the strategic points of the regions. A neutral zone shall be reserved on the right bank of the Rhine between the stream and a line drawn parallel to the bridgeheads and to the stream and at a distance of ten kilometres from the frontier of Holland up to the frontier of Switzerland. The evacuation by the enemy of the Rhinelands (left and right bank) shall be so ordered as to be completed within a further period of sixteen days, in all, thirty-one days after the signing of the armistice. All the movements of evacuation or occupation are regulated by the note (annexure No. 1) drawn up at the moment of the signing of the armistice.

Six. In all territories evacuated by the enemy there shall be no evacuation of inhabitants; no damage or harm shall be done to the persons or property of the inhabitants. No person shall be prosecuted for offences of participation in war measures prior to the signing of the armistice. No destruction of any kind shall be committed. Military establishments of all kinds shall be delivered intact, as well as military stores of food, munitions, and equipment not removed during the time fixed for evacuation. Stores of food of all kinds for the civil population, cattle, etc., shall be left *in situ.* Industrial establishments shall not be impaired in any way and their personnel shall not be removed.

Seven. Roads and means of communication of every kind, railroads, waterways, main roads, bridges, telegraphs, telephones, shall be in no manner impaired. All civil and military personnel at present employed on them shall remain. Five thousand locomotives and 150,000 wagons in good working order, with all necessary spare parts and fittings, shall be delivered to the associated powers within the period fixed in annexture No. 2, and total of which shall not exceed thirty-one days. There shall likewise be delivered 5,000 motor lorries (camione automobiles) in good order, within the period of thirty-six days. The railway of Alsace-Lorraine shall be handed over within the period of thirty-one days, together with pre-war personnel and material. Further, the material necessary for the working of railways in the countries on the left bank of the Rhine shall be left *in situ.* All stores of coal and material for the upkeep of permanent ways, signals, and repair shops shall be left *in situ.* These stores shall be maintained by Germany in so far as concerns the working of the railroads in the countries on the left bank of the Rhine. All barges taken from the Allies shall be restored to them. The note, annexure No. 2, regulates the details of these measures.

Eight. The German command shall be responsible for revealing within the period of forty-eight hours after the signing of the armistice all mines or delayed-action fuses on territory evacuated by the German troops and shall assist in their discovery and destruction. It also shall reveal all destructive measures that may have been taken (such as poisoning or polluting of springs and wells, etc.). All under penalty of reprisals.

Nine. The right of requisition shall be exercised by the Allied and United States armies in all occupied territories, subject to regulation of accounts with those whom it may concern. The upkeep of the troops of occupation in the Rhineland (excluding Alsace-Lorraine) shall be charged to the German Government.

Ten. The immediate repatriation without reciprocity, according to detailed conditions which shall be fixed, of all Allied and United States prisoners of war, including persons under trial or convicted. The Allied Powers and the United States shall be able to dispose of them as they wish. This conditions annuls the previous conventions on the subject of the exchange of prisoners of war, including the one of July, 1918, in course of ratification. However, the repatriation of German prisoners of war interned in Holland and in Switzerland shall continue as before. The repatriation of German prisoners of war shall be regulated at the conclusion of the preliminaries of peace.

Eleven. Sick and wounded who cannot be removed from evacuated territory will be cared for by German personnel, who will be left on the spot with the medical material required.

II. Disposition Relative to the Eastern Frontiers of Germany

Twelve. All German troops at present in the territories which before belonged to Austria-Hungary, Roumania, Turkey, shall withdraw immediately within the frontiers of Germany as they existed on August 1, 1914. All German troops at present in the territories which before the war belonged to Russia shall likewise withdraw within the frontiers of Germany, defined as above, as soon as the Allies, taking into account the internal situation of these territories, shall decide that the time for this has come.

Thirteen. Evacuation by German troops to begin at once, and all German instructors, prisoners, and civilians as well as military agents now on the territory of Russia (as defined before 1914) to be recalled.

Fourteen. German troops to cease at once all requisitions and seizures and any other undertaking with a view to obtaining supplies intended for Germany in Roumania and Russia (as defined on August 1, 1914).

Fifteen. Renunciation of the treaties of Bukharest and Brest-Litovsk and of the supplementary treaties.

Sixteen. The Allies shall have free access to the territories evacuated by the Germans on their eastern frontier, either through Danzig, or by the Vistula, in order to convey supplies to the population of those territories and for the purpose of maintaining order.

III. Clause Concerning East Africa

Seventeen. Evacuation by all German forces operating in East Africa within a period to be fixed by the Allies.

IV. General Clauses

Eighteen. Repatriation, without reciprocity, within a maximum period of one month in accordance with detailed conditions hereafter to be fixed, of all interned civilians, including hostages (persons?), under trial or convicted, belonging to the allied or associated powers other than those enumerated in Article Three.

Nineteen. The following financial conditions are required: Reparation for damage done. While such armistice lasts no public securities shall be removed by the enemy which can serve as a pledge to the Allies for the recovery or reparation for war losses. Immediate restitution of the cash deposit in the National Bank of Belgium, and, in general, immediate return of all documents, specie, stocks, shares, paper money, together with plant for the issue thereof, touching public or private interests in the invaded countries. Restitution of the Russian and Roumanian gold yielded to Germany or taken by that power. This gold to be delivered in trust to the Allies until the signature of peace.

V. Naval Conditions

Twenty. Immediate cessation of all hostilities at sea and definite information to be given as to the location and movements of all German ships. Notification to be given to neutrals that freedom of navigation in all territorial waters is given to the naval and mercantile marines of the allied and associated powers, all questions of neutrality being waived.

Twenty-one. All naval and mercantile marine prisoners of the allied and associated powers in German hands to be returned without reciprocity.

Twenty-two. Surrender to the Allies and United States of all submarines (including submarine crusiers and all mine-laying submarines) now existing, with their complete armament and equipment, in ports which shall be specified by the Allies and United States. Those which cannot take the sea shall be disarmed of the personnel and material and shall remain under the supervision of the Allies and the United States. The submarines which are ready for the sea shall be prepared to leave the German ports as soon as orders shall be received by wireless for their voyage to the port designated for their delivery, and the remainder at the earliest possible moment. The conditions of this article shall be carried into effect within the period of fourteen days after the signing of the armistice.

Twenty-three. German surface warships which shall be designated by the Allies and the United States shall be immediately disarmed and thereafter interned in neutral ports or in default of them in allied ports to be designated by the Allies and the United States. They will there remain under the supervision of the Allies and of the United States, only caretakers being left on board. The following warships are designated by the Allies: Six battle cruisers, ten battleships, eight light cruisers (including two mine layers), fifty destroyers of the most modern types. All other surface warships (including river craft) are to be concentrated in German naval bases to be designated by the Allies and the United States, and are to be completely disarmed and classed under the supervision of the Allies and the United States. The military armament of all ships of the auxilary fleet shall be put on shore. All vessels designated to be interned shall be ready to leave the German ports seven days after the signing of the armistice. Directions for the voyage will be given by wireless.

Twenty-four. The Allies and the United States of America shall have the right to sweep up all mine fields and obstructions laid by Germany outside German territorial waters, and the positions of these are to be indicated.

Twenty-five. Freedom of access to and from the Baltic to be given to the naval and mercantile marines of the allied and associated powers. To secure this the Allies and the United States of America shall be empowered to occupy all German forts, fortifications, batteries, and defence works of all kinds in all the entrances from the Cattegat into the Baltic, and to sweep up all mines and obstructions within and without German territorial waters, without any question of neutrality being raised, and the positions of all such mines and obstructions are to be indicated.

Twenty-six. The existing blockade conditions set up by the allied and associated powers are to remain unchanged, and all German merchant ships found at sea are to remain liable to capture. The Allies and the United States shall give consideration to the provisioning of Germany during the armistice to the extent recognized as necessary.

Twenty-seven. All naval aircraft are to be concentrated and immobilized in German bases to be specified by the Allies and the United States of America.

Twenty-eight. In evacuating the Belgian coast and ports Germany shall abandon *in situ* and in fact all port and river navigation, material and supplies, and all arms, apparatus and supplies of every kind.

Twenty-nine. All Black Sea ports are to be evacuated by Germany; all Russian war vessels of all descriptions seized by Germany in the Black Sea are to be handed over to the Allies and the United States of America; all neutral merchant vessels seized are to be released; all warlike and other materials of all kinds seized in those ports are to be returned and German materials as specified in Clause Twenty-eight are to be abandoned.

Thirty. All merchant vessels in German hands belonging to the allied and associated powers are to be restored in ports to be specified by the Allies and the United States of America without reciprocity.

Thirty-one. No destruction of ships or of materials to be permitted before evacuation, surrender, or restoration.

Thirty-two. The German Government will notify the neutral governments of the world, and particularly the governments of Norway, Sweden, Denmark, and Holland, that all restrictions placed on the trading of their vessels with the allied and associated countries, whether by the German Government or by private German interests, and whether in return for specific concessions, such as the export of shipbuilding materials, or not, are immediately cancelled.

Thirty-three. No transfers of German merchant shipping of any description to any neutral flag are to take place after signature of the armistice.

VI. Duration of Armistice

Thirty-four. The duration of the armistice is to be thirty days, with option to extend. During this period if its clauses are not carried into execution the armistice may be denounced by one of the contracting parties, which must give warning forty-eight hours in advance. It is understood that the execution of Article III and Section Eighteen, under IV, shall not warrant the denunciation of the armistice on the ground of insufficient execution within a period fixed, except in the case of bad faith in carrying them into execution. In order to assure the execution of this convention under the best conditions, the principle of a permanent international armistice commission is admitted. This commission will act under the authority of the allied military and naval Commander-in-Chief.

VII. The Limit For Reply

Thirty-five. This armistice to be accepted or refused by Germany within seventy-two hours of notification.

A heavy German artillery barrage prevented the delegates from getting back to the German lines until evening, but on November 9th General Headquarters in Spa were able to cable the gist of the armistice terms to the Foreign Office in Berlin. Hindenburg immediately cabled a vigorous protest against the armistice terms to the War Ministry in Berlin.

An attempt must be made to procure the modification of the following points in the Armistice terms.

1. Extension of the date of evacuatin to two months, the greater part of this time being needed for the evacuation of the Rhine Provinces, the Palatinate and Hesse, otherwise the Army will collapse, as the technical execution of the terms is absolutely impossible.
2. The right wing of the Army must be allowed to march through the corner of Maestricht.
3. Abandonment of neutral zones for reasons of internal order, at least must be restricted to ten kilometers.
4. Honorable capitulation of East Africa.
5. A considerable reduction must be effected in the railway material to be surrendered; otherwise industry will be seriously endangered. With re-

gard to Paragraph 7, only a small number of personnel can be left; more detailed arrangements required at this point.

6. Army only provided with 18,000 motor lorries, fifty percent available for use; surrender of number demanded would mean complete breakdown of Army supply system.

7. Only 1,700 pursuit-bombing aeroplanes in existence.

8. If there is to be one-sided surrender of prisoners of war, at least present arrangements as to treatment of latter must remain in force.

9. The blockade must be raised so far as food supplies are concerned. Commissioners to deal with regulations of food supplies are on the way.

If it is impossible to gain these points, it would nevertheless be advisable to conclude the agreement.

In case of refusal of points 1, 4, 5, 6, 8, 9, a fiery protest should be raised, and an appeal addressed to Wilson.

Please notify Government of outcome of these matters at earliest possible moment.

Von Hindenburg

The Chancellor, however, paid little heed to these protests and cabled the Armistice Commission:

You are authorized to sign the armistice. You will at the same time add the following declaration to the protocol: "The German Government will make every effort to execute the conditions imposed. The undersigned, however, conceive it to be their duty to call attention to the fact that execution of certain points of these conditions will plunge the population of unoccupied parts of Germany into the misery of starvation. The abandonment of all provisions in the territories to be evacuated—provisions which were destined to feed the army—as well as the curtailment of the traffic facilities which is equal to an abstraction, while the blockade is at the same time maintained makes the nourishment of the nation and any organized distribution impossible. The undersigned therefore request that they be allowed to negotiate on such alterations of these points as will ensure the question of nourishment." I also agree that the Supreme Army Command be permitted, through His Excellency Erzberger, to effect the capitulation of East Africa in an honorable manner, and furthermore to arrange for the march of our troops through the corner of Maestricht.

Imperial Chancellor

The War Costs at a Glance

Charles F. Horne, Ph.D.

THE GREAT EVENTS OF THE WAR, VOL. II, 1923

With the Armistice in force, the war came to an abrupt halt. The smoke cleared slowly and the devastation of cities, the loss of life, mangled bodies and scattered families lay revealed.

The facts of the death, destruction and financial cost of the war staggered the civilized world. The following mass of statistics in round figures were compiled bringing in to full view the unbelievable price that was paid for the Allied victory.

COST IN HUMAN LIFE

Army deaths	8,000,000
Civilian deaths	8,000,000
Permanent human wrecks from wounds, etc.	6,000,000
Total human loss (chiefly of males)	22,000,000

COST IN PROPERTY DESTROYED

France (Factories, farms, public works, etc.)	$10,000,000,000
Belgium, (Factories, farms, public works, etc.)	5,000,000,000
Other surviving countries	13,000,000,000
Russia (losses really incalculable)	20,000,000,000
Ships (chiefly British)	3,500,000,000
Cargoes	4,500,000,000
Total direct property loss	$56,000,000,000

COST IN MONEY

Government expenditures by Allies	$105,000,000,000
Government expenditures by Central Powers	65,000,000,000
Increased charitable expenditures	2,000,000,000
Loss by bankruptcy of Russia, Turkey, etc.	30,000,000,000
Total direct money loss	$202,000,000,000

HUMAN LIFE COSTS

TOTAL CASUALTIES OF ARMED FORCES

	Mobilized	*Dead*	*Wounded*	*Prisoners*
British Empire	8,654,280	873,980	2,525,927	279,357
United States	4,165,483	123,547	231,722	4,994
France	7,500,000	1,385,300	3,000,000	446,300
Italy	5,615,000	496,921	949,576	485,458
Belgium	267,000	20,000	60,000	10,000
Serbia	707,343	322,000	28,000	100,00
Montenegro	50,000	3,000	10,000	7,000
Rumania	750,000	200,000	120,000	80,000
Greece	230,000	15,000	40,000	45,000
Portugal	100,000	4,000	15,000	200
Japan	800,000	300	907	3
Russia	12,000,000	1,700,000	4,950,000	2,500,000
Totals	40,839,106	5,144,048	11,931,132	3,958,312
German Empire	11,000,000	1,718,246	4,350,122	1,073,620
Austria-Hungary	6,500,000	800,000	3,200,000	1,211,000
Turkey	1,600,000	300,000	570,000	130,000
Bulgaria	400,000	201,224	152,399	10,825
Totals	19,500,000	3,019,470	8,272,521	2,425,445

CIVILIANS SLAIN

Armenians*	1,100,000
Greeks (in Turkey)*	900,000
Syrians*	150,000
Serbians	650,000
Poles and Lithuanians	500,000
Rumanians	275,000
French	40,000
Belgians	30,000
British (by U-boats)	20,620
Neutrals (by U-boats)	7,500

* The first three items which represent the total of official Turkish massacres, were estimated by the Eastern relief commission in 1920 at almost double these figures. These form the closest available approximations to the number of civilians massacred, starved or dying from privation as a direct result of the ravages of war. They do not include deaths from privation in uninvaded regions. These were especially heavy in Austria-Hungary and Russia.

Epilogue

President Wilson arrived in Europe in mid-December where he found his ideas for a League of Nations unpopular with the French and English. His 14 Points that were to be the basis for the peace treaty was dissipated in the debates that followed during the many conferences relating to the final draft of the treaty. His main object, the League of Nations, was embodied in the treaty, but it was to become the principle reason that the new Republican Senate refused to ratify it. The Peace Treaty of Versailles was never recognized by the United States, and eventually, in 1920, a law was passed ending the war with the Central Powers.

The League of Nations suffered a severe handicap through the refusal of the United States to become a member and through the persistence of all members in regarding national sovereignty and interests as superior to mutual concession. As a rule the League of Nations settled successfully such disputes as involved the smaller nations, but it foundered because the powerful nations could not be persuaded into mutual compromise.

The league decay began with the Second Sino-Japanese war in 1931 and the withdrawal of Japan from the league.

Another serious failure was the inability of the league to stop the war of Bolivia and Paraguay (1932–1935) over the Chaco where more than a million lives were lost. Germany, under Adolf Hitler, withdrew from the league in 1933 and remilitarized the Rhineland in 1934, denounced the Treaty of Versailles in 1936, and seized Austria in 1938.

Encouraged by the league's inaction, Italy under Mussolini attacked Ethiopia in 1935 and actively interfered in the Spanish Civil War in 1936, then bowed out of the league in 1937.

In just about the time it took to grow a crop of young men of army age, Germany decided to reap the harvest. In 1939 World War II picked up steam and forged ahead.

Index